THE GUARDIAN BOOK
OF MUNICH

The good man and the bad man had come to terms. How? If the good man had not become bad, nor the bad man good, how could they come to terms? Justice is not elastic. The point is that it was made expedient at Munich, though nobody questioned such expediency for days afterwards. Relief ran ahead of logic.
Ronald Blythe, *The Age of Illusion*

The Guardian Book of Munich

R.H. Haigh
D.S. Morris
A.R. Peters

WILDWOOD HOUSE

Published by
Wildwood House Limited
Gower House
Croft Road
Aldershot
Hants GU11 3HR

Distributed in the United States by
Gower Publishing Company
Old Post Road
Brookfield
Vermont 05036
USA

British Library Cataloguing in Publication Data
The Guardian book of Munich
1. Munich Agreement (1938)
I. Haigh, R.H. II. Morris, D.S. III. Peters, A.S.
940,5312   D727

The reports in this book, all from the pages of the
Manchester Guardian, were selected by three independent
historians who also wrote the annotations, introduction
and appendices.

Every effort has been made to obtain permission to reproduce
the letters included in this volume but the publishers would be
pleased to acknowledge any additional copyright holders at
the first opportunity.

ISBN 0-7045-0533-9

Printed and bound in Great Britain by
Billing and Sons Limited, Worcester.

Contents

vi

Maps

Acknowledgements

A number of people have made our task in producing this book a great deal easier than would have otherwise been the case. Michael Harkin, Social Sciences Librarian at the Central Library in Manchester, responded most readily to our request for microfilmed copies of the *Manchester Guardian* and by so doing greatly reduced the time and effort expended on producing the manuscript. Roger Hines, Margot Madin, Ray Thompson and Laura Tolley of the Eric Mensforth Library, Sheffield City Polytechnic, all gave willingly of their time and never failed to meet the many arduous demands we made on them.

Joanne and Ann Gould cheerfully undertook the mammoth typing effort entailed in preparing the manuscript for publication and did so with a speed and accuracy which exceeded our most optimistic expectations.

Finally, we dedicate this book to our families.

R.H. Haigh
D.S. Morris
A.R. Peters
Sheffield, 1987

Editors' Introduction
to the Series

The historian is blessed with many advantages. He can assemble all of the available facts relevant to any particular past event, analyse each in turn, assemble his accumulated knowledge into a comprehensive and logically sequential pattern and present a rationally sound appraisal of all the elements which have contributed both directly and indirectly to a social phenomenon considered by him or by others to be worthy of special attention.

In marked contrast to the historian stands the journalist. Not for him the luxury of wide-ranging and detailed information; instead he is confronted by a complex blend of fact, rumour and innuendo which falls far short of being comprehensive in character or cohesive in format. Working from partial information he can at best offer his reader a rational assessment of what he has gleaned from a multiplicity of sources, with but little hope or opportunity of being able to verify and validate every element of his story by reference to other knowledgeable or accepted authorities and accounts.

Yet despite the advantages enjoyed by the historian and despite the disadvantages which beset the journalist, there is an immediacy about journalistic accounts which the historian can only try to capture in his own scholarly labours. Social events rarely happen in a causal sequence, decisions are invariably taken on the basis of limited knowledge, and the complexity of societal phenomena makes total comprehension and a fully rational response an impossibility. Perhaps, therefore, the historian may be not unreasonably accused of enforcing a rationality and order on to events which is largely his own, and of attributing motives which accord with his perceptions rather than being the motives which underlay human actions at the time of his chosen event.

In short, the journalist offers a 'snap shot' of the world as he perceives it in the present, an assessment which has an immediacy even though it affords an interpretation which may well lack comprehensiveness. The historian, working from accumulated past knowledge and enjoying the benefit of hindsight, is able to offer a fuller account of past events but one which will almost inevitably fall short of conveying the immediacy which is a feature of the journalistic report.

Let it not be forgotten that the work of a journalist can, of itself, be a factor which influences the actions of others. Journalistic accounts are themselves elements which are capable of influencing the perceptions and behaviours of social actors and can, therefore, be an integral part of significant events in man's social activities. The historian may point to past 'errors' and may influence current and future events by so doing, but it is most unlikely that his work will ever, by its very nature, be as significant a determinant of current events as that of the journalist.

simply to state that in order to gain an understanding of a past event and to acquire an appreciation of it that was available to the majority of those living at the time it was unfolding, it may well be more fruitful to give consideration to journalistic accounts of the day rather than simply being restricted to the more academically oriented accounts of historians. Journalists offer living history, historians offer considered history. Neither is of itself better than the other, nor are the two mutually exclusive. We have chosen to utilise the former to provide an insight into the origins and causes of the Munich Agreement of September 1938 and, by so doing, have consciously sought to offer a counterbalance to the many voluminous and more profoundly academic accounts which have been produced over the years.

Whether or not we have succeeded, indeed whether or not we should have even attempted such an exercise, must be left to the judgement of the reader.

R.H. Haigh
D.S. Morris
A.R. Peters
Sheffield, 1987

Editors' Introduction

The international conference which assembled on 29 September 1938 at Munich had a two-fold task confronting it. First, it had to provide a solution to the 'problem' of three million German-speaking people then residing within the frontiers of Czechoslovakia. Secondly, it had to make every possible effort, constrained only by the perceived limits of diplomatic negotiations, to prevent the outbreak of a war in Europe coupled with the probable re-drawing of Czechoslovakia's frontiers with her neighbouring countries.

On the face of it, therefore, the Munich Conference and the Agreement which emanated from it were remarkably successful. The German-speaking population resident in Czechoslovakia was incorporated into Hitler's Third Reich, and war did not break out in Europe as a result of that Agreement. The Munich Agreement could simply be described as yet another step on the road to lasting peace which was the declared aim of all governments in the aftermath of the First World War.

However, 'Munich' was, and to a certain extent still is, regarded by many as a particularly unsavoury example of international chicanery; and the 'Munichites,' those British politicians who had either participated in, or supported, the Munich Agreement, were effectively denied office in the cabinets which were formed after the fall of Neville Chamberlain in 1940. One needs to delve deeper to discover why.

The Munich Agreement constituted in the eyes of many politicians qualitatively much more than the granting of justifiable German demands. It was ultimately seen, first by a few and then by the many, as not only or even simply a national disaster, but an international humiliation for Britain and France.

For the Czechoslovakians, the Agreement signalled the end of their country in all but name. They were left with what could only be described as a rump. Under the terms of the Agreement, they lost some 11,000 square miles of territory; 2,800,000 Sudeten-Germans and 800,000 Czechs from their population; plus all their formidable frontier defences, which were regarded as being second in strength only to the Maginot Line. If this were not disastrous enough, from an economic point of view the results of the Agreement were even more catastrophic.

They lost 66 per cent of their coal; 80 per cent of lignite; 86

per cent of chemicals; 80 per cent of cement; 80 per cent of textiles; 70 per cent of iron and steel; 70 per cent of electric power; and 40 per cent of their timber. From the political standpoint, Czechoslovakia as a country was well aware that it appeared to be only a matter of time before the rest of her territory was absorbed into the Third Reich. And such proved to be the case.

There was for many years a simplistic approach towards the interpretation of international politics in interwar Europe which was neither pro-appeasement nor anti-appeasement, in an attempt to understand Munich. Similarly, the 'Men of Munich' cannot be dismissed as simply stupid, callous, clever, unprincipled, brave, determined, cowardly, etc. Everyone involved in those turbulent times, both appeasers and anti-appeasers, were essentially individuals of their time, with all that that entailed.

These men could feel emotion for Czechoslovakia, but their rational judgement told them that what they desired was not possible in practical terms.

This book offers a view of the events of 1938 through the archives of the *Manchester Guardian*, but it is essential to have a brief overview of the previous twenty years in order to set that archive material within a framework for analysis.

Czechoslovakia came into being following the breakup of the Austro-Hungarian Empire in 1918. The gap that was left by such a breakup was for many years underrated by contemporary commentators. The formation of Czechoslovakia meant that a new country was being forged out of the remnants of other areas which, for literally hundreds of years, had thought of themselves as anything but Czechoslovakian.

The new country in 1919 comprised the provinces of Bohemia, Moravia and part of Silesia, which were formerly in Austria; and Slovakia and Sub-Carpathian Russia, which were formerly part of Hungary. It came into being on 28 October 1918 and was formerly recognised on 10 September 1919 with the Treaty of St Germain. The new state was landlocked and surrounded by Germany, Poland, Rumania, Hungary and Austria.

Its total population in 1934 numbered some 14,739,536, but it was the make-up of this population that was important; the ethnic minorities comprised the undermentioned numbers of the sum total:

3,231,688 of German race	All former subjects of
691,923 of Hungarian race	the Austro-Hungarian
549,169 of Russian and Ukrainian race	Empire
81,737 of Polish race	

Herein lay the seeds of discontent, a discontent on which Hitler via the Sudeten-Germans was to capitalise during 1938.

Although for the first ten years of her life Czechoslovakia

prospered, the world economic crash of 1929 had tremendous economic repercussions on her, with foreign trade falling to a catastrophically low level and unemployment rising eleven-fold in the period 1929 to 1933.

What became known as the Sudeten problem, i.e. the demands being made by the Sudeten-German people to be 'reunited' with Germany, was fermented by the formation of the Sudeten-German Party under the leadership of Henlein and financed by Hitler.

What made the Czechoslovakian situation much more poignant and significant was that she constituted the one democratic state in Central Europe, created from the ashes of a war which had been fought to make the 'world safe for democracy'.

Within the context of the interwar period one of the most-used and least-understood of words is 'appeasement' with regard to the foreign policy strategy pursued by the victors of World War One and particularly Great Britain. Appeasement could and indeed, does, have more than one interpretation over the twenty-year cycle. The first type of appeasement, which can be used to span the immediate postwar period, through the 1920s and up to the early 1930s, is a tremendous desire for peace, following the horrors of the First World War, coupled with a willingness to accept what were regarded as legitimate claims by those nations who had been defeated in that war. However, by the 1930s the second type of appeasement represented what can only be construed as a full retreat in the face of one's potential enemies. This retreat was exemplified by the surrendering of one's potential strength and by losing out constantly in the military, diplomatic and strategic spheres.

It is possible to trace the change in the emphasis of appeasement by taking a brief look at some of the major diplomatic and military events between the end of the First World War and the time of the Munich Agreement.

The insistence of the framers of the Treaty of Versailles, on the 'War Guilt' notion and the demand that Germany's responsibility for the conflict should be exercised by the payment of 'just' reparations was undoubtedly instrumental in paving the way for future conflicts. It is not our intention to enter into debates about the 'moral validity' or otherwise of that Treaty, but it is important to point out that the above clauses, and the arbitrary drawing of geographical and ethnic boundaries of the countries created out of the ruins of the economic and politically bankrupt Austro-Hungarian Empire, played a vital role in the development of interwar diplomacy in Western Europe. We have suggested that this is crucially important with regard to Czechoslovakia, whose national majority outnumbered its national minority by a ratio of only 2 : 1.

The future role to be adopted by the French on diplomatic

stage in Europe was embodied in the Treaty of Locarno in 1925, which saw the development of the rapprochement between Britain, France and Germany. The Treaties guaranteed the Franco-German and Belgo-German frontiers; arbitration treaties between Germany on the one hand and France, Belgium, Czechoslovakia and Poland on the other; and treaties of mutual guarantee between France on the one hand and Czechoslovakia on the other.

The Locarno Agreement symbolised the desire of the Western Nations to woo Germany rather than Bolshevik Russia, a movement which had received a setback when the Treaty of Friendship between Russia and Germany was signed at Rapallo in 1922. More than anything, however, it demonstrated the attitude of the French in international relations, following as it did their abortive attempt to force reparation payments out of Germany by the re-occupation of the Ruhr in 1923. It could be loosely interpreted as the French asking all the other nations, 'What can you do for us?' At the same time it signified the abdication of the French to any claim to leadership of the powers on the Western European mainland. This, we suggested, was to be the mainspring of the French international diplomacy from Locarno up to and beyond Munich in 1938.

For Britain, Locarno also marked a further turning away from Europe and a movement back to those areas of the world where she perceived her real material interests lay, namely the Empire, and in particular the Far East in the face of ever-increasing Japanese competition and expansionism.

Locarno, then, was the embodiment of the first kind of appeasement. The dividing line between the two definitions of appeasement can be said to be the Japanese invasion of Manchuria in 1931. By that time the major powers were wrestling with almost overwhelming economic difficulties in their own countries, but by 1935 the Japanese had established the puppet state of Manchukuo which consisted of territory equivalent in size to the whole of Great Britain, France, Germany, Italy and Spain combined, and contained a total of 100,000,000 people within its borders.

This second type of appeasement was not only military, but also political and diplomatic. Militarily the Japanese action in Manchuria and later in China was never seriously challenged by the Western Powers or the League of Nations. In a military sense the Western Powers were paying the price both of the outcome of the Washington Naval Treaty and the continued failure to make the League of Nations a genuinely effective organisation.

Yet there were clear reasons why Great Britian did not wish to interfere with the Japanese action in Manchuria. Britain was very concerned with the stability of the Far East, not least because a large part of her Empire was situated there, and also because of her very lucrative trade with China. It was felt in many British circles that the Japanese invasion would lead to greater stability in China, and hence greater benefits to Britain in the way of trade. The

Japanese invasion was seen as a counter to the conflicting Nationalist and Communist elements within China.

There seemed to be a certain historical justification for this opinion. Great Britain and Japan had been allies in the past, and it could be argued that Great Britain was willing to let Japan become a 'second partner' in the Far East trade as a concession for her contribution to the maintenance of stability in that part of the world. It could be further argued that as Great Britain and the USA were involved in economic rivalry in the Far East, it would be to Britain's advantage to give her tacit support to the Japanese. Further arguments in favour of this stance were that, because of economic difficulties at home, Britain was willing to forgo some of the trading concessions in the Far East, thereby reducing some of the cost of maintaining adequate forces there to safeguard her concessions, and being able to concentrate on the stability so necessary in India and other parts of Asia if she was to maintain her very favourable terms of trade in those areas as well.

However, whatever the reasons that could be advanced, no really tangible moves were made to stop Japanese aggression in China, and British policy towards Japan must be construed as the second type of appeasement. The 1930s witnessed an ever-increasing growth of this kind of appeasement as Abysinnia, Austria and Czechoslovakia were all lost as the Allies retreated before their opponents.

Furthermore, this pattern was maintained via the Spanish Civil War 1936–1939 when the British and French Governments pursued a policy of non-intervention, described by Pandit Nehru as 'the greatest farce of our times', whilst being fully aware of the massive interventionist role being played by Germany and Italy, which far outstripped the limited intervention of the USSR.

Hitler's annexation of Austria in 1938 again met with no perceptible response from either the British or the French, even though this was a direct attack on the basis of the Versailles Treaty and enabled the Germans to outflank much of the Czech frontier defences.

It is, therefore, difficult to justify this policy of appeasement pursued through the 1930s by Britain and France on any conceivable grounds. Where Appeasement in the 1920s could mean:

> ... appeasement in 1920 was a shrewd policy, designed to end division of Europe into the warring camps of 1914. It was also a cautious policy, aimed at dissociating Britain from French hostility to all aspects of German recovery. It was a policy which depended for its success upon European economic co-operation and upon the revision of all clauses in the Versailles Treaty Whose alteration could be shown to be conducive or even essential to European peace. It was a practical policy, one of

whose aims was to stimulate trade and recreate the flourishing and confident business activity of the pre-war years. ...

(Martin Gilbert, *The Roots of Appeasement*, Weidenfeld and Nicolson, 1966, pp.79–80)

appeasement in the 1930s would be described savagely, but accurately as:

Save my skin, and damn my conscience,
and negotiations win.

(Louis MacNeice, *Autumn Journal 1938*)

Appeasement as a policy depended on at least two factors. Those who were willing to appease, and those who were willing to be appeased. Britain and France chose the former and consequently Germany assumed the latter role.

However, in order to understand further why the policy of appeasement became the essence of British foreign policy it is necessary to undertake an overview of the events leading up to Munich, not least because the *Manchester Guardian* reporters' and the correspondents' work which we have edited, operated within such a framework.

Britain emerged from World War One battered physically, socially and economically almost beyond belief. Her economy was in tatters; the USA had assumed an international economic dominance which she was never to lose; the political parties were divided on the causes, outcome and effect of the Great War. The old political order was facing up to the new challenge from the Labour Party. Before any long-lasting recovery could be mounted Britain, along with the rest of the world, was hit by the tidal wave of the Wall Street Crash, and thereafter until the outbreak of war in 1939 mass unemployment dominated the political scene.

It was imperative that Britain adopt a foreign policy which would enable her to rebuild her ravaged economy and get her returning troops back to work; this required stability both in Europe and those areas where Britain enjoyed her biggest trading concessions, i.e. the Empire.

The central issue in Europe could be seen as essentially a simple one. Were Britain and France to coerce Germany into co-operation, to intervene physically in order to keep her militarily impotent to preserve Versailles? Or were they to accede to what could be described as her more reasonable demands and win German friendship in that way?

France was justifiably concerned with the problem of security against a further invasion of her territory and hence would have preferred a weak and divided nation on her borders, while reinforcing this position with strong military alliances. As a result her reparation demands were always, from the British point of view, pitched at an impossible level and French diplomacy resulted in a series of military alliances with central European states. These treaties ranged from the 'Little Entente' with Czechoslovakia, Yugoslavia and Romania to the Franco-Russian alliance of 1935, and were intended to balance potential and real German power.

Unfortunately, France, weakened as she was by the excesses of the Great War, was unwilling to intervene physically across the Rhine after the economic results of her occupation of the Ruhr in 1923. She was ultimately prepared, quite surprisingly in view of their differing long-term aims, to place her dependence upon Britain. For example, if Germany was to be deterred by overwhelming military strength the Royal Navy had to underwrite the land power deployed by the French Army; alliances with Central European armies were not enough.

The British view, in apparent direct contradiction to that held by France, was that Germany should be re-integrated into the European community as soon as possible. A weak Germany was a hindrance to general economic recovery, and potentially vulnerable to a Bolshevik-style revolution. In the event of Germany falling to communism, Poland's position would become untenable.

Perhaps more important is that simultaneously a generally more sophisticated view of the causes of the First World War was beginning to emerge in Britain, and at least a significant part of British opinion believed that Germany had been unjustly treated by the framers of the Versailles Treaty, and that she was entitled to some redress if she were ever to make any further progress. The scapegoat in the British view for this state of affairs was France. The way to redress this was appeasement. The harshness of the Treaty was ascribed to French folly. France was 'blamed' for having encouraged Britain to agree to an excessive punishment of the Germans. Therefore, it was argued, justice could be done by helping Germany to take her rightful place in Europe as a Great Power.

One can suggest that the position established after Versailles could only be maintained if Britian was willing to assist in its maintenance. As this was not to be the case, Germany's industrial power and potential, her growing population and dynamism coupled with vast amounts of American capital invested in her economy could only result in her once more becoming probably the most powerful state on the Western European mainland.

The Treaty of Rapallo had already served to remind Britain of the possibility of an Eastwards-oriented Germany. Locarno was to redress the balance, but its non-aggression clause deprived France of the military initiative given her by Versailles.

Therefore, if the League of Nations collapsed, and if Britain and France lacked either resolution or the inclination to act, Germany's eastern neighbours would be isolated unless they could secure support from the USSR. It could conceivably be argued that the beginnings of the Munich Crisis already existed in embryo after the Treaty of Locarno. As it happened, Britain's support for the League was to be tempered with a fair degree of caution, and was indeed to appear a good deal more half-hearted than was probably the case.

Certainly, after its collapse the policies of Baldwin and Chamberlain were to lead to such isolation, and to the eventual dismemberment of both Czechoslovakia and Poland. However, one must also consider the reluctance of either France or the USA to offer any effective military support to Britain before condemning the British Government for inaction.

The League was without any means of bringing military or naval pressure to bear and had to resort to ineffectual 'sanctions', and the USA's Fleet with its nearest Pacific base at Honolulu was unable to challenge the Japanese Pacific Fleet in its home waters. Even a League-backed intervention by Britain would have been of little help, with the Singapore naval base well out of effective range, so that the Japanese invasions of Manchuria and China were never seriously challenged. All in all Britain was now paying the price both for the failure to arm the League, and for the negotiation and acceptance of the terms of the Washington Naval Treaty.

Following the 1931 political crisis and the landslide victory of the National Government, Britain was governed by an administration which consisted largely of men who were sceptical as to the worth of the League, doubtful about the whole idea of collective security and deeply concerned with enormous economic problems. They were also bitterly hostile to the USSR and any other type of 'left wing' government, and hence when Hitler seized power in 1933 were far more concerned with his anti-communist stance than with his well-publicised hostility to democracy. Traditional balance of power diplomacy was instrumental in their support for the somewhat rickety 'Stresa Front' of April 1935, but when Hitler denounced the remaining disarmament clauses of the Treaty of Versailles, no action was taken or even seriously contemplated.

Therefore, when the Ethiopian crisis tested the whole principle underpinning the notion of collective security, the ineffectuality of the League if it were not backed by resolute military action or the threat of it destroyed both the concept of collective security and the League.

Whatever their motive, the Ethiopian débâcle marked the end of the last semblance of the League's credibility as an instrument for keeping the peace, and by 1936 Neville Chamberlain was speaking against the sanctions applied against Italy as being 'the very mid-summer of madness'.

This articulation of Britain's stance became even more

pronounced when Hitler remilitarised the Rhineland in 1936. Although the British government gave a direct undertaking to support France in the event of an attack, the positive results of this agreement were negligible, five days of staff talks which were then broken off and not resumed until May 1939. The most probable reason for this state of affairs was, we submit, the total unwillingness of the French to commit themselves to any situation which demanded offensive action of them.

The outbreak of the Civil War in Spain in July 1936 added further evidence to the Fascist powers that Britain and France would not act, even in the face of a significant potential threat to their fundamental interests.

The non-intervention decision crippled the Spanish Republic and, as Franco suffered no such similar handicap, almost guaranteed a Nationalist victory. The Civil War itself acted as a divisive force within British politics, not only between 'left and right' but also within 'left and right'. Albeit with hindsight, British policy seems to have been motivated by a combination of timidity in the face of the Axis powers, anti-communism, ideological divisions, and a continuing faith that the policy of appeasement could still work.

From a strategic position, however, the Spanish Civil War was more than just a Civil War, for given the possibility of an Anglo–French–German conflict at some time in the future, a possibility that simply couldn't be ruled out, the probability of opening the Atlantic and Mediterranean coasts of Spain to hostile ships and aircraft left the Chiefs of Staff curiously unmoved. It must be remembered that Franco's victory was won largely on the men and materials provided by the Axis powers, Italy and Germany.

Similarly, the Anschluss of 1938 met with no perceptible British response and only a marginal one from the French, even though this was a direct attack on the Treaty of Versailles, and as early as March 1938 it was clear that Britain had little or no intention of assisting Czechoslovakia should the Germans move east, as evinced by an oft-quoted memorandum of that date to the French government.

The British argued that there was 'little hope' that military operations by France and the Soviet Union could prevent the occupation of Czechoslovakia; the British, even if they entered the war, could do no more than offer the 'economic pressure' of blockade, which was not an inconsiderable contribution, but essentially a long-term rather than a short-term measure.

Therefore, it is possible to argue that the fate of the Czechs was sealed before the Munich talks ever took place, and that rather than Munich being a special case, it was the logical continuation of a process of events whose roots lay much deeper than in the contemporary circumstances of 1938.

The central figure for the Western European Powers was to be Neville Chamberlain, who had succeeded Baldwin as Prime Minister on 28 May 1937. He became Prime Minister after a lengthy period of ministerial office. Of his previous nineteen years of continuous membership of the House of Commons, eleven had been spent in ministerial office. Chamberlain's perception of politics was apparently influenced by his belief that the qualities of individuals were more important than institutions, and he constantly argued that in a Cabinet the Prime Minister and his Cabinet Ministers constituted the most important element. This facet of his thinking was to be given full rein in his personal diplomacy in the Czechoslovakian crisis.

Although in the early 1930s Chamberlain had been a much more convinced supporter of rearmament than most of his colleagues, by the time he became Prime Minister he inherited the 'double line' policy of previous British governments of trying to combine rearmament for purposes of deterrence with a search for peaceful settlement. His attitude had also changed between 1933 and 1937, in that whereas he formerly saw Germany as posing the long-run threat and was more in favour of deterrence he was latterly convinced that rapprochement was the answer, and consequently this was given preference over other considerations.

Chamberlain further pinned his faith in the policy of appeasement because he seemed to accept the generally-held contemporary belief that another World War could only arise from international misunderstanding. To his way of thinking no statesman could possibly contemplate war as a means of pursuing his own ends. Therefore, his reaction to Hitler was to pursue a personal initiative as British Prime Minister to show that it was still possible to inject some 'old-fashioned diplomacy' into the international situation.

However, his view of foreign affairs, whilst not at all naive, was a personal one, and although he continued an agreed policy of appeasement, there is little doubt that by the time of his flights to negotiate with Hitler at Berchtesgaden, Godesberg and Munich, he had made appeasement into his own personal policy, and it is on that level that it must be finally judged.

There was opposition in the British Parliament to appeasement, but at best it was fragmented, and at worst it seemed to comprise a very strange set of bedfellows and mavericks.

The names of those opponents to Chamberlain's foreign policy within his own party bear testimony to that 'maverick' implication. Churchill, L.S. Amery, Harold Macmillan, Robert Boothby, Brendan Bracken, Duncan Sandys and ultimately Anthony Eden. Although this list includes some of the most important figures in the post-Chamberlain Conservative Party, it has to be remembered that in 1938 Chamberlain had the almost total support of his party, and the dissenters were relatively few in number.

Within the Labour Party at the same time there were anti-appeasers, but it must not be forgotten that there was still a not insignificant group of out-and-out pacifists in the Labour ranks, including its leader in the first half of that decade, George Lansbury. The party was also divided constantly between the views of those such as Hugh Dalton who wanted rearmament even if such a policy entailed a cut in the Social Services; but the maintenance of these services was a consistently central plank in Labour's platform. On the other side a significant body of opinion within the party viewed rearmament for possible use against fascism as acceptable provided that it was conducted under the aegis of a Labour/Socialist government. However, this same group could not accept rearmament carried out by a National/Conservative government, their class enemies, as such rearmament could be used against themselves, as shown by Aneurin Bevan's comment that if they agreed to this policy they were 'putting a sword in the hands of our enemies that may be used to cut off our own heads'.

These differences contained within the Left in Parliament made it easier for Chamberlain, with his large majority, to prevent an effective opposition policy from emerging and offering what would possibly have been seen as a credible alternative government. This in turn meant that anti-appeasement within the Conservative ranks never really united with the anti-appeasers in the Labour Party until the Norway debate. Therefore anti-appeasement tended to be conducted on different levels by different groups of people, and Chamberlain was easily able to divide and conquer.

Outside Parliament there were influential anti-appeasers notably in the Trade Union Movement, many of whose leaders and even more of the rank and file members were under no illusions as to what a Fascist and Nazi regime meant to movements such as theirs. They had appreciated the fact that almost the first action of the new regions in Italy and Germany had been to destroy the trade unions in those countries.

Among military thinkers J.F.C. Fuller and B.H. Liddell Hart, both later to gain such eminence, were ostracised by the armed forces and most of the government for the expression of their views.

A final group of House of Commons men who could be termed to a certain degree anti-appeasers were the 'Francophiles', those who shared the French distrust of Germany. They numbered among their ranks Sir Austen Chamberlain (Neville's half-brother), Duff Cooper (who resigned following the Munich Agreement) and Brigadier-General E.L. Spears. They constantly urged, following Hitler's accession to power, that the former allies of the Treaty of Versailles should once more stand together. However, in making this appeal they obviously ran the risk of alienating the many people to whom the Treaty represented a morally corrupt revenge exacted by France.

Thus the anti-appeasement lobby and the anti-appeasers themselves were never able to combine into an effective group and certainly not until well after Munich did they appear to have the inclination to do so.

Of course, appeasement could be seen as a response to harsh reality. The sheer cost of rearmament made it difficult to see how Great Britain could adequately finance both the defence of the Empire and a viable European Expeditionary Force. It was also arguable that a continental commitment could only involve her in another war of attrition like World War One, in a geographic area where she had no vital economic interests, and render defenceless those valuable areas of the Far and Middle East which were vital to the recovery of her economic well-being. The dilemma, in short, was practical as well as moral.

But by the time of the negotiations over Czechoslovakia in 1938 which is the topic of this book, Hitler had for years been spelling out the four aims necessary to be achieved in order to secure Germany's pre-eminence within Europe, i.e. the abrogation of the Treaty of Versailles; the bringing within the Reich of all the German minorities bordering on Germany in addition to the whole of Austria; to dominate Europe economically; and finally to establish *"Lebensraum"* in Eastern Europe, that is to occupy and colonise a vast stretch of it.

One final thought before reading the *Manchester Guardian's* views of these momentous events. As Chamberlain left London to fly to Munich he quoted Hotspur's speech from Shakespeare's *Henry IV, Part I,* Act II, iii: ''out of this nettle, danger, we pluck this flower, safety.' Perhaps it would have been better to have heeded the advice which Hotspur was spurning in that speech: 'The purpose you undertake is dangerous; the friends you have named uncertain; the time itself unsorted; and your whole plot too light for the counterpoise of so great an opposition.'

R.H. Haigh.
D.S. Morris.
A.R. Peters.
Sheffield,
March, 1986.

Chronology of Munich
1938

February
4   War Minister, von Blomberg, and von Fritsch, the army commander-in-chief, are dismissed. Hitler becomes supreme commander of the Wehrmacht. Von Ribbentrop replaces von Neurath as Foreign Minister.

20   Anthony Eden resigns as Foreign Secretary and is replaced by Lord Halifax.

March
12   German occupation of Austria.

13   Annexation of Austria by Germany (the Anschluss) is announced.

April
16   Anglo-Italian agreement negotiated.

24   The Sudeten German Party under Konrad Henlein demands autonomy for the Sudeten area of Czechoslovakia.

28–29   Daladier and Bonnet in London.

May
20–22   The scare over Czechoslovakia, Czech mobilisation. The 'weekend crisis'.

30   Hitler's directive to the Wehrmacht for the destruction of Czechoslovakia.

July
23   Lord Runciman 'invited' to Czechoslovakia.

August
3   Runciman departs to commence his mission to Czechoslovakia.

September
7   Benes offers to meet the Sudeten German demands.

8   Talks between Prague and the Sudeten German Party broken off by the latter.

13   Rioting in Sudetenland.

15   Prime Minister Chamberlain flies to Berchtesgaden to confer with Hitler on the Sudeten crisis.

18   Daladier and Bonnet in London.

SELECTED REPORTS FROM
THE MANCHESTER GUARDIAN
21 FEBRUARY to 7 NOVEMBER 1938

PROTECTING GERMANS OUTSIDE GERMANY
Hitler's Claim to Safeguard Them

CZECHO-SLOVAKIA AND THREAT OF INTERVENTION

From our own Correspondent

Berlin, February 20.

Herr Hitler, who spoke for almost three hours in the Reichstag this afternoon, disappointed those who expected sensational developments or even much light upon the meaning of the events of February 4. His statements upon Austria were bald.

There were times, in fact, when even the ranks of the brown and black uniformed deputies fidgeted restlessly, as for example after an hour's recital of masses of statistics of the success of domestic economic policy. Herr Hitler, in fact, merely reaffirmed virtually all the known features of his foreign policy and contributed nothing new. This time there was no further offer of a German 'peace plan.'

Germany and Italy, Herr Hitler declared, had the same attitude to Spain. The victory of the Madrid Government, he said, would disturb the existing balance in Europe. That Herr Hitler vouchsafed so few details about the Austrian agreement and did not plainly show that Austria would rapidly be assimilated within the Reich, as party and other quarters were expecting indicates, according to the view of some observers here, that in deference to the Italian wishes this process is not to be hastened unduly.

Italy, it is suggested, has been encouraged to go ahead with her Spanish policy, which is shared by Germany. According to this view the London negotiations with Italy through Count Grandi have not been a success.

THE FOREIGN PRESS

Herr Hitler declared that relations between Germany and her Western neighbours were poisoned by the press. Germany would answer this press 'campaign' against her with Nazi thoroughness.

Foreign observers were greatly puzzled as to the meaning of Herr Hitler's phrase declaring that the press agitation was a danger to peace which had made him strengthen the German Army sufficiently to secure the country against these attacks being turned into bloody force.

Referring to what he describes as foreign interference with German internal affairs, Herr Hitler declared that British M.P.s would do better to concern themselves with the verdicts of British courts martial in Palestine than with those of German courts. This sally, like other sallies aimed at Britain, was warmly applauded. ...

GERMANS OUTSIDE GERMANY

The most significant passage was Herr Hitler's claim to the protection of all Germans living outside the Reich frontier. He gave a warning to Czecho-Slovakia without mentioning that country by name. This is regretted by Czech quarters here as opening the door to continual intervention on behalf of the active Sudeten German minority in Czecho-Slovakia.

Two States alone outside Germany's borders included over 10,000,000 Germans, Herr Hitler declared. They were prevented against their own will from joining the Reich. Separation from the Reich, however, could not deprive them of their rights. Self-determination had been promised solemnly in President Wilson's Fourteen Points as the condition of an armistice, and it could not be disregarded simply because Germans were concerned.

Those seeking by force to prevent the easing of European tension would one day cause force to be employed. Germany would find a way of enforcing respect for her interests as England did throughout the world.

Among those German interests, he emphatically stated, was the protection of all Germans unable to secure political freedom and freedom for their political viewpoint.

p.15

FRENCH OPINION OF SPEECH
Hitler No Longer a 'Defender of Europe's Peace'

From our own Correspondent

Paris, February 20.

In substance as well as in tone, Hitler's speech is considered in Paris to be the most violent and the most menacing he has yet made. The following are the principal points specially noted here:

1. Hitler no longer makes any serious pretence of being a 'defender of European peace';
2. He virtually declares that the policy of Berchtesgaden will be persevered in, and that woe to the Czechs if they do not submit to his demands in favour of the German majority;
3. He declares more explicitly than ever before Germany's refusal to tolerate a victory of the Spanish Government;

4. Germany gives Japan unqualified support;

5. The speech is strikingly anti-British, and Hitler no longer thinks it necessary to keep up even the illusion that Germany may, under certain conditions, return to the League of Nations;

6. The speech does not contain the slightest guarantee of Austrian independence;

7. France is treated merely with contempt, as a country clinging to a dead democratic ideology and incapable of putting her house in order economically. ...

There is a wide disparity of views regarding Hitler's speech, in both its content and tone, between Berlin and Paris.

Saturday 5 March   *p.13*

CZECHO-SLOVAKIA'S FIRM REPLY TO GERMANY
No Interference to be Permitted

TO DEFEND INDEPENDENCE WITH ALL ITS STRENGTH
The Status of the German Minority

From our own Correspondent

Vienna, March 4.

In a speech before the Prague Parliament to-day the Premier of Czecho-Slovakia, Dr. Milan Hodza, replied to Herr Hitler's speech to the Reichstag and Field Marshal Göring's speech delivered earlier in the week. Dr. Hodza said:

> We seek peace, but if it is our destiny to have to defend ourselves we will do so with all the intensity of our technical and moral resources. The Czecho-Slovak Government will defend its independence and all the attributes of the State with all the forces at its command.

THE GERMAN MINORITY

As to Herr Hitler's reference to the protection of the 10,000,000 Germans outside Germany's frontiers, Dr. Hodza said the German minority in Czecho-Slovakia (about 3,000,000) enjoyed all rights. If Herr Hitler thought to extend the protection of Germany to the Germans in Czecho-Slovakia, this was an intervention in the internal affairs of the Czecho-Slovak State.

While hoping to establish friendly relations with Germany, Czecho-Slovakia must reject any intervention in her internal affairs.

5

Clarity was necessary because it created goodwill, loyalty, and peace, while unclear statements produced uncertainty, distrust, and superfluous discussion.

The home of the German people in Czecho-Slovakia had been within the present boundaries since time immemorial. Under the circumstances it was the duty of the Czecho-Slovak State to arrange the life of the German minority in a way that they should recognise it as their home.

Dr. Hodza thought that the most important problem was to eliminate the psychological hindrances in the way of an understanding between Germany and Czecho-Slovakia. Nevertheless Czecho-Slovakia would have to reject any interference with the sovereignty of the State. A fruitful collaboration was only possible on a basis of equality and non-intervention.

'NOT AFRAID'

Dr. Hodza expressed the hope that ways for a reconciliation within the borders could be found:

> We were not afraid for one thousand years and we are not frightened to-day, because we believe in the unity of the hearts and in the sanity of all layers of our population. We wish for tranquillity and peace.

Dr. Hodza stressed Czecho-Slovakia's good relations with Austria, Hungary and Italy. He noted with satisfaction the statement by Mr. Chamberlain in the House of Commons, which he regarded as an assurance of the continuity of British policy. This was one of the most decisive elements in European peace. It was indisputable that Great Britain had consolidated her position in the world as a protector of peace, not only in relation to the vital interests of her own Empire, but in Central Europe also.

Dr. Hodza emphasised Czecho-Slovakia's intention to stand loyally by all the international agreements to which she was committed. He declared his faith in the mission of the Little Entente, to which Czecho-Slovakia was a party with Rumania and Yugo-Slavia. France's agreement with the Soviet Union no less than that with Czecho-Slovakia, he said, was a potent instrument of peace, and he noted with approval recent speeches by the French Premier and the French Foreign Minister. ...

The Czechoslovakian government was still apparently convinced that both Britain and France would be prepared to come to her aid should the situation arise, whereas a matter of a few months later Sir Horace Wilson would write 'If we two, Britain and Germany, came to an agreement regarding the settlement of the Czech problem, we shall simply brush aside the resistance that France or Czechoslovakia herself may offer to the decision.'

FRENCH CONCERN OVER CZECHO-SLOVAKIA
Reported Statement to Britain

From our own Correspondent

Paris, March 13.

As might be expected, the news of what is in fact a German annexation of Austria caused great indignation in France as well as profound uneasiness. It is held that the British Government has a great responsibility for the destruction of Austrian independence, which is a violation of a treaty signed by Great Britain and one more affront to the League of Nations, under whose protection Austria was placed. The view is that Mr. Chamberlain and Lord Halifax became responsible by rejecting the French proposal made immediately after the Berchtesgaden ultimatum that firm representations should be made in Berlin by the British and French Governments jointly. Had the British and French Governments, it is believed, told Hitler that they would not tolerate any further action against Austria he would have refrained from it. ...

The chief concern now is to prevent similar action against Czecho-Slovakia. The Czecho-Slovak Government has declared in reply to questions from Paris and London that it will resist any German attempt to intimidate Czecho-Slovakia and that if German troops invaded Czecho-Slovakia because an ultimatum had been rejected the Czecho-Slovak Army would resist by force. I understand that M. Delbos, the Acting Foreign Minister during the interregnum, informed Sir Eric Phipps, the British Ambassador here, yesterday that the cause of Czecho-Slovakia was the cause of France and that the same information has been given by the French Ambassador in London.

The Anschluss with Austria was yet another step by Germany which seriously weakened the position of France on the Western European mainland, coming as it did in the wake of the re-militarisation of the Rhineland and the outbreak of the Spanish Civil War. All these events were major potential threats to the defensive policies adopted by the French in their interwar military and diplomatic policy planning.

BRITAIN'S REPLY
Premier Announces Further Defence Efforts

HITLER'S VIENNA TRIUMPH
France Solemnly Renews Pledge to the Czechs

While Herr Hitler was making a conqueror's progress through the streets of the Austrian capital yesterday afternoon Mr. Chamberlain in the House of Commons was announcing that Germany's actions would force Britain to take still further defence measures. The Premier's words were:—

We must consider a new situation quickly, but with cool judgement. And I am confident that we shall be supported in asking that no one, whatever his preconceived notions may be, shall regard himself as being excluded from any extension of the national effort which may be called for.

In regard to our defence programmes, we have always made it clear that they were flexible and they would have to be reviewed from time to time in the light of any new development in the international situation. It would be idle to pretend that the recent events do not constitute a change of the kind we had in mind.

Accordingly we have decided to make a review, and in due course we shall announce what further steps we may think it necessary to take.

Mr. Chamberlain brushed aside the official German pretence that 'forcible pressure' was not exerted by the Reich. ... Mr. Chamberlain declared that the methods adopted by Germany throughout these events 'call for the severest condemnation' and must prejudice the Government's hope of promoting international co-operation. ...

FRANCE'S PLEDGE TO CZECHO-SLOVAKIA

Mr. Chamberlain recounted in his speech the German assurances to Czecho-Slovakia, but said nothing of the British position.

Yesterday France gave Czecho-Slovakia a solemn pledge that she is determined to honour her agreement with Czecho-Slovakia in the event of attack. The pledge was given by M. Blum, the Premier, and M. Paul-Boncour, the Foreign Minister, to the Czecho-Slovak Minister in Paris, and the French Ambassador in London was instructed (says Reuter) to inform the British Government of this determination.

Again, it seems entirely appropriate for the Czechoslovakian attitude to be fundamentally determined by the strong and repeated assurances given to her by France. Although Great Britain was less emphatic, there appeared little tangible evidence to suggest that Britain would be tardy in coming to Czechoslovakia's aid in the face of German threats.

p.22

LETTERS TO THE EDITOR

HITLER'S SEIZURE OF AUSTRIA
The 'Mein Kampf' Policy

To the Editor of the Manchester Guardian.

Sir,–Hitler moves on! His declared policy in 'Mein Kampf' is–

1. To tear up the Versailles Treaty.
2. Occupy the Rhineland.
3. Gain complete control of Austria.
4. Gain lands in Czecho-Slovakia or the Ukraine.
5. Seize colonies if he cannot get them by negotiation.
6. Subjugate France.

It may be we can only look on, but at least let us do it clear-eyed and hear no more about Germany's self-respect. I have often been puzzled at the kind of Germany decent Germans find worthy of respect.–Yours, &c.,

K. M. WALKER,
31, Swan Court, Chelsea, London, S.W.3, March 12.

From the above letter it is clear that the writer had both read and understood 'Mein Kampf' even if His Majesty's Government might not have done so.

FRANCE AND MR. CHAMBERLAIN
Not Last Word?

STAND WANTED ON CZECHO-SLOVAKIA

From our own Correspondent

Paris, March 16.

Mr. Chamberlain's speech has not been a disappointment here, for nobody expected anything better. ...

... the French Government is convinced that if France had to mobilise to protect Czecho-Slovakia the British Government would be on her side. ...

NOT MR. CHAMBERLAIN'S LAST WORD?

What is hoped here is that Mr. Chamberlain has not said his last word and that he may yet make a definite and public statement of policy. Meanwhile the French Government has informed the British Government that, should the occasion arise, France will fulfil all her obligations under her treaties of alliance with Czecho-Slovakia to the letter. This action shows that something has changed at the Quai d'Orsay. The French Government may now be expected to take an initiative sometimes instead of always waiting for the British Government to take one.

It is earnestly hoped here that it will be recognised in England that the situation is critical and that a definite attitude will be adopted in time, as nobody knows what Hitler may be going to do – he might attack Czecho-Slovakia at any moment.

The 1930s witnessed a gradual but clearly perceptible move by France to becoming subordinate to Great Britain in foreign policy matters. Yet, paradoxically, France had much less cause to act as an appeaser than had Britain. All the gains made by Germany as a result of French policy weakened France's position in Europe much more than they did Britain's.

RUSSIA AND THE CZECHS
Promise of Support

Moscow, March 15.

The Soviet Union would go to the aid of Czecho-Slovakia if she were attacked provided France did likewise, Reuter was informed by an authoritative spokesman here to-night. This would be in accordance with the pact of mutual assistance between the Soviet Union and Czecho-Slovakia.

Asked how such aid could be carried out in the absence of a common frontier, the spokesman replied, 'A corridor must be created'. (The 'corridor' would have to be by way of Rumania in the south or by way of the Baltic States in the north.)

The above would be referred to in later months by the Western Allies as yet another ploy by the USSR to insinuate its influence further into Europe under the guise of a friendship pact with Czechoslovakia. The 'corridor' idea was never a realistic one as it would have required the acquiescence of states who were never likely to have given their permission for Soviet troops to cross their territory.

Thursday 17 March   *p.20*

LETTERS TO THE EDITOR

BRITAIN AND THE DICTATORSHIPS
A Way to Save Czecho-Slovakia and Spain from Austria's Fate

To the Editor of the Manchester Guardian

Sir,–Yesterday's debate showed Parliament to be at last thoroughly aroused as to the dangers of allowing aggression to go unchecked. But the Government gave no indication whatever as to how it proposes to meet the danger except by (1) strengthened armaments, (2) consultation with France beforehand, (3) remonstrance afterwards. As to the rest, the Prime Minister deprecated 'hasty decisions'. That has the advantage that it allows public opinion to be mobilised to affect such decisions. How can this best be done?

In the most powerful speech of the debate Mr. Churchill gave his own solution in a series of vivid and arresting phrases. As the only alternative to being 'edged and pushed farther down the slope in a disorderly, expostulating crowd of embarrassed States', resulting in 'a general landslide' of the small countries into the orbit of the Fascist dictatorships, he suggested 'a stand while there is still a good company of united, very powerful countries that share our dangers and aspirations'. This should take the form of 'a solemn treaty for mutual defence against aggression', its forces marshalled in 'a grand alliance' with concerted staff arrangements – the whole to rest upon the Covenant of the League. This plan offered a strong step towards collective security for ourselves and others, and though he did not deny its risks he believed them to be less than in waiting till, 'when all else has been thrown to the wolves, we are left to face our fate alone'.

Here surely is a definite policy for which those of all parties who believe in it should unite. But there are two instalments of it which call for immediate action. The two countries in the most pressing danger to-day, both vital to the success of Mr. Churchill's proposed combination and both with special claims on ourselves, are Spain and Czecho-Slovakia. The former has shown already what a democracy on its defence can do when possessed by the belief that 'it is better to die on your feet than live on your knees' (President Azana). The latter has an equally brave spirit and far better resources. As Mr. Churchill ironically remarked, her army is only two or three times as large as ours and her munitions supply only three times as great as that of Italy. Nevertheless, neither nation probably can hold out for ever against Great Powers aided by internal rebellion, if all their natural allies desert them.

As to Spain, Sir Archibald Sinclair said rightly that the success of General Franco meant that her whole resources, 'her man-power, economic wealth, strategic position, islands, and colonies will pass over to the credit of Germany and Italy and will be used to reinforce the structure of their war machine'. At this stage it seems to me unrealistic to urge (as some speakers did) the withdrawal of foreign man-power. That could not be done quickly enough. Not man-power but overwhelming superiority in munitions and aeroplanes, plus their own inferiority in food supplies, is destroying the Spanish Republican. The one practicable remedy to-day is to abandon the tragic, dishonourable farce of non-intervention and to permit and encourage the supply of arms from our own and other democratic countries.

As to Czecho-Slovakia, it seems probable that Austria's fate was precipitated by Mr. Chamberlain's declaration three weeks ago that small nations could expect no protection from the League, nor (as the rest of his speech implied) from ourselves. Mr. Eden's policy was at least to leave the Dictators guessing. The result of the change will be the same for Czecho-Slovakia unless the Government makes it perfectly plain that France and Russia will find us by their side if they fulfil their treaty obligations to resist her destruction. Those who flinch from this do not seem to realise what would be the result if France resisted alone and were defeated. As Mr. Churchill has recently reminded us, France is at least as necessary to our defence as we are to hers.

The notable point of yesterday's debate was the consensus of opinion, irrespective of party, as to these dangers, though on the Spanish question 'class prejudice and property sense' (to quote Captain Liddell Hart) still blind the strategic sight of some. The next few weeks offer an opportunity, which may be the last, of rallying public opinion to the support of collective security and, as a beginning, to effective defence of the two threatened democracies whose fate is now hanging in the balance. I suggest, therefore, that those who share these beliefs should concentrate on these points.–Yours, &c.,

ELEANOR F. RATHBONE,
House of Commons, March 15.

Eleanor Rathbone was an independent MP representing the English Universities, and a critic of the National Government's foreign policy toward Germany and Italy. For the key points of Mr. Chamberlain's speech see reports of Tuesday 15 March.

p.20

THE TIME TO MAKE A STAND IS NOW

To the Editor of the Manchester Guardian

Sir,–In to-day's leader you say: 'There must come a time when the democracies, and any other countries that are with them, make a stand.' That time is surely now. The tactics of Germany render it likely that an early and sudden threat of force will be presented to Czecho-Slovakia in pursuit of the all-Germany policy. To rely upon some action of the League in protection of a member might be of no avail, as in the case of Austria, though the full powers of the League might be invoked in support of a stand already taken. A stand by whom? By the three Great Powers who are members of the League but have a special concern to protect Czecho-Slovakia–Britain, France, and Russia.

France has already declared her intention to stand by her plain formal obligation to safeguard the independence of Czecho-Slovakia. If in the fulfilment of this pledge she should be engaged in war with Germany, could we withhold our armed assistance? If we were unwilling to do our part and left France to co-operate alone with Russia the issue would be precarious. Only if we now express without delay our intention to act with France and Russia would the balance of power be so strongly against Germany as to deter Hitler from forcible action.

13

The Parliamentary debate and the press comments indicate how reluctant we are to commit ourselves to any co-operation with Soviet Russia, discredited as she is by recent revelations of brutality and injustice. But though her efficiency for military action may be impaired by what has taken place there is no reason to doubt that her fighting force (especially in the air) is far greater than during the Great War. However hateful, therefore, such an alliance may be to our Government, any immediate policy of action likely to deter Hitler from his next contemplated coup requires an early announcement of common action with France and Russia for the protection of Czecho-Slovakia. Why shirk this unpleasant duty, the only reasonable protection against the further quick aggression of a Germany which regards all its pledges as 'sacred' only in the sense that they may help to deceive gullible Governments into a too-late 'waiting' policy?–Yours, &c.,

J.A. HOBSON,
Hampstead, March 15.

Hobson was a noted economist and author of 'The Evolution of Modern Capitalism and Imperialism'.

Wednesday 23 March   *p.6*

PROBLEMS OF BRITISH FOREIGN POLICY
Spain Still the Most Dangerous Issue

CZECHO-SLOVAKIA: A CONFLICT THAT MIGHT AFFECT OUR VITAL INTERESTS

From our Diplomatic Correspondent

London, Tuesday Night

The views of the British Government on foreign affairs are not as directly discernible as they used to be, because exceptional precautions are being taken to prevent them from becoming known, while official optimism is being spread so as to promote the public illusion that things are, if not exactly well, not at all as bad as some people make out.

There is, of course, no question of any kind of formal censorship or pressure. But a few hints have sufficed to lighten the emphasis on the seriousness of the situation in the picture theatres and on the wireless by reducing news reel references and discussion to a minimum.

Not for many years has there been so little contact between the press as a whole and those responsible for the conduct of foreign policy. The change that came about when Mr. Eden resigned is as perceptible as ever, though there is one rather significant exception. Between those who favour an isolationist policy (if it can be called a policy) and certain members of the Cabinet there is a certain intimacy which is reflected in several ways, especially in the excessive optimism those of 'isolationist' tendency are helping to spread.

CZECHO-SLOVAKIA

With regard to Central Europe, there will be no direct guarantee to defend the independence of Czecho-Slovakia against a German attack. On that point there is agreement between the Government and many of their more serious critics – namely, that such a guarantee cannot be given.

But the fact remains that a German attack on Czecho-Slovakia would have far-reaching consequences that could not leave Great Britain unaffected. It is taken for granted here that if the Czechs are attacked then they will fight, and it is clear that a war in the very heart of Europe, and one that may go on for weeks (the fighting quality of the Czech Army is rated very high by experts here), could not be localised, as the Spanish civil war could be. The French and Russian guarantees make it as good as certain that the war would become general almost from the beginning.

It seems most unlikely that Germany will attack Czecho-Slovakia seeing that she has the possibility of exercising what Lord Halifax would call 'peaceful' pressure on that terribly endangered country. Germany would run the risk of losing everything by an armed attack on Czecho-Slovakia, whereas she still has much to gain in Central and Eastern Europe by her 'peaceful' methods.

A QUESTION OF DEFENDING BRITAIN

Even if it is impossible for Great Britain to give a specific guarantee with regard to Czecho-Slovak independence, it is equally impossible to give the Germans (or anyone else) even an indirect guarantee that Great Britain will remain neutral in any conflict that may arise out of a German–Czech war. It may be said that the independence of Czecho-Slovakia is not a vital British interest as the independence of Spain certainly is, but a conflict spreading as the result of German aggression might affect British vital interests very quickly.

The question resolves itself not into one of defending Czecho-Slovakia but of defending Great Britain; it is not one of right or wrong, or of the treatment of minorities, or of what the Sudetic Germans want or do not want or have a right to have or not to have, or of the justice or injustice of Hitler's claims, but simply of the security of Great Britain, which may have to be defended against the consequences of an attack on Czecho-Slovakia just as they had to be defended against the ultimate consequences of the attack on Serbia in 1914.

One may therefore expect that Mr. Chamberlain will leave the world in no doubt that Great Britain would regard a German attack on Czecho-Slovakia as a very grave matter indeed. It may also be expected that the terrible gravity of the whole European situation will be emphasised by a further increase in the speed and volume of British rearmament.

From a strategic position, the Spanish Civil War was more than just a civil war, for given the possibility of an Anglo—French—German conflict at some future time, a possibility that simply could not be ruled out, the probability of opening the Atlantic and Mediterranean coasts of Spain to hostile ships and aircraft apparently left the British Chiefs of Staff curiously unmoved.

Friday 25 March   *p.11*

WHEN WE WOULD FIGHT
Premier Defines British Obligations

CZECHO-SLOVAKIA'S CASE
No Direct Pledge But Warning to Aggressors

Mr. Chamberlain, the Prime Minister, made his statement on foreign policy to a crowded House of Commons yesterday.

Mr. Chamberlain's chief declarations were—

1. There can be no direct guarantee to Czecho-Slovakia and no pledge of automatic help to France if she became involved in war because of her commitments to Czecho-Slovakia;
2. Non-Intervention in Spain is still the best policy; and
3. There is to be a big acceleration of the rearmament programme in which defence requirements must take priority in respect of both men and materials. ...

The Premier offered the British Government's help in the solution of questions likely to cause difficulty between the German and the Czecho-Slovak Governments.

Many varied reasons have been advanced for Chamberlain's somewhat extraordinary initiative in undertaking to mediate between Czechoslovakia and Germany, one of which is that he saw himself in the role of the 'honest broker', i.e. not directly concerned but wishing to avert the possibility of a conflict which had the almost inevitability of dragging Britain or at least her interests into the struggle.

16

CZECHO-SLOVAKIA

Since the union of Austria and Germany Dr. Hodza, the Premier of Czecho-Slovakia, and Dr. Benes, the President, have both made formal declarations on the subject of the German minority in their country. It would be hard to find two more statesmanlike speeches in the history of modern politics than these. The Czech Government is in a most difficult position. It must strive to conciliate the German minority and by timely concessions to deprive Germany of any excuse for intervention, yet it must avoid the danger which faces all those who would negotiate with Hitler's Germany – that conciliation may be mistaken for weakness. The official demands of the Sudeten Germans in Czecho-Slovakia cannot be conceded without disrupting Czecho-Slovakia herself. That, indeed, may be their purpose. Dr. Hodza, however, has promised a new 'minority statute' which shall meet their more reasonable claims, and has invited, as also did Dr. Benes on Saturday, the German leaders to discuss these problems with the Government. As earnest of its good intentions the Czech Government has already proposed to hold this year the municipal elections which were postponed last year to the annoyance of the German minority, and on Saturday Dr. Benes signed a decree granting a wide amnesty to political prisoners. As this pardon applies chiefly to offenders under the Defence of the Republic Act, the Sudeten Germans stand to gain the greatest benefit. The calm confidence and generous spirit of Dr. Benes's speech compel admiration in themselves; but the internal policy of the Czech Government deserves the active support of the great European Powers, for on its success their peace may depend.

The problem of Czech–Sudeten relations had been exacerbated in 1935 by the formation of a Sudeten–German party. This party, although not advocating union with Germany, did support the idea of self-government. The Czech government resisted any such move, as it foresaw that it would be the first step from a unitary to a federal structure. The logical progression of such a move would be that each of the ethnic minorities in Czechoslovakia would in turn demand self-government and so gravely weaken the structure of the state as a whole.

These fears were not unfounded as the Anschluss had ensured that Czechoslovakia's position vis-a-vis Germany had been enfeebled in that her formidable frontier defences had been outflanked and she was now guarding a frontier which was only part of her boundaries with Germany/Austria.

BIG DEMANDS ON CZECHO-SLOVAKIA
Change in Country's Foreign Policy

HENLEIN'S SPEECH

Carlsbad, April 24.

Eight demands were made by Herr Konrad Henlein, leader of the Sudeten Germans, in his eagerly awaited speech at the party congress here to-day.

Herr Henlein said that to pave the way to peaceful developments they thought that the legal order of the State should be constructed on the following lines:–

1. Full equality of status between Czechs and Germans.
2. Guarantee of equality by recognition of the Sudeten Germans as a legal personality.
3. Determination and legal recognition of the German regions within the State.
4. Full self-government for these German regions.
5. Legal protection for every citizen living outside the region of his own nationality.
6. Removal of injustices inflicted upon us since 1918. Reparation of the damages caused thereby.
7. Recognition and realisation of the principal 'German regions and German officials'.
8. Full liberty to profess German nationality and the German political philosophy. ...

Leader ## 'HIGH TIME'

The careful phrases of the official communiqué issued at the end of the Anglo-French conversations in London yesterday reveal no secrets in the French translation, however, the stilted language of diplomacy is broken by a curious phrase – almost slang – which may or may not express an emotion common to Mr. Chamberlain and M. Daladier, to Lord Halifax and M. Bonnet. 'The Ministers', it runs, 'have agreed that it is high time in the present circumstances that the two Governments should continue and develop their policy of collaboration and consultation concerning defences. 'High time': it is a striking phrase. One would not build too greatly on this slender foundation, but it suggests at least that the Ministers of both countries were aware, in spite of their reference to 'appeasement' (blessed word!) in Europe, that there is no time to lose. It would suggest, too, that our special correspondent was right when he wrote that the chief result of the conversations would be to strengthen the military alliance between France and Britain. Reports have all agreed that a measure of co-operation is contemplated betwen the Air Forces of the two countries and that there is to be some mutual arrangement for the buying of aeroplanes and raw materials. These measures go farther, perhaps, than two independent States have ever gone before in peacetime alliance, certainly farther than Britain and France had gone in 1914 – but few will dare to criticise them. It is legitimate to point out that when danger threatens even Mr. Chamberlain is forced to turn to 'collective security' for safety instead of relying only on his good right arm.

The immediate danger, of course (though one might not guess so from the communique), is Central Europe – and, in particular, Czecho-Slovakia. The Czech Government is understood to have presented a memorandum to the British Government stressing the critical nature of the situation and stating how far it is prepared to go in making concessions to the claims of the Sudeten Germans. The French Government is also understood to have outlined a scheme by which the British Government might strengthen Czecho-Slovakia and the other small countries of South-east Europe against the German advance by buying more of their exports and so making them less dependent on Germany. The current number of the 'Bulletin of International News' contains an admirable summary of the extent to which South-east Europe is now economically dependent on Germay since the union with Austria. If 'Grossdeutschland' had been in existence last year it would have taken just under half the exports from Bulgaria and Hungary, over a third from Turkey and Yugo-Slavia, over a quarter from Greece and Rumania, and one-fifth from Czecho-Slovakia and Poland. Even before the Anschluss Germany was already the chief market for every country in South-east Europe except Albania. For Britain to reverse this process would be an immense task, made more difficult by our existing trade agreements with other food-producing countries. Moreover, though most, if not all, of these small countries are anxious to become less dependent on Germany, they are held in subjection by their 'frozen credits' in Germany which they cannot afford to lose. As the 'Bulletin' also points out, the 'recession' in the United States and the threat of a new world-wide depression are likely to increase the German grip.

It is unlikely, therefore, that even with the best intentions the British Government could save the peace of Central Europe by economic action. There is, we must remember, no time to lose; the Germans boast of a settlement 'by the autumn'. The Czech problem is one of peculiar difficulty. It is unlikely that Germany will annex the Sudetenland by force, for the Czech Army is strong enough to prevent another version of the policy of the 'accomplished fact', and there can be no doubt that war would bring in France and maybe Britain. But such an open use of force may not be necessary. By economic power, by gradual encirclement, by internal disruption Germany may secure the downfall of the Czech Government. The road to Prague may lie through Bucharest, Budapest, and even Warsaw as much as through Carlsbad, and it is unfortunate that Czecho-Slovakia should be on bad terms with all her neighbours and not only with Germany. German irredentism flourishes on the complaints of the Hungarian and Rumanian minorities as well as on its own soil. Strategically, moreover, Czecho-Slovakia is now cut off by land from both of the two countries pledged to her support – France and Russia; in war it would be impossible to defend her except by defeating Germany. Yet, carefully handled, a peaceful and just solution, such as is described in the Anglo-French communiqué, is not impossible. Two factors should prove advantageous: first, Germany does not want war, and, secondly, not all the Germans in Czecho-Slovakia want to be under the German Government. The Czech Government is prepared to make far-reaching concessions. If these are firmly supported by the French and British Governments, and if the German Government is made to understand that it will be responsible for their rejections, there is good hope that the Czech concessions may be accepted by the German minority. But it is a condition of success that the British Government should show itself actively interested in this and every other problem of Central Europe.

On 28 May 1938 Hitler issued orders that the Sudeten-German question must be settled, once and for all in that year and certainly not later than 1 October. He did not deviate from that self-imposed timetable.

p.17

ANGLO-FRENCH MILITARY CO-OPERATION
German Dislike of London Talks

TALK OF COUNTER-ACTION IN ROME NEXT WEEK

From our own Correspondent

Berlin, April 29.

There is little doubt that Germany is disturbed by the military agreements which are reported here to have been made between France and Britain during the London conversations. In some quarters here it is thought that it would not be surprising if they found their counterpart in Rome when Hitler meets Mussolini next week.

The great strength of the German delegation – which in all amounts to about 300 – is particularly remarked. The Army, Navy, and Air Force are strongly represented, while a substantial part of the Foreign Office, including the eminent jurist Dr. Gaus, as well as the Foreign Minister and the leading departmental chiefs, are travelling to Rome. A mutual military assistance pact is talked of as a distinct possibility in certain Berlin political quarters.

German misgivings about the French and British attitude to Czecho-Slovakia as a result of the London conversations appear to be at least as great as the misgivings about the military aspects. This is understandable. Germany has for long discounted some form of Anglo-French defensive alliance in the attainment of her Continental arms, but Germany has never wished to have to collide with Britain in attempting to obtain that settlement of accounts with Czecho-Slovakia which unofficial quarters here are fairly sure is to come about by the late summer. To a considerable extent the view of a division of powers, or super-spheres of influence, as between this country for the Continent of Europe and Britain overseas, has continued to inspire German policy in its main lines in spite of the pact with Japan, and Germany's colonial claims. Until now Germany has not yet really contemplated a complete break with that policy. ...

CAMPAIGN AGAINST CZECHS

In the press it is declared that the Danubian area is to Germany what the sea routes of the world are to Britain in respect of foodstuffs and raw materials. Naturally, writes one paper, we attach the same value to these Continental markets for food and raw materials not being blocked as England does to the freedom of her sea connections.

The campaign against Czecho-Slovakia is, in fact, in full swing again here. A Czecho-Slovakia hostile to Germany, it is declared, is the same menace to Germany as a hostile Ireland would be to Great Britain – the more so since only a land frontier separates the former countries and Czecho-Slovakia has, additionally, an alliance with Russia.

The 'Angriff', the Nazi official evening organ, begins to-night a series of articles entitled 'Not Moscow but Prague' in which allegations are made that the Czech Government treats Sudetic German workpeople in an inhuman fashion, particularly in the radium mines. Pictures are shown of naked emaciated miners suffering from cancer contracted at their work in the radium mines, which resemble those exhibited in the anti-Bolshevik exhibitions here, where alleged victims of starvation and slaughter in Russia were shown with gruesome details.

FRENCH VIEWS ON THE LONDON TALKS
The Military Side Emphasised

PLEASURE & DOUBTS

From our Correspondent

Paris, April 20.

French opinion regards the decisions of the London talks with a paradoxical mixture of profound satisfaction and serious anxiety. The development of the Entente into what is generally described as being virtually a defensive alliance between France and Great Britain is warmly welcomed.

It is generally believed that an understanding has been reached which provides in case of war for unity of command of the two Armies under French direction and of the two Air Forces under British direction, with British reserves of petrol stored in France and British use of French aerodromes. It is believed also that there is agreement on the principle of joint purchases of war material and also of foodstuffs for war emergency, and that France has agreed to pool her agricultural resources and general food supplies with those of Great Britain.

It is suggested in the 'Temps' to-night that both of these understandings will be helped forward by the immediate establishment of a permanent mission for working out the details of military co-operation and a permanent board.

NAVAL DEFENCE

With regard to naval defence, it is believed that it is proposed to re-establish the division of responsibility of the naval agreement of 1907, under which France was charged with the security of the communications of both countries in the Mediterranean and Great Britain with the protection of the Channel and Atlantic coasts of France. It is even considered in some quarters that Franco-British defensive co-operation is in future pledged in regard to the whole of Western Europe and the whole of the Mediterranean instead of being limited, in the case of Great Britain, to assistance in the event of unprovoked attack by Germany on France.

All this is considered to be highly satisfactory, as is also the prospect of British financial co-operation with France, which is inferred from Sir John Simon's answer to a question in the House of Commons yesterday.

HESITATION ABOUT CENTRAL EUROPE

Nevertheless France remains anxious because Great Britain is not willing to take the firm stand over the Central European danger which, in the French view, would prevent that danger from materialising but is disposed to hesitate in the very way which is considered here to be likely to lead to catastrophe.

France looks at the strength of Franco-British defence as an element in a wide collective-security system which shall include Czecho-Slovakia and the whole of the Little Entente as well as Russia, and not as a step to the Four-Power Pact towards which the British Government would like to lead France.

French opinion is convinced that a declaration by Great Britain to the effect that the destruction of Czecho-Slovakia would not be tolerated would be sufficient to save that country from attack, as her own defences are by no means negligible, but that the absence of such a declaration will tempt Germany to launch a course of South-eastern aggression which may easily sweep away Yugo-Slavia and Rumania, as well as Hungary, and may rapidly carry German power to the Black Sea as well as to the Adriatic.

GERMANY WAITING FOR SIGNS OF WEAKNESS?

Both the 'Populaire' and the 'Humanité' to-day express their conviction that Germany is waiting for any show of weakness by France and England on this matter in order to take action.

This view is not confined to the press of the extreme Left, for M. Burè takes the same line in 'L'Ordre'. Moreover, several papers of the Right insist that France cannot fail to carry out her treaty obligations to protect Czecho-Slovakia if attacked. It is recognised that the British Government is aware of this and will consequently make every effort by diplomatic means to persuade Germany not to precipitate the crisis, but the feeling here is that the moment has not yet come when approaches towards Germany can usefully be made.

Monday 16 May   p.6

REDUCING CZECHO-SLOVAKIA TO A VASSAL STATE

From our Diplomatic Correspondent

London, Sunday.

Herr Henlein in his visit last week was not officially received here, but his visit was not a private one. He is an instrument of German foreign policy, an instrument that is being used to sever the connection between Prague and Moscow and to make Czecho-Slovakia a vassal of Germany.

There is no question of a German–Czech war. Herr Hitler himself believes, rightly no doubt, that an armed attack on Czecho-Slovakia might lead to a general European conflict, for which Germany is not prepared.

It is even doubtful whether Herr Hitler wants the break-up of Czecho-Slovakia. It would seem that he wants to preserve Czecho-Slovakia within her present frontiers and to exercise a domination over her through the Sudeten Germans. If the country were to break up, the Polish and Ukrainian minorities would be incorporated in Poland and the Hungarian minority in Hungary. This would mean the joining of Poland and Hungary, so that Germany would not have access to Rumania.

'SALIENT' FOR GERMANY

But if Czecho-Slovakia remains intact and becomes a vassal of Germany's Germany will be in a position of enormous strength. For Germany Czecho-Slovakia is a kind of salient whence she can achieve a political, military, and economic hegemony over the South-eastern European countries, especially over Rumania, whose oil and corn belt she needs. Czecho-Slovakia is a key position, though one that also has an intrinsic value to Germany.

Later on, perhaps in a few years' time, if Germany decides to 'solve' the Polish 'problem' she will be in a position to do so almost irresistably if she has control over Czecho-Slovakia.

'Home rule' for the Sudeten Germans is a step towards the capture of this key position. When the Sudeten Germans have got 'home rule', or something like it, they will come under German domination while remaining within the Czecho-Slovak frontier. Only Czech control can save them from German control. With 'home rule' they will be just as little the masters over their own territory as the Austrian National Socialists are masters of Austria.

'Home rule' for the Sudeten Germans means that they will exchange the freedom and equality they now enjoy under the Czechs for vassalage under the Germans of the Reich. But as vassals they will be the instruments for reducing the Czechs to vassalage as well. Perhaps there will be a time when 'home rule' for the Czechs will be a European issue.

A most prescient article which correctly forecasts the outcome of a Czechoslovakia absorbed by Germany and its effects on the 'Polish question'. Henlein arrived unannounced, in London on the evening of Thursday 12 May.

RUSSIA & DEFENCE OF THE CZECHS
Question of Staff Talks

From our own Correspondent

Geneva, May 17.

According to information from a well-informed French source M. Bonnet, the French Foreign Minister, in the course of a conversation with Mr. Litvinoff, the Russian Foreign Minister, in Geneva last week, asked Mr. Litvinoff what measures Russia would be prepared to take in the event of an attack on Czecho-Slovakia. Mr. Litvinoff replied that the matter was one for the Russian General Staff acting in agreement with the French and Czecho-Slovak General Staffs and that it would be impossible to draw up a plan without conversation between the three General Staff concerned.

It had been agreed, Mr. Litvinoff said, when the Franco-Soviet Pact was signed on May 2, 1935, that there should be conversations between the French and Russian General Staffs, but hitherto the French Government had always refused to allow such conversations to take place, although the Russian and Czecho-Slovak Governments had repeatedly asked for them. Clearly if there is to be any effective joint action on the part of France and Russia for the defence of Czecho-Slovakia it cannot be improvised at a moment's notice.

The opinion in international quarters here is that if the French Government does not agree to the military conversations in question it will have to be assumed that the French Government has no serious intention of defending Czecho-Slovakia if that country is attacked.

At the same time a German military attack on Czecho-Slovakia is considered to be very unlikely for the reasons given by your diplomatic correspondent in the 'Manchester Guardian' yesterday, one of which is that with the aid of the British and French Governments Herr Hitler will get all he wants without resorting to force.

The correspondent in Geneva made a remarkably accurate assessment in this article of the role played by Great Britain and France in the subsequent Munich negotiations.

THE CZECH CRISIS

It was as recently as March 11 that reports of German movements heralded the downfall of independent Austria. With the third week of May reports of similar movements on the Czech frontier have opened up a much graver crisis, for Czecho-Slovakia is not a State that would yield to a military demonstration were one intended, and no one could set bounds to a conflict should one break out. That the position has its grave dangers – though there is no reason why it should not be held in hand, and held it will be if there is any sanity left in Europe – is clear from a mere survey of the week-end's events. The German Government denied that there had been any troop movements which were not of a purely routine nature; the Czecho-Slovak Government, no doubt remembering the sequel to the events of Friday, March 11, has taken the precaution of calling up a number of reservists. For some time feeling between Czechs and Sudeten Germans has been rising, each side accusing the other of provocation and violence, and it was expected that there might be some disorders yesterday, which was the first day of the municipal elections. In fact there seems to have been no disorder, but, though it had nothing to do with the elections, two Germans were shot on the frontier, and a fresh stimulant was provided for the violent campaign of the German press against the Czechs. On Saturday the British Ambassador in Berlin was twice at the Foreign Office seeking assurances that no serious troop movements were taking place, and yesterday he again saw Herr von Ribbentrop, for the purpose, it may be assumed, of urging on the German Government the necessity of a reasonable course of action.

There is nothing in any 'incidents' either within Czecho-Slovakia or on the border that could conceivably justify any country in imperilling peace. It would be strange if there were not some incidents in a country now disturbed, as was Austria before, by the pressure of the National Socialist power. The Nazis accuse the Czechs of terrorism, just as they accused Herr von Schuschnigg in the same way, but others, including the German Democrats in Czecho-Slovakia, affirm with much detailed evidence that the violence comes from the Nazi side. In any event, nothing is more certain than that the Czech government is ready to exert, and will exert, every effort to protect the Sudeten German minority from any form of persecution: how should it do otherwise since it is in desperate case and must at any cost avoid provoking the German Government? There is no ground for any threat or danger of war in any 'incidents' or 'disorders' arising out of minority questions; there is nothing of that kind that cannot be dealt with by the ordinary means of peaceful international intercourse, and only if there are any who seek a pretext for violent means will violence be used or even threatened. Whether or not Germany now seeks to ground herself on the supposed ill-treatment of the Sudeten Germans, the deeper danger lies in the demands which, through Herr Henlein, she is making on the Czech Government and in the inability of that Government to grant them. The question is whether Germany is willing to allow her spokesmen and the Government to negotiate peaceably for a settlement that may be compatible with the continued existence and security of Czecho-Slovakia or whether she proposes to have her own way willy-nilly.

Herr Henlein has put forward certain demands, and the Czech Government has made its own proposals. Herr Henlein asks for 'a complete revision of Czech foreign policy', by which he means the abandonment of the alliances with France and (in particular) Soviet Russia: he asks that the Sudeten-German community should be accorded not only autonomy but a 'legal personality' of its own, which would make it more amenable to control from Germany: and, of course, the Sudeten Germans must have full liberty to express the Nazi 'philosophy'. These are large demands to make of a State which is to remain independent, and they are the demands not merely of Henlein but of Germany. The Czech Government, on it side, has proposed a scheme which means a large measure of autonomy for the Sudeten Germans and proportional representation for them and the other minorities in the appointment of officials, the allocation of contracts, and the like. The Germans have refused to enter the discussion until they receive 'guarantees' that peace, order, and freedom of speech will be maintained. In this critical situation there are several things that the British Government can do. If specific 'incidents' threaten danger, it can immediately propose that international inquiry into the responsibility which is the only right solution and it can offer to play its full part in such a mission; it will not be forgotten that during the Russo-Japanese war this country, while under great provocation and when feeling was strong against Russia, did not hesitate to submit the Dogger Bank 'outrage' to an international court. In the broader field the British Government cannot exert itself too strongly to impress on Germany the reasons why the differences between the Czecho-Slovak State and the Sudeten German minority should be allowed to go forward to full and peaceable discussion. The reasons from the stand-point not only of the local peace but of European and world peace are manifest, and there is reason to believe that the Government has expressed them firmly during the week-end. Herr Hitler has always congratulated himself that his sweeping successes have been gained by peaceful means. It is impossible to believe that he will not recognise the responsibility that rests on him now.

BRITAIN WILLING TO ACT AS MEDIATOR

From our London Staff

Fleet Street, Sunday Night.

The Cabinet met for an hour this evening to consider the events which have taken place in Czecho-Slovakia and Germany since Friday.

It is recognised that the situation is extremely critical, and the immediate aim of the Government is to secure a breathing space so that passion may abate on both sides of the frontier. To this end the Government is doing its utmost, both in Prague and in Berlin, to make acceptable a policy of moderation.

No attempt is being made here at present to sift the highly confused and contradictory evidence about the shooting incident reported on Saturday, and the timing of troop movements, for it is held that it would be dangerous to pronounce any judgment until the facts of the week-end can be seen more objectively.

The practical steps which the Government has taken have been to urge upon Prague the avoidance of more incidents and the need for hurrying a settlement with Herr Henlein. In Berlin the British Government is pointing to the merits of patience and of moderation in press comments.

If it is possible, the British Government would gladly act as mediator in the conflict, but it must have the confidence of both sides first. Once a breathing space has been secured the British Government will return to its original policy of trying to smooth out the difficulties in the way of a settlement of the Sudeten-German problem.

This declared willingness by Great Britain to act as a mediator with regard to Czecho-Slovakian—German relationships would ultimately lead to the despatch of Lord Runciman in August 1938 and the visits by Prime Minister Chamberlain to Berchtesgaden, Godesburg and Munich in September, 1938.

NO 'AUTOMATIC WAR'

Paris, May 22.

Official quarters emphatically deny the report that a spokesman of the French Foreign Office last night said:

If Germany crosses the Czech frontier it will automatically start war. France will furnish the utmost help to Czechoslovakia if she is the victim of aggression.

'No such statement was ever made,' Reuter was informed to-day. It is true that M. Bonnet, the French Foreign Minister, yesterday reiterated to both the British and Soviet Ambassadors that France would completely fulfil her obligations to Czechoslovakia in case of necessity. It is emphasised, however, that French obligations depend on the Locarno Treaty, in which there is no question of automatic action. This does not weaken the fact that France would act loyally if circumstances warranted.

The above article highlights the continued ambiguous approach of France to the Czechoslovakian problem, in that she had unequivocal treaty obligations towards Czechoslovakia but constantly fudged the manner in which these obligations would be met.

Tuesday 24 May

CZECH AND GERMAN

Mr. Chamberlain's statement on the Czech crisis in the House of Commons was bare but sufficient. So long as the Opposition is satisfied that, on the whole, the Government is taking the right course it will not complain of lack of information. There is a nice distinction between reticence and secrecy, and for once the Government is on the right side. Yet Mr. Chamberlain managed to reveal what are obviously the two main objects of his policy. First, to restrain the German Government from taking precipitate action by reminding her of the grave consequences which might follow; secondly, to urge the Czecho-Slovak Government to arrive at a settlement with the Sudeten-German minority while there is still time to do so. Some success, it would seem, has already been achieved in the first aim, and, in Mr. Chamberlain's words, 'the situation appears to have somewhat eased'. But since the crisis was manufactured in Germany and consisted really in nothing but a sudden increase of German pressure, it is clear that the wind may rise again as quickly as it has fallen. It is therefore all the more important to take advantage of the lull to hurry on negotiations for a lasting settlement. Here, too, Mr. Chamberlain had something to announce. Herr Henlein, who had been formally invited by the Czech Government to discuss the proposed Nationality Statute on May 21 and who had refused on the ground that 'peace and order' had not been guaranteed, has now consented to see the Czech Ministers. So at least there are to be negotiations and the Sudeten Germans have shown themselves capable of making at least one small concession. It is a promising start.

In this country much energy is still expended by private individuals in discussing the rights and wrongs of the situation and whether the Allies were wise to put the historic claims of the Bohemian frontier before the new principle of self-determination. In general this attitude is praiseworthy, but it is no longer relevant to the present case. The British and French Governments have both advised the Czech Government to go to the utmost in making concessions, and by that they mean far farther than is necessary to fulfill the demands of justice. (As it is the Sudeten Germans have little to complain of.) The Czech Government itself is very willing to put expediency before its rights. The real problem is now to find a solution which will satisfy the Sudeten Germans, deprive the German Government of any excuse to continue its intervention, and yet prevent the disruption of the Czech State. We do not yet know whether such a solution is possible, but we do know that it must be attempted. One of the main difficulties is ignorance as to what exactly the Sudeten Germans want, and whether what they want is also the wish of the German Government. It is possible, for instance, that the Sudeten Germans want autonomy in Czecho-Slovakia but not union with Germany, while the German Government may want the inclusion of all the Sudeten Germans in the boundaries of the Third Reich. On the other hand, it is also possible that the German Government is really more interested in using the Sudeten Germans to break up or gain control of Czecho-Slovakia as a means to achieving its imperialist aims in South-east Europe. If that were true the German Government might be satisfied with some quite reasonable concession now, believing that it would help in the end to win some greater gain. In this belief, again, it might be right or wrong.

The actual position of the German minority in Czecho-Slovakia is no less complicated. There are about three and a quarter million Germans, or 23 per cent of the total population. Though the great majority of these live in the old district of Bohemia bordering Germany, they do not all do so, and even in the Sudetenland proper there are strips and enclaves inhabited by a majority of Czechs. So mixed are the two peoples that it would be quite impossible to draw a boundary which would not leave many Germans outside or many Czechs inside. There are also some

700,000 Hungarians and 80,000 Poles in Czecho-Slovakia, and it is clear that the Czech Government will be morally obliged to offer them the same concessions as are offered to the Germans. But if, in spite of the difficulties, it were decided to grant the Germans 'Home Rule' or autonomy, it would mean that the most important part of the Czech frontier with Germany would be under the control of Germans and not Czechs – obviously an unfortunate position. On the other hand, if the Germans had Home Rule and the right to keep order in their own districts, the German Government could hardly intervene on the ground that the Sudeten Germans required protection and that the Czechs could not keep order. As this is its favourite argument at present, the point is important. Yet how is it possible to grant the Germans Home Rule of any kind without also surrendering to the Nazi majority the German Jews, Socialists, and pacificsts who live in the same districts? Then there is the question of the Czech Government's foreign policy, and especially its pact with Russia. No minority can possibly claim to control a country's policy, but since everything is really dependent on Germany this too must be taken into consideration. Most of these points must be decided by the Czechs themselves, and the British Government can do little more than preserve an atmosphere in which negotiation is possible. But it should be remembered that, as Mr. Winston Churchill has pointed out, the more we encourage the Czechs to concede the more we are morally bound to support them if the concessions should fail.

p.16

FRENCH RELIEF AT PASSING OF WEEK-END CRISIS
The Danger that Still Remains

GERMANY SHOWN THAT CZECHO-SLOVAKIA IS NOT ALONE

From our own Correspondent

Paris, May 23.

Paris heaved a sigh of relief this morning when it found that 'nothing had happened' in Czecho-Slovakia. Nevertheless, nobody imagines that all danger has passed, and the French Government will not relax its vigilance. Herr Henlein's absence from Czecho-Slovakia during the election is regarded as rather ominous.

Although the French Government is seconding the British Government in its efforts to persuade the Czech Government to go to the utmost limit of concessions compatible with the preservation of the Czecho-Slovak State – and the comprehension and sense of responsibility generally of the Czech Government in this matter is given the highest praise everywhere – it is still doubted whether any solution can be found that Germany will accept.

This week-end is nevertheless believed to have had a salutary effect on Germany insofar as it must have convinced her that Czecho-Slovakia is not alone or helpless and certainly cannot be regarded as another Austria.

According to a number of reports Germany was afraid not only of French intervention supported by Britain, and of Russian intervention, but she was not even sure of Poland. While Poland would have intervened on Germany's side or at least have remained neutral, if Czecho-Slovakia had been left to her fate by the Great Powers, she might have acted entirely differently in the event of a general conflict. ...

There appears little doubt that a combined Czech—French—British force would have been more than a match, militarily, for Germany. This was certainly the perception of Hitler's military leaders such as Keitel and Jodl, who informed Hitler of the parlous nature of their military position.

Wednesday 25 May   *p.11*

DEMAND FOR DEMOBILISATION OF CZECH TROOPS
First Stages of Prague Talks

GERMAN PRESS ATTACKS ON BRITAIN
Denial that Crisis Ever Existed

From our Correspondent

Berlin, May 24.

The conversation between Dr. Hodza, Premier of Czecho-Slovakia, and Herr Henlein, leader of the Sudeten Germans, on Monday introduced a quieter note to-day in the views and comments voiced here on the Sudeten questions. Emphasis is laid on the wording of the statement issued by the Sudeten party, in which it is said that this meeting opened the conversations. As long as these talks continue it is felt the immediate danger of an acute crisis is checked. Rumours that Herr Henlein is in touch with Herr Hitler remain speculation as long as German official quarters strictly deny any direct interference of the Reich in the issue on hand. Herr Hitler was still in Bavaria to-day.

It is quite generally said here to-day, however, that it would be of little use to discuss the minority statute prepared by Prague as long as law and order is not assured. Originally the placing of police control in the hands of the Sudeten Germans was demanded.

This demand – in which there appears to be much interest here – is upheld, but a new demand has now been added. It is that Czecho-Slovakia should demobilise the soldiers which it had called into service shortly before the election began.

REASON FOR DEMAND

If the reported attacks of Czech police and military on innocent Sudeten pedestrians gave rise to the demand that the Czechs should surrender police control to the Sudeten Germans, the reported frontier violations have given rise to the demand that Czecho-Slovakia should reduce the number of its soldiers now under arms. If these two demands are not fulfilled, it is intimated, fresh incidents might occur which would be fraught with danger to peace.

Germany takes the line that the calling to arms of a number of Czech soldiers – described here as a mobilisation – was a mobilisation against Germany. The Reich showed great calm and self-control by not ordering a counter-mobilisation. This view is brought out most clearly in an inspired and important communiqué issued in the middle of last night. The communiqué describes how the Reich quickly denied rumours that it was mobilising, and then continues:

Nevertheless the Czechs called to arms one year of the reserves and mobilised technical troops. This leads to the conclusion that the assertion of a German mobilisation was merely invented in order to produce a pretext for Czech mobilisation. The Czechs overlooked, however, that such an irresponsible proceeding might have the result that Germany after all might adopt those measures for her own protection, which, until then, had not been taken, and had been quite correctly denied. In spite of this Czech manoeuvre, and in spite of further provocations, Germany preserved her calm and refrained from resorting to measures which seemed only too natural.

As a result of this it is now asked that Prague shall not only make peace with the Sudeten Germans but also with greater Germany.

ATTACKS ON BRITAIN

Great Britain, British diplomacy, the British press, and Mr. Chamberlain are the target of violent attacks here to-night. They have arisen from the strong annoyance felt here over British and other reported press comments which regard the lessening of the tension as the work of British diplomacy. The 'Deutsche Allgemeine Zeitung', for instance, writes:

A legend is spread around the world by the propaganda machine of the Entente. It is that Germany was about to disturb the peace and that only Great Britain's determined attitude saved the world in the last minute from a new catastrophe. Mr. Chamberlain is regarded as the saviour of peace. Paris congratulates Prague and London, and Prague and London congratulate one another. Peace was not menaced by Germany, therefore it could not be saved by Britain.

The 'Kölnische Zeitung' writes:

Of what does this British diplomatic success consist? Merely of having pretended to 'prevent' something which never was fact and never was intended.

GERMAN PEOPLE AGAINST WAR

The grave charges against Prague, the alarming news of incidents and frontier violations, have been read by the German public with much attention. The danger of a conflict was not denied over the week-end, but the general wish is that no such conflict may arise, as the population still has a keen memory of the devastations such a war is apt to entail.

Thursday 26 May   *p.6*

ITALY'S SYMPATHY WITH GERMANY
'British and French Lies'

Rome, May 25.

Solidarity with Germany in 'her indignation at the lies of the British and French press' is voiced in Italian newspapers and political quarters to-day. The 'lies' referred to are suggestions that the firm attitude of Britain and France, but primarily of Britain, has dissuaded Germany from an act of aggression against Czecho-Slovakia. These suggestions are denounced not only as entirely untrue but harmful to international relations.

Italian quarters praise the moderation of Germany and approve the German protest to Prague over alleged frontier incidents. 'The most noticeable residue to the critical days now passed is a sharp controversy between the German and the British newspapers,' says the 'Stampa.' 'Paris stays quietly behind the scenes rejoicing that another Power has taken on the task of racing Germany in the front line.'–Reuter.

The dilatory stance being adopted by France was by now one of the focal points for correspondents of the 'Guardian' throughout Europe.

CZECH'S MOVE FOR PEACE
Henlein's Demands

ACCEPTED AS BASIS OF DISCUSSION

Prague, June 10.

The Czecho-Slovak Government have agreed in principle that the memorandum in which the Sudeten Germans set forth their demands can serve as a basis of discussion. Naturally it will have to be modified, and it is probable that it will be discussed simultaneously with the Minorities Statute. The jurists will endeavour to assimilate the two drafts into a homogeneous whole that will be acceptable to all parties.

According to present plans the negotiations will begin next Tuesday and are likely to take some time. The question of local automomy is hedged in with all kinds of thorny problems, but what is important is that the two parties should come together in a spirit of mutual understanding.

HENLEIN'S MEMORANDUM

The Sudeten memorandum is based on the eight demands made by Herr Henlein in his speech at Carlsbad on April 24. These were –

1. Full equality of status for Czechs and Germans.
2. This equality to be guaranteed by a recognition of the Sudeten Germans as a legal entity.
3. The determination and recognition of the German areas within the State.
4. Full self-government for these areas.
5. Legal protection for every citizen living outside the area of his own nationality.
6. Removal of injustices inflicted on the Sudeten Germans since 1918 and reparation for the damage caused.
7. Recognition and realisation of the principle 'German regions – German officials'.
8. Full liberty to profess German nationality and the German political philosophy.

The Czecho-Slovak Minister in Paris arrived in Prague to-day and had interviews with Dr. Hodza, the Prime Minister, and Dr. Krofta, the Foreign Minister, and he is dining with President Benes to-night. The Minister had long conversations with M. Bonnet, the French Foreign Minister, in Paris yesterday, and no doubt is the bearer of advice from the French Government.—Reuter.

Wednesday 15 June   *p.20*

LETTERS TO THE EDITOR

GERMAN OPPOSITION TO HENLEIN
How Social Democratic Voters Are Intimidated

To the Editor of the Manchester Guardian

Sir,—I ask your kind permission to say a few words to the British public about the situation in the Sudeten German region of Czecho-Slovakia from the standpoint of a democrat.

Herr Henlein's party had great success at the municipal elections on May 22 and 29, and in all probability it will follow it up in the remaining elections on June 12 by inducing something like 88 per cent of the voters to support its list of candidates. But in explanation of this result it must be categorically stated that the atmosphere and conditions in which the elections in the Sudeten German districts are being held are inevitably not normal.

It must be borne in mind that the voting is taking place along the frontier, in a region which, as the whole population is acutely aware, may become a theatre of war. The propaganda of the Henlein party systematically works upon the consciousness of this and upon the knowledge of the savage reprisals which war would bring. The Sudeten German democrats and Socialists are assured day after day that the invasion of Hitler's armies is coming and that when it does come they – the democrats and Socialists – will be hanged on the nearest tree. The wives and even the children of our supporters in the Sudeten region are intimidated with the same threat. Unhappily this method proves extremely effective. The ordinary Sudeten German regards the Czechs as humane but the Nazis as barbarian. The simple man infers that the safest thing is to conform to Nazidom, for he feels sure that even if war comes there will be no Czech reprisals on the German civil population.

The secrecy of the ballot no longer exists in the Sudeten German region. Every conceivable means of pressure is being applied to the population to induce them to decorate their houses or flats with portraits of Henlein and placards of the Sudeten German party. The occupants of any dwellings not placarded are the target for organised threats and intimidation. The result in some of the entirely exposed border towns – for instance, Joachimsthal, near Karlsbad – has been that only half the members of the German Social Democratic party (of Czecho-Slovakia) ventured to vote Social Democrat. Wives begged their husbands not to vote, but to bring their Social Democratic voting-paper home. If war came the ballot-paper would then be a protection for the family as evidence of having voted for Henlein.

In the small urban and rural districts systematic pressure was carried on against the Socialist candidates. They were sent for by their employers and threatened with dismissal; those who were out of work were warned that they would never again be given employment by any factory owner or builder of their district; these employers are almost without exception enrolled members of the Henlein party. In our distressed areas, where for more than five years past the population has been suffering severely from unemployment, that threat amounted to a death-warrant for the candidate's whole family. In two cases subordinate officials of the German Social Democratic party were driven by this pressure to suicide. If in such circumstances 12 per cent of the electors voted against Henlein, I ask the impartial British public whether that is to be regarded as an unimpressive result!

The members of the Socialist minority among the Sudeten Germans are in a situation of complete material dependence, and the tactics of the Henlein party aim at forcing them to surrender by an economic and social boycott. I am sorry to have to say that, though the Government condemns this terrorism, it has not taken adequate practical steps to protect its loyal German population.

Unhappily the political tactics of our Government are actually helping Herr Henlein to obtain the maximum of success at the elections. The principles on which the promised Nationalities Statute is to be drafted have been communicated to the London and Paris Governments, but not to our own public. This has left the anti-Henlein group among the Sudeten Germans in uncertainty as to the scope for existence which the Czech policy will allow them. Under such circumstances even moderate-minded Germans who desire a solution of the Sudeten German question without external interference are voting for the Henlein party, hoping in this way to induce the Government to make larger concessions. Only after the Nationalities Statute has been placed in front of them will the Sudeten Germans be able to decide whether they shall try to secure democratic equality of rights by peaceful means or whether they shall work for Nazi hegemony in Central Europe, even at the cost of a war. It is in the interest of European peace that the Sudeten Germans should be compelled to make this choice quickly through the publication of the Nationalities Statute. I am thoroughly convinced that a large part of the Sudeten German population, perhaps even the majority, will prefer a peaceful arrangement to a war, which would mean absolute ruin to their own region.

In the elections that have been held the mass of the Czech people have plainly been voting for the parties of national accommodation. The National Democratic party (National Union), which is the proponent of the past mistaken policy of the national State, has been beaten everywhere and has sunk to insignificance. The Czech people has thus given its leaders carte blanche for an honourable peace with the moderate Sudeten Germans. Our soldiers obeyed the mobilisation order with admirable courage when the frontiers of the Republic were threatened. The Sudeten German democrats and the democrats of Europe are entitled to demand similar courage of the Prague Government and to call upon it to place before the Sudeten Germans and the other nationalities of the Republic a serious attempt at the satisfaction of their just claims in respect of their vital interests.–Yours,&c.,

W. JAKSCH.

Prague, June 7.

(Herr Jaksch is a Social Democratic member of the Czecho-Slovak Parliament and the leader of the Sudeten-German 'Activists' (in opposition to Henlein).)

Friday 17 June   p.6

GERMAN ESSAY ON INVASION OF CZECHO-SLOVAKIA
The Need for a Short Campaign

From our Correspondent

Warsaw, June 16.

The current issue of 'Der Deutsche in Poland', a weekly paper of the German Catholics in Polish Upper Silesia, prints a military essay sketching a plan for a campaign against Czecho-Slovakia. This essay won a prize offered by the German Military Academy; it is stated to have been written by Colonel Conrad, the Chief of Staff of the 18th Reichswehr Corps, now stationed in Salzburg, Austria.

The plans foresee a quick, short, but very fierce war in which German tanks and aeroplanes are to play a dominating part. Czecho-Slovakia, he declares, must be submerged within fourteen days, the quicker the better, and for two reasons–

1. Because Germany cannot, for lack of food and raw stuffs, go in for a long war.
2. Because Czecho-Slovakia's allies will hardly have time to come to her assistance.

38

THE TAKING OF PRAGUE

'We should concentrate', Colonel Conrad declares, 'large masses of troops and war material on Czecho-Slovakia and attack her from the north, south, and west by the German armies now in Silesia and Austria.' He gives other particulars how to carry on the war against Czecho-Slovakia to make foreign intervention impossible. He says no cost should be too much for Germany in her attempt to destroy the Czech Maginot Line, thrash the Czech Army, and take Prague. The taking of Prague would paralyse Czech defence.

He points to what he calls Mussolini's quick victory in Abyssinia, and says this was possible because Mussolini was able to take Addis Ababa. If Madrid had been taken in 1936 no foreign intervention would have been posible and Franco's victory won long ago.

He excludes Polish help for the Czechs, saying that Poland would either remain neutral or take Teschen herself. Hungary would come in and take Slovakia. Yugo-Slavia should not be feared, he says. She would never fight against Germany, and Rumania is too weak to count.

As regards France, he advises Germany to go slow with her at first and concentrate on defeating the Czechs. When this is achieved France, he says, will hesitate to risk a war with a victorious Germany.

NO DECLARATION OF WAR

Russia, the plan fears, particularly the Russian Air Force, but says that quick German action on Czecho-Slovakia would make Russian help impossible. According to the plan Germany should not declare war on the Czechs, which would only enable them to prepare. The German Army, he says, is always ready. S.A. (Storm Troops) and S.S. (Nazi Guards) men should infiltrate into Czecho-Slovakia first and then the German Army should make a sudden advance to free the Sudeten Germans, who could immediately be called up to serve in the German Army.

The Colonel Conrad referred to in the above article had a noteworthy precognition of the pattern any future European conflict, based on the issue of the sovereignty of Czechoslovakia, would take. It could have served as a blueprint for subsequent German conquests of France and the Low Countries.

LORD HALIFAX ON BRITAIN'S ROLE AS PEACEMAKER
'Short Cuts' Not Possible in These Days

NO REAL DIVISIONS ON THE PURPOSES
OF OUR FOREIGN POLICY

From our London Staff

Fleet Street, Tuesday.

Lord Halifax followed the example of other Foreign Secretaries of recent years when he consented to speak at the annual dinner to-night of the Royal Institute of International Affairs. Those, however, who had gone to the dinner hoping to hear some comment on the immediate matters which have been occupying the Non-Intervention Committee to-day were disappointed. Lord Halifax, who extolled the work of the institute and suggested that men of means should contribute to its support, outlined broadly the principles on which present British foreign policy is based.

'My own reading of British foreign policy', he said, 'is that, however intimate our relations may be with any other Power, as they happily are with France to-day, we are always trying to feel our way towards a wider sense of unity in international relations. Sometimes we succeed, sometimes we fail – for success does not lie in our hands alone – but the purpose remains the same.

'You will therefore find British policy repeatedly emphasising what unites nations instead of what divides them, and for the same reason we are not interested to secure so-called diplomatic successes and win the plaudits of the crowd if by so doing we prejudice the attainment of our principal objective.

RESTRAINT MISTAKEN FOR WEAKNESS

'No one with knowledge would pretend that the role of peacemaker was an easy one. That role is one that demands great patience and fairness and at the same time firmness and strength. Motives are frequently misunderstood, restraint and cool heads are liable to be mistaken for weakness. Moreover, he who seeks peace cannot succeed unless others are animated by the same spirit, for no peace can endure which is not built upon respect for law and justice.

'Nor will such a policy ever appeal to the mind which hankers after short cuts and feels that if only we had Lord Palmerston still with us we could rapidly and decisively impose British solutions on an acquiescent world. We, unhappily, have to work under different conditions and with different instruments. If our voice is

40

to carry conviction abroad it must be the voice of a united nation. Whatever may be the party differences as to particular actions of Governments, there is no real divergence of view in any quarter upon what ought to be the purpose of British policy. No body of men with the actual responsibility and the full knowledge of government would in present circumstances take any very different action from our own.

'None of us has any desire to do anything to embarrass any other country: we have no wish to cramp legitimate development, or to encircle any nation with a ring of potential enemies. Still less do we wish to interfere with a system of government with which we may not happen to agree. We are none of us out for sinister motives to improve political relations with Governments of a different political complexion from our own in order to influence the course of political development at home. Every sensible Englishman knows that kind of suggestion to be wholly untrue.

PEACE THROUGH RESPECT FOR LAW

'But we are all alike determined to throw all our weight on the side of securing world peace through respect for law based on just settlements: we have no use for a world society in which law would be expected to be the obedient handmaid of lawless force; and we are all resolved to preserve British rights and liberties against attack from whatever quarter, within or without the State, these may come.

'No British Government could hope with any success to conduct a foreign policy which was not broadly acceptable to the whole nation, and that is a fact which both here and elsewhere should always be borne in mind. A great mistake would be made abroad if it was ever thought that our domestic controversies upon the day-to-day conduct of foreign policy would in the least degree affect the primary instinct of our people to stand solidly together in any real emergency. They have always done so and would do so again.'

ISOLATION WINNING FEW CONVERTS

Other points in Lord Halifax's speech were:– 'In spite of all its attractions, I doubt whether the gospel of isolation is winning many converts. Our people would feel instinctively that to try and cut clear of lending a hand when things are difficult was an unworthy attitude for a great nation and was not pulling the weight in the world that might rightly be expected of it.

'In their hearts the British people do not believe that isolation is likely to prove practicable. This does not mean that we, any more than the United States of America, want to see our country involved in quarrels that do not concern us, but it does mean that we realise that facts may be more powerful than the wills of men and that once war starts it is impossible to predict where it may not end.

'Three qualities – respect for law, recognition that law must rest upon consent, and toleration – are quite indispensable to any sound or constructive approach to the international problems of to-day. Their possession of these in particular degree does seem to call the British people to play a very distinctive part in the guidance of world movements.'

THE GOVERNMENT AND THE COVENANT

Referring to the League of Nations, Lord Halifax said: 'In spite of all set-backs and hopes destroyed the fact remains that if the world is to survive it must find some reasonable basis for international relations, whether it does it through the Covenant or by some other road.

'Events have made the full application of the Covenant impracticable to-day – and it is no service to refuse to acknowledge facts. But that is no reason why a country like ours, which believes the spirit of the Covenant to be the right spirit in international affairs, should not continue to practise that spirit in our dealings with other nations. And that is what we are trying to do.'

It appears remarkable now that Lord Halifax, the British Foreign Secretary, could still have been expounding in positive terms the role of the League of Nations as late as June 1938.
The League had suffered at worst a series of diplomatic and military disasters and at best the ignominy of being almost totally ignored.

Friday 1 July *p.6*

DR. BENES'S HOPES: CLAIMS OF THE SUDETENS

Prague, June 30.

'I am convinced that in a very short time, in a few days or weeks, we shall have solved our nationalities problem in a just and reasonable manner,' declared President Benes in a speech here to-night.

'We shall maintain our economy and our finances in a sound state and we shall come out of the present crisis with increased strength. We are determined to settle these questions in a spirit of goodwill with all our nationalities. We count on all parties showing a sense of fair play. In the interests of our own country as well as international collaboration we are prepared to go to the extreme limits consistent with the political conditions and possibilities and needs of our State.

42

'I still believe that European peace can be saved,' said the President.

Sudeten German demands were formulated to-night in a communique issued after a full meeting of the party's Parliamentary group.

It was unanimously decided that it was incompatible with membership of the party for Sudeten Germans to allow their children to attend Czech schools. A basic solution demanded a complete revision of the political conception and political entity of the Czechs. Only thus could the necessary reconstruction of the State on the basis of the equality of the peoples as national groups be realised.

It was emphasised that the representatives of Herr Henlein had made it clear that they regarded this reconstruction in the sense of a big demand for autonomy as indispensable, and that no half-measures would be considered adequate.–Reuter.

Monday 4 July   *p.11*

PRAGUE ADVISED NOT TO DELAY
Further Representations by Britain and France

Prague, July 3.

Great Britain and France have, it is understood, made further representations to the Czecho-Slovak Government urging them to expedite a solution of the nationalities problem.

The British Minister, Mr. Basil Newton, called on Dr. Hodza, the Prime Minister, yesterday, and the French Minister saw him on Friday. An official statement issued last night says that they 'informed the Czecho-Slovak Government of the views of their Governments on the present situation'.

It is unlikely that there will be any important negotiations between the Government and the Sudeten German party within the next few days, as Ministers have to attend various gatherings connected with the Sokol (physical training) festival, which lasts until Wednesday.

It is hoped, however, that an agreed text of the Government's proposals, including the Nationalities Statute itself, will be completed before the end of this week. The fact that President Benes is to preside over the meeting of the political sub-committee of Ministers indicates the solidarity of the Government block in facing the grave responsibility that will have to be taken in regard to the Nationalities Statute.

Whether, however, the Government proposals go far enough to be acceptable to the Sudeten Germans it is impossible to say, as the exact nature is not yet known.

A statement from Sudeten German party headquarters yesterday declared that a recent article by Herr Kundt, one of the party's deputies in the Chamber, should not be regarded as a rejection of the proposals. The full text of the proposals, it is added, will not be communicated to the party until next week, and until then the attitude of the party cannot be defined.–Reuter.

Wednseday 13 July   *p.12*

FRENCH PREMIER RENEWS PLEDGE TO CZECHO-SLOVAKIA
'Sacred and Cannot be Evaded'

REFERENCE TO HITLER'S 'PEACEFUL ASPIRATIONS'

From our own Correspondent

Paris, July 12.

Diplomatic reports from Germany in the last few days have been far from reassuring, and their 'synchronisation' with threats coming from Japan, Italy, and Franco's Spain have not passed unnoticed in Paris.

M. Daladier, the Prime Minister, speaking in Paris to-night, felt obliged once again to emphasise, this time perhaps more strongly than ever before. France's determination not to allow Czecho-Slovakia to be invaded. 'The solemn undertakings we have given to Czecho-Slovakia', he said, 'are sacred and cannot be evaded.' But while his speech was implicitly a warning to Germany, it was also explicitly an ardent appeal to Germany not to rush Europe into war and to allow the Czech Government to reach a peaceful and lasting settlement of the Sudeten question.

Without even alluding to Austria, M. Daladier said that he desired to 'be confident in the peaceful aspirations which the Chancellor of the Reich has always publicly proclaimed.' The word 'publicly' was perhaps calculated to give some elasticity to the meaning of the phrase.

NOTHING PROVOCATIVE

At the same time M. Daladier was careful not to say anything that Germany could interpret as a provocation. In speaking of the 'criticial week-end' of May 21 he suggested that the crisis had been averted not only by the firmness of France and Britain and Czecho-Slovakia herself but by 'a meeting of the free and spontaneous goodwill' of everybody concerned, including Germany.

44

A few listeners in Paris actually wondered whether this undeserved compliment to Germany's pacifism – a compliment contrasting so strongly with the Tamerlane-like speeches of Hitler's fellow-dictator – will not be interpreted as another sign of 'democratic' humility. But the extreme firmness of M. Daladier's remarks on France's duty towards Czecho-Slovakia should meet this objection.

In the second part of his speech M. Daladier dealt with the French internal situation, and said that he preferred to restore France's economy and finances slowly but surely instead of being carried away by 'the fantasy of the illusionists'. While it was too early to look back on the work done by the Government and to say how this work would be continued it was sufficient to say that he (M. Daladier) had an indestructible confidence in the future of France.

He claimed that great improvements had already been made in the industrial and financial fields, and he thought that progress would be facilitated by the present signs of an economic world recovery. Tourists were coming to France in large numbers, and the balance of trade had improved. The Government was determined, he said, to protect the franc, to maintain internal order, and (this was an allusion to the threatened strike of the Government officials) all the public services.

'We shall also maintain the integrity of France and of her overseas empire,' he said, 'and revive the power of labour and production, and above all that noble feeling of brotherhood which in all decisive moments has safeguarded the greatness of our country.'

Daladier's words quoted above were not backed up by his subsequent actions, although he remained subordinate to Great Britain in foreign affairs and almost obsequious to Germany.

Monday 18 July *p.14*

GERMANY'S MOTIVES IN THE NEW CZECH CRISIS
British Pressure on Prague Wanted

HOPE THAT BRITAIN WILL ADVISE CONCESSION OF SUDETEN DEMANDS

From our own Correspondent

Berlin, July 17.

The Berlin correspondent of the Essen 'National Zeitung' makes the attitude of the German Government clear in an important article in to-day's issue, dealing with the visit of Sir Nevile

Henderson to the German Foreign Office on Saturday. Although in general such discussions between high Foreign Office officials and Ambassadors are not of a startling character (the correspondent writes), the conversation between Sir Nevile Henderson and Herr von Weizsäcker is attended with deep universal attention in view of the latest development in the Spanish and Czecho-Slovak questions.

In contrast to the relatively clear and not unfavourable situation in respect of Spain, the Czecho-Slovak problem at the present moment must be regarded as especially serious and dangerous. It is understood that the conversation between Sir Nevile Henderson and Herr von Weizsäcker was mainly concerned with this the most burning of all European questions. Without doubt it led to a further clarification of the news of each side.

Britain (the correspondent continues) has announced its interest in Prague's policy and in the position of the Sudeten Germans, especially in the critical days of the second half of May, and has taken steps in Prague in this connection.

BRITAIN AND THE LAST CRISIS

Britain had put forward the view (which the paper emphatically rejects) that it prevented war in May, and that it will now be listened to when it advises far-reaching concessions to the Sudeten Germans. Nevertheless it is clear that the Czech Government has passed over the eight cardinal points of the Sudeten German claims and will force its own minority programme upon the nationalities without regard for the consequences.

The cause of the tension (the correspondent of the 'National Zeitung' continues) is not the irreconcilability of the Sudetens but the arrogance of the Czechs, who find themselves falsely in security and within the protection of their Western European friends.

The British Government will, after its latest inquiries, (the paper continues) be able to judge with what feelings the German people and its Government follow the practices of the Czech officials and how far removed Germany is from regarding the previous British step in Prague as positive and contributing to European peace.

CONCEDE SUDETEN DEMANDS

If the British Government wishes to prove its great interest in the Czech question in the light of the European situation it must use its influence in the near future more strongly and effectively in Prague against the Czech manoeuvres of deception, and it must advise the Czech Government to reverse its policy and concede the Sudetic claims.

Berlin is not convinced (the paper continues) that the British Government is concerned with the Czech problem only for appearance's sake or for securing a future position. Nevertheless so far its efforts have produced so little in the way of tangible success that there is every reason for regarding the latest developments with anxiety and scepticism.

Germany and England, the correspondent states, are at one in the wish to preserve peace. The British Government is still of the opinion that a far-reaching solution of the Sudeten question must be made by the Czecho-Slovak Government. This makes it Britain's duty to put forward its wishes and advice where its influence is felt. Only then can it be said that it has fulfilled the duty which it took upon itself for various reasons.

Wednesday 20 July   *p.11*

HITLER'S SOUNDINGS IN LONDON
Making Sure Britain is Not Bluffing on Czecho-Slovakia

From our Diplomatic Correspondent

London, Tuesday.

The visit of Herr Hitler's adjutant, Captain Wiedemann, to this country is none the less important for being qualified as 'informal'. The French Government is being kept informed of all that passes in the conversations with Captain Wiedemann here. Yesterday he had an 'informal' talk with Lord Halifax at the Foreign Secretary's private house in London.

It matters a great deal to Hitler that he should really know the attitude of the British Government towards the Central European problem. Indeed, it is no exaggeration to say that a mistaken view on Hitler's part may lead to a European war. If Hitler thinks that Great Britain will remain passive in a war between Germany and Czecho-Slovakia, that war is almost as certain as anything can be in politics, for the Germans believe that they can 'contain' the French Army and Air Force. They are strengthening their western defences for this very purpose.

But if Hitler cannot count on British neutrality – that is to say, if the diplomatic action taken by the British Government on May 21 (the week-end of the frontier crisis) both in Berlin and in London was not a bluff (and Mr. Chamberlain's recent letter to M. Daladier ought to have left no doubt that it is not) – then the risk of going to war with Czecho-Slovakia must appear excessive in Hitler's eyes.

Herr von Ribbentrop has all along been inclined to believe that the British Government was bluffing. The German military leaders are not, as is generally supposed, on the side of the 'moderates' this time. They were quite critical, indeed apprehensive, of the reoccupation of the Rhineland and of the invasion of Austria, but events proved that they were wrong and that Hitler was right. Now it is Hitler who is critical and apprehensive – that is to say, of an armed attack on Czecho-Slovakia – while the military leaders believe the attack to be feasible. Hitler is certainly right now, as he was on the two previous occasions, and it is again clear that in political judgement he is superior not only to his generals but also to some of his political collaborators.

A conference on this subject was held in Berlin the other day. Hitler, Ribbentrop, Göring, Goebbels, General Keitel, General Brauchitsch, and others were present. Hitler remained non-committal throughout the conference. Goebbels, strange as it may appear, was for 'moderation', though the reason is that he believes that Czecho-Slovakia can be coerced by propaganda and other 'peaceful' means. But on the whole it is Hitler and the other National Socialist chiefs (Göring and Ribbentrop excepted) who are for 'moderation', while the German General Staff are for action, their reason being not only that they believe, as Ribbentrop does, that Great Britain is bluffing, but that her rearmament is still so backward that she cannot play a decisive part in a European war before the year 1940.

The question whether Great Britain is bluffing or not is therefore of primary importance. There can be little doubt that if Hitler believes that she is not bluffing the war with Czecho-Slovakia will not come this year.

(Reuter reports from Berlin that Sir Nevile Henderson, the British Ambassador in Berlin, last night saw Baron von Weizsäcker, Secretary of State, at the Foreign Office, presumably with reference to the Czecho-Slovak question.)

Thursday 21 July   *p.11*

ANGLO-FRENCH HARMONY
Talks in Paris

EARLIER AGREEMENT RE-EMPHASISED

From our own Correspondent

Paris, July 20

During the day Lord Halifax had a long talk with M. Daladier, the Premier, and M. Bonnet, the Foreign Minister, and this evening the following statement was made:–

The visit to Paris of their Majesties the King and Queen of England has given Lord Halifax, M. Daladier, and M. Bonnet occasion to examine the international situation as a whole as well as questions of special interest to the two countries. In the course of these talks, which took place in the spirit of mutual confidence which inspires Franco-British relations, the Ministers, once again showing their common will to pursue their action of appeasement and conciliation, noted that the complete harmony of their views, established during the visit of the French Ministers to London on April 28 and 29, was entirely maintained. ...

BRITAIN AND CZECHO-SLOVAKIA

It is understood that while no new decision was taken regarding Czecho-Slovakia, Lord Halifax assured the French Ministers that Britain would adhere to the firm attitude against aggression which she had adopted in April and May. While various possibilities concerning the best way of 'treating' the Czech problem were examined, it appears that it was decided to 'wait for developments' and in the meantime to make further inquiries into the state of negotiations between the Czech Government and the Sudeten Germans.

It does not seem that the French showed themselves much impressed by suggestions coming from certain British quarters regarding an eventual 'neutralisation' of Czecho-Slovakia, nor did they wish certain essentials of the Czech problem to be overlooked. The possible 'limits of concessions' that could reasonably be suggested to the Czechs were discussed. Whether the possible 'four-Power arbitration' of the Czech–Sudeten dispute – a suggestion which has been mentioned in some quarters here – was also discussed is extremely doubtful. It savours too much of Four-Power Pact politics, and so is scarcely acceptable to the French Government.

Saturday 23 July   *p.11*

HITLER'S SOUNDINGS IN LONDON
Danger of the Czech Crisis Coming to a Head

NO GREAT REASON FOR OPTIMISM

From our Diplomatic Correspondent

London, Friday.

The results of the visit of Captain Wiedemann, Herr Hitler's adjutant, to London have been entirely negative, unless he himself has obtained some clear impression, whether true or erroneous, as to what British policy really is. What he had to say in conversation with authoritative persons here was so vague that it does not allow any definite conclusion with regard to German policy.

In view of the several discrepant reports that have been published here with regard to his mission, it is necessary to repeat what has been stated in this correspondence more than once – namely, that its chief purpose was to find what the British attitude would be if Germany goes to war with Czecho-Slovakia. It does not follow that he asked any direct questions on this subject: indeed, it is rather unlikely that he did so, using instead various vague proposals as a means of sounding or sensing the British attitude.

AMBASSADOR'S TALK WITH PREMIER

The German Ambassador, Herr von Dirksen, who leaves for Germany to-morrow, had a long talk with the Prime Minister to-day. The talk was quite general – no specific proposals of any kind were made. The suggestion that the independence of Czecho-Slovakia might be guaranteed by Great Britain, Germany and France is an old one, but it was not discussed to-day, and indeed, it would, unfortunately, have little relationship with present-day realities.

Reports, chiefly emanating from Paris, that pressure has again been brought to bear on the Czecho-Slovak Government by France and Great Britain as the result of recent Anglo-French discussions are untrue. The Minorities Statute is now ready, and will be submitted to the Czecho-Slovak Parliament shortly. It will be subject to public debate and possibly to amendment. For the time being, the statute will have to take its course. Later on, perhaps, if there is a deadlock between the Czech and the Sudeten German points of view, mediatory efforts by France and Great Britain may be possible.

The view that seems to prevail here no less than in Paris, Prague, and Warsaw is that the German–Czech crisis will not come to a head until early next year. But it must be admitted that there is a certain undercurrent of uneasiness here lest the crisis come to a head in August.

GERMANS SENDING ARMAMENTS

Prodigious quantities of war material have been passing through Vienna during the last three weeks. The trainloads arrive after dark and pass on the Czecho-Slovak frontier, where work on the German defensive and offensive positions is going on apace.

There is no justification for the official optimism which has crept into some of this morning's papers. This optimism is certainly not felt by those responsible for the conduct of British foreign policy or by those in touch with them. A grave crisis is possible in the near future, even if it may not be likely. That the German–Czech conflict is capable of solution for a long time to come, if at all, is not seriously believed by any responsible observer here, and the danger of an armed conflict is realised by all, even if it is not regarded as immediate.

Monday 25 July   *p.18*

LETTERS TO THE EDITOR

AUTONOMY FOR THE SUDETEN GERMANS
Lord Noel-Buxton's Argument

To the Editor of the Manchester Guardian

Sir,–The Czecho-Slovak Government is apparently putting the finishing touches to a series of measures designed to rectify the grievances of the Sudeten Germans. But the Government bills are the responsibility of the Government and do not represent an agreed solution of the question. Unless the Sudeten districts are given a wide measure of autonomy, the reforms that are carried through Parliament will not amount to a settlement. So long as an unresolved conflict persists, there remains the danger of incidents, in consequence of which Germany's help might be called for, and war might break out without any deliberate design on the part of the German Government. In short, the grant of autonomy is an essential safeguard to the peace of Europe. Our interest in the matter is scarcely less than that of the Czechs themselves: it is our duty to make our views powerfully felt in Prague. ...

NOEL-BUXTON.
18, Cowley Street, Westminster, London, S.W.1, July 22.

Noel-Buxton was first a Liberal then a Labour M.P. and a member of Ramsey MacDonald's first two Labour Governments. He was ennobled in 1930.

BRITISH ADVISER FOR THE CZECHS
Offer to Send Lord Runciman

PLAN THAT WILL BE ACCEPTED WITH GRATITUDE
Prague Parliament Summoned

From our Central European Correspondent

Prague, July 25.

It is confirmed here that the British Government has offered the services of Lord Runciman as mediator or advisor in the dispute between the Government and the Sudeten Germans. It is believed that the Government will accept the offer with thanks. An announcement to this effect will probably be made to-morrow.

Czecho-Slovak official quarters deny that there is any official information about an alleged German–Czecho-Slovak Pact or a neutrality pact, either directly or though the mediation of the British Minister in Prague, or through any other source. The influential 'Lidove Noviny' to-day expresses indignation at the suggestion that it is possible to negotiate on such vital matters without consulting the country which is most concerned. The newspaper in this matter voices the feelings of the country. The Czechs certainly would not agree to a neutrality pact guaranteed only by Great Britain, France, Germany, and Italy. This would, presumably, mean that Czecho-Slovakia would have to disarm and open the gates to the Nazis whenever Hitler decided to strike. In that case French, British, and Russian help would arrive too late.

PACT THAT COULD BE ACCEPTED

But a neutrality pact could be considered if it was guaranteed not only by the four Powers but also by Russia as well as by the neighbours of Czecho-Slovakia, including Poland, Hungary, and Rumania. A ten-year non-aggression pact has never been rejected by the Czechs, but it cannot be accepted at the price of renouncing the French and Russian alliances. Czecho-Slovakia has not understood that the British Minister in Prague has urged her to make further concessions than she is ready to make. The Czecho-Slovak view is that the Prague Government is ready to make far-reaching concessions to the Sudeten Germans. Official quarters are convinced that when the final draft of the law is published foreign public opinion will be completely satisfied that the Czechs have gone to the utmost limits of possible concessions.

Parliament has been summoned for August 2. The bills dealing with the nationality problems are still being drafted. In Czecho-Slovakia Paliamentary bills are never published until the final draft is ready. Moreover the Germans are difficult to negotiate with, and the full truth about the negotiations cannot yet be made public. In addition the Government will give ample time to all parties to consider the bills before they are made public.

To-day the Political Committee, which has six members, is considering the final draft of the bill for the reform of the Administration.

Lord Runciman, a former Cabinet Minister, was to be despatched to try and find a solution or a compromise between the two sides, and although the Czechs objected to the whole mission in the first place, British pressure persuaded them to allow Runciman to get on with his work.

With this action, the British Government, in a paradoxical move had, despite their professed lack of interest in Central Europe, assumed an open responsibility for the solution of the Sudeten dispute and the possible protection of Czechoslovakia; a burden which militarily was a French and Czech problem, and one which the British would find, in the absence of a French commitment to military action, an impossible one to assume.

Wednesday 27 July   *p.10*

Leader   **THE ROAD TO PRAGUE**

Lord Runciman is going to Prague as 'a mediator and investigator independent of his Majesty's or any other Government'. (We trust, however, that the British Government will buy his ticket.) So Mr. Chamberlain said yesterday in the House of Commons when announcing what is, for better or for worse, the most daring initiative in European affairs taken by the National Government since that unhappy day when Sir Samuel Hoare led the sanctions brigade into action at Geneva only to sound the retreat a few months later. The very fact that this move suggests a more active foreign policy disposes one to approve it, and closer consideration can only confirm this approval. Lord Runciman's mission will prove finally to all who doubt it (including certain persons in this country) that the British Government is really interested in Central Europe, for if the fate of Czecho-Slovakia had been a matter of indifference to us we should not have taken this responsibility. When that is admitted the criticism that we have no right to interfere in the internal affairs of Czecho-Slovakia also falls to the ground. If we run the risk of war on Czecho-Slovakia's account, then it is reasonable that we should have some say in the present negotiations. The French Government, which is in exactly the same situation, has already given the plan its blessing, and the Czech Government, which alone might reasonably have objected, actually requested it. Finally, even if we take the gloomiest view, Lord Runciman's visit will make certain that negotiations will continue for a little (no small gain in these days), and the Germans are not likely to bomb Prague so long as he continues to investigate.

The crux of the matter lies rather in the kind of advice which the British Government and Lord Runciman ('independently') offer to the Czech Government. Yesterday Mr. Chamberlain told the House of Commons that so far from 'hustling the Czech Government' the British Govenment had advised it not to be hasty. That is all to the good, but it is not quite the point. There have been reports that in the last few days the British Government has been urging the Czech Government to concede all the demands of the Sudeten Germans, though these demands are clearly not compatible with Czecho-Slovakia's freedom and independence. Mr. Chamberlain did not answer this point directly, but said that hitherto the British Government had abstained from making definite suggestions. But this is a matter of fundamental importance. No one, perhaps, who is informed about the situation now expects a 'just' settlement or even, for that matter, a permanent settlement. Events have moved too far for that. The best we can hope for is a settlement which will satisfy the Sudeten Germans for the present but which will not lead to the disruption of the Czech State. There is, unfortunately, good reason to believe that the German Government itself is not really interested in the happiness and prosperity of the Sudeten Germans but in furthering its own expansionist aims in South-east Europe. If that is true it would be better to leave the Czechs to man the walls themselves than to go to them as friends merely in order to open their gates to the enemy. Yesterday Mr. Chamberlain said : 'Let no one imagine that though we seek peace we are willing to sacrifice even for peace British honour and British vital interests.' These are brave words, but we should have preferred an assurance that the British Government, in its search for peace, is not ready to sacrifice the honour and vital interests of Czecho-Slovakia.

The Czech Government has not yet published the text of its Nationalities Bill, and will not do so, if possible, until agreement has been reached with the Sudeten Germans. But enough is already known to make clear that there is still a considerable gap between the maximum concessions of the Czech Government and the minimum demands of the Sudeten Germans. That is why the British Government has decided to send Lord Runciman to Prague. His duty will be to bridge the gap. Mr. Chamberlain admitted that the Sudeten Germans have not yet given their consent to his mediation, but it is unlikely that they will refuse since the German

Government apparently has no objection, and in a sense Lord Runciman's mediation itself will be a recognition of their demand to be treated as a legal entity. But it is also clear that Lord Runciman must fail unless he can persuade the Sudeten leaders to make some concessions on their side. Opinions differ as to whether Herr Henlein will or can concede anything, but it is a promising sign that little is now heard of the former German demands that Czecho-Slovakia should abandon her alliance with Soviet Russia; in a recent interview Herr Henlein stated that they would 'leave defence demands and foreign affairs in the hands of the central Government'. There is one point which should be carefully considered by both Herr Henlein and the German Government. If they insist on full autonomy and refuse to make even the most reasonable concessions, Lord Runciman will be bound to report to the British Government that the Czech Government is not to blame for the breakdown. If, on the other hand, the Czech Government, on the advice of Lord Runciman, makes concessions which it would not otherwise have made, the British Government will be morally responsible for seeing that it does not suffer thereby.

Thursday 28 July *p.12*

RUSSIANS SUSPICIOUS OF LORD RUNCIMAN

From our Correspondent

Moscow, July 27.

The Soviet press takes up a suspicious and critical attitude toward Lord Runicman's mediation in Czecho-Slovakia. 'Izvestia' groups its reports under the sub-heading 'England's inter-ference in the internal affairs of Czecho-Slovakia', and pub-lishes correspondents' assertions that Britain will demand from Prague sacrifices incompatible with the security of the Czecho-Slovak State.

Although the Soviet Union was right to be sceptical with regard to the roles being played by Great Britain and France vis-à-vis Czechoslovakia (see also article on p.171) there existed counter arguments.

From October 1917 the Soviet Government had openly declared its aim of supplanting liberal—democratic societies by soviet-style regimes. To this end it had assisted the birth and growth of Communist Parties, and had not only guided their policy, strategy and tactics, but had also assisted on a large scale with finance and personnel.

Sections of the British Opposition believed that Chamberlain refused to negotiate with the Soviet Union because of a fear of ultimate Soviet expansion in Europe and this was coupled with what could be described as a pathological hatred of Communism by significant numbers of this party.

LORD RUNCIMAN ON HIS MISSION
Told by 'Two Parties' That He Would be Welcome

'I DID NOT ASK FOR THIS JOB'

Lord Runciman, who is to mediate between the Czechs and the Sudeten Germans, arrived in Prague yesterday. The negotiations proper between the Czech Government and the Sudeten German party were to have begun yesterday, but by common consent they were postponed because of Lord Runciman's arrival. Dr. Hodza, the Premier, met the Sudeten leaders, however, to discuss future procedure.

LORD RUNCIMAN'S STATEMENT

Lord Runciman yesterday evening met representatives of the press and made the following statement:

In the first place I have to make it quite clear to you and to many other people that I did not ask for this job. Two parties told me before we left England that my presence would be welcome, and I have to thank the Lord Mayor, the representatives of the Ministers, and of the Sudeten Germans for the kind welcome I received to-day.

I come as one who has had forty years of experience in various phases of political activity in my country. I have learnt that permanent peace and true tranquillity can be secured only on a basis of mutual consent.

Personally, I hope to be the friend of all and the enemy of none. I would say to you, gentlemen of the press, that your assistance will be valuable to help in solving the troubles that have to be settled.

These troubles can and will be explored, and in due course we may hope to get to the bottom of some of them, especially if we set to work in a spirit of goodwill and the exercise of patience.

With the members of his staff Lord Runciman has made the Alcron Hotel his headquarters. A whole suite of rooms has been reserved for him for a month, but the proprietor has been warned that they may be needed for a second month or longer. The staff includes Mr. Geoffrey Peto, formerly his Parliamentary Private Secretary; Mr. Ashton-Gwatkin, head of the Economic Department at the Foreign Office: and Mr. R.J. Stopford. Mr. Ian Henderson, of the Consular Service, who has been acting as one of the two British observers in Czecho-Slovakia, is joining the party in Prague.

REPLY TO SUDETENS

Dr. Hodza yesterday received the German delegates, Herr Kundt and Dr. Roshe, and afterwards the Sudeten party headquarters issued the following communiqué:–

The discussion confirmed the talks and future procedure between the Government and the Sudeten party delegates. Dr. Hodza has given the following reply to the five questions submitted on Saturday by Herr Kundt:–

1. The texts of the Nationalities Statute and Language Bill handed to the Sudeten German party remain valid, with the reservation that they will serve as basis for the discussion in detail on the same footing as the memorandum of the party of June 7.
2. The latest proposals handed over regarding self-government are to be regarded as the definite proposals of the Government with the same reservation.
3. With regard to the Sudeten party memorandum of June 7, in so far as it goes beyond the proposals of the Government in the matter of the Nationalities Statute, Language Bill, and self-government proposals, a reply will be given at the latest after the negotiations dealing with the measures at present under consideration.
4. The same applies to the definite attitude of the Government to the entire contents of the German memorandum.
5. The present conversations between the Sudeten party and the Government will continue and will assume an official character. The method of discussion will be altered only should there be any new developments outside present conditions.

Discussing Lord Runciman's arrival, the 'Narodny Politika', an independent Czech organ, says that the success of his mission will probably depend on the position in the Far East. If there is peace he may have a chance of success, but if there is war he is foredoomed to failure. In any event any solution can only be temporary, adds the paper, for what Germany wants is a complete change in Czecho-Slovak policy in favour of the Reich.

The importance of the Far East in British calculations cannot be over-emphasised. Following the Japanese invasion of Manchuria in 1931 it had taken merely four years before she had established the puppet state of Manchukuo, which consisted of territory equivalent in size to the whole of Great Britain, France, Germany, Italy and Spain combined, with a total of 100,000,000 population within its borders.

The Japanese action had never been seriously challenged by either the Western Powers or the League of Nations. Yet there were reasons why Great Britain did not wish to interfere with the Japanese action in Manchuria. Britain was very concerned with the stability of the Far East, because large parts of her Empire were situated there, and also because of her very lucrative trade with China. It was felt in many British circles that the Japanese invasion would lead to greater stability in China, and hence greater benefits to Britain in the way of trade. The Japanese invasion was seen as a counter to the conflicting Nationalist and Communist elements within China.

Thursday 11 August   *p.16*

LETTERS TO THE EDITOR

ACTIVITY ON THE GERMAN FRONTIERS
Motor-Lorries, Road-Making, and Fortifications

To the Editor of the Manchester Guardian

Sir,–We send you a copy of a letter which we addressed on July 31 to the leaders of the French General Confederation of Labour, the French Socialist, Radical Socialist, and Communist parties, and the British trade unions and parties:

Dear Friends,–As a group of the united free trade unions engaged in illegal activity in Germany, we feel bound to inform you of some alarming, authentically established steps taken by our Government; since we feel bound by democrats and friends of democratic France and Czecho-Slovakia to join in watching over their security. The sending of Lord Runciman to Czecho-Slovakia is regarded here, among the anti-Fascist mass of the population, as a concession to the dictators and an intervention in the internal affairs of the Czecho-Slovak Republic; it has consequently aroused disturbed feelings mixed with depression. Such concessions do absolutely no service to peace but only increase the aggressiveness of the aggressors.

Recently, in the course of only the past week, the following things have happened in this country in our region (along the borders of Czecho-Slovakia), and probably everywhere:

1. All post offices were instructed by telegram to place as many passenger omnibuses as possible, with their drivers, at disposal. One post office in a small town provided as many as seven omnibuses. The private omnibus companies have

58

to provide relief vehicles to carry on the services as far as is possible.

2. All motor-lorries in anything like usable condition must be given up by the factories, with their chauffeurs.

3. All unmarried building workers and married ones without children, and Sudeten Germans who have arrived lately among us, were withdrawn from road and building work, no matter how urgent, and at once conveyed to other places.

All included 1–3 (omnibuses, workers, chauffeurs, and lorries) are going to the Rhineland and Saar Territory for work on fortifications. A chauffeur's wife wept heartrendingly at her husband's departure, believing that he was already off to the war.

One man refused twice to obey the order; on this he was arrested and sentenced to four months' imprisonment for sabotage of the Four-year Plan. The men are being sent from the labour exchanges, at whose disposal they are compelled to be placed by their employing authorities as 'on leave'.

As, however, in our region (under the mobilisation orders which have now been distributed) even men of forty have to report at 9 a.m. on the second day of mobilisation, it is being said that the men sent away will at once be reorganised directly from their new place of work, according to their training. The purpose of this will be to prevent extensive scenes of farewell (like the one just mentioned), because that means a disturbance of the mobilisation.

It can be imagined what masses of motor-vehicles and men have been sent altogether in the last week to the western frontier. But considerable numbers of men are already being assembled along the Silesian and Polish frontier for fortification work.

4. At present all roads leading from farther inland to the Czecho-Slovak frontier are being prepared for the deployment, at full pressure, with increased gangs and additional shifts. For this Sudeten Germans are being employed in special numbers, irrespective of their normal occupation; they are being brought over in thousands, great promises being made to them, and are being drilled and trained and formed into legions. The date fixed for the completion of all these roads is August 31. Further work on all dwellings for frontier officials and Custom-houses started or half-finished was suddenly stopped a fortnight ago as no longer needed; in any case the material was needed for more urgent purposes. This was officially stated to the master craftsmen employed on the work or working under contract.

We feel it our most urgent duty to inform you of these surprising occurrences or steps taken by our Government. Since the motors are being sent to the western frontier from such distances, and also vast masses of workers, the only possible purpose must be to conceal the steps taken from the local population.

We beg you all to take action accordingly, especially politically, in order not to weaken the peaceful forces in the country (which are daily growing more powerful) by such steps as the Runciman mission. May 21 was the critical date of the new increase in an enormous measure of the anti-war feeling in our country, and it is necessary to fight to increase and organise further the forces supporting collective security, as revealed on May 21. Do not forget the strength of the peace forces in our own country, if they are duly strengthened from without.

We may add to the letter the further detail that on July 22 and 23 all tours already arranged by the 'Strength through Joy' organisation in our district were cancelled. Money already paid was not returned, but those who demanded it were informed that the tours would take place later.–Yours. &c,

THREE SOCIAL DEMOCRATS,
Eastern Germany (via Prague), August 5.

Monday 15 August   *p.8*

KNOWN AND UNKNOWN

So far Lord Runciman's mission follows an even course, and public opinion in this country tends to assume that the course must continue to be even until a happy end is reached; in a reasonable world, and since we have sent a peacemaking mission, how can it be otherwise? Unfortunately, the world is far from reasonable. The mission has begun well, but nothing else was to be expected. Lord Runciman is a mediator. In Czecho-Slovakia they know that war may come out of the present crisis at least as easily as peace, and all sides are anxious to appear before him as people desiring only the peaceful attainment of their just rights. Lord Runciman has been seeing the Czech Government and President Benes, the Parliamentary leaders of the Sudeten Germans (as the representatives of the complaining party), and some leading industrialists. While he is familiarising himself with their views the discussions are carried a step farther: the Sudeten leaders meet the chief members of the Czech Cabinet and of the Czech Coalition parties sitting together. But at the same time the Czech officers warn the Government that it must not go too far; it must not yield so much to the Sudetens that they and those who manipulate them may be able to undermine the Czecho-Slovak State from within. If when a settlement was being worked out, it was necessary only that Czechs and Sudeten Germans should be satisfied, the difficulty would still be great but not insuperable. But behind the Sudetens is Herr Henlein, who, whatever he may intend to do, has not seen Lord Runciman and behind Herr Henlein stands Herr Hitler, with whom alone it rests to say whether the Sudetens are to be allowed

60

to accept the most generous offers that the Czech Government can make to them without fatally endangering the State.

Calm as is the atmosphere of the Prague discussions – and to keep the temperature down is one of the tasks of the Runciman Mission – it would be extreme folly for the people of this country not to realise that there is great danger ahead and that it may easily come sooner and more suddenly than anyone anticipates. What matters is Berlin. The alternative of peace or war lies with Herr Hitler; all else can be got over. And if one looks over the German border at the present moment there are two things to be seen, and both disquieting. There is, first, the violent campaigning of the German press against Czecho-Slovakia. It is possible to argue that this may have no more serious intention than to put pressure on the Czechs by intimating to them that the 'patience' of Germany in the face of Czech 'provocations' is, from day to day, almost at an end. It is, however, much more than possible, it is certain, that this unsleeping propaganda is designed to keep the mind of the German people in a state fit to be used at any moment by the German Government for its own purposes not only of 'peaceful' pressure but of intimidation and, if need be, war. The British Government has now in Prague an 'observer' who can be sent to report the truth about such 'incidents' as the alleged murder of a Sudeten by a Czech, although in fact he was murdered by another German. The idea ought to be extended. There might well be half a dozen observers – British if no 'neutrals' will join in – to report immediately on 'incidents' and prevent lying rumour from getting a good start.

Then there is the immense military activity now going on in Germany. The drive to complete the lines of Germany's defensive fortifications, especially on the west, is not to be easily explained. It is not the making of the lines, for that is inevitable, that excites general apprehension, but that it should apparently be done as a work of emergency, at the cost even of some dislocation of civilian life, to be finished within a fixed time. For what object? If one were to inquire of the informed in Europe they would give one of three answers. The most hopeful would say that since Germany fears that she may be interfered with by France, or by France and Britain, in settling the Czech problem (however she may propose to settle it) she is giving herself greater freedom of action by building an impregnable line of defences; she will soon, in effect, say to the West 'You can no longer interfere.' A middle school would say that her intention is ruder – plain intimidation; on this view she would say to Czecho-Slovakia 'They can no longer help you.' A third school, which is as authoritative as the other two, goes farther still and believes that Germany can only be making so tremendous an effort because she contemplates settling the Czech question, if she thinks fit, by force. The nervous anxiety that is reported from inside Germany indicates that there, too, whatever view is taken of these military measures, it is not a pleasant one. For the moment there is a calm while Lord Runciman sees what he can do; it ought to be true that so far from merely pressing the Czechs (as some people expect) to make surrenders which may be fatal to them he will also press the Sudeten Germans, and through them their masters, the arbiters of peace and war, not to demand what is known to be impossible. But some of those arbiters, it is to be feared, are men who are concerned only to believe that what they will they can. They may already have forgotten what Mr. Chamberlain has more than once said clearly, that it is impossible to set limits to such a war as would arise out of Czecho-Slovakia, and it would be a service to peace if a way were found of repeating a truth which, to the general danger, may have by now been forgotten.

p.9

NAZI GOVERNMENT'S MILITARY ACTIVITIES
Nervousness of the German People

MANOEUVRES AND RUSHED WORK ON FORTIFICATIONS
Germany Forms a Sudeten Legion

The matter that is still dominating Europe is the great military activity in Germany. Many thousands of reservists have been called up, civilian property has been commandeered on a large scale, and big manoeuvres are about to begin on the frontiers of France and Czecho-Slovakia. These activities are on so great a scale that telegrams from Germany report that the public is becoming increasingly nervous.

The Czech Army is also holding manoeuvres, but in order not to offend Germany they are not on a big scale.

SOUNDINGS IN BERLIN

Britain and France have made inquiries in Berlin about the situation and are said to have received some reassurances.

In Czecho-Slovakia Lord Runciman is continuing his efforts. Last week he brought the Czech Ministers and the Sudeten leaders together and the negotiations then begun will be continued this week. Apart from this there appears to be no marked change in the situation.

RUSHED WORK ON FORTIFICATIONS

Fresh news continues to arrive about Germany's rush to complete the fortifications on her frontiers in the west and also in the east. So many men have been taken away that work on the Munich underground railway has almost stopped.

Our Warsaw correspondent reports that some workers in Upper Silesia have protested and have refused to work on the fortifications and others have come to blows with the police. Pamphlets saying 'the Nazis are pushing Germany into another war' are being circulated.

The much-vaunted German fortifications known as the 'West Wall' were in reality at this time much more akin to a gigantic builder's yard rather than a system of fortifications. In August 1938 the German Generals were informing Hitler that in the event of a war with both Czechoslovakia and France they could only defend their western fortifications for a maximum of three weeks.

Tuesday 16 August *p.9*

GERMAN PUBLIC DISTURBED BY MILITARY ACTIVITIES
Dangers of an Uncontrolled Government

HITLER RETURNS TO BERLIN AND MEETS ARMY CHIEFS

(Herr Hitler, who attended the Army manoeuvres near Berlin yesterday, returned to the capital in the evening and had a conference with Field Marshal Goring and some of the heads of the Army and the Air Force.)

Berlin, August 15.

The German manoeuvres which have aroused such wide-spread interest began to-day, and Herr Hitler himself watched military exercises of troops of all arms at Juterbog, the Aldershot of Germany, a short distance from Berlin.

Reports from parts of Germany indicate that the general public is becoming seriously alarmed over the extent of the manoeuvres, especially as so many reservists have been called to the colours and the press campaign against Czecho-Slovakia continues unabated. The main centres are Bavaria and Saxony on the Czecho-Slovak border and on the left bank of the Rhine along the French frontier. They are being carried on quite openly, but no one is allowed to approach the scene of operations.

WHOLESALE DREAD OF WAR

The public apprehension over the manoeuvres may fairly be attributed to a wholesale dread of war, for it cannot be denied that the Germans of to-day have no desire for military adventure. This fact and the knowledge that the Reich Government can act without consulting the nation in any way have undoubtedly given rise to a feeling of helplessness and alarm. Hitherto anxiety has been more prevalent in the country generally, but now it has spread to Berlin.

Numbers of Post Office vans have been commandeered in Berlin to transport workers to the fortification areas. Charabancs generally engaged in sightseeing tours of the capital are now being used by the Post Office.

The calling up of able-bodied citizens under Field Marshal Goring's decree for the mobilisation of labour continues. No fewer than 250 persons employed in the Ufa film studios have been taken from their works, and some 150 employees from the department store of Wertheim. ...

FRENCH AIR CHIEF'S VISIT

Paris, August 15.

General Vuillemin, the Chief of the French Air Staff, is to pay a visit to Germany. He leaves Le Bourget by air to-morrow morning and will stay until Sunday.

General Vuillemin, who will be accompanied by French air officials, is returning the visit paid last year to the French Air Force by General Milch, the Secretary of State of the German Air Ministry.–Reuter.

During the above visit General Vuillemin allowed himself to be bluffed regarding the strength of the Luftwaffe. He saw the He-100 fighter and believed it to be in full production, whereas in reality only three test prototypes existed. After looking at the He-111 bombers in construction, he confided to the French Ambassador 'I am shattered,' and further suggested that 'should war break out as you expect late in September, there won't be a single French plane left in a fortnight.'

His subsequent report on his visit made a tremendous impact on the perceptions of M. Bonnet, the French Foreign Minister.

HITLER AND THE EUROPEAN RIDDLE
The Choice He Has To Make

WHAT WILL INFLUENCE HIM IN HIS DECISION
Weighing the Risks and the 'Prize'

From our Diplomatic Correspondent

London, Tuesday.

It is recognised here, and no doubt in other European capitals, that the dispute between the Czecho-Slovak Government and the Sudeten Germans is only an aspect of the wider struggle for power in Europe.

The view expressed in your leader columns on Monday is widely accepted – namely, that the decision between peace and war lies with Herr Hitler. It is not believed here that Hitler has made up his mind in any final sense. It is, however, known that he is not in a very accommodating mood and that he has a strong bias in favour of a 'settlement' which will not only give the Sudeten Germans the 'rights' they demand but will establish a German ascendancy over Czecho-Slovakia.

There is what may be loosely called a 'war party' in Berlin – a number of persons, that is to say, who play a leading part in the conduct of German policy and believe that Germany can afford to run the risk of going to war with Czecho-Slovakia. It is not clear whether Herr Hitler shares their views; it is still possible that he will, in the end, decide for at least a temporary settlement with Prague – always provided that Prague goes a long way in satisfying the demands of the Sudeten Germans.

THE RISK

There are German officers of high rank who are not at all convinced that the outcome of a war would be favourable to Germany. But among others there is a 'now or never' mood. While recognising certain hazards, they believe that Germany can break the resistance of the Czechs before there can be any effective intervention by the Western Powers.

Having crushed Czecho-Slovakia, Germany would soon be master of the Danubian Basin, a prize her 'war party' appears to regard as well worth those parts against Germany, but it is also believed that such a plan would be fatal to Poland herself no less than to Czecho-Slovakia, for there would be complete rupture between Poland and the Western Powers, and she would be left alone to face Germany and Russia.

ALARM IN GERMANY

The German internal situation also seems to be influencing German policy. That there is great alarm in the German western and south-eastern frontier regions is certainly true. It is true, also, that the German people do not want war. Indeed, the fear of war is probably greater in Germany than anywhere else in Europe, including even Czecho-Slovakia. But the decisions in the next few weeks will hardly be affected by what German people want or do not want.

Although there is no effective opposition to the National Socialistic dictatorship, discontent has grown steadily. Enthusiasm over the Anschluss has worn off. Indeed, little setbacks endured by the dictatorship are beginning to cause greater rejoicing than its triumphs – the recent defeat of Schmeling in New York, for example, was received with general delight throughout Germany, even amongst National Socialists, so that the 'Völkischer Beobachter' had to explain in a leading article that no loss of national prestige was involved.

The German working class is particularly discontented, so much so that, although there is no organised sabotage in the factories, there is a perceptible difference between the willingness with which men work for war and peace. In some of the war industries the slowness and apathy of the men, despite high wages and piece-time work, come very near to ca' canny.

Germany has been given to understand quite plainly that the attitude of Great Britain in the event of a European conflict resulting from a German attack upon Czecho-Slovakia was defined by Mr. Chamberlain in his statement in the House of Commons on March 24. That statement was a very grave warning indeed, and the British Government has not departed from it by one hair-breadth.

But just as in 1914 Germany disbelieved the warnings addressed to her, so now she is far too little impressed by the warnings addressed to her, while she places too favourable an interpretation (from her own point of view) on the circumstance that Great Britain is not encouraging the Czechs to anticipate help from this country in the event of a war. It is clear that Great Britain cannot give Czecho-Slovakia any specific guarantee, but it is equally clear that she cannot remain indifferent to a general conflict. Now, as in 1914, Germany misjudges the situation, believing that this country must be telling all the truth in Prague (as in Paris 24 years ago) and bluffing in Berlin.

Germany is sceptical whether France will help Czecho-Slovakia in the event of war. But even if there were certainty in Berlin that France would help her Central European ally, the German 'war party' would, apparently, remain as strong as it is now.

It is convinced that the German defences in the west will 'contain' a French attack until Czecho-Slovakia has been crushed. It is difficult to tell whether this belief is justified or not. Some objective observers rate the Czech armies' power of resistance very high. ...

The conquest of Czecho-Slovakia would, if rapidly achieved, justify the existence of the new army – which is to a large extent Herr Hitler's creation. Leading National Socialists believe also that armed victory in the heart of Europe would stimulate patriotic fervour and make Germany appear irresistible. It would also give her access to further supplies of raw materials, especially Rumanian oil and grain.

It is true that a long and arduous conflict would probably mean the end of the National Socialist dictatorship, and of a good deal more. But it is feared that the National Socialist leaders Hitler included, may be inclined to take the risk and to take it soon. That is the reason why the European situation is recognised both here and in Paris as being very grave.

Hitler's whole strategy was based on the concept of the 'Blitzkrieg' (lightning war) both in military and economic terms. Germany possessed armaments in width necessary for Blitzkrieg tactics but lacked armaments in depth equally necessary for a more prolonged conflict.

Saturday 20 August   *p.11*

THE SHADOW OF GERMANY
Friends In Need

CZECHO-SLOVAKIA'S ALLIES
German Strategy

By our Special Correspondent

If Germany is able to create a 'fait accompli' as she did in the Rhineland and in Austria – that is to sy, if she can invade Czecho-Slovakia unresisted or rapidly overcome all resistance and then confront the Western Powers with her main armies unweakened and entrenched behind her almost impregnable western defences – then Czecho-Slovakia will have been lost and the main – and perhaps the only – barrier to the German domination of Eastern and South-eastern Europe will have fallen.

The semicircle of mountain and forest that divides Bohemia from the Reich forms a defensive line of immense natural strength. It has been made almost impregnable by the Czechs. The Germans would hardly attempt to break through this line. It is more likely that they would attempt the invasion of Czecho-Slovakia by closing in on her from the north and south simultaneously, from Upper Silesia and from the region round Vienna, and so penetrate her defensive girdle in its two weakest places, the so-called 'Moravian gap' and the frontier zone north of Bratislava.

TWO GAPS

The 'Moravian gap' is poor in natural defences but has been covered with a network of fieldworks, machine gun nests, artillery positions, and so on that would inflict heavy losses and perhaps long delays on the invader.

The Czechs fortified their Austrian frontier in anticipation of the 'Anschluss'. The frontier zone north of Bratislava offers another natural 'gap' which, if invaded would expose Brno (Brunn) to capture. If a German converging or 'pincer' movement through the two 'gaps' were to succeed Czecho-Slovakia would be cut in half and the Czechs would be severed from the Slovaks. The loss of Brno alone would deprive Czecho-Slovakia of the main railway junction between east and west.

Czecho-Slovakia has relatively weak defences against Hungary. The River Danube offers a formidable obstacle along some hundred miles of the Czecho-Slovak–Hungarian frontier. In the region beyond the point (the town of Szob) where the Danube turns southwards the Czech defences are quite inadequate, but are rapidly being strengthened.

It is doubtful whether Germany would invade Hungary or attempt to secure Hungarian co-operation against Czecho-Slovakia for to do so would almost certainly bring Yugo-Slavia into the war. ...

RUSSIAN AID

Rumania will almost certainly allow the passage of Russian war material, troops, and aeroplanes to Czecho-Slovakia. Poland will certainly deny Russia the right of way. Russia will perhaps do all in her power to help Czecho-Slovakia but that power is limited. Her own western communications are few. Only one Rumanian railway line (and that not a main line) gives her access to Czecho-Slovakia. Even then the remaining distance to the war zone would be very great. It is doubtful whether the Czechs have sufficient personnel, adequate aerodromes, repair shops, and spare parts to maintain a Russian Air Force of any size, even if they do possess some of the types of aeroplanes which the Russians would dispatch to their help. The Russian air bases would be at least 600 or 700 miles from the war-zone, while Germany would be able to carry out air raids in rapid succession and at short range.

As Czecho-Slovakia is a much more concentrated target than Germany and is bound to remain on the defensive, her Air Force even if augmented by Russian 'planes could hardly play a decisive part in a war. It would mainly serve to attack the German lines of communication and marching columns and so contribute – perhaps heavily – towards arresting an invasion.

The real value of the alliance between Prague and Moscow is not so much military as political and psychological. It has been followed by improved relations between Moscow and Bucharest. Rumania, relieved of anxiety with regard to her eastern frontier, would be the better able to help Czecho-Slovakia. Like the Franco-Soviet Pact, the alliance between Moscow and Prague is chiefly intended to counteract the chances of an alliance between Moscow and Berlin. The Red Army and Air Force are enthusiastically cheered whenever they are shown in the picture theatres in Prague, and the prospect – illusory as it may be – of Russian help on a gigantic scale has done much to keep up the spirits of the Czech public. As for Russian political influence, there is absolutely none of it in Czecho-Slovakia. It is nonsensical to maintain that Czecho-Slovakia is 'an outpost of Bolshevism' in the very heart of Europe. The Czecho-Slovak Communist party is of no consequence whatever; the Czechs are as alien to the spirit of Muscovite Communism as they are to the spirit of Fascism or National Socialism.

GERMANY'S POSITION

Czecho-Slovakia cannot be sure of immediate armed help from any of the Powers. Germany cannot count on the neutrality of the Western Powers, and it is certain that France will at least threaten her in the west if she goes to war with Czecho-Slovakia. She cannot count on the neutrality of Yugo-Slavia. Polish and German troops may invade Czecho-Slovakia together and share the country out between them, but Poland may also turn against Germany. Germany cannot even be sure of Italian neutrality.

She would therefore have to keep divisions along her eastern and western frontiers, and perhaps even on the Brenner, so that the forces available for the invasion of Czecho-Slovakia would be limited. She is preparing to 'contain' a French attack by means of a vast system of flexible defences in the west, while her preparations along the Czecho-Slovak border reveal plans for an offensive carried out with a tremendous weight of metal rather than with overwhelming numbers of men.

It is clear that if the first German onset failed the chances of intervention by neutral or semi-neutral Powers would grow with every day the Czechs were able to withstand the invader. Czecho-Slovakia has many friends while Germany is without a real friend in Europe.

This article echoes the comments being made repeatedly to Hitler by his generals. Indeed Göring had commented in 1938 that '... England and France do not stand alone on the opposite side, but are always in a position to draw on the immense reservoir (of) raw materials in America.'

LETTERS TO THE EDITOR

HITLER'S AIMS TO CZECHO-SLOVAKIA
The Lesson of Austria

To the Editor of the Manchester Guardian

Sir,–In the different papers which I am reading, English included, I find frequent reference to the so-called Czecho-Slovak–German conflict. The authors vary in their views about it, yet almost all regard the affair as a local 'nationalities' problem. But let me quote Mr. Stivin, M.P., on this point, as he put it in the Czecho-Slovak daily 'Pravo Lidu' on July 31:

> ... it is not a question of 'nationalities' in Czecho-Slovakia but of the Czecho-Slovak ironworks, coal and metal basins, grain, sugar, meat; of the Hungarian wheat and corn; of the Rumanian petroleum; of the Ukrainian fertile plants; of an access to the Black Sea; of the German Drang nach Osten (thrust towards the East).

This old German ambition Hitler carefully nurtured in his book 'Mein Kampf'.

Hitler's failure to get hold of us on May 21, which was due to miscalculating the readiness of the democracies to confront his violence, up to that time unchecked, did not at all take away his appetite. He has always shown extraordinary patience and stubborn perseverance in pursuing his object. So it is evident that he will never want to give up the realisation of his imperialistic dreams, but is determined to overcome our resistance in another way – underground. By internal means, forcing us to rewrite our liberal Constitution and reorganise our democratic State. By external means, manufacturing propaganda to confuse and blind our friends and bluffing war in order to extort the 'key to our house' – namely, self-govenment for the so-called, 'Sudetens'. But we in our turn do not want to give up our determination ever to yield to his threats nor fall into his traps. We do not want to become subjects for his terroristic rule as it is exemplified in the cruel oppression of minorities in Germany. We do not want to betray our old national culture and our newly won liberty, for which our own fathers have bled not so long ago.

Hitler's course of proceeding against Austria and her fate stand as a warning to us. His failure to annex her two years ago did not dissuade him from pursuing his plans. He only changed his manner of approach. He worked covertly, corrupting law and order and authority by his alluring Nazist pledges, made the people believe that their annexation would be their salvation, compelled Schuschnigg to set Seyss-Inquart, his accomplice, in power – and Austria tumbled like a ripe apple into his hands. His present tactics against us are similar. It is the same trap, adjusted to our size and wits. And we see through it all too clearly.

We are glad of Lord and Lady Runciman's presence in our country because it means some sort of a truce for us in the highly dangerous circumstances, and we hope his Lordship will see what is what with the Germans and what with ourselves in our State. His task is certainly a herculean one. It amounts to harmonising two diametrically opposite life conceptions, Democracy and Nazism. Can it ever be done? Hitler's goal is known. He needs our country to build a German thoroughfare to the east. A settlement of the conflict, which settlement Lord Runciman is trying to bring about, could be only a cover to Hitler for his great plans of world conquest. And a settlement – should the miracle happen and Lord Runciman succeed in his peace-making effort – by itself could be of no value to Hitler unless it granted such additional concessions to the Henlein Germans as would in their time gradually undermine this State's law and order and authority, paralyse its power of resistance; in short, end in a disintegration of democratic Czecho-Slovakia and make us an easy prey to Hitler-like Austria. However, the democratic Czecho-Slovak people – Czecho-Slovaks, Germans, Poles, and Hungarians alike – are on the look-out for any possibility of such an outcome and would be heard of tremendously should it threaten.–Yours, &c.,

A COMMON CITIZEN OF CZECHO-SLOVAKIA,
Prague, August 16.

Tuesday 30 August   *p.9*

THE NEW CZECH PROPOSALS
Sudeten Germans and the Home Rule Plan

From our Diplomatic Correspondent

London, Monday Night.

The outlook to-day is perhaps a little more hopeful than it has been for several weeks. It is difficult to believe that the German Government, and even Hitler himself, can have remained wholly unaware of the dangers made manifest above all by the attitude of the British Government, which Germany would bring upon herself if she were to go to war with Czecho-Slovakia. Hitler is certainly an 'extremist' and shares the ultimate aims of the German 'war party', but he has in the past been able to judge the international situation with some shrewdness. If he can correctly assess it now he will at least hesitate, so it would seem, before starting on an enterprise that might bring disaster on his country and on himself.

It is perhaps of some significance that the new Czech plan for granting the Sudeten Germans a large measure of home rule has not been rejected in advance by the Sudeten German party and has not been denounced as intolerable by the German press and wireless. This would seem to show that the Sudeten German party and the patron, Hitler, are in favour of negotiating on the basis of the new Czech proposals. The speech made by Herr Frank at Oberleutensdorf on Sunday would seem to bear this out, all the more so as Herr Frank is one of the 'extremists' amongst the Sudeten German leaders. In his speech he declared that 'the next few days and weeks will be devoted to negotiations'.

It is, of course, possible that Germany wishes to remove the impression that she is intractable. If negotiations begin it does not follow that after a while an 'incident' may not be staged to show the world and the German public that it is hopeless to negotiate with the Czechs, and that all Hitler's unexampled efforts on behalf of peace have been in vain. But, for the time being, the fact that some sort of accommodation is being shown by the Sudeten German party is welcomed here, for it is not impossible that it is the outcome of a wish, felt by the party and by the German Government, to find a peaceful rather than a warlike solution.

p.13

CABINET MEETS IN FRANCE
Looking to London

HOPING FOR ACTION BY BRITAIN

From our own Correspondent

Paris, August 29.

... A statement on the European position was made by the Foreign Minister, M. Bonnet. The French Government takes a very serious view of the present situation and the failure of the Runciman mission as yet to achieve anything concrete. Nevertheless there is no tendency here to over-estimate its gravity, and things are being faced with great calm.

The deepest interest is being taken in the Cabinet discussions in London and in the instructions the British Ambassador in Berlin is expected to take back with him. There are hopes that the action the British Ambassador in Berlin is then expected to take will prove fruitful.

Again, even at this late stage, the French government is still demonstrating its eagerness to subordinate its role to that of the British.

Wednesday 31 August   *p.8*

Leader   **IN SUSPENSE**

Ministers met yesterday in London, but nothing was announced except that they were agreed about what had already been done (Sir John Simon's speech) and about 'the policy to be pursued in the future'. Sir Nevile Henderson, our Ambassador, returns to Berlin to-day. Whatever his instructions, there are two things that we would like to have both the German Government and the German people know: that in the opinion of this country there is no shadow of a reason why peaceful negotiations should be abandoned for force and that the use of force would in all probability not be 'local' (Spain and the Far East are no analogy) but would almost certainly lead to the unspeakable calamity of a wider war from which we should find ourselves unable to stand aloof. The Government must choose its own means, but its duty to the simple interests of this country compels it to make clear privately anything in these two propositions which it believes not to be clear already. The other centre of action is Prague. It had been announced yesterday that a meeting would take place between President Benes and the Sudeten German leader Herr Henlein. One version had it that Herr Kundt, the Parliamentary leader of the Sudetens, would meet the President. The purpose was to discuss the new plan for satisfying the Sudetens which Lord Runciman had explained to Herr Henlein on Sunday. Herr Henlein did not attend, but Herr Kundt and a colleague did. This may mean something less encouraging than the gesture which the presence of Herr Henlein himself would have indicated, but at the same time something less than rejection of the new concessions. The nature of these concessions is still unfortunately unknown in detail, and a German newspaper complains that opinion in this country 'credits Czecho-Slovakia with a conciliatory attitude because it is said to have made some undefined proposals'. British opinion knows a better reason why the Czechs are conciliatory: it is that, should there be a war, their country will be made a shambles.

Since the German Government is completely silent one must study the press, or, as one should rather say, its press. There are two phenomena to be seen, one of which is extremely discouraging. It is the implacable persistence with which the newspapers represent the Sudeten Germans as a misused and even tormented body that must be rescued from its oppressors by the German action. The Nazi 'Angriff', one of the most powerful organs of the party, writes of the 'bloody and violent methods of the Czechs' and declares that 'the shameful acts of the unleashed mob lie like a cloud of horror over the tortured land'. The 'Deutsche Allgemeine Zeitung' complains that the British press 'itself keeps silence about this incredible terrorism'. This is unfair. Yesterday at least three newspapers which have correspondents in Prague spoke of the incidents of which so much is made in Germany. The 'Times' correspondent spoke of ' a doleful list of week-end brawls among men the worse for drink', said that 'the incidents represent little more than what happens in a rowdy election campaign elsewhere', and reported that it was being asked why the Czech Government did not 'stop the sale of heavy drink on Saturday and Sunday nights'. The 'Daily Telegraph's Prague message spoke of 'a number of more or less trifling incidents' which, but for the political tension, could be regarded as 'night brawls' while our own correspondent said that the increasing number of incidents was 'alarming' and that there had been 'clashes, mostly originating in inns, between Germans belonging to different political camps or between Czechs and Germans'. In times of high political excitement and incipient war fever it has been common enough in the past for newspapers of their own accord to exaggerate 'incidents' telling against the rival country threatened by popular passion. But in Germany to-day there is no popular passion, and this campaign must be the deliberate policy of the Government. Its purpose can only be to make the German public believe that the oppression of the Sudeten Germans justifies, and even demands, whatever it is that the German Government now intends to do.

The other side of the German press during the last few days has been its discussion of Sir John Simon's speech. This too is significant. In the old days Germany's press would have given us different points of view written by men of independent judgment. Now it is the Government's point of view that we get everywhere; the writers whatever their papers or their names say what they must say, what they are told. This at all events gives us a pretty clear idea of the impression which the speech has made not on the public – for about that we must hope but cannot know – but on the Government itself. The Government, then, appears to be somewhat surprised and extremely resentful. We are told that to expect, in Sir John Simon's words, 'contributions from all concerned' is to put the blame for any disaster that may occur on the Sudeten Germans, although it should be, and must be, obvious that this country, in its anxiety to avert the use of force, has been anxious for the Czech Government to concede to the Sudetens whatever degree of self-government does not involve, directly or indirectly, the destruction of the State. We do not seek to put the blame on the Sudeten Germans, for they are not their own masters: it is never to be forgotten that Herr Henlein, when he came to London, gave a clear impression that he was then only demanding what could be reasonably granted by the Czech Government. It is to the German Government and to Hitler that we have always to look as being those wholly responsible for the Sudeten Germans' actions, and a study of the German press leaves little doubt that the intention of Sir John Simon's speech was understood by them. They can still, unhappily, refuse to believe it: how to convince them – if any doubt remains – is perhaps the matter now to be taken in hand.

Thursday 1 September p.8

Leader **THE GERMAN DEMANDS**

The Czech problem would at least be clearer, if not simpler, if it were known exactly what the Sudeten Germans want and what Herr Hitler will allow them to accept. These two things, of course, are not necessarily the same. To say (as the Sudeten Germans sometimes say themselves) that they want autonomy is not enough, for there are obviously many degrees of autonomy. Under the existing laws, for instance, they have in their hands the administration of all parishes, towns, and districts where they form a majority of the population and to that extent are autonomous. On the other hand, 'complete autonomy' can be enjoyed only by sovereign States, such as Canada and Australia within the British Empire. The Sudeten Germans generally say that what they want is 'racial autonomy,' but no one knows exactly what that means. Certainly it means more than local self-government (in German 'Selbstverwaltung'), which Dr. Hodza, the Czech Premier, has already promised them, and more even than 'territorial autonomy,' which is another favourite phrase. For any fuller explanation one must look to the Eight Points put forward by Herr Henlein in a speech at Carlsbad on April 23 this year and the Fourteen Points contained in a memorandum (sometimes called the Kundt memorandum) presented to the Czech Government by the Sudeten party on June 7. ...

For Henlein's 'eight points' see article on p.87 and for the Sudeten-German fourteen points see pp.127-9.

LORD RUNCIMAN SENDS A MESSAGE TO HITLER
Taken to Berchtesgaden by Henlein

SUPPORT FOR CONTINUANCE OF NEGOTIATIONS SOUGHT
Nazi Leaders in Conference

The most important development yesterday in the Czech crisis was a visit by Henlein (the leader of the Sudeten German party) to Hitler, at Lord Runciman's request.

Lord Runciman, believing in Henlein's 'genuine desire for peace,' asked him to deliver a message to Hitler hoping that he will approve of the continuance of the present negotiations.

Henlein therefore went to Berchtesgaden yesterday. Although he was (as far as can be discovered) in Hitler's house for about three hours, he was apparently not received by Hitler, as a communiqué issued by the Propaganda Minister yesterday said:

> Henlein arrived at Berchtesgaden this afternoon and put up at a local hotel. He will not make his visit to the Führer until to-morrow.

However, a conference appears to have been held in the house. It is known that Field Marshal Göring, Herr Hess (Hitler's deputy), and Dr. Goebbels were present. The conference will be resumed to-day, when Herr von Ribbentrop, the Foreign Minister, is expected to be present.

Göring returned to Berlin last night in a special train. It was noticed that more plainclothes policemen than usual were with him.

In Prague the executive of the Sudeten German party met to consider the new Czech plan. An obscure statement issued after the meeting said that the committee considered the political situation and drew the necessary conclusions. This statement is probably purposely obscure as the party leaders in Czecho-Slovakia must await the decisions which Hitler and his Ministers are expected to make to-day.

DANGER OF GERMAN ILLUSIONS ABOUT BRITAIN'S ATTITUDE
The Tactic of Lulling Europe's Fears

MAGNITUDE OF GERMANY'S MILITARY PREPARATIONS

From our Diplomatic Correspondent

London, Friday Night.

It would seem that Hitler's long-expected 'peace offensive' has begun. The interview he has given to a correspondent of the 'journal' is highly characteristic of his method. The friendliest words are addressed to France, while the main polemic is concentrated on Czecho-Slovakia, though in a veiled form. There is the familiar denunciation of 'Bolshevism' and the pronouncement that the 'absorption of other territories by Bolshevism' cannot be tolerated. Hitler's thesis with regard to Czecho-Slovakia has all along been that she has always been an 'outpost of Bolshevism,' that she is under 'Bolshevik' domination by reason of her alliance with Russia and that she has been absorbed, or is at least about to be absorbed, by 'Bolshevism.'

The interview is in full keeping with Germany's military preparations – that is to say, purely defensive preparations in the west and offensive preparations in the east against Czecho-Slovakia.

A WORLD-WIDE MORAL COALITION

It is believed here that Hitler will develop his 'peace offensive' during the Nuremberg Congress. For some time the German Government has been considering whether it would not be useful to open discussions about the limitation of aerial armaments and the possibility of confining aerial warfare to objectives of military importance. It seems likely that the Czech proposals for a new Minorities Statute wil be accepted as a basis of temporary negotiation. In this way Germany may hope to escape from the rather unfavourable position in which she has been placed internationally.

Whereas she now appears as a potential aggressor, she will, if her 'peace offensive' is successful, impress the world as a peacemaker. The attitude of Great Britain and the solidarity (whether real or apparent) of public opinion both in this country and elsewhere (except Italy and Japan) can hardly have failed to make an impression in Berlin. Germany finds herself confronted with a world-wide moral coalition (so to speak) that would endeavour to stay her hand if she were to attack Czecho-Slovakia. The purpose of Hitler's 'peace offensive' will be to break up this coalition. ...

PLAYING FOR TIME

Hitler is clearly playing for time (though it may be for no more than a short time) and is delaying his reply to the Czech proposals. A little time, especially if filled in by a 'peace offensive,' and the crisis will have been forgotten. ...

It seems very doubtful indeed whether Hitler, and, indeed, even German observers with some knowledge of this country, believes that the British Government really takes the international situation as seriously as it professes to take it (Hitler is no doubt mistaken, but it is not the reality but their impression of the reality that will determine his actions).

GERMANY'S MILITARY PREPARATIONS

Meanwhile German military preparations continue. They are increasing in volume and have become much more extensive than is generally realised. Germany has, by now, carried out something more than a normal mobilisation. She has mobilised her whole Army, Navy, and Air Force, a considerable number of reservists, and a vast army of workmen.

The purpose of Hitler's recent visit to the Western frontier regions was, apparently, to deepen the impression which German military preparedness has made on the Western Powers. The German public is in rather a defeatist mood. This is especially true of the Rhineland and of the multitudes who are working on the Western fortifications. A 'peace offensive' in addition to his personal tour would help to counteract defeatism.

Labour on the western defences did not begin as recently as is generally supposed. It began soon after the reoccupation of the Rhineland. Work on the defences that lie close up against the French frontier began last winter. After May 21 it was intensified in a prodigious manner, hundreds of thousands of workmen from all parts of the Reich (including Austria) being conscripted for forced labour in the west. At the present time the number of men engaged in the work must be about 500,000, if not more; it certainly exceeds 400,000.

LETTERS TO THE EDITOR

OPINION IN CZECHO-SLOVAKIA
The Alternatives for Britain

To the Editor of the Manchester Guardian

Sir,–I have just returned from nearly three weeks in Czecho-Slovakia, where I have been fortunate enough to be in close touch with many people intimately connected with the Government of the State – the Lord Mayor of Prague (school-fellow and close personal friend of President Benes), the Governor and Vice-Governor of Sub-Carpathian Russia, university professors who are also advisers to or members of the Administration, members of the Foreign Office, and others. In addition I have travelled from the German border on the west to the farthest point of Sub-Carpathian Russia on the east and from Bratislava on the Hungarian frontier to the south to the Tatra Mountains on the border of Poland in the north. Wherever I have been I have made it my business to find out as accurately as I could the mind of the people on the present situation. May I, therefore, trespass on your space to give the results of these first-hand investigations.'

From the Government to the man in the street, from west to east and from south to north, there is one dominant opinion and one only – that if Great Britain will to-day speak one strong word of warning to Hitler there will be no war. Failing that, that nothing can prevent war. (As a corollary it is added that if war comes, Britain will be dragged in willy-nilly with the rest.) Far from the feeling of satisfaction with Sir John Simon's speech that the 'Times' Prague correspondent purports to have discovered, there was in Prague on Sunday a feeling of intense disappointment that the British Govenment had not yet found it expedient to make a more definite statement than that made by Mr. Chamberlain in March.

To any observer with an open mind the position is perfectly clear. The demands made by the Sudeten German party will never be satisfied because they are not genuine demands. They are merely a pretext for causing trouble, and as fast as one is met another will spring up in its place. As one professor and member of Parliament said to me: 'Nothing will satisfy the Germans except the complete extinction of the Czech nation – and then they would blame us for killing their potential converts!'

But even taking the demands as genuine, there is a limit beyond which the Czecho-Slovak State (and in this the nation is at one with the Government) cannot go. As the Lord Mayor of Prague put it: 'There is life with dishonour or death with honour,

79

and if it comes to that choice we prefer death to life, on such terms.' Certain further concessions can and will be made, but the demand for complete racial autonomy cannot be granted if only for the reason that it would maroon 700,000 Czechs in German districts – and the treatment of a minority in a German district would not compare favourably, to put it at its lowest, with the treatment of any minority in the Czecho-Slovak Republic, where, in fact, as well as according to the Constitution, 'Czech nationals who belong to racial, religious, or linguistic minorities enjoy the same treatment and security as ... the other foreign nationals. There is no solid German fringe round the border of Bohemia as is drawn on a map now being circulated by the Sudeten German party.

The unanimous opinion in Czecho-Slovakia to-day is that Hitler will undoubtedly try a bold stroke in the very near future. If the Powers then show they are not prepared for the fate that overtook Austria to be repeated in Czecho-Slovakia some general will (temporarily) lose his job and no more will come of it. If, on the other hand, the Powers say nothing, Germany's march to the Black Sea will begin, and once in possession of Hungarian corn, Rumanian oil, and all the other things he now covets no Power on earth can withstand her. Even if she does not get as far as that Europe will have become involved in a war the end of which no man can foresee. 'The one thing that can stop Hitler to-day,' said one Government adviser, 'is the certain knowledge that if she fights she will lose. Therefore the strength against her must be shown to be such that she dare not take the risk of starting a war.'

Czecho-Slovakia to-day is a State of more complete fair play and good treatment for every section of the population, than is to be found anywhere else on the continent of Europe. There can be no compromise between the safety and security of that State and the demands of the German bullies. It seems that only public opinion can force the necessary statement out of the reluctant, sealed lips of our Government. Can public opinion be mobilised in time?–Yours, &c.,

F.L. JOSEPHY.
1, Alvanley Gardens, Hampstead, London, N.W.6, August 31.

NEW CZECH OFFER
Announcement After Five-Hour Ministers' Council

REPLY TO SUDETEN LEADERS
Henlein Pressing For Full Carlsbad Demands

There were two sudden developments in the Czech crisis last night – on the Sudeten side against any compromise and on the Government side for a still more generous offer.

The Sudeten German leaders, after a conference with Herr Henlein, announced that they stood by the whole of the Carlsbad demands. A communiqué they issued ended with the words–

All reports that have been received show an untenable situation that can be altered only by the prompt and complete realisation of the eight Carlsbad points.

While the Sudeten Germans were in conference at Eger the Czech Inner Cabinet Council was in session in Prague discussing the limit of the concessions it can now offer to the Sudetens. Late last night, after a meeting of many hours, it was announced that the Ministers had 'drawn up a definitive plan which will be submitted with minimum delay to the Sudeten party'

The main demands of the Carlsbad programme are that there should be full equality of status between Czechs and Germans; the recognition of the Germans as a legal entity; full self-government for the German regions; and full liberty to profess German nationality and German political philosophy. The latest Czech Government proposals are not yet known, but it was understood on good authority in Prague last night that they go far on the way to satisfying the full Sudeten demands. ...

CONCESSIONS BY CZECHS
Going a Long Way

SACRIFICES ALL ON ONE SIDE
To-day's Discussions

Paris, September 6 (2 a.m.).

The communiqué announcing that the Czecho-Slovak Inner Cabinet has drawn up a plan for the settlement of the Sudeten German problem is of 'capital importance,' says a Prague message to the Havas Agency.

81

The new proposals drawn up by the Government for presentation to the Sudeten party are described in the communiqué as 'definitive.' That is a significant word on the eve of the Nuremberg Congress, states the message. ...

Since the proposals are described as 'definitive' it must be that Lord Runciman considered that the Prague Government could go no farther in the matter of concessions.

HAVE THE SUDETENS AGREED?

In these circumstances the question is to know whether the Sudetens, to whom the outline of the proposals was communicated in the course of secret conversations during the past two days, have agreed to them. If they have a solution is in sight. If not the question of force is left open. But from what indications can be gathered here and there it would appear that the first hypothesis is the true one. Under pressure from Great Britain the Czechs seem to have given way.

On what bases? No information is yet forthcoming on this subject but the intransigence of speeches made yesterday by various Sudeten leaders in Sudeten districts leave little doubt on the subject. Sudetens declare that they would not modify in any way their claims set forth in the eight points by Herr Henlein at Carlsbad. Even taking into account the demands of party oratory, it is therefore unlikely that the Sudetens have made any concessions, and everything points to the Czechs as the side which has made the sacrifices.

Fresh discussions are announced for to-morrow, doubtless in order officially to communicate the new proposals to the Sudeten party and to obtain their agreement.–Reuter.

FRANCE TAKES PRECAUTIONS
Frontier Defences

ALL ARMY LEAVE CANCELLED
Britain Consulted

From our own Correspondent

Paris, September 5.

Although there are no outward signs of nervousness in the streets of Paris to-day, an undercurrent of deep anxiety is to be observed.

The important concentrations of troops observed in the last few days in the Rhineland were beginning to cause serious concern to the French Government, but the decision to answer this

82

concentration with a reinforcement of the French effectives on the frontier was postponed as long as possible. I understand that the latest steps were taken after consultation with the British Government and with its full approval.

After the speeches made yesterday by Dr. Goebbels and the various Sudeten leaders there is little indication of what the last reassuring paragraph of the French communiqué is based on, unless the French Government has really serious grounds for believing – which is by no means certain – that these menacing speeches are not, as is commonly supposed here, a fitting introduction to what Hitler himself will say at Nuremburg this week. ...

Wednesday 7 September   *p.9*

TERMS OF CZECH OFFER
Nine Points Conceding Most Sudeten Demands

EXTENSIVE SELF-GOVERNMENT
Proposals Would be Put in Force as Soon as Possible

The new Czech offer to the Sudeten Germans was published in Prague late last night. It consists of the following nine points:–

Proportional employment of officials according to the population both for present and future appointments.

Employment of officials in the districts of their nationality.

Local regions to have police of their own nationality.

New language law based on complete equality.

Assistance to depressed Sudeten industrial areas, including a loan of £5,000,000.

Self-government for the national minorities in the areas in which they show a majority. All questions not dealing with national unity to be dealt with locally. Guarantees for the integrity of the frontier and the unity of the State.

Special departments for the Minorities in the central administrations.

Protection for citizens against denationalisation.

The plan to be put in force as soon as possible, detailed proposals being worked out in collaboration with the Sudeten Germans.

These, in brief, are the Government's proposals, and they meet most of the eight Carlsbad demands.

THE MINORITIES OF CZECHOSLOVAKIA

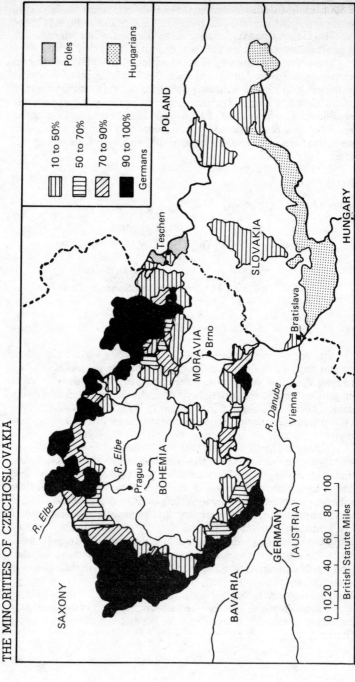

The Czech offer is already known to the Sudeten Germans, but of whether it has been accepted there is no definite news.

The only indication of the Sudeten attitude was to be obtained from a meeting Herr Kundt and Herr Sebekowsky had yesterday afternoon with the Runciman mission. The proposals were explained to the Sudeten leaders, and the result of the meeting was believed to have been favourable.

After this meeting the two Sudeten negotiators visited Dr. Benes, the Czech President. To-day they are expected to see Dr. Hodza, the Premier.

Herr Henlein, the Sudeten German leader, arrived in Nuremberg last night. ...

p.18

LETTERS TO THE EDITOR

THE GERMAN-CZECH CRISIS
'Now Is the Moment for Britain to Speak'

To the Editor of the Manchester Guardian

Sir,—May I as one who has frequently visited Czecho-Slovakia and has discussed its problems with Dr. Benes, Dr. Hodza, and Herr Henlein, be permitted to support the view expressed by your diplomatic correspondent regarding the danger of Herr Hitler's coming 'peace offensive'? This is purely a tactical political move on the part of Germany to throw dust into the eyes of Britain and France.

Germany does not intend to accept anything less than 100 per cent of her own demands, which, if granted, would mean the establishment within Czecho-Slovakia of a German National Socialist State, which can but lead to the disruption of the Czecho-Slovak Republic. Consequently Germany, to avoid the odium of rejecting a basis for negotiation, is now putting up her own terms, which are a mere variant of Henlein's 'Carlsbad eight points,' in the hope of putting the Czechs in the position of bearing the odium of rejection. This, in the view of Berlin, should result in Germany having a 'case' in the eyes of the world for taking violent action and throwing the blame and responsibility for it on Prague. Alternatively, so Berlin thinks, such a situation might well cause Britain and France to urge Prague to give in to Germany's demands. In either case Germany would get what she wants, at the expense of Czecho-Slovak independence, either by war or by blackmail.

Surely the time has come when our Government should realise that the 'equitable compromise' they and the Runciman Mission are supposed to be working for is not possible of attainment for the simple reason that Herr Hitler does not want it. Therefore, the time for urging further concessions from Dr. Benes is past, and the time for saying, 'Thus far and no farther' to Herr Hitler is now at hand. Otherwise it means an interim peace purchased at the price of Czecho-Slovak integrity. And this, in turn, means only the postponement of war, which, when it comes, will in consequence be fought on terms more advantageous to Germany, because of the weakening of Czecho-Slovakia in the meantime.

The Czech–Sudeten question has long since ceased to be a minority problem. If it were only that it could be settled at once. It is now purely and simply a question of power politics – Is or is not Germany to be allowed to dominate Europe from the Baltic to the Balkans? On the actual minority question itself the Czechs have shown themselves to be ready to meet every grievance. What the Czechs cannot be expected to do – and what they quite rightly refuse to do – is to permit Germany to establish within the frontiers of the Republic a replica of herself, complete with suppression of Czechs, non-Nazi Germans, and Jews, and owing its allegiance not to Prague but to Berlin.

I feel strongly that at this critical moment it is particularly necessary to point out these truths. Urging Prague to give way all along the line will not preserve the peace. Telling Berlin that the limit has been reached, and that if Germany passes that limit she will have to face a European coalition, including Britain will preserve the peace.

Now is the moment for Britain to speak. Yours, – &c.,

C.F. MELVILLE

Elmside, Bridge Road, Chertsey, Surrey, September 5.

WILL GERMANY RISK WAR?

To the Editor of the Manchester Guardian

Sir,–The opinion expressed by Miss Josephy in your issue of September 5 is corroborated by two Germans with whom I have recently talked. I saw them separately, but both agreed about the Sudeten Deutsch. One said:

> You probably know more about it than I do, for we are so kept in the dark. We never heard of them till lately. Is war likely? If Hitler thinks he can seize the place without any Power resisting he will do so. But he will not risk war.

The other said:

The Sudeten? That has all been worked up from outside.
Hitler does not care about them. He uses them only as an excuse
to annex their land. It is the land he wants. The Germans in
the South Tyrol have been far more badly treated than the
Sudeten, who were satisfied until Hitler interfered. There is a
lot of discontent in Germany. The workpeople complain of
having to leave their jobs in order to do compulsory labour on
fortifications. They are no better than slaves. Hitler may think
that a victory would popularise him. But if he sees there would
be a strong resistance he will hardly dare a war, unless it were
sure to be a very short one. The country is not provisioned for
a long war. There is already shortage of many things. If Hitler
is shown it must be a long war he will at least postpone it. To
my mind it all depends on the firmness of France and England.

As, for obvious reasons, no clue must be given to my
informants I cannot sign by name. – Yours &c.,

LONDONER,
September 5.

'WHY SHOULD BRITAIN BE INTERESTED?'

To the Editor of the Manchester Guardian

Sir,–May I be permitted to thank your correspondent Miss
F.L. Josephy for summarising so succinctly the real issue in Czecho-
Slovakia? 'If,' she says, 'the Powers say nothing Germany's march
to the Black Sea will begin and once in possession of Hungarian
corn &c., and all the other things she now covets no Power on earth
can withstand her.' That was always the excuse of the cannibal
chief for attacking his neighbour. The argument was not unknown
in our political life. I remember Grey, in 1908, in the House of
Commons defending our acquisition of what we politely called 'a
sphere of influence' in Southern Persia because Russia was stated
to be in Northern Persia and a menace to India. In 1914 Russia was
our ally. In 1922 Mr. Lloyd George's Government would have had
us fight Turkey in the interest of Greece and European civilisation.
To-day Turkey and Greece have settled their differences and live
in peace.

Why should we be interested in Czecho-Slovakia? It is
probably fair to say that not one in a hundred thousand of our
population knows where it is situated. Twelve months ago they had
probably never heard of it. The facts are these. In 1922 our
Government, through the Prime Minister (Mr. Lloyd George), and
it comprised Balfour, Curzon, and Austen Chamberlain, definitely

informed the French, who wanted us to guarantee Poland, with which it had a treaty and which it described as its 'eastern frontier,' that 'participation in military enterprise in Central and Eastern Europe could not be contemplated.' Poland is now neutral. ...

ELLIS W. DAVIES
Craig Wen, Caernarvon, September 5.

Thursday 8 September   *p.9*

SUDETENS' NEW MOVES
Czech Offer Accepted as Basis of Negotiation

THEN HITCH OVER INCIDENT
Finally Agreement to Consider Resuming Talks

The Sudeten German leaders yesterday accepted the new Czech proposals as a basis for negotiations.

No sooner had they done this than they decided to 'interrupt the negotiations becaue of an incident reported from a Sudeten German town. Then late last night, after seeing the Czech Premier, they agreed to reconsider the situation to-day.

Their acceptance of the Government's proposals was announced as follows—

It was decided to continue to negotiate with the government on the basis of these proposals with a view to the realisation of the Carlsbad eight points.

At that point in the discussions, says the special communiqué, news was received of an incident at Mährisch-Ostrau, in which two Sudeten deputies were alleged to have been beaten.

The Sudeten Germans thereupon brought to an end their discussion of the plan, and decided to interrupt negotiations with the Czech Government. Their communiqué says:

The incident at Maehrisch-Ostrau demonstrates that the Government does not control the situation sufficiently to begin the discussion in detail in the present circumstances with any success or with the possibility of bringing them to a peaceful conclusion.

The German newspapers, which are strongly critical of the Czech offer, were last night as one in their chorus of indignation at the alleged use of 'riding whips against Germans,' as the incident was described. ...

CLEAR WARNING TO GERMANY
Labour's Demand

A STAND — AT ANY RISK
'Call Parliament'

From our Special Correspondent

Blackpool, Wednesday Night.

Late to-night the meeting of the three executives of the Labour movement agreed on a statement of Labour's attitude toward the international crisis. This statement will be placed before the Trades Union Congress in the morning. It makes two main points, first that 'the British Government must leave no doubt in the mind of the German Government that it will unite with the French and Soviet Governments to resist any attack on Czecho-Slovakia,' and secondly it demands the immediate summoning of Parliament. ...

Friday 9 September   *p.11*

SUDETENS REFUSE
Why They Cannot Negotiate at Present

'PRAGUE NOT IN CONTROL'
Premier Promises to Deal With Ill-Treatment of Germans

The Sudeten German party last night announced that it could not negotiate with the Czech Government.

The general reason given was that the Government could no longer maintain order in the country. The Sudeten German leaders are to prepare a memorandum giving the 'many reasons' why they cannot enter into discussions.

The announcement was made after there had been a long meeting between Dr. Hodza, the Czech Premier, and the Sudeten German delegates. Dr. Hodza promised the Sudeten leaders that those responsible for the ill-treatment of the Sudeten Germans in the Mährisch-Ostrau region would be punished with all severity.

An official Czech investigation has shown that a number of Sudeten Germans arrested in that region have, in fact, been ill-treated.

From a number of Sudeten districts last night minor incidents were reported.

BRITISH CABINET TO MEET

A meeting of the British Cabinet has been called for Monday

morning. The announcement was made after a day of discussions in Downing Street, where the Premier, Lord Halifax, and Sir John Simon had twice met. Lord Halifax has postponed his visit to Geneva – he was to have left London to-day.

The Cabinet is to meet at 11 a.m. Hitler is expected to make his pronouncement of policy on the Sudeten German question in the evening of that day.

M. Bonnet, the French Foreign Minister, Colonel Beck (Poland), and M. Spaak (Belgium) have postponed their departures for Geneva, where the League Council opens to-day.

The Trades Union Congress yesterday endorsed, with hardly any criticism, the joint declaration calling for a firm stand by Britain against aggression – whatever the risks. ...

BRITAIN AND HITLER
A Further Warning? Führer Not Yet Convinced

From our Diplomatic Correspondent

London, Thursday Night.

The fear is growing here that Hitler does not desire a genuine settlement, and if there is a settlement of any sort it will only have the purpose of tiding over the period that will lead to the long-anticipated and long-prepared attack on Czecho-Slovakia. But it is also thought, and rightly, that if time can be gained much else can be gained.

The German attack may at first take on some indirect form. The Sudeten German party may, for example, declare after some real or imaginary 'incident', that the Czecho-Slovak Government is no longer able to exercise its authority in the Sudetenland and that party will therefore assume power and see to the maintenance of law and order. This would be equivalent to a declaration of independence as a preliminary to union with the Reich. Any attempt of the Czecho-Slovak Government to enforce its authority would then be met by German intervention.

This is one of the ways, though only one, in which an armed conflict could be brought about by Hitler. There are no illusions left here with regard to the possibility or even the likelihood of such methods. Throughout the present crisis it has been evident – and on this point too, there have been no illusions here that only one thing can be decisive – namely the impression made by the Western Powers, and above all by Great Britain, on Hitler. Does he believe that the warnings uttered by Mr. Neville Chamberlain and Sir John Simon are serious, or does he think them bluff?

The answer can hardly be in doubt. Hitler is not convinced that if Germany goes to war with Czecho-Slovakia the conflict will spread and, in the end, involve the Western Powers. In other words, he does not really believe that Great Britain 'means business' even to the extent indicated by Mr. Chamberlain and Sir John Simon.

HITLER'S ADVISERS

Hitler's advisers on foreign affairs, especially Herr von Ribbentrop, argue that the Western Powers will be unable to give Czecho-Slovakia effective help against a German attack before the year 1940. They also argue that the Third Realm enjoy widespread sympathy in Great Britain, and they can quote innumerable utterances by well-known persons and articles in leading newspapers.

It may be that Hitler has not made up his own mind, but the trend of events during the last few days can hardly have failed to incline him towards the 'war party,' who believe that Czecho-Slovakia must be attacked in the very near future (though not until a situation has been created in the Sudetenland that will appear to justify German action, if not in the eyes of the world, then at least in the eyes of the German people).

Hitler himself would seem to be more convinced than ever of the irresistible power of National Socialism and of the new Germany. One concession after another has been wrung from the Czechs – and while the Western Powers pretend that there is a crisis and even some danger of a European war, they make no serious technical preparations to meet the danger. The very limited precautions taken by them cannot possibly impress Hitler.

ANOTHER BRITISH WARNING?

The principal aim of British and French diplomacy during the last few weeks has not been achieved and it will be necesary to convince Hitler of what is, after all, only true, that Great Britain is in earnest.

The British Government has not been unaware that the warning uttered by Sir John Simon might not suffice and that some further action might, after an interval, be necessary. What further action will be taken cannot be anticipated at the moment. But whatever it is it may decide the issue between peace and war in Europe.

It is widely assumed that Hitler will make a definite pronouncement with regard to Czecho-Slovakia at the Nuremberg Congress on Monday. There is no evidence whatever in support of this assumption. Hitler's speech may be of the highest importance – and it may be quite empty.

The recent Czech proposals have made a very favourable impression on the 'moderates' in the Sudeten German party. They would, if carried out, mean peace and the possibility of economic recovery in the Sudetenland. They would also remove the fear of war which is gripping the hearts of a growing number of Sudeten Germans.

On the other hand, the proposals have disappointed the extremists precisely because they are so reasonable, and because they meet the wishes of these same extremists. Like Hitler himself, the 'extremists' do not want a permanent settlement and are afraid lest a conciliatory spirit spread amongst the Sudeten German population.

The 'incident' at Mährisch-Ostrau is the reply to the latest Czech proposals. Such incidents, some of them spontaneous (though not serious in themselves), others deliberately arranged, are exploited with the design of perpetuating the tension.

Saturday 10 September   *p.11*

MAKING IT CLEAR TO HITLER
New Measures of a Practical Kind Under Consideration

MUSSOLINI'S POSITION IN THE CRISIS

From our Diplomatic Correspondent

London, Friday Night.

Germany's attitude grows more menacing every day. Her mobilisation gains in amplitude; it goes far beyond anything that is generally known. There are movements of German troops in the direction of the French and the Czecho-Slovak borders. About a week ago the German military preparations were intensified (vast as they were even then). The indications now are that she would be in the position to go to war with Czecho-Slovakia and to 'contain' a French invasion in two or three weeks.

Russia is carrying out military preparations near her western border. General Bluecher, who is regarded as the ablest of the very fine commanders who have survived the 'purge', has been transferred from the Far East to the west. It is believed both here and in Paris that Russia would go to war almost automatically as soon as Czecho-Slovakia was attacked.

HITLER AND HIS GENERALS

It is now fully recognised here that British warnings have not made the slightest impression on Hitler. Some of his generals are against a war with Czecho-Slovakia just now because they believe it will lead to a general war in which Germny would be defeated. It is true that General Beck, the German Chief of Staff, offered his resignation, but it is not certain whether the resignation has been accepted.

It would, however, be a mistake to base any hopes on any disagreement between Hitler and his generals. Whatever independence of spirit the Reichswehr may have had (and it never had much) it was broken months ago. The generals as a whole may have views of their own, but if Hitler gives the signal they will march. Nor is it at all certain that all his generals will venture to disagree with him; some of them will give exactly the advice he wants them to give him.

It is an illusion to suppose that Germany's economic position has a restraining influence on Hitler or on any of the National Socialist leaders. The opposite is rather the case. ...

BRITAIN AND HITLER

With regard to Great Britain, expectations of 'strong action' have been raised by articles in the press especially in the evening papers. There is no question as yet of going beyond Sir John Simon's statement the other day. One would have thought that it matters a great deal to Hitler whether he can count on British neutrality or not in a European conflict. He certainly cannot count on British neutrality. But thanks very largely to the influence of Herr von Ribbentrop he believes he can.

The question is therefore what must be done to make him believe what is known to be true by all who know the language of diplomacy. This question is being examined in all its aspects by the French and British Governments working in closest collaboration.

All forecasts of what will be decided upon are premature, but there can be no doubt that measures will be taken – including some of a practical kind – to convey the seriousness of a British warning to Hitler.

The issue between peace and war now depends on whether Hitler understands that warning or fails to understand it. His tactics in the immediate future would seem to be clear. He regards the recent Czecho-Slovak proposals as unacceptable. In recent conversations, he and Henlein agreed that the Sudeten Germans must have control even in those areas where they are a minority. Hitler's real demands, of course, go far beyond the Carlsbad programme. He has for some time been considering the advisability of demanding a plebiscite in the areas inhabited by the Sudeten Germans. ...

SUDETENS NOW AGREE
Negotiations to be Resumed in Prague To-day

CONVINCING HERR HITLER
France and Britain Considering New Warning Action

The Sudeten Germans agreed last night to resume negotiations to-day with the Czech Government.

Agreement was reached at a long meeting last night between the Sudeten negotiators, Herr Kundt and Herr Rosche, and the Czech Premier, Dr. Hodza. At an earlier meeting the Sudeten leaders had handed over a memorandum of the alleged ill-treatment of Sudeten Germans.'

The report on the alleged beating of the Sudeten deputies at Mährisch-Ostrau received in London from Major Sutton Pratt, the British observer in Czecho-Slovakia, shows that the incident has been 'very much exaggerated.

LONDON: FURTHER WARNING

The British Premier yesterday again spent almost the whole day in discussions of the crisis with Lord Halifax and Sir John Simon – discussions that will continue to-day and will include a meeting at Mr. Chamberlain's request, with Mr. Attlee, the Opposition Leader.

Our diplomatic correspondent says that the British and French Governments, in close co-operation, are considering what further step shall now be taken to impress upon Herr Hitler the gravity of the crisis.

Last night it was announced that the Admiralty are bringing the First Mine-sweeping Flotilla up to complement and that four mine-laying destroyers are to be brought up to full commission from reserve.

NUREMBERG: AMBASSADOR SEES RIBBENTROP

Sir Nevile Henderson, the British Ambassador to Germany, yesterday saw Herr von Ribbentrop, the German Foreign Minister, at Nuremberg. Later Herr von Ribbentrop reported to Herr Hitler on the meeting. Sir Nevile had arranged to return to Berlin to-day, but early this morning it became known that he had decided to stay in Nuremberg.

Herr Hitler conferred with the Sudeten German leaders Herr Henlein and Herr Frank.

General von Brauchitsch, Commander-in-Chief of the German Army, arrived in Nuremberg, and will stay there until the Nazi party rally ends.

France has decided to call up a number of naval reservists. There is great activity at Brest and at Toulon, where the Atlantic and Mediterranean fleets are assembled. ...

Monday 12 September *p.11*

HITLER SPEAKS TO-NIGHT
May Demand Plebiscite for Sudeten Germans

NO DIRECT BRITISH APPROACH
Danger of the Führer's Counting on Our Neutrality

Hitler speaks to-night, but there is still no certainty that with the speech will come the turning-point in the crisis. There were indications last night that he may demand that the Sudeten Germans shall decide by plebiscite whether their areas shall remain in Czecho-Slovakia or to go Germany.

The British Cabinet meets this morning; any decisions will be communicated to the French Cabinet, which meets this afternoon.

Yesterday, in a speech at Nuremberg, Hitler made his first public reference to the German–Czech dispute:–

I see before me a Germany happy in its unity. There are other Germans to whom this happiness is at present still denied. Our hearts fly out to them, just as we know that their hearts are with us at this hour.

The previous day at Nuremberg Field Marshal Göring had made a violent attack on the Czechs – 'these ridiculous dwarfs in Prague,' – behind whom, he said, was Moscow. And Dr. Goebbels, the Propaganda Minister, in a speech at night had made his text the Bolshevik menace of Czecho-Slovakia, with Prague as 'the centre of the Comintern.'

Göring spoke of Germany as being stronger to-day than ever before in her history, with the greatest Air Force in the world and impregnable fortifications in the West. His speech contained slighting references to Britain.

THE PRAGUE NEGOTIATIONS

Dr. Benes, President of Czecho-Slovakia, in a conciliatory broadcast on Saturday appealed to his countrymen to preserve their calm and explained the latest attempt made by his Government

95

at heavy sacrifice to secure a solution of the Sudeten German problem.

Dr. Hodza, the Czech Premier, on Saturday saw the Sudeten German negotiators, and it was announced that negotiations would be resumed on Tuesday. ...

p.14

AMERICANS AND THE CRISIS
No Commitments

POSITION SIMILAR TO BRITISH

From our own Correspondent

New York, September 11.

President Roosevelt has gone to the bedside of his son James at Rochester, Minnesota. James, who is suffering from a septic ulcer, was to undergo an operation to-day at the famous Mayo Clinic there.

The European crisis has caused all domestic problems to be laid aside temporarily. President Roosevelt is in contact almost constantly with officials at Washington and elsewhere regarding the situation, of which he takes a grave view.

When the President said that the United States had no obligation of any kind to take part with England and France in an effort to curb possible German aggression against Czecho-Slovakia, he indicated no change in the United States policy. He was forced to make the disclaimer because wild and exaggerated reports about the extent of American commitments were in circulation here. It was being said that this country had undertaken definite obligations to use force against the Germans if necessary, and many persons had become greatly alarmed. Whatever Mr. Roosevelt's own wishes are, it would, of course, be impossible for him to assume any such obligation in the present state of American opinion.

Actually this country's position is not unlike Great Britain's, and this fact is doubtless not accidental. The United States refuses to make any definite pledge of action. At the same time Mr. Roosevelt and Mr. Cordell Hull repeatedly, in recent addresses, warned aggressive Powers that any conflict now would be a matter which may involve the whole world.

THE NEUTRALITY LAW

The next session of Congress will probably see a determined effort by Mr. Roosevelt to obtain a modification of the neutrality law to enable aid to be given to the democratic Powers should conflict occur. It is suggested that one such change might be the end of the rigid embargo on munitions, so as to permit them to be sold on the 'cash and carry' basis. This means, of course, that no credits would be permitted and American ships would not be used to carry them.

An attempt might also be made to modify the Johnson law. which forbids further loans to the Government in arrears on war debts. ...

GÖRING'S SABRE-RATTLING SPEECH
Reminiscent of Imperial Germany

'STRONGEST AIR FORCE' & 'WESTERN DEFENCES IMPREGNABLE'

From our Special Correspondent

Nuremberg, September 11.

Field Marshal Göring's sabre-rattling speech made at the Labour Front meeting yesterday is a foretaste of what may be expected when Chancellor Hitler winds up the Nazi Congress to-morrow night with his big statement on foreign policy.

Using frank, blunt, everyday language, full of coarse expressions – one a phrase quite unprintable – Field Marshal Göring swept his audience of 30,000 Nazi working men into a frenzy. Nazi anger against Prague (suppressed so far because the Sudeten German problem had been banned from Congress speeches) was worked up to a dangerous pitch by this dynamic aggressive speech, which was also broadcast to millions of Germans.

In every sentence the Air Minister left no doubt that Germany is now strong and formidable on land, in the air, and on the sea, and refuses to tolerate interference or advice from anyone.

'FOLLOW HITLER BLINDLY'

He also appealed passionately to all German workers to follow Herr Hitler blindly, because he has built up a powerful, invincible Germany. 'Germany to-day is ready to take on all comers' was the essence of Göring's speech, and it reminded one irresistibly of some of the speeches delivered in Germany in pre-war Kaiser days. German commentators claim that the speech makes it clear that in future Germany intends to go her own way in spite of the efforts of those who try to stop her. One writer says:

Hermann Göring's speech has given the German people the proud feeling that we have become strong enough to establish our own destiny. We have the strength, the will of the Leader.

Field Marshal Göring denounced the Czechs as 'a people without culture' and describing the Czech Government as 'those little dwarfs in Prague,' charged them with oppressing the Sudeten Germans. 'We cannot tolerate our German brothers being harried,' he shouted. His violent attack on the Czechs called forth loud shouts of 'Shame!' Moscow and Jewish Bolshevism, he declared, are really behind Prague, egging on the Czechs to defy Germany.

RUDENESS TO ENGLAND

He was also rude to England. Instead of jabbering about peace so much he said, she ought to be bringing peace in her own 'old Jewish State' (Palestine). ...

Germany, he declared proudly, was never so strong in her history as she was to-day. She was growing stronger every year, and no one could stop her. He dealt at length with the Four-year Plan measures brought in during the past two years to make the nation economically independent and powerful on the military side. Enormous food reserves had been secured, a large raw-material industry had been created, and all land possible had been placed under cultivation. A powerful armaments industry looked after the needs of a large Army, a growing modern fleet and an Air Force which was, he claimed, technically and numerically the strongest in the whole world.

'WESTERN DEFENCES IMPREGNABLE

The fortifications in the west, he said, guaranteed the Reich against all attacks, and no power on earth could break through these new forts into Germany – a warning to France. ...

A UNITED FRANCE READY FOR ALL EMERGENCIES
'Attracting Forces of Wisdom & Reason'

Paris, September 11.

M. Albert Sarraut, Minister of the Interior, made a fervent declaration of French preparedness for war in a speech at Noyon (Oise), amid the former battlefields to-day. At the same time he appealed to Germany to maintain peace. He said:–

'Let there be no mistake about this abroad where echoes of our divisions – more apparent than real but magnified by interested propaganda – might tend to foster guilty aspirations. Tomorrow if the law of danger and duty called France would instantly find herself again of one accord, as she has been every time she has been confronted with foreign peril.

'A sense of common safety demands that we should all gather more closely than ever around the head of the Government of National Defence, whose clear resolution, firm hand, and far-seeing patriotism have brought to the highest degree of preparedness our incomparable army, which is both our safeguard and pride. The country stands with its face turned towards destiny as a compact, homogeneous, and unbreakable block to which the forces of wisdom and reason that are still so powerful throughout the world will unfailingly be attracted.

'In that way human peace will once again be saved.

'Already the forces of wisdom and reason are abandoning their attitudes of waiting and reserve and no longer hesitate to proclaim firmly the duties which certain eventualities would impose on them. They have several times sent out pressing appeals which, while not neglecting due consideration for the self-esteem and honour of the peoples to whom they have been addressed, nevertheless convey warning devoid of all ambiguity.

'The democracies of the world unite at this moment their initiatives and efforts with the object of maintaining peace, a lasting peace with all peoples in honour, and with respect for the independence of all of them.'

NAZI ATTACKS ON DEMOCRACY
The 'Red Menace in Czecho-Slovakia'

GOEBBELS'S SPEECH

Nuremberg, September 10.

Dr. Goebbels, the Propaganda Minister, spoke of the 'Red Menace in Czecho-Slovakia' when he addressed the Nazi party rally at Nuremberg. Bolshevism in that country might 'lead to a dangerous development' he said.

'The Communists in Czecho-Slovakia,' Dr. Goebbels declared 'acquired the Government's support by aiding President Benes's election and by voting for the Government military budget in 1935. Thus they proved the agreement between their aims and those of the Government. Prague is now the centre of the Comintern for Europe. The Government must know this, yet it tolerates such a terrible state of affairs.

'There would be no hope if we had not seen through this system. We face the united front of democracy and Bolshevism, and therefore these two hate us. We do not want to conquer the world, but we want to defend our nation. We sought loyal and dependable friends in the world; we found them and will continue to find them. Arms cannot produce ideas, but as Germany has proved, ideas can produce arms.

'Our leader gave us the great idea of liberty. He has given us the weapons with which to defend our ideas and their political and economic results. Now we are not afraid of anyone. The world shall not believe that by the use of pressure it can prevent us from claiming our right to live.

'The greater the crisis, the stronger our feeling of security. The Führer leads the Reich and gives us his orders and we are happy to obey them'. ...

SIR N. HENDERSON
Back in Berlin To-day

From our own Correspondent

Nuremberg, September 11.

Sir Nevile Henderson, British Ambassador, leaves Nuremberg by train at 1 10 to-morrow morning for Berlin. He will not be here therefore to hear Herr Hitler speak to-morrow night, but will listen in to the speech on the wireless in the British Embassy.

Sir Nevile has been in Nuremberg for five whole days. During this time he has met Herr Hitler at the diplomatic tea-party, Field Marshal Göring, Herr von Ribbentrop, German Foreign Minister, and last night he sat next to Dr. Goebbels at a bivouac given in honour of the foreign guests by Herr Himmler's S.S. organisation. The British Ambassador to-day had half an hour's conversation with Baron von Neurath, the former Foreign Minister. Sir Nevile has also met during the past few days Herr Rudolf Hess and other Nazi leaders. All rumours that he had met Herr Hitler to talk about politics are denied by Sir Nevile Henderson. No such meeting has taken place, and it was not sought, it is stated.

Tuesday 13 September   *p.11*

HITLER'S ANGRY SPEECH
'Self-Determination' the Right of the Sudetens

GERMAN AID, IF NEED BE

Hitler's speech at Nuremberg last night made no definite announcement of German policy towards Czecho-Slovakia except that of determination to defend the Sudeten Germans against Czech 'oppression' if that did not cease. Hitler's tone was angry, and there were bitter references to Czecho-Slovakia and to the democracies, Britain in particular.

The vital passages of the speech follow. It will be noted that Hitler did not in explicit terms demand a plebiscite, and that though he declared that the Sudeten Germans demanded the right of self-determination, he also said that it was 'up to Prague to come to an agreement' with them:–

> Herr Benes indulges in tactics; he speaks; he organises negotiations. This cannot go on. This is not a matter of phrases but of right.
>
> The Germans demand the right of self-determination. Herr Benes shall not give them mere gifts but their rights.
>
> I demand that the oppression of 3,500,000 in Czecho-Slovakia shall end or – (drowned by cheers) ... the free right of self-determination shall take its place.
>
> It is up to Prague to bring about an agreement with the Sudeten Germans.
>
> If the democracies should be convinced that they must protect with all their means the oppressors of the Germans, then this will have grave consequences.

A 'UNITED FRONT' AGAINST GERMANY

In his speech Hitler declared that the German minority was robbed of its right of self-determination, ruined economically, and threatened with destruction by the brutality of the Czechs, for whom the democracies were prepared to fight. And he spoke of the 'united front from the Bolsheviks down to the democracies' against Germany. ...

DEMONSTRATIONS IN SUDETEN AREAS
How Prague Received the Speech

From our Central European Correspondent

Prague, September 12.

The impression in Prague after the speech of Herr Hitler is that the war danger has at least been considerably postponed. It had been expected that Hitler's speech would be filled with violent outbursts against Czecho-Slovakia, so that the country was prepared for this.

The allusion to the fortifications in the west as being ready at the end of this year is read here as an indication that Hitler is not yet ready for a major war.

Violent as part of his speech has been, Hitler has not committed himself to any definite plan concerning the Sudeten German areas, though he mentioned self-determination twice. But an outright recommendation of a plebiscite was missing.

The hatred against Dr. Benes was evident in his speech and in this regard the speech recalled the invective which Hitler was wont to use against Dr. Schuschnigg in the pre-Anschluss days.

The reaction in Prague naturally is not favourable to the speech, but a certain relief is noticeable. The 'Prager Presse,' the mouthpiece of the Foreign Office, writes as comment in its late edition that the German Chancellor has been constantly misinformed about Czecho-Slovakia and that thus his conclusions are based on wrong information. The final official attitude must be, however, awaited.

The Cabinet Council met to-night to take measures, if necessary, to deal with any unrest or dangerous demonstrations should they take place in the Sudeten German regions. Much depends, of course, on the attitude of the Sudeten Germans, who naturally will feel that Germany, with its 75,000,000 population is now pledged to stand behind them.

There were big demonstrations in those areas after the speech, and in Carlsbad a crowd of 8,000 proceeded through the town shouting 'Out with the Czechs and Jews!' Many of them wore Swastika armlets and sang the 'Horst Wessel' song. The atmosphere rather suggested the pre-Anschluss atmosphere in Graz and Linz, in Austria, in March. But no serious incidents have so far been reported.

CZECHS WANT INTERNATIONAL GUARANTEE
Memorandum to British Government

CABINET MEETING APPROVES THE STEPS TAKEN TO WARN HITLER

From our Diplomatic Correspondent

London, Monday Night.

There was considerable unanimity at to-day's meeting of the Cabinet, attended by all its members except Lord Stanley and Lord Hailsham, who are out of the country. Those members of the Cabinet who have held that the attitude of the Government was not sufficiently 'firm' are, on the whole, rather more satisfied as the result of to-day's meeting. The Cabinet was in agreement that the steps taken by Sir Nevile Henderson at Berlin and Nuremberg to convey the attitude of the British to the German Government (or rather to Hitler) were as much as could be humanly done in the present circumstances.

The Czecho-Slovak Minister Mr. Jan Masaryk called at the Foreign Office to-day. He submitted a memorandum setting forth the reasons why the Czecho-Slovak Government cannot accept the proposal which Germany is expected to make for a plebiscite in those regions of Czecho-Slovakia that are populated by national minorities. It would seem that Mr. Masaryk pointed out that if the recent Czecho-Slovak proposals for a new Minorities Statute are accepted by the Sudeten Germans it is desirable that the Czecho-Slovak Republic have some form of international guarantee that will preserve her from disruption. There will be a very real danger of this because the national minorities will obtain such a huge measure of home rule that they will, if they choose, and if they receive sufficient support from neighbouring Powers, be able to break up the Republic from within.

The views of the Czecho-Slovak Government on this subject have, it would appear, the support of the French Government.

p.14

AMERICAN VIEW

Washington, September 12.

The strident and aggressive tones of Herr Hitler's speech brought a measure of reassurance to the United States capital. People here seem to believe that the actual degree of menace in the speech was in inverse ratio to the fiery tones of the Führer's voice. 'The bark was alarming, but the bite has at least been postponed.' Such is a fair summing up of opinion here, although it is recognized that Europe has gained only a respite from the fears of the past few weeks.

Particular attention is focused here on Hitler's claims regarding his previous forbearance and his apparent admission that the Siegfried Line defences are not yet ready.–Reuter.

FRANCE'S REACTIONS TO THE HITLER SPEECH
The Tension Unrelieved

CABINET'S DECISIONS: A REMARKABLE COMMUNIQUE

From our own Correspondent

Paris, September 12.

What are France's reactions to Hitler's speech? Until a late hour to-night the general public did not know much about the speech, and there was a remarkable lack of any excitement in the streets. 'Well, he hasn't declared war right away – that is always something,' was the popular view taken of the speech; and some people said that he had not burnt his bridges – which was also a good thing – and that perhaps last night's interpretation of the British attitude as telegraphed from London had to be thanked for that.

Official spokesmen declared that they preferred to give a considered opinion, of the speech tomorrow. 'Its gravest aspects,' it was declared in official quarters 'is that it has not changed the situation in any way for the better.' But actually I gather that official spokesmen are much more disturbed by the speech than they are willing to admit openly, particularly those who (like M. Bonnet himself) listened to the venomous outpourings on the wireless and to the wild rejoicings of the Nuremberg Congress.

Competent observers do not entirely agree with the view that Hitler 'has not burnt his bridges,' and his treatment of Czecho-Slovakia as an ephemeral growth, presumably to be swallowed up by the great German Empire, and his way of denying the Czechs the right to give 'little presents to the Sudeten Germans to keep them quiet' scarcely leave in his mind, it is felt here, much room for a peaceful settlement of the Sudeten problem which would leave Czecho-Slovakia a sovereign State.

FORTIFICATIONS 'BLUFF'?

French military experts to whom I spoke to-night of Hitler's extravagant description of the new Rhineland fortifications described them as 'the biggest piece of bluff in the whole speech'. 'We know what our fortifications cost us and how long it took to build them. And we are inclined to think that the German Generals would not support Hitler's claim that the new Rhineland fortifications are impregnable.'

Before the speech, when I asked a prominent member of the Cabinet what he thought of the statement of the British attitude received here from London last night, he said, stressing his words 'I am very, very satisfied indeed.' 'And the suggestion of new Czech concessions?' 'We shall see about that later; it is no good rushing the Czechs into suicide, and I do not think your Government wants to do it anyway.' ...

A SUDETEN ULTIMATUM
Prague Given Six Hours to Withdraw Martial Law

HENLEIN ACTS ON ITS EXPIRY
Dr. Hodza Told That No Further Negotiations are Possible

DAY OF 'INCIDENTS': 12 DEAD

Last night the German–Czech crisis became acute.

Hitler's speech, with its pledge of German backing to the Sudetens, had been followed by serious rioting and disorders in a number of the German Sudeten areas. Eight Sudeten Germans and Czechs lost their lives, and there were attempts by the Sudetens to capture public buildings and railway stations.

The Czech Government thereupon imposed emergency police measures in eight Sudeten departments. By night further incidents brought the death-roll to eight Czechs and four Germans.

At 5 p.m. the Sudeten German leaders, after a conference at Eger, sent an ultimatum, delivered at 6 p.m. to Dr. Hodza, in which they accused the Prague Cabinet of having broken a pledge to discuss any important new measures with them, and demanded the immediate withdrawal of 'martial law' and of the State police, leaving mayors and municipal councillors (that is, the Sudeten German majority) to take care of order.

If this were not done by midnight, said the ultimatum, the Sudeten leaders would 'decline all responsibility for all future developments.'

Another Sudeten announcement said that the German Sudeten leaders were now demanding a plebiscite as the only thing that would satisfy their excited followers.

PRAGUE SUGGESTS DISCUSSION

The Czech Cabinet, after a meeting last night, sent a reply to the Sudeten ultimatum which, it is learned, while not an acceptance, did not close the door to further negotiations.

Later it was reported that Herr Kundt, the chief Sudeten negotiator, was on his way by road to Prague in response to Dr. Hodza's suggestion that it might be possible to reach an agreement that would lead to pacification.

After the meeting of the Czech Cabinet, which lasted two hours, Dr. Hodza had talks with Mr. Basil Newton, British Minister in Prague, and M. de la Croix, French Minister.

THE ULTIMATUM EXPIRES

The Council of Ministers met again and shortly before midnight, when the ultimatum expired, resolved to take no further cognisance of it. There was no news of Dr. Kundt.

HENLEIN'S REFUSAL

At 12 15 this morning Henlein, through his secretary, notified Dr. Hodza that under the circumstances further negotiations are not possible. The news was communicated by the Czech Minister in London.

Herr Henlein had stated that the circumstances relieved the Sudeten Germans who had been conducting the negotiations of their duties and expressed gratitude to them for what they had done.

The Czech Minister in London stated that this news was telephoned to him by Dr. Hodza himself, who expressed the view that the British public should know of this latest development.

BRITISH CABINET AND THE SPEECH
Hitler's Failure to Appreciate Our Attitude

London, Tuesday Night.

The impression formed by the British Government of Herr Hitler's speech is, first of all, that it does not finally bang the door on a settlement but leaves it ajar in the sense that it is possible for the negotiations to be continued.

On the other hand, it is recognised that the speech had solved no problem nor made any concrete suggestion as to how the way may be cleared towards reaching a solution, and has therefore done very little to remove the menace which is causing Europe and the world such great anxiety.

The immediate sequel of the speech has been the series of very grave incidents to-day in Czecho-Slovakia of which we do not yet see fully the results, but which show how electric the atmosphere is and how great is the need for calmness in treating the situation.

What is noticed by the Government, besides the references in the speech to the Sudeten German problem and its direct reactions on that problem, is the failure of the speech to appreciate or make proper allowance for the attitude of Great Britain.

A DANGEROUS DISTORTION

This omission is considered remarkable, for this country has realised and acted upon the urgency of the Czech problem. Indeed, there was rather a suggestion in the speech that we had either failed to recognise the problem or even that we, with other democracies, were trying to obstruct a settlement. Nothing, it is urged, could be farther – more dangerously farther – from the truth than that.

Great Britain, it is claimed, can truthfully say she has never failed to recognise the urgency of the problem and in many respects the justice of the demands that the Sudeten Germans have put forward. But while recognising that side of the problem, Great Britain also recognised all the time that if resort was had to violence in the attempt to solve it, the interrelation of force involved was such that the consequences of such resort to violence would be quite immeasurable.

No one, it is felt, can safely or securely predict events. No one can say when, how, or in what precise form vital decisions may be forced upon Governments. But it is worth making quite clear that however anxious the British people are to see a settlement effected of a problem that they recognise is a real one, it is quite impossible to suppose that Great Britain could stand aside from a general conflict in which the integrity of France might be menaced.

HOPE IN NEGOTIATIONS

Everybody must be anxious that nothing should be done that would lessen the chances of a peaceful issue from our anxieties. Everything shows how essential it is to restrain the reaction to provocation on one side or the other and give the negotiations, in spite of all the difficulties of the highly charged atmosphere, a chance to proceed and reach what it is believed should not be impossible if they are allowed to go on – a peaceful settlement.

Great progress, it is pointed out, has been made in the negotiations, and that progress shows clearly to any impartial onlooker how morally unjustifiable it would be for any action from any quarter to be taken which must bring hope of issue through negotiations to an end.

INTERPRETING HITLER'S SPEECH

From our own Correspondent

Paris, September 13.

If it is true that last night Paris heaved a sigh of relief at the thought that Hitler 'had not yet declared war,' it is equally true that the considered opinion of official quarters this morning was very far from optimistic, and as the day advanced and reports of rioting and bloodshed in the Sudeten areas reached Paris this opinion became frankly pessimistic.

The press on the whole tried this morning to be as cheerful as possible. Several papers said that 'the door had not been closed for a settlement' – though none of them saw very clearly how such a settlement was possible with Hitler in his present frame of mind. It was noted that Hitler had completely ignored the efforts made by Lord Runciman and the enormous concessions the Czech Government had granted the Sudeten Germans, and it was felt that it would be worse than useless at the present stage to press the Czech Government to concede more than it had already done.

STRASBOURG CATHEDRAL

But in spite of all the boasting about Germany's invincibility, French observers clearly detected in Hitler's speech his fear of becoming involved in a war with France and Great Britain and his desire to limit his war to Czecho-Slovakia. Hence his reference to Strasbourg Cathedral that he was giving France (as if it was his to give) as a peace offering; and also his many details about the western fortifications – which were apparently intended to intimidate the French and also to allay any misgivings that must certainly exist in Germany that the 'localised' war might still develop into a general war.

The moral drawn from Hitler's speech was that Britain and France could still exercise a decisive influence by a show of strength, energy, and determination not to tolerate the invasion of Czecho-Slovakia under any pretext. Even M. Bailby, who has not been a friend of Czecho-Slovakia owing to her links with Soviet Russia, writes in 'Le Jour' to-day:

> France must, in agreement with England, have the courage while there is still time to say 'No.' Germany will not attack France and England. Germany wants to attack the weakest opponent in the hope of defeating him at the first blow. France and England must still try to exhaust every possibility

of arbitration, and they must warn Hitler that if he plunges
Europe into war he and his country will be the first victims.

THE AUSTRIAN PARALLEL

This afternoon the gloom in Paris deepened when it was
learned that violent disorders had broken out in the Sudeten
country. 'The first consequences of Hitler's speech,' one of the
evening papers remarked. The question is inevitably asked
whether the moment will not come when, after creating violent
trouble in the Sudeten country, the Sudeten leaders will not, after
the manner of Dr. Seyss-Inquart in Vienna, appeal to Hitler to come
and save them. ...

Regarding a plebiscite, the French Government holds that
the Czech Government would be in its perfect right to refuse it. Hitler
has made it perfectly plain that the 'martyrdom' of the Sudeten
Germans is only a pretext for destroying Czecho-Slovakia, and a
plebiscite – for which the Sudeten Germans have in any case
never asked – would inevitably be conducted in the familiar
atmosphere of Nazi terrorism.

The curious absence of any reference in Hitler's speech to
the aid Soviet Russia would give Czecho-Slovakia in case of war
is attributed here to two motives. First, by trying to intimidate
England and France into inactivity, Hitler is hoping to prevent
automatically a Russian intervention in Czecho-Slovakia's favour,
and secondly, it is believed here he did not wish to speak of a
possible Russian invasion, as it might have damped the
enthusiasm of his audience with their faith in a lightning victory
over Czecho-Slovakia.

HITLER'S STRATEGY

From our Diplomatic Correspondent

London, Tuesday Night.

The more Hitler's speech at the Nuremberg Congress is
studied the more sinister it appears. Hitler has, so to speak,
carried the crisis one stage farther. He has not simply left things
where they were before, but, while throwing the responsibility
for a rupture on the Czecho-Slovak and British Governments –
he is ostentatiously moderate in his references to France, – he
has made the initiative pass from the British Government to
himself.

He allows the negotiations between the Sudeten German
party and the Czecho-Slovak Government to go on, but does not
suggest that the Czech propoals are acceptable even as a basis.

In fact, although he does not say so explicitly, he implies in the plainest manner that he has no use for the proposals.

He insists on 'self-determination' and declares that he will put an end to the 'wrongs' which he grossly exaggerates, endured by the Sudeten Germans. He calls the attention of the Western Powers to his armed strength and the invulnerability of his western defences. He speaks of Czecho-Slovakia and of her President, Dr. Benes, in terms that seem to rule out an amicable settlement. He refers to Great Britain in terms of envenomed hatred and scorn.

Meanwhile the 'incidents,' some of them deliberately engineered, continue and the prodigious German warlike preparations are intensified. It now seems impossible that Hitler could revert to the Czecho-Slovak proposals as a basis for negotiation. Unless his speech turns out to have been a deceptive signal indeed, these proposals are dead.

A PLEBISCITE UNDER THREAT

What is the alternative? 'Self-determination' – in other words, a 'plebiscite.' A 'plebiscite' means the extinction of Czecho-Slovakia. 'Self-determination' is demanded under the threat of war. Hitler is confident that the public will not understand what this 'right,' if carried out at all, by himself (as it would be if carried out at all), really means in practice. 'What he says amounts to this: 'Allow me to make myself master of Czecho-Slovakia and you will be spared a European war.' He promises by implication to employ only 'peaceful means' (terrorism, invasion by armed irregulars, and so on), but not open warfare, unless, of course, the Czechs resist, in which case war will have been 'forced upon him.'

ANGLO-FRENCH TALKS IN PARIS LAST NIGHT
Ambassador Called from the Opera

TWO MEETINGS WITH M. DALADIER IN ONE DAY

From our own Correspondent

Paris, September 13.

The Sudeten ultimatum confirmed the worst fears entertained in Paris during the afternoon. Sir Eric Phipps, the British Ambassador, who had seen M. Bonnet, the Foreign Minister, and M. Daladier earlier in the day, was at the Opéra-Comique this evening when at nine o'clock he suddenly left to see M. Daladier at the War Office once again – it is believed at the French Premier's request.

The view apparently taken by the British Government was that Lord Runciman was perhaps still the 'last hope,' and it was said that he continued to be in contact with both the Sudeten leaders and the Czech Government.

ADVICE TO CZECHS

The French Government, while deeply disturbed by the latest events in Czecho-Slovakia, apparently took the view that these events were still 'internal' and did not directly involve Germany, and it would appear that the Government urged moderation on the Czech Government so long as the conflict could not be officially regarded as 'international.' It is partly as a result of consultations with Paris that the Czech Government agreed to-night to take a conciliatory line in spite of all the provocation it had suffered. ...

The situation late to-night was still extremely strained, but although there was some talk of a possible general mobilisation order at the moment of writing this seems highly improbable.

The French Cabinet had met again this morning under the chairmanship of M. Lebrun, the President of the Republic, who had hastily returned to Paris from his summer residence at Ramboullet. M. Lebrun was informed in detail of all the military measures that had already been taken and that would, if necessary, be taken within the next few days.

It is considered probable that if the tension does not relax several classes of reservists may be called up in the course of the week.

A STATE OF EMERGENCY

Prague, September 13.

The Czech Government proclaimed a state of emergency in eight departments of Czecho-Slovakia – all in the Sudeten German part of the country. This state of emergency, which resembles in various ways martial law, is a police measure which permits the authorities to restrict personal liberty, to carry out house searches without warning, to control correspondence, forbid meetings and the publication of newspapers, and also provides special regulations regarding the manufacture, distribution, or carrying of arms and the use of party emblems.

REPUDIATION OF HENLEIN

Prague, September 14, 1 a.m.

The Sudeten German Democratic party has issued a statement dissociating itself from the attitude adopted by the Henlein party. The party condemns the 'warmongering policy of Herr Henlein,' and adds that his party does not speak on behalf of the whole German population – Exchange Telegram.

p.13

MARTIAL LAW HELD BACK TO LAST MOMENT
Prague's Reluctance to Act

NOT ORDERED TILL EXCESSES WERE IN FULL SWING

From our Central European Correspondent

Prague, September 13.

The situation has rapidly worsened during the last 24 hours. The natural consequences of Hitler's inflammatory speech were soon seen in the attitude of the Sudeten German population, which began dangerous demonstrations and excesses. The scenes in most of the Upper Bohemian towns reminded me of similar spectacles in Austria shortly before the taking over of power by Hitler. But Czecho-Slovakia is not Austria and has a reliable police.

The Czech authorities hope not to be compelled to employ stronger measures against Sudeten German demonstrators. ...

INTERPRETING HITLER'S SPEECH
Views of the Dominions: 'Another Breathing-Spell'

'MANNERS OF A DRILL SERGEANT'

– American comment

The following are among the views expressed in the Dominions on Herr Hitler's speech at Nuremberg on Monday night:–

AUSTRALIA

The Melbourne 'Sun' accuses Hitler of being deliberately evasive and leaving the world in the dark. Herr Hitler, the paper says, has thrown the onus of finding the exit from the difficulties on the other Powers. The references to Britain and France, however, show that he is properly mindful of their insistence on a solution without destroying or impairing Czech sovereignty. He said nothing to modify his hopes of eastward expansion, but his grudging admission that his forces were standing for law and order cannot be disregarded. ...

SOUTH AFRICA

Lobby opinion in the South African House of Assembly indicates no undue concern. While admitting that menace might be read into the speech, the feeling is that it may mean much or nothing and that the whole position is still as indefinite as before. The speech has given rise to little speculation and no qualms. ...

CANADA

The Ottawa 'Journal' says Hitler's speech may not have gone far to ease the world's anxiety. 'Yet,' says the paper, 'It does give another breathing-spell – a remaining chance to work out some solution to avert a conflict.' ...

NEW ZEALAND

'Those who hoped Hitler's speech would convey some assurance of peaceful intention hoped in vain,' says New Zealand's national daily, the 'Dominion.' 'The effect,' it continues, 'must undoubtedly be to increase the tension of the situation. It is likely to harden the resistance of the Sudetens to compromise, thus prolonging the crisis and placing the situation at the mercy of circumstances.' ...

MOSCOW SILENT
Press and Radio Ignore Hitler's Speech

From our Correspondent

Moscow, September 13.

The Soviet press continues its policy of avoiding direct comment on the European crisis. More news columns have warned the public of the growing seriousness of the sitaution, but more remarkable has been the careful avoidance of giving any authoritative expression of opinion. The official attitude seems to be that the Soviet Government has made clear its intention to carry out its commitments and that at present it is unnecessary to make any pronouncement until the crisis is resolved one way or the other.

News dispatches do not observe the same reserve. British policy is consistently criticised and the distrust of England's negotiations is indicated in a sub-heading, 'A Letter From London,' wherein emphasis is laid on reports that England is preparing to force Czecho-Slovakia to submit to Hitler's demands for the dismemberment of the country, with France abetting.

'Pravda,' the only Moscow newspaper published to-day, completely ignores Hitler's speech, and the Russian broadcasting stations, both yesterday and to-day, also make no mention of it. As the broadcast from Germany was completely 'jammed' in Soviet territory the public generally has no knowledge that it was delivered.

There is no indication from official sources that the Soviet Govenment is taking any special military measures. 'Pravda' is printing a series of articles on the history of the Communist party and to-day's article, headed 'The Leninist Theory of Socialist Revolution,' expounds the distinction between Imperialist war, which Communists are bound to oppose, and war of defence, in which Communists can take part.' ...

UNITED STATES

The 'New York Herald Tribune,' in a leader headed 'Still standing to arms,' says:

Millions listened to a single voice shouting its rounded, grandiose, essentially meaningless phrases throughout the world. By turns sarcastic, solemn, and shrill, delivered against the roaring background of cadenced 'Sieg Heils' – for all the world like the mindless roars of an American football crowd – it sounded unbelievably sinister and violent. ...

Thursday 15 September   *p.9*

PREMIER TO SEE HITLER
Flying to Berchtesgaden This Morning

LAST MINUTE PEACE EFFORT
Führer's 'Very Ready' Reply to Mr. Chamberlain's Telegram

Mr. Chamberlain is flying to Berchtesgaden to-day to see Herr Hitler in the hope of finding a peaceful solution of the crisis.

The announcement, made last night at No. 10, Downing Street, was that the Prime Minister had sent to the German Führer

114

and Chancellor through his Majesty's Ambassador in Berlin the following message:—

> In view of the increasing critical situation I propose to come over at once to see you with a view to trying to find a peaceful solution. I propose to come across by air and am ready to start to-morrow.
> Please indicate the earliest time at which you can see me and suggest place of meeting. Should be very grateful for very early reply.
>
> NEVILLE CHAMBERLAIN.

Hitler replied that he would be 'very ready' to meet the British Prime Minister to-day. The meeting will be at Berchtesgaden. The Premier will reach Munich about one o'clock, and there will be a short halt there before the 'plane goes on to Berchtesgaden.

MR. CHAMBERLAIN'S STAFF

Mr. Chamberlain will be accompanied by Sir Horace Wilson and by Mr. William Strang, of the Foreign Office, and he will leave by British Airways from Heston about 8 30 a.m.

The announcement was broadcast at 9 5 from the Berlin wireless station.

The news of the Prime Minister's decision had been given to the Opposition leaders earlier in the day, and it is understood that they expressed their approval. The French Government had also been consulted.

Incidentally, it is believed that this will be the Premier's first journey by air.

SUDETEN LEADERS' NEW DEMAND

The expiry of the Sudeten Germans' six-hour ultimatum to the Prague Government at midnight on Tuesday was followed in a quarter of an hour by the announcement by Henlein, their leader, to Dr. Hodza, the Czech Premier, that 'under the circumstances further negotiations are not possible.'

Under the ultimatum, it will be recalled, the Sudetens declined 'all responsibility for future developments' but yesterday seems, in fact, to have been a quieter day than Tuesday, though the death-roll was eleven. ...

FRENCH PREMIER'S TALK WITH MR. CHAMBERLAIN
Need of 'Exceptional Step' Agreed

'THE TWO GOVERNMENTS SEE EYE TO EYE'

–M. Daladier

From our Own Correspondent
Paris, September 14.

The news of Mr. Chamberlain's visit to Hitler to-morrow was received in Paris with such astonishment that many people simply refused to believe it. It is claimed that the idea was first suggested to Mr. Chamberlain by M. Daladier (who on a number of occasions in the past had shown faith in the virtue of direct talks with Germany). ...

No doubt the good reason that will be given by Mr. Chamberlain for the visit will be that he is determined to save peace, but it is sincerely hoped that this remarkable step will not be interpreted by Hitler as weakness on the part of France and England.

M. BONNET: 'ITS A FINE THING'

Paris, September 14.

M. Bonnet, the Foreign Minister, spent twenty minutes in conversation with M. Daladier, the Premier, at the Ministry of War late to-night, and on leaving, when asked what he thought of Mr. Chamberlain's visit to Herr Hitler, remarked 'It's a fine thing'. –Exchange Telegram.

French reservists who had been called up and were leaving for the Maginot Line region heard the news of Mr. Chamberlain's visit. The serious faces of the young soldiers lit up when they obtained special late papers and the train departed with a cheerful contingent.–Reuter.

PRAGUE 'ELECTRIFIED'

Prague, September 14.

The news of Mr. Chamberlain's impending visit to Herr Hitler has electrified Prague. The information was conveyed to a few newspapers at 9 28 p.m. by the German broadcasting station at Königswusterhausen. Special editions of the newspapers were printed and at this moment they are being eagerly seized from every newsvendor in the centre of the city. ...

Attention now centres round the question as to whether or not the British Prime Minister will be able to convince Herr Hitler that restraint is necessary in dealing with Czecho-Slovakia.

Foreign diplomatists expressed relief at the news. There is, however, some apprehension to be noted in that there is a fear that Czecho-Slovakia might be called upon to make sacrifices to an extent which the Government could not feel itself able to go. – Exchange Telegram.

AMAZEMENT IN WASHINGTON

Washington, September 14.

Amazement amounting almost to disbelief was registered in Government quarters when the news of Mr. Chamberlain's decision was flashed here. Observers here could not recall any occasion when a British Premier had found it necessary to hasten to the Continent and plead personally with a ruler widely regarded as threatening the peace of the world.

BERLIN HEARS THE NEWS
Warm Appreciation

RELIEF OF THE MAN IN THE STREET

From our own Correspondent

Berlin, September 14.

The news that Mr. Neville Chamberlain is to fly to-morrow from London to Berchtesgaden to meet Herr Hitler to discuss a peaceful solution of the Sudeten German issue has caused a tremendous sensation here. Its completely unexpected character has surprised not only German official quarters but also the general public. The news was first announced late this evening by the official German News Agency. ...

HITLER AND RIBBENTROP

... Herr Hitler, I understand, was in Munich all day to-day, and Herr von Ribbentrop, the German Foreign Minister, was with him also. It was in Munich that Herr Hitler received the message from the English Prime Minister. Although the general public are not sure what it is all about, they will undoubtedly be much relieved to-morrow at the idea of an attempt at a peaceful settlement. The papers to-night have continued to harp so much on 'the Czech atrocities' that the atmosphere has seemed both tense and choking.

As Mr. Chamberlain cannot speak German and Herr Hitler cannot speak English, the famous German Foreign Office interpreter Herr Schmidt will be present at the meeting. ...

RELIEF IN THE DOMINIONS
Canadian Premier on Mr. Chamberlain's 'Truly Noble Action'

CANADA

Ottawa, September 14.

The coming meeting has created a very favourable impression here. A revival of optimism is noticeable in all quarters.

Mr. Mackenzie King, the Canadian Prime Minister, has issued a statement revealing that he has cabled Mr. Chamberlain expressing the 'deep satisfaction' with which he and his Cabinet colleagues learned of his proposed meeting with Hitler. The statement said:

I am sure the whole Canadian people will warmly approve this far-seeing and truly noble action on the part of Mr. Chamberlain. Direct personal contact is the most effective means of clearing away the tension and misunderstandings that have marked the course of events in Europe in recent months.

Mr. Chamberlain has taken emphatically the right step. The world will hope that to-morrow's conference will create an atmosphere in which at last a solution may speedily be found of the problems which threatened peace.

–Reuter.

IN SOUTH AFRICA

Capetown, September 14.

News of Mr. Chamberlain's proposed journey to Germany was broadcast to theatre crowds in the cities and the more solitary listeners on the veld. 'Like the sunshine breaking through the clouds of a gloomy day,' is the general comment here. The British Prime Minister's action is the subject of glowing tributes in Lobby quarters and among prominent persons of the Union.
–Reuter.

MR. DE VALERA'S PRAISE

Geneva, September 14.

In an interview with Reuter Mr. De Valera warmly commended Mr. Chamberlain:

Another world war would be appalling, and if Mr. Chamberlain succeeds in averting it he will deserve the gratitude of all the peoples of Europe. His method is the right method, and all right-minded people will pray that his mission may be successful, and that it may be the beginning of the foundations for a real peace based upon an honest attempt to be whole-heartedly just.

p.12

FRENCH PRESS VIEWS
Doubts and Hopes

EUROPE'S BALANCE OF POWER

From our own Correspondent

Paris, September 14.

The 'Matin' to-day argues that France is not legally bound to intervene in the 'internal affairs' of Czecho-Slovakia, and it ignores the fact that the Sudeten rights are not such an 'internal' affair as all that. Even the much more responsible 'Temps,' while saying that the entry of German troops into Czecho-Slovakia would be 'fatal,' almost accuses the Czech Government of dilatory tactics, and (with a curious perversion of the historical facts) says that the Czechs should be able to appreciate the demands made by the Sudetens, 'demands which are so like those the Czechs themselves used to make in the days of the Austro-Hungarian monarchy.'

Opinion on the Left is rather divided. While the Communist 'Humanité' believes that a show of strength on the part of the Western democracies can alone save peace in Europe. M. Blum still thinks that a settlement between the Sudetens and the Czechs is possible, and he suggests that order should be restored in the Sudeten country (for in the present state of disorder an agreement is difficult) by sending there an Anglo-French police force. Like the 'Temps,' M. Blum thinks that Lord Runciman may still have an important part to play in Czecho-Slovakia.

Many Left wing deputies, on the other hand, showed themselves much dissatisfied with M. Daladier's statement last night, and asked 'whether the Czechs were the people to whom counsels of wisdom and appreciation should be sent.' Some of them also expressed the view that any more pressure on Benes might create an upheaval among the Czechs themselves, and if Benes were forced to resign and a military dictator took his place, the danger of a German invasion would certainly increase enormously.

'Pertinax,' feeling no doubt the way the wind is blowing, asks to-day, rather in the form of a rhetorical question, whether after the absorption 'in one way or another' of Czecho-Slovakia by

119

Germany (and the absorption would include the Skoda works, not an inappreciable asset) it may still be possible to prevent German hegemony over the whole of Central and Eastern Europe, and whether there is another line of retreat left there. He clearly believes that the surrender of Czecho-Slovakia would tip the balance of power in Europe heavily in Germany's favour.

p.13

THE CZECH ARMY
Well-Trained, Well-Armed Force Behind Mountain Wall

2,000 Fighting Aircraft

From a Military Correspondent

I recently paid a brief visit to Czecho-Slovakia and I was given an opportunity to see the Army and Air Force which would be opposed to Germany in the event of war.

My impression on the whole were entirely favourable, both as regards physique and training. The Czech is an ideal soldier, short and stocky, and obviously capable of great endurance. As a race, the Czechs willingly submit to discipline, yet have independence and great individuality. They are eager to learn and are intensely patriotic.

MILLION RESERVES

The Czecho-Slovakian standing Army amounts to approximately 200,000 men, divided into some fourteen divisions, frontier guards, and four brigades of cavalry. This could be increased by probably 1,000,000 men drawn from the reserves, forming some 24 to 26 divisions at war strength. In addition, there are some 200,000 older men, a large number of whom are veterans of the Polish Legions, who fought for the Allies in Russia, France or Italy, or in the German or Austrian armies.

The Sokol movement, which exists throughout the country and is devoted to the training of youths, produces a type of recruit, when of suitable age, readily absorbable into the Army. The reserves of the Army undergo a month's training every year, and are ready to take their place in the ranks.

One is rather apt to think that Czecho-Slovakia is a nation composed of many races. Such is not the case. With the exception of the German or Sudeten population which are scattered along the Bohemia–German frontier, and amount in all to some 3,500,000 people, the Czecho-Slovaks themselves with 10,000,000 people represent an overwhelming majority of the population.

There are a considerable number of Sudeten Germans in the ranks. These are divided among the infantry regiments, and would undoubtedly serve as loyally and as well as the Czechs themselves. There are no Sudeten German officers.

The Army has gradually improved in training and equipment year by year. A French mission of some 200 to 300 officers took charge of the organisation on the creation of the Republic. These have been gradually reduced until only one general and a few staff officers remain, and the Army to-day is under the command of its own generals and trained by its own officers.

The officer class consists of veterans of the Great War, those trained in French Staff colleges, and the juniors who have been trained at Prague during recent years. There is no aristocracy in Czecho-Slovakia, and the officer corps has been found entirely from the upper middle classes. The N.C.O.'s appear to be rather too young, but they are intelligent and smart in drill and appearance and much better turned out than the rank and file. One is impressed by the keenness of all ranks and the alacrity with which orders are obeyed. ...

STRONG DEFENCES

The crest of the Bohemian hills on the German frontiers belong to Czecho-Slovakia. These have been strongly fortified with many blockhouses and armed with the latest artillery and rendered as invisible as possible. Work is going on incessantly making the defences of Czecho-Slovakia more secure. The occupation of Austria by Germany has rendered it necessary to extend these defences to Bratislava on the Danube. Part of the defences in this region of Southern Moravia consists of a flooded area, which would be extremely difficult for an attacking force.

As regards arms, the Czech Army is self-supporting. Quite apart from the Skoda works, where much heavy armament is being made, the Czechs have arms factories at Brno, and at places scattered among the Moravian hills. These factories are working day and night, and before the present situation arose were supplying the armies of other nations. The whole country, Bohemia, Moravia, and Slovakia, is agriculturally rich and the question of food supply will not cause any difficulty.

The Czecho-Slovakian Air Force is actually part of and under the command of the Army. I would say that it consists to-day of 2,000 military 'planes and some 15,000 men. Doubtless this could be considerably increased in case of war by 'planes manufactured in the great armament works. New aerodromes have recently been built to accommodate a largely increased number of 'planes. In my opinion the Czech will fight determinedly to defend his country, and even when he is driven out of Bohemia will retire to his defensive positions in the Moravian mountains and continue to resist.

121

I doubt very much whether the Czecho-Slovakian Army, excellent as it is, and established in strong natural and artificial defences, could hold out for a considerable time against vastly superior numbers.

SOVIET PUBLIC NOW HEARS OF HITLER'S SPEECH
Attack on British Policy

From our Correspondent

Moscow, September 14.

The Soviet public generally obtained its first knowledge of the venom of Hitler's last Nuremberg speech to-day when 'Pravda' and 'Izvestia' published liberal extracts from comments in the press of Britain, France, Czecho-Slovakia, and the United States. Sufficient was published to acquaint the public with the gravity of the resulting situation, though any text or summary of the speech is still not available.

Careful selection from the foreign press puts the emphasis on certain interpretations. American and British papers' view that the speech dealt the death-blow to Mr. Chamberlain's policy is given prominence, as well as the opinion that the possibility of a settlement is lessened by the German attitude and that the co-operation of Britain, France and the Soviet Union for peace is more essential than ever.

Direct comment is barred as before, in the daily press, but the weekly 'Journal de Moscou' attacks British policy as being directed towards compelling Czecho-Slovakia to abandon resistance to the German demands.

The Soviet public shows eagerness to buy newspapers, queues forming each morning at the stalls. The fact that copies of the principal newspapers are available throughout the day in spite of this eagerness indicates that the demand has been anticipated and extra copies printed, because the papers are usually sold out at an early hour.

This evening a 'black-out' as practice against air raids was carried out in parts of Moscow.

MR. CHAMBERLAIN'S DEPARTURE
Brief but Hopeful Message Before His First Flight

From our London Staff

Fleet Street, Thursday.

At about 8.30 on this cool and sunny morning the diplomatists, Cabinet Ministers, and journalists in Heston Aerodrome stood looking up, hat in hand, while the noisy, silver, flashing 'plane bearing the Prime Minister circled once round their heads and so faded to a faint gleam and a faint mutter in the direction of Germany.

Two officials from the German Embassy, Dr. Kordt, the Chargé d'Affaires, and Baron von Selzam, the First Secretary, were among the first to arrive for this extraordinary farewell. Both were in the full formality of top-hat and morning coat. Lord Londonderry, in a countrified battered soft hat, was there; he looked extremely pleased, and so did Lord Brocket, who so recently visited 10, Downing Street on his return from a Nuremberg tea-party. Lord Halifax, placid as usual and in his usual rather funereal garb of long black overcoat and bowler hat, arrived with Lady Halifax, driven by Sir Alexander Cadogan. Lord Halifax was heard to say something about 'the beautiful day' and 'a good omen.' Journalists were admitted through the barrier to the precincts of the waiting 'plane; cars carrying news-reel cameras crossed the skyline, fancy-bred monsters they seemed in a scene whose ordinariness made the occasion all the more improbable.

PREMIER'S ARRIVAL

Mr. Chamberlain drove up, with him Sir Horace Wilson, and Mr. William Strang of the Foreign Office, his two companions for the Berchtesgaden talks. The Premier looked tanned and positively debonair – grey Homburg genially lifted to his friends, spick and span umbrella, grey suit and big, soft grey tie. There was a sporting look about him; perhaps, though it did not seem so, he was forcing a cheerfulness, or perhaps he was just glad to be rid of decisions for a few hours. Yet one noticed his slightly nervous flush, as though of a man who dislikes drama in the everyday. He had a word with the Germans, a brief consultation with Lord Halifax and Sir Alexander Cadogan. Then, as he moved to the 'plane, there was a slight demonstration from beyond the barrier – 'Long live Czecho-Slovakia': a demonstrator was removed. Mr. Chamberlain paid no attention at all. At the door of the 'plane he turned; the photographers called for Lord Halifax; a photograph was taken.

As the Premier turned away again a microphone was unexpectedly put before him and immediately, in his clipped, unemotional voice, he made his unpremeditated speech: 'I am going to meet the German Chancellor because the situation seems to me to be one in which discussion between him and me may have useful consequences. My policy has always been to try to ensure peace, and the Führer's ready acceptance of my suggestion encourages me to hope that my visit to him will not be without result.'

There was warmth in Dr. Kordt's reply: 'I congratulate you on your magnamimous gesture, and wish you God-speed.' Mr. Chamberlain entered the 'plane and again the photographers loudly entreated him; so he stuck his head out of the window; and this time with a quite unprecedented gaiety, he waved his hat and his free hand and laughed. Voices from beyond the barrier again called out, 'Stand by Czecho-Slovakia,' but there were shouts at the same time of 'Good luck' and hats came off and people – even the journalists – were cheering. Yet there was a constraint about this cheering; some, no doubt, welcomed his fine gesture but feared its outcome; others who entirely approved seemed to feel the inadequacy of ordinary applause. And so Mr. Chamberlain began his first flight in such circumstances and at the age of sixty-nine.

PREMIER RETURNS TO-DAY
To Consult Cabinet After Seeing Hitler

A SURPRISING DEVELOPMENT
Official Communiqué Promises Further Talk
'In a Few Days' Time'

RUNCIMAN TO SEE PREMIER

Mr. Chamberlain is returning to London this morning by air, after a talk last evening with Herr Hitler at his home near Berchtesgaden. The announcement was made by the German News Agency in Berlin as from Berchtesgaden:–

The Führer and Chancellor had a conversation with the British Prime Minister at the Obersalzburg to-day, in the course of which a comprehensive and frank exchange of views about the present situation took place.

The British Prime Minister is returning to England to-morrow in order to discuss matters with the British Cabinet.

In a few days' time a further conversation will take place.

The British Ambassador stated, says an unofficial report, that the next meeting would not be at Berchtesgaden.

THE NEXT MEETING

A Reuter telegram speaks of depression in press quarters at Berchtesgaden as a first reaction, but a later message said that opinion looks forward to the next meeting 'with hope.' In Berlin political quarters regard Mr. Chamberlain's decision to return to London as an indication that he realizes the urgency and seriousness of the position. It was believed there early this morning that Mr. Chamberlain would be back in Germany by to-morrow.

Strong rumours are current in Paris of the imminence of a meeting between Hitler, Mussolini, M. Daladier, and Mr. Chamberlain in the near future, but semi-officially the news is described as 'premature.'

LAST NIGHT'S TALK

The British Prime Minister had reached Munich soon after midday in a four-hour flight from Heston and had then gone on to Berchtesgaden by train and thence to Hitler's home by car. On the steps he was greeted by the Führer with outstretched hand.

With Herr Schmidt acting as interpreter, the private talk between Mr. Chamberlain and Herr Hitler following after tea and concluded in two and a half hours' time.

Mr. Chamberlain looked extremely tired when he returned to his hotel.

LORD RUNCIMAN RECALLED FOR CONSULTATION

Lord Runciman is returning to London to consult with the Prime Minister. An official statement issued by the mission early this morning in Prague read:

At the invitation of the Prime Minister, Lord Runciman, accompanied by Mr. Ashton-Gwatkin, is returning to London for a consultation with the Prime Minister and his colleagues in connection with the Berchtesgaden conversations.

Meanwhile Lord Runciman appeals to all parties to refrain from any act which will aggrevate the existing situation pending the result of the further consultations contemplated in the near future between the British Prime Minister and the Führer.

HENLEIN'S SECESSION DEMAND

The Sudeten leaders and the German press, far from

regarding Mr. Chamberlain's visit as calling for a truce, yesterday proceeded to new extremes in their campaign against the Czechs.

Herr Henlein, the Sudeten leader, issued a proclamation in which, with the usual charges of oppression and military terrorism, he announced his aim to secession, but still did not mention the word 'plebiscite.' It included the following:–

All our efforts to induce the Czech people and their responsible statesmen to treat us honestly and justly have failed.

In this hour I stand before you, the German people and the civilised world, and declare: We want to live as free Germans. We want liberty and work in our Fatherland. We want to return to the Reich.

At the same time that their headquarters at Asch the Sudeten leaders called on 'every Sudeten German to defend his life and that of his family against the murderous and plundering Czech hordes.'

The Prague authorities as a result of these steps are issuing a warrant for the arrest of Henlein and other party leaders. Henlein is said to be in Bavaria. ...

GERMAN CROWDS CHEER

Berchtesgaden, September 15.

Herr von Ribbentrop had welcomed Mr. Chamberlain at the airport, saying in English 'I greet you in the name of my Führer and his country.' 'Thank you,' answered the Prime Minister.

Driving to the station between a cheering crowd that shouted 'Heil!' and saluted, Mr. Chamberlain raised his hat and bowed acknowledgement. At the railway station the royal reception hall had been decorated with British and German emblems and vases of flowers. Here the British visitors were welcomed by two well known Nazi leaders – General von Epp, Governor of Bavaria and head of the German Colonial League, and Herr Adolf Wagner, party leader in Bavaria.

During the journey the British visitors took lunch with their German escort who included Herr von Ribbentrop and Baron von Weizsäcker.

Meantime preparations were being made in Berchtesgaden to receive them. The royal suite at the hotel was carefully inspected by two detectives early to-day and a Union Jack hoisted, flanked by two Swastika banners.

One of the largest crowds ever seen at Berchtesgaden frantically shouted, cheered, and threw their hats into the air when the Prime Minister arrived. Hats were flung high into the air, and there were cries of 'Hurrah!' ...

GERMAN VIEW
'Premier Back by Saturday'

DANGER OF DELAY
'Very Guarded Optimism' at Berchtesgaden

Berchtesgaden, September 16.

The official communiqué issued last evening spoke of 'some days' as the period for the next meeting between Herr Hitler and Mr. Chamberlain, but actually the present intention is that the meeting shall take place before the end of this week, if all goes well. For the moment the place of meeting is being kept secret, but it will not be either Berlin or Berchtesgaden.

Last night Mr. Chamberlain was closeted in his private suite with Sir Horace Wilson and Mr. Strang discussing the results of his talk with Herr Hitler. The talk itself lasted two hours and thirty-five minutes, while the conversation over the teacups lasted twenty-five minutes.

Up to an early hour this morning telegrams from London were being delivered to Mr. Chamberlain by motor-cycle dispatch rider. Mr. Chamberlain plans to leave Berchtesgaden this morning at 9 30 by car for Munich, and then will return to London by the same aeroplane by which he came.

As far as can be gathered from quarters in close touch with Herr Hitler last night the afternoon's talk was useful to both sides. It is believed that Herr Hitler did not by any means do all the talking. Mr. Chamberlain is believed to have made the most of this opportunity to put the British case fairly and squarely before Herr Hitler.

The general feeling is that last evening's talk has cleared the air somewhat, so that both sides now know where they stand. Early this morning the general mood here was one of very guarded optimism. ...

p.12

THE PREMIER AND HIS MISSION
Czech Assent Needed for Any Agreement

From our Diplomatic Correspondent

(This article was written before the news that the Premier was returning to-day.)

London, Thursday.

The visit of Mr. Neville Chamberlain to Berchtesgaden has, naturally enough, roused a good deal of emotion. It has been welcomed with great joy in some places as signalling the end of the European crisis and in others with resentment as a capitulation.

It is neither of these, least of all the latter. On the purely human side it must be said that no one acquainted with the facts will deny that Mr. Chamberlain's action is courageous and high-minded. He is fully aware that it will have aroused anxiety in some quarters, and for understandable reasons, but the dangers of the situation have become so fearful that such considerations have to be waived.

THE NECESSITY FOR SOME SUCH VISIT

It has been evident that there would be little hope of averting European war if Hitler were not informed of the British attitude. The British Ambassador in Berlin, Sir Nevile Henderson, has not seen Hitler since June.

Hitler has in his present state of mind been very inaccessible and has sometimes seemed to be living in another world (though some at least of his actions have been realistic enough). There is good reason to believe that he was – and still is – convinced that whatever happens in Central Europe Great Britain would not go to war. He has consistently been encouraged in this belief by Herr von Ribbentrop. It has long been considered necessary here that a person of some authority should leave Hitler in no doubt as to the attitude of this country. The choice wavered between M. Daladier and Mr. Chamberlain. It fell on the latter, for France is an ally of Czecho-Slovakia and has a pact with Russia, whereas Great Britain has no formal ties with either of those two countries. In any case, Mr. Chamberlain is better able than anybody else to speak with authority about the British attitude.

There is no question of 'letting Czecho-Slovakia down.' Mr. Chamberlain takes no proposals, no new plans with him to Berchtesgaden. He will explain British policy and call Hitler's attention to the possible consequences of a German attack on Czecho-Slovakia. But he will also be open to suggestions from Hitler.

It may be that Hitler has made up his mind to annex the Sudeten German regions whatever happens and to attack Czecho-Slovakia if she resists. In that case Mr. Chamberlain will have failed in his mission (unless Hitler changes his mind at the last moment), although it will have been made clear to the world that Great Britain did her utmost to avert disaster.

Hitler may declare that the Czecho-Slovak problem is one that concerns only Berlin and Prague and not London or Paris. This view is, of course, unacceptable in Paris, as it is here.

It is not at all sure that the possibility of a plebiscite will be considered. That a plebiscite as conceived by Hitler would have all the consequences outlined in the article in to-day's 'Manchester

Guardian,' (in other words, that it would mean the extinction of the Czecho-Slovak Republic) is realised here better, perhaps, than in Paris.

CZECH ASSENT NEEDED FOR ANY AGREEMENT

But whatever solution is proposed it will require the assent of the Czecho-Slovak Parliament. After all, Czecho-Slovakia is an independent sovereign State, and has the right to say 'so far and no farther' if her independence and sovereignty are menaced, and in case of armed attack to invoke her alliances.

It may be that wider issues – for example, Anglo-German relations as a whole – will be discussed at Berchtesgaden. Mr. Chamberlain goes with an entirely free hand in an eleventh-hour effort to avert a European war without prejudice to the independence of Czecho-Slovakia.

SUDETENS GO TO GERMANY
Over 5,000 Cross

The German News Agency declared in Berlin last night that more than 5,000 Sudeten Germans have so far fled to Germany. Entire families are said to have arrived at the German frontier. A camp for them has been established at Zittau, Saxony. Many of the refugees who crossed the frontier near Zittau are reported to be young men who had received calling-up orders. Others are said to be Sudeten German party officials against whom warrants have been issued. ...

p.13

NEW ZEALAND PREMIER'S 'I THINK HE WILL SUCCEED'

The Dominions press also praises Mr. Chamberlain's decision. The New Zealand Premier, Mr. Savage, yesterday described it as 'an historic gesture in the cause of peace.' He reasserted that New Zealand is firmly behind Great Britain, and went on:–

What Mr. Chamberlain has done merits our deepest admiration. Faced with a problem of the greatest magnitude he has shown himself a man big enough to deal with it in a big way. I personally think he will suceed in averting the possibility of war.

Melbourne, September 15.

The Melbourne 'Argus' writes: 'Mr. Chamberlain, a pilgrim of peace, old and wearied, goes as one inspired, scorning tradition, defying etiquette. British hearts are filled with pride and thankfulness.' ...

The 'Sydney Herald' declares, 'Only a nation conscious of its strength and the justice of its cause could make such a gesture.'—Reuter.

SUSPICION IN MOSCOW
'New Sacrifices'

From our Correspondent

Moscow, September 15.

Official views on Mr. Chamberlain's visit to Germany or on his prospects of achieving results that might ensure a just peace are not obtainable in Moscow, where the press has reported the Premier's decision briefly and without comment.

The Soviet attitude is that Mr. Chamberlain's whole policy is based on appeasement of the aggressors by concessions, and official quarters are believed to be watching the latest move warily, expecting new sacrifices to be demanded from Czecho-Slovakia. Such a development has already been hinted at in the press here before the announcement of the Berchtesgaden meeting.

The Runciman Mission has apparently lost heart entirely and retired into the British Legation, according to a Tass dispatch from Prague.

A 'MAGNIFICENT GESTURE'

Mr. George Lansbury, who has just returned from a European trip, during which he had interviews with many famous figures, said to a reporter yesterday: 'Everybody throughout the world must welcome Mr. Chamberlain's courageous step. Every man and woman who even thinks about prayer will pray that it will be successful. In that prayer I most sincerely join and I hope that the result of the Chamberlain–Hitler talk will be a great step forward to a real world peace and understanding.'

'A BETRAYAL'

The University Labour Federation yesterday sent the following telegram to the National Executive of the Labour party:–

'Regard Mr. Chamberlain's flight to Hitler prelude to the betrayal of Czecho-Slovakia. Urge the Executive to organise for a national campaign against a plebiscite or further concessions imposed on Czecho-Slovakia – Meredith, University Labour Federation.'

M. BLUM ON MR. CHAMBERLAIN'S 'NOBLE AUDACITY'
French Praise for His Mission

BUT FEARS OF A FOUR-POWER PACT REVIVED

From our own Correspondent

Paris, September 15.

Mr. Chamberlain's journey to Berchtesgaden is announced under spectacular headlines in all the Paris papers, and the keynote of most of the comments is approval and admiration for his bold undertaking. 'The fact that the British Premier is a man of seventy,' says the 'Temps,' makes his decision all the more moving.'

M. Blum praises Mr. Chamberlain for his 'noble audacity in his will for peace,' and, on the other extreme, M. Doriot, the pro-Nazi leader of the Parti Populaire hopes that the meeting will 'lay the foundations for the future statute of Europe.'

In so far as Mr. Chamberlain's journey may 'save peace' nearly everybody welcomes it, though there is one commentator who, parodying Mr. Chamberlain himself, says that he will 'eat his hat' if any good comes out of the Berchtesgaden meeting. Further, there are a certain number of observers who are rather alarmed precisely because Hitler may attempt to lay what M. Doriot calls 'the foundations for a new European State,' based on the Four-Power Pact or something of the kind.

FRANCE'S ATTITUDE TO CZECHS

The loudest dissenting views are those of the Communist 'Humanite,' which says that Mr. Chamberlain's visit can only increase Hitler's arrogance and feeling of impunity, and of papers like the 'Ordre' and the 'Epoque,' which largely reflect the views of the French General Staff, and which refuse the surrender by France of her influence in Europe and of the abandonment (in one way or another) of Czecho-Slovakia. For there is a widespread feeling that the attitude of the French Government in the last few days was one that could only encourage Hitler in his belief in France's ultimate indifference to the fate of Czecho-Slovakia and in her desire to avoid a war at almost any price. And by 'almost any price' is meant almost any 'reorganisation' of Czecho-Slovakia short of an invasion by Germany of that country.

M. de Kerillis for instance finds this attitude extremely shortsighted and considers that it would be fatal for France to allow Germany to absorb Czecho-Slovakia 'in any shape or form' and especially to eliminate her as a military ally of France. No doubt it may be too early yet to speak of the ultimate policy that may be decided by the French Government should Hitler try to carry out his avowed intention of, in the long run, destroying Czecho-Slovakia altogether. Much will depend on the outcome of the Hitler–Chamberlain talks.

In Paris to-day quantities of sand were being distributed to most houses as a precaution against incendiary bombs.

An important conversation took place today between M. Daladier, the Premier, and M. Herriot, the President of the Chamber of Deputies. It is probable that the question of calling Parliament in the very near future was considered.

Saturday 17 September p.15

CZECHS AND PLEBISCITE
Minister's Statement

Prague, September 16.

The Deputy Prime Minister, M. Bechyne, in an interview appearing in the 'Lidove Noviny,' states:

> There can be no Government in Czecho-Slovakia which can accept a plebiscite, since no such Government could survive such a step by more than one hour.
> I can assure the public there will be neither plebiscite nor international police in our country.

It is generally believed among foreign observers here that President Benes told Lord Runciman that the Czech Government has not deviated by one inch from its position in regard to plebiscites or separations as defined in a note to London and in a verbal statement to the British and French Ministers in Prague last Monday.–Exchange Telegram.

MR. CHAMBERLAIN ON HIS MEETING WITH HITLER
Last Night's Consultations

TALK WITH THE KING: CHEERING CROWD
OUTSIDE THE PALACE

Immediately after the arrival at No. 10, Downing Street, early last evening of Mr. Neville Chamberlain, accompanied by Lord Halifax, and Lord Runciman, the 'Inner Cabinet' met. Sir John Simon and Sir Samuel Hoare, with the Government's diplomatic advisers, had awaited them at No. 10.

A great crowd had waited for the Premier in Whitehall and Downing Street and gave him a thunderous reception. Among them was Sir Thomas Inskip, Minister for the Co-ordination of Defence, who waved as Mr. Chamberlain's car went by. Crowds surged round the entrance to No. 10 as the Prime Minister stepped from his car. Mrs. Chamberlain was the first to greet her husband. Arm in arm they stood smiling on the steps of No. 10, and faced a battery of photographers and cinema operators.

Even after Mr. Chamberlain had gone in repeated efforts were made by hundreds of people in Whitehall to pass the police into Downing Street in order to cheer outside No. 10. Police, reinforced by mounted men, insisted on their remaining in Whitehall.

OUTSIDE THE PALACE

At 9 30 p.m. the Premier went to Buckingham Palace and remained with the King for an hour and a quarter.

Crowds at the Palace gates had grown to several thousand by the time he left, and there was a big cheer as they recognised Mr. Chamberlain. Looking tired, he waved to the crowd as his car passed out of the gates. In spite of the efforts of extra police cheering men and women surged forward and brought the car almost to a standstill. When the crowd gave way the Premier drove to No. 10, Downing Street, where he was again cheered by the big crowd in Whitehall. ...

A LETTER FROM THE KING

A black-bordered envelope bearing the royal crest was handed to Mr. Chamberlain by a private secretary. It had been brought to the airport by special courier, and was a personal letter in the King's handwriting. Slowly the Premier read the contents of the letter, covering three pages, and then he made some comments to Lord Halifax.

All the time the people on the aerodrome building were waving and shouting 'Bravo! Well done, Neville!' Mr. Chamberlain, smiling broadly, waved his hat in acknowledgement, murmuring 'Thank you very much.'

PREMIER'S STATEMENT

In his statement Mr. Chamberlain said:

I have come back again rather quicker than I expected after a journey which if I had not been so preoccupied I should have found thoroughly enjoyable.

Yesterday afternoon I had a long talk with Herr Hitler. It was a frank talk; it was a friendly one; and I feel satisfied now that each of us fully understands what is in the mind of the other. (Cheers.)

You won't, of course, expect me to discuss now what may be the results of that talk. What I have got to do now is to discuss them with my colleagues, and I would advise you not to accept prematurely any unauthorised account of what took place in the conversation.

But I shall be discussing them to-night with my colleagues and with others, especially with Lord Runciman, and later on – perhaps in a few days – I am going to have another talk with Herr Hitler. Only this time he has told me that it is his intention to come half-way to meet me. (Laughter and cheers.) He wishes to spare an old man another such long journey.

As he finished his speech and moved towards his car with Lord Halifax people took off their hats and cheered him. With Lord Halifax he entered a car and drove away to Downing Street amid continuous cheers from the people massed outside the main gates. The two advisers who had flown with him from Munich also went on to Downing Street – Sir Horace Wilson to No. 10 and Mr. Strang to the Foreign Office, where shortly Mr. Ashton-Gwatkin, Lord Runciman's adviser, who had reached Croydon from Prague with Lord Runciman at 5 30 p.m. also arrived.

FOREIGN OFFICE CALLERS

There were many callers at the Foreign Office during the day. Count Grandi, the Italian Ambassador, saw Lord Halifax for the first time since the beginning of the crisis. Another caller was the Archbishop of Canterbury, who spent some time with the Foreign Secretary.

Lord Halifax also requested Mr. Attlee, Leader of the Opposition, and Mr. Arthur Greenwood, Deputy Leader, to call on him, and they were told of the latest developments in the situation. ...

BIG DUMPS OF ARMS
Czech Discoveries

SUDETENS AND THE 'ANSCHLUSS'
Many Opposed

From our Diplomatic Correspondent

London, Friday Night.

The Czech authorities have discovered large quantities of arms, including machine guns of German origin, in the headquarters of the Sudeten German party in various parts of the Sudetenland. Ammunition and hand grenades were also found.

Documents belonging to the Sudeten German party, and seized by the Czech police, reveal that an armed insurrection in a large scale had been planned. It was timed to begin soon after Hitler made his speech at Nuremberg. It is believed that the plan was not carried out because Czech resistance promised to be too formidable.

It is a symptom of some significance that the Sudeten German population as a whole are not following the lead of their chiefs. Nearly all the more serious incidents have been confined to the Eger district, where the Sudeten German movement has always been strongest. In other districts the party chiefs have been unable to incite the masses to acts of resistance against the Czech authorities.

Dislike of National Socialist tactics is spreading in the Sudetenland. The 'moderates' in the Sudeten German party (who appear to be more numerous than is generally supposed) want Home Rule, but do not wish to be incorporated in the Third Realm. A large number of Sudeten German members of the Czecho-Slovak Parliament who belong to the 'moderate' wing of the party have appealed to the Czecho-Slovak Government to resist Hitler's demands and to protect them if the German authorities demand their extradition.

Several of the leaders of the party – and not only 'moderates' – such as Jundt and others, repudiate Herr Henlein's proclamation demanding the 'Anschluss' with the Reich.

RUSSIAN FEARS
'Czecho-Slovakia to be Sacrificed'

FOUR-POWER PACT

From our Correspondent

Moscow, September 16.

The selection of comments from the foreign press published to-day in 'Pravda' and Izvestia' on Mr. Neville Chamberlain's visit to Herr Hitler are unfavourable or critical in tone. The complete absence of direct comment on the European crisis continues, and both newspapers devote leading articles to the discussion of trade union problems.

The Tass Agency suggests that the German leaders are seizing on Mr. Chamberlain's visit as an opportunity to achieve a general settlement of Anglo-German relations, and the Czech press is quoted as believing that Czecho-Slovakia is to be sacrificed to this end.

A suggestion that Mr. Chamberlain is organising a four-Power conference excluding Russia is advanced by the Geneva correspondent of 'Izvestia,' who remarks: 'It is easy to imagine the fate of Czecho-Slovakia at the hands of such a conference.' A four-Power pact is the Kremlin's great anxiety and the suggestion recurs in the press whenever a darkly suspicious mood prevails.

'Serious diplomatic quarters' are quoted as regarding Hitler's anxiety to rescue his 'German brethren' as disingenuous and that his real aim is to force Czecho-Slovakia to repudiate the French and Russian treaties and to neutralise the country, which is considered to be the key to German hegemony in Europe.

Expanding the idea of Mr. Chamberlain's as a 'humiliation,' the Geneva correspondent of 'Izvestia' asks: 'Who can imagine Pitt's seeking an interview with Napoleon to beg for peace?'

VISIT AS A HITLER TRIUMPH

From our own Correspondent

Geneva, September 16.

The Berlin correspondent of the Basle paper, the 'National Zeitung' says that in the opinion of the man in the street in Germany Mr. Chamberlain's visit to Berchtesgaden is the most sensational event of Chancellor Hitler's extraordinary career. It is pointed out that the affair of Austria was less difficult than that of Czecho-Slovakia, a country protected by pacts binding it to the great democracies, and that in this case Hitler's chance of success appeared to be almost nil. ...

ANGLO-FRENCH PLAN
Complete Agreement Announced at Midnight

'POLICY FOR PEACEFUL SOLUTION'
Hope of More General European Settlement Later

The French Premier and Foreign Minister flew to London yesterday morning and for over eight hours in all were in conference with Mr. Chamberlain and his three collegues, who have acted as an 'Inner Cabinet' during the crisis.

The French Ministers did not leave Downing Street till ten minutes past midnight.

The following official communiqué was issued from Downing Street:–

> After full discussion of the present international situation the representatives of the British and French Governments are in complete agreement as to the policy to be adopted with a view to promoting a peaceful solution of the Czecho-Slovak question.
>
> The two Governments hope that thereafter it will be possible to consider a more general settlement in the interests of European peace.

The Cabinet, it was announced last night, will meet this morning to consider the result of the Anglo-French discussions.

The French Ministers will leave London this morning by air for Paris, where the Cabinet has been summoned.

The Czech Government has not yet been consulted.

AN EVENTFUL WEEK-END

Of the many developments in the crisis during the week-end one of the most important was the announcement by Mussolini in a speech at Trieste yesterday that if the policy of 'plebiscites for all minorities' which Italy backed failed to secure peace Italy would range herself, were the conflict to become more than local, by the side of Germany. ...

MUSSOLINI SPEAKS

In his speech yesterday Mussolini, who spoke of the Prime Minister as 'the flying messenger of peace,' said:

> Confronted with the problem which at this moment agitates Europe, the solution has only one name – plebiscites: plebiscites for all the nationalities who demand them, for the

137

nationalities which were forced to become part of that State which wanted to be great Czecho-Slovakia and which to-day reveals its organic inconsistency.

At a certain moment events assume the headlong motion of an avalanche, so that it is necessary to act quickly if disorders and complications are to be avoided.

We hope that in these final hours a pacific solution may be reached. We hope otherwise that if this is not possible the eventual conflict may be limited and circumscribed.

But if this does not happen and it were to end in a ranging of forces of universal character for or against Prague, let it be known that Italy's position is already chosen.

CZECH ATTITUDE TO DOWNING STREET TALKS

… The Czech Government took it for granted that it would be consulted before any decisions were reached, the message said.

DR. HODZA'S REJECTION OF A PLEBISCITE

Dr. Hodza, the Czech Premier, broadcasting to the nation yesterday, claimed that it was as a result of the strong measures that the Government had taken that there had been no serious consequences of the Sudeten leaders' revolt, and these measures would be continued as long as was necessary.

Dr. Hodza rejected the idea of a plebiscite as a solution of the nationalities problem.

p.14

ANTI-CZECH FEELING HARDENS IN GERMANY
'Atrocity' Tales Having Their Effect

From our Correspondent

Berlin, September 18.

Matters were in suspense here to-day, as everybody is awaiting the outcome of the British–French discussions in London. Thus what might have already been a Sunday full of trouble once more passed off comparatively quietly here – the emphasis being on 'comparatively.' Undeniably there is much tension in the atmosphere here and anxiety is felt by those who have menfolk. People go about with serious faces. The display windows of the local branches of newspaper offices are besieged. The public reads the news in silence and walks away in silence.

The continual stream of allegations of Czech atrocities is having its effect. Many people are heard voicing genuine indignation. It is not astonishing as they have been reading news for about a week with headlines such as these:

MOSCOW ARMS CZECH BANDITS.
REFUGEES TELL TERRIBLE TALES.
CHILDREN TORN FROM THEIR MOTHERS.
GERMANS CHASED.

Likewise the feeling is gradually spreading that Russia is backing Prague, for would Prague be so bold, the public asks, if it had not a powerful ally at the back of it? Even if the two countries have no joint frontier, the man in the street argues, the Russians could send weapons just as they sent them to Spain.

HENLEIN'S LEGION

The most important news of to-night is the announcement in a message of the German News Agency from Dresden stating that the Sudeten German Free Corps has 40,000 men who will be divided into four groups. Late to-night Conrad Henlein issued a proclamation to the Sudeten Germans, according to a German News Agency message dated from Berlin, which contains the following sentences:–

The hour of liberation is nearing. Therefore do not despair but hold out. Offer resistance. Hundreds of thousands of Sudeten Germans are joining the ranks of the Free Corps. They are willing to risk their blood and life for the freeing of the home country from the Czech yoke.

The proclamation is signed 'The Command of the Sudeten German Free Corps.' The number of Sudeten Germans who have so far crossed the frontier is given at 80,000 to-night.

'LIQUIDATION OF CZECH STATE'

The German view is well formulated in an editorial of the 'Deutsche Allgemeine Zeitung' this morning, which writes:-

By its procedure against the Sudeten Germans Prague has drawn the line between Czecho-Slovakia and the German element. Thus the German element has been excluded from this State and certainly does not have to show it any more loyalty. This State is in the process of dissolution. The protection of the Sudeten German population is primarily the concern of the German Reich. But the speedy liquidation of the Czech State is in the interests of all Europeans.

To-day no one in the world can say any more that support of our German comrades is an 'unprovoked' pact. The Czecho-Slovakia of 1919 has vanished, and if criminal elements in Prague threaten to drag innumerable innocent people with them into the abyss they must be prevented from doing so. There is no other question with which a British Cabinet Council or a meeting of British and French Ministers can occupy itself. We are in the midst of a race between an international discussion and a local development which is separating two peoples.

p.15

FRANCE AND THE CRISIS
Looking to Britain

THE TRANSFERRED INITIATIVE

From our own Correspondent

Paris, September 18.

Among the most remarkable features of the present crisis have been, especially during the past week, (1) the unwillingness, one might even say the inability, of the French Government, divided by internal dissensions, to take any clear decision, and (2) the great eagerness with which it has been handing the 'lead' and the responsibility over to England. It was not apologetically but almost with paternal pride that M. Daladier claimed the credit for Mr. Chamberlain's Berchtesgaden trip.

The change in the respective positions of Britain and France in relation to the Czech crisis has been remarkable. The Franco-Czech alliance was during the May 21 crisis and until the end of July what Pertinax calls 'Factor No. 1.' From the end of July to the beginning of September 'Factor No. 1' was the Runciman mission; everything revolved round it. In the last fortnight the French could have revived the Czech alliance as 'Factor No. 1,' but they have hitherto failed to do so and are again looking to London for guidance.

GERMANY'S INCREASING DEMANDS

As 'Ce Soir' remarks to-night, the hesitations of the French Government during the last fortnight have had the effect of accumulating more and more German obstacles in the way of a peaceful settlement of the Sudeten question. In the German view all the immediate demands of the Sudetens are now out of date; even the demand for a plebiscite is out of date; a Henlein Legion that may at any moment attempt to march into Czecho-Slovakia is the latest surprise Hitler has sprung on Europe. Nothing is lacking short of an actual invasion of Czecho-Slovakia by the German Army, and it would seem that Hitler, after watching France closely, has come to the conclusion that nothing short of such a German invasion can persuade France to mobilise.

Will this belief be contradicted by the Anglo-French talks in London to-day? That is the question Paris has been asking. And another question asked is: In what capacity have the French Ministers really gone to London – is it as the allies of Czecho-Slovakia in search of British support or is it as people who in their state of indecision are hoping to receive some guidance from Mr. Chamberlain?

FRENCH OPINION STIFFENS

The apparent contempt with which Hitler had treated France in the last week and his apparent belief that nothing need be feared from her has in the last 24 hours produced a notable stiffening in the state of French public opinion. No doubt there are still many Frenchmen, especially in the countryside, who say, 'Why bother about the Czechs?' but the feeling is growing that Hitler's arrogance is such that it is impossible to say to what lengths it will go, and the growing tendency is to say that 'apart from the Sudeten question' France cannot abandon Czecho-Slovakia, her Eastern alliances, retrench herself (to use M. Flandin's phrase) behind the Maginot Line and hope for the best.

The problem, it would seem, is now (from the French point of view) how to give Germany satisfaction on the Sudeten question and yet to save Czecho-Slovakia, not only as a State but also as a military ally, and to set down firmly the limits beyond which Germany will not be allowed to go without the risk of war with France and Britain. Will M. Daladier be sufficiently firm on this point?

One can even read in one of the French papers to-night that 'Germany will not believe in French firmness unless the British Government proclaims its intention to introduce conscription in Britain' – an unconscious indication of the tendency to make England responsible for French hesitations.

A STATE OF EMERGENCY
Czech Decree

Prague, September 18.

The Cabinet decided late last night to introduce the state of emergency throughout the country for a period of three months. This measure will enable the authorities to take strict measures for the control of traffic, to make domiciliary visits, and to empower the authorities to establish a curfew where necessary. It was gathered that there was a desire in certain quarters to take even more drastic measures, but the Cabinet, and particularly President Benes, who came up from the country especially to preside over the meeting, showed firmness and resisted the pressure.

Some idea of the nature of this pressure is evident from an article in the 'Prago Lidu,' the organ of the Social Democrat party, which states: 'We may not be able to wage a successful war against Germany, but in any case, we can precipitate the whole of Europe into war.' It is this state of mind which is making the task of President Benes increasingly difficult.

Even in some Czecho-Slovak quarters there is a feeling that any solution will be preferable to a plebiscite, with its attendant delays, excitement, and agitation. In Sudetenland there can be little doubt about the feelings of the great majority of the followers of Herr Henlein. The leaders were in favour of an agreement within the Czech frontiers, but national sentiment and Nazi propaganda have undoubtedly had a tremendous effect upon the local population.

The Permanent Committee of the Chamber has been summoned for to-morrow in order to confirm the decision of the Government to dissolve the Sudeten German party.

There is some evidence to-day in Prague of the precautionary measures that are being taken by the Government. There was a distinct scarcity of taxis in the street, because large numbers have been used for military purposes, such as taking reserves to their barracks. Petrol stations and garages have been instructed to limit their sales of petrol to private customers and to keep a reserve of fuel for military needs.—Reuter.

A FIVE-HOUR CABINET
Saturday's Crowded Hours in Downing Street

Saturday's meeting of the British Cabinet had been its longest meeting since the crisis began.

For five hours and ten minutes the Ministers were in conference at No. 10, Downing Street, and heard for the first time from Mr. Chamberlain the full account of his talks with Hitler. During part of the meeting Lord Runciman was present. One of the first decisions was to invite the French Premier and Foreign Minister to London on the following day.

Mr. Joseph Kennedy, the American Ambassador, paid two visits to the Premier during the day, the second lasting an hour and twenty minutes. One visitor to the Foreign Office was Count Grandi, the Italian Ambassador.

THE LABOUR DEPUTATION

When the Cabinet meeting finally broke up Mr. Chamberlain received at No. 10 a deputation from the National Council of Labour, which placed before him the views of the Labour and trade union movements on the international situation. It is understood that Labour still takes the view that the independence and integrity of Czecho-Slovakia must be maintained. the deputation comprised Mr. Herbert Morrison, M.P., Dr. Hugh Dalton, M.P., and Sir Walter Citrine, general secretary of the T.U.C.

No official statement was issued after the deputation had left, but it is understood that there was some plain speaking by the three members. It is believed that they made it clear to the Premier that the Labour and trade union movements stood rigidly by the joint manifesto issued at Blackpool a week ago. In this it was stated that the British Government should leave no doubt in the mind of the German Government that they would unite with France and the Soviets to resist any attack on Czecho-Slovakia.

Whether the Labour movement will modify its attitude as a result of Saturday's talks is not known, but the whole position is being reviewed once again at to-day's meeting of the National Council of Labour.

DOMINIONS INFORMED

Dominion High Commissioners called at the Dominions Office after the Cabinet meeting. They remained for a considerable time, and were informed by Mr. Malcolm MacDonald, the Colonial Secretary, of the Cabinet discussions.

THE KING

During Saturday the King was kept informed of the matters under discussion by the Cabinet.

Tuesday 20 September   *p.11*

CZECHS TO ACCEPT
Decision Early To-day After Five Hours' Council

TO AVOID WAR AND BLOODSHED
The Next Step : Mr. Chamberlain's Second Visit to Hitler

France and Britain are awaiting Czecho-Slovakia's reply to the Anglo-French plan submitted to it yesterday.

Discussions between the Czech Cabinet, leaders of parties, and President Benes went on until shortly before one o'clock this morning. Our Central European correspondent, telephoning from Prague soon after midnight, said it was believed that, faced with the alternative of war without Western support, Czecho-Slovakia would accept the plan, possibly with reservations.

At 1 30 the following message was received from Reuter's Prague correspondent:–

It is learned authoritatively that the Czecho-Slovak Government has decided to accept the recommendations of the British and French Governments, but to ask for more concrete explanations so as to be able to reply in detail.

This decision was reached at a five-hour meeting of the Cabinet Council under President Benes, which ended at 12 45 this morning.

The Cabinet is meeting again under President Benes at 11 a.m.

The chief consideration governing the discussions was the determination to avoid war and bloodshed.

THE SECOND VISIT TO HITLER

It is possible that the reply may be received by to-night in which event it was suggested in London late last night that Mr. Chamberlain's second visit to Hitler may be made to-morrow.

Meanwhile the German campaign of provocation continues unabated, and on the Czech frontier the Henlein Legion of 40,000 Sudeten German refugees, fully equipped with the most modern war material, announces that it is preparing a campaign of raids.

OUTLINE OF THE PLAN

No official or semi-official statement has been issued of the plan which the Franco-British conference devised and forwarded to Prague. It is believed in responsible quarters in London (says our London correspondent) that its proposals are:

1. Areas in Czecho-Slovakia with a predominant German population to be ceded without a plebiscite.
2. Other areas to remain in the Czecho-Slovakian State under the federal system proposed in Dr. Benes's Fourth Plan.
3. An international commission to 'rectify' the new boundaries.
4. The independence of Czecho-Slovakia within these boundaries to be guaranteed by Great Britain, France, Germany, Italy, Poland, Hungary, Rumania and Yugo-Slavia.
5. The neutralisation of Czecho-Slovakia and cancellation of her treaties of alliance.
6. The interchange of populations to be arranged by which German sympathisers within Czecho-Slovakia can go to the new

German provinces and the population in these provinces that does not wish to remain there can go within the new boundaries of Czecho-Slovakia.

BRITISH AND FRENCH CABINETS MEET

M. Daladier, the French Premier, and M. Bonnet, the Foreign Minister, returned from London to Paris by air yesterday morning and at once reported to the French Cabinet. After a meeting which lasted ninety minutes it was officially announced that the attitude of M. Daladier in the London conversations and the policy agreed upon there had been unanimously approved. The communiqué said that the two Ministers gave the Cabinet an account of the negotiations and 'the conditions under which agreement had been reached with the British Government.'

The British Cabinet at a two-hour meeting also approved the plan.

During the day Mr. Kennedy, the American Ambassador, again saw Mr. Chamberlain.

Count Grandi, the Italian Ambassador, was among the day's callers at the Foreign Office. ...

THE OPPOSITION AND THE PLAN
Deeply Disturbed

From our Political Correspondent

London, Monday Night.

The British Cabinet spent two hours to-day in finally passing the Anglo-French plan. Now it waits to hear from Prague before meeting again.

Mr. Attlee, the leader of the Labour party, and Mr. Arthur Greenwood, the deputy leader, saw Mr. Chamberlain to-night, and so did Sir Archibald Sinclair. This can be said for the Labour and Liberal parties, that they are profoundly disturbed by the accounts of the plan appearing in to-day's press and just hoping that the plan is not as bad as that. Their leaders, who called on the Prime Minister to-night presumably now know the plan, but their followers have to await its official publication.

No hint can be given here when that can be expected, but it cannot be before Mr. Chamberlain has had his second meeting with Herr Hitler. When the meeting is over Mr. Chamberlain cannot any longer delay to meet Parliament, but no date has been or can be fixed for its summoning until it is known when he is coming back from Godesberg. To-night it has not even been settled when he will go to Godesberg, and it is evident that the time cannot be fixed until the Czech reply has been received.

PRAGUE A GLOOMY CITY
Czech Government Preparing Its People for Surrender

OUTBURSTS OF PUBLIC ANGER FEARED

From our Central European Correspondent

Prague, September 19.

In this sad and desperate city to-day people are walking about with gloomy and set faces. Czecho-Slovakia feels herself betrayed by her allies. There had been doubts here for some time about the attitude of Mr. Neville Chamberlain and M. Bonnet, but it had been hoped that M. Daladier would remain firm and would realise what an efficient alliance the Czecho-Slovak Army offered to France.

The change of atmosphere came almost overnight. Last night everybody still hoped that the allies would stand by and this explaining how it came about that on Thursday Dr. Benes told the French and British Ministers that a plebiscite meant war, and that as late as yesterday Dr. Hodza, the Premier, declared that a plebiscite was impossible.

People in Prague talk of Great Britain's 'third Abyssinia,' and the man in the street still maintains 'We must fight even if we go down.' But whether responsible quarters will accept the great responsibility for such a decision is doubtful.

GOVERNMENT'S APPEAL TO PEOPLE

This afternoon a manifesto was issued by the Government, saying that reports had been published in the world press on the results of the negotiations. The Czecho-Slovak Government asked its public to accept this news with the calm knowledge that all constitutional factors – the President and the Government, as well as the political representatives of the Czecho-Slovak people – were ceaselessly active and constantly in communication with the Governments of the friendly States. The Government would consider the situation and the results of the Anglo-French conversations from the point of view of the necessities and actual vital interest of the Czecho-Slovak State.

The manifesto exhorted the people to remain calm and place complete confidence in the responsible constitutional authorities, but whether these will accept the great responsibility of risking a war is doubtful. ...

ENDING RUSSIAN ALLIANCE

This naturally would end the French and Russian alliances with Czecho-Slovakia. One must remember that Dr. Benes only

146

negotiated the pact with Russia because Britain refused to guarantee the Czecho-Slovak frontier.

Under these terms Herr Hitler has attained his aim, because the breaking of the alliance between Czecho-Slovakia and Russia was more important to him than the incorporation of the Sudetens.

The afternoon papers published the reported text of the conditions to be imposed on Czecho-Slovakia. Official quarters replied that the reports were all guesses. But by now they probably know that these guesses, unfortunately, are not very far from the truth.

What will be the answer of Czecho-Slovakia?

During the afternoon the 'Inner Cabinet' considered the outline of the Anglo-French proposals which had been communicated, and this evening a full Cabinet Council was held and discussions were proceeding at a late hour.

THE SUDDEN CHANGE

Yesterday the atmosphere was grave and serious but hopeful. To-day the situation has greatly changed. The man in the street is certainly for war – a refusal to yield in face of German bullying 'If we go under, let us perish with honour,' say most people. But, after all, what could Czecho-Slovakia obtain now by going to war under the changed circumstances of to-day?

To-night for the first time all neon signs were extinguished in Prague, apparently as a first step in air-raid precautions.

It is now clear that the curtailment of the public liberties was imposed so that the Government could remain master of the situation, even in face of possible outbreaks of public indignation.

September 20, 12 30 a.m.

It is probable that a decision on the Czech Government's reply will be reached in the early hours of to-day. It is believed that it is likely to be an acceptance with modifications, as against the alternative of war without Western allies. ...

LABOUR PARTY'S DISMAY
'Shameful Betrayal'

AN INTERNATIONAL CONFERENCE
Invitations Sent

The National Council of Labour held three meetings in London yesterday. At its third meeting, which lasted until 10 30 p.m., it received a report from Mr. Attlee and Mr. Greenwood, fresh from a long talk with Mr. Chamberlain. The following official statement was issued at the end of the meeting:–

The National Council of Labour, earnestly desirous of maintaining peace, views with dismay the reported proposals of the British and French Governments for the dismemberment of Czecho-Slovakia under the brutal threat of armed force by Nazi Germany and without prior consultation with the Czecho-Slovakian Government.

It declares that this is a shameful betrayal of a peaceful and democratic people and constitutes a dangerous precedent for the future.

The National Council of Labour expresses its profound sympathy with the Czecho-Slovakian people in the grievous anxieties through which they are now passing. It reaffirms its convictions that enduring peace can be secured only by the re-establishment of the rule of law and the ending of the use of lawless force in international relations.

The Council will meet again this morning. An invitation has been sent to the Socialist and Trade Union Internationals and French Socialist and trade union leaders to come to London for a conference, and it is expected that they will be at this morning's meeting.

The Labour Opposition at this period represented at least three strands of opinion within its ranks and there still remained a significant group of pacifists includng the Labour Party Leader of the early 1930s, George Lansbury. There were also re-armers such as Hugh Dalton who were demanding rearmament even if the result of such a policy entailed a cut in social services; the maintenance of such services was a major plank in Labour's platform. The third grouping comprised those who, although they favoured rearmament against Fascism, felt it to be only acceptable provided such rearmament was under the aegis of a Labour/Socialist government. They were less willing to sanction such policies being carried out by a National/Conservative Government, i.e. their perceived class enemies. Indeed Aneurin Bevan, a member of this group, likened such a policy to'putting a sword in the hands of our enemies that may be used to cut off our own heads.'

FRENCH CABINET ACCEPTS THE PLAN
Emphasis on British Responsibility

VIRTUAL BREAKDOWN OF POST-WAR SYSTEM OF ALLIANCES

From our own Correspondent

Paris, September 19.

The French Cabinet held a meeting this morning and, according to the communiqué.

The Cabinet gave its unanimous approval to the statements and the attitude of the Premier and to the solutions that have been proposed in agreement with the British Government.

It is understood that at least two members of the Cabinet showed profound dissatisfaction with the outcome of the London talks, but they were prevailed upon not to make their feelings public, as this, it was said, would add a new difficulty to an already sufficiently difficult situation.

'SENTENCED WITHOUT A HEARING'

After the Cabinet meeting M. Bonnet, the Foreign Minister, had an hour's conversation with M. Osusky, the Czech Minister in Paris, and submitted to him the Anglo-French plan. In leaving the French Foreign Office M. Osusky looked profoundly perturbed, and bitterly remarked to the journalists outside: 'Here you see the condemned man. He has been sentenced without even being heard.' M. Osusky's bitterness is understandable, as it is he who in the last two years has assembled the most impressive collection of French assurances of help, assistance, and loyalty to the Franco-Czech Pact.

No doubt the French are not refusing even now to come to the assistance of Czecho-Slovakia, if she were actually invaded by Germany, but it seems clear that the London plan is hardly compatible with the assurances the Czechs have been repeatedly given by France.

THE FRENCH CLAIM

What did the French have to say in their own defence? There is not the least doubt that the French weakened their position terribly last week by their show of indecision and by their request to Britain to take the lead. But at the same time it is now claimed here that as a result of the Berchtesgaden meeting the British Government went, in their eagerness to satisfy Hitler's demands, considerably beyond what the French would have expected.

And it is said that M. Daladier, spent some rather disagreeable moments in London yesterday, for when he reminded the British Government that France was after all bound to Czecho-Slovakia by certain precise treaty obligations he received a somewhat disagreeable reply to the effect that if France wished to carry out these treaty obligations she could do so but should not expect too much from Britain at this stage.

It would be interesting to know exactly whether this story is told by the French in self-justification or whether it is substantially true.

THE FORECASTS OF THE PLAN

Although reports on the terms of the London plan as published in the French press agree in essentials they do not agree in every detail. It is for instance not clear yet what parts of the Sudeten country were to be handed over to Germany. Some reports say parts with a German population of 70 per cent or more, others say 50 per cent or more.

Nor is it clear whether there is to be a plebiscite in the other predominantly German parts. As regards the 'neutralisation' of what will remain of Czecho-Slovakia and the guarantee to be given her, there is some doubt whether Russia is to be included among the guarantors. According to most reports she is not. It is reasonably asked in Paris: Is not the inclusion of Italy merely calculated to mark the rebirth of the Four-Power Pact, which was at one time at any rate, dear to Mr. Chamberlain's heart?

No doubt the only good feature of the arrangement from the French point of view is the inclusion of Britain among the guarantors, and it is understood that this was granted very grudgingly and after no less than three hours' consultation among the British Ministers while the French were waiting outside.

The proposed exchange of populations as part of the frontier revision is also considered reasonable as far as it goes.

The French have, of course, no illusions on what it all means to them. It means the virtual breakdown of their post-war system of alliances. The question now arises whether Hitler and the Czechs will accept the plan. If Hitler does not and insists on wiping out Czecho-Slovakia altogether, either now or in the near future, it is not doubted that France will go to war.

HITLER'S REAL INTENTIONS IN CZECHO-SLOVAKIA
Destruction of the Republic

DEMAND FOR ALL REGIONS WITH MORE THAN 50 P.C. OF GERMANS

From our Diplomatic Correspondent

London, Tuesday Night.

Czecho-Slovakia accepts the Anglo-French proposals with reservations that are meant to make the proposals compatible, if carried out, with her sheer existence as an independent State. She is determined to fight for her independence even if she has to fight single-handed.

Each demand made by Hitler or by the Sudeten German party has been followed by demands more exorbitant. When Henlein, the leader of the party and Hitler's chosen instrument, was in London early this year he represented the demands of his party as being so moderate that the Czechs could have granted them without any difficulty. When he was asked to explain why he had made his now famous Carlsbad speech, in which he had put forward eight points summarising demands of an extreme character, he explained his purpose had been chiefly demagogic and that the real demands of his party were not nearly as extreme as the speech seemed to convey.

EARLIER SCHEMES REJECTED

The Czechs made three successive proposals in the hope of negotiating an agreement with the Sudeten German party. None of these proposals was even considered. Then, under strong pressure from the British Government, they made their fourth set of proposals, which completely satisfied some, and partly satisfied others of the Eight Points in the Carlsbad speech. But even this was not enough. Hitler and the Sudeten German party shifted their ground and left no doubt that their real demands were much more extreme that had ever been admitted.

In his discussion with Mr. Neville Chamberlain at Berchtesgaden Hitler demanded that all regions with a population that is more than 50 per cent Sudeten German must be separated from Czecho-Slovakia and transferred to Germany. This demand was embodied in the Anglo-French proposals that were submitted to Czecho-Slovakia yesterday.

Although these proposals go so far that Czecho-Slovakia cannot accept them and survive, they do not go far enough for

Hitler. He is again shifting his ground. Last night the German Ministry of Propaganda gave the German press confidential instructions to attack Czecho-Slovakia with the utmost virulence and to demand that the Czecho-Slovak State be destroyed. These instructions have been carried out – they certainly represent the policy of the German Government.

THE MAIN AIM

There has never, since the beginning of the present conflict between Berlin and Prague, been the slightest doubt in the mind of any informed and objective observer that Hitler's purpose is not merely to annex the Sudetenland but to destroy the Czecho-Slovak Republic. It is only the French and British Governments who have held that there can be any serious compromise between Hitler and the Czechs or that he will ever be satisfied with any concessions that are compatible with the continued existence of Czecho-Slovakia as an independent State. Even if such concessions had been accepted by Hitler, it could never have been seriously doubted that acceptance on his part would only have been provisional and that he would only have waited for the opportunity to accomplish the total destruction of the Czecho-Slovak Republic, which, quite apart from the fact that it stands in the way of his schemes not merely of Eastern and South-eastern European but also of Western European conquest, is intolerable to him because the Czechs are a democratic people. A country that rules without terrorism, concentration camps, and anti-Semitic outrages is not regarded as worthy of continued existence, especially as a neighbour.

FRANCE'S 'LOST' PRESTIGE
Russian Comment

CHIEF BLAME FOR BRITAIN

From our Correspondent

Moscow, September 20.

The reported terms of the Anglo-French settlement of the crisis clearly indicate that the fears expressed in the Soviet Union just before Lord Runciman's departure for Prague have been fully realised.

The summary of distrustful Soviet views published in the 'Manchester Guardian' on August 3 reads like an inspired prophecy of the developments – an end to Czecho-Slovakian sovereignty, revision of the map, dismemberment of the State, neutralisation of

Czecho-Slovakia, and renunciation of her treaties of alliance in which the Soviet Government has a vital interest.

The hopeful opinion was then expressed that the Czechs would not yield to pressure on them to neutralise their State, and a leading article in to-day's 'Pravda' declares that the fate of Czecho-Slovakia depends on the firmness of its Government, which is supported by the bulk of her people. Both the leader-writer and the Geneva correspondent of 'Izvestia' dwell on the effect of the settlement on France's prestige and future.

ALSACE-LORRAINE

'French prestige in Europe is liquidated' the latter holds, and the former sees France betraying her own interests if only because Hitler's programme includes Alsace-Lorraine. While the tone towards France is thus pitying and reproachful, Britain is arraigned as betraying her ally France and sacrificing Czecho-Slovakia for the sake of friendship with Germany.

The press does not comment on the fact that the Soviet Government was not consulted in spite of Russia's important stake in the outcome of the settlement plan, but complains that Czecho-Slovakia, the nation most affected, was not consulted.

FRANCE AND THE 'SURRENDER'
Sharp Reaction of Public Opinion

From our own Correspondent

Paris, September 20.

If M. Daladier is feeling unhappy about the result of the Anglo-French talks in London on Sunday, the same can hardly be said of M. Bonnet, who seems to be taking the betrayal of Czecho-Slovakia rather more philosophically. On the whole M. Flandin's doctrine of 'retrenchment behind the Maginot Line' – a doctrine supported by M. Caillaux and M. Chautemps and other old politicians who claim to speak 'in the name of rural France' – has triumphed for the time being.

Why M. Flandin and his friends should expect that France will in the long run be left in peace behind the Maginot Line while German hegemony is being established over Central and Eastern Europe is not clear. With Czecho-Slovakia gone, or virtually gone, the future of the Franco-Soviet Pact becomes very doubtful, especially if, as is believed by many, Mr. Chamberlain shows a desire to subscribe to a four-Power pact which would be principally directed against Russia so as to divert Germany's energies from the west – at least for a time.

'Is nothing going to stop Hitler? Are we going to have the whole of Europe against us?' is the theme of the anxious questions heard on buses and in cafés from people of every kind. ...

The Army, as General Gamelin told M. Daladier on the previous Monday, was in perfect shape and he added that it could indefinitely prevent an invasion both by Germany and by Italy. No doubt the Air Force was a weak spot and the organisation of A.R.P. insufficiently advanced; but with a better backing from Britain than she had ever had before why was France's diplomatic game so very much feebler than was warranted by her military position?

The advice being offered to the French Government at this time by the French military leaders was invariably one of despondency and defeatism and was totally lacking in any strategic initiative.

p.9

PREMIER SEEING HITLER TO-MORROW
Czechs Want Discussions

FRANCE AND BRITAIN REPLY: 'TIME PRESSES'
Prague Urged This Morning To Accept

The Czecho-Slovak reply was given to Britain and France last night. It asked for further discussions of the proposals.

Early this morning the British and French Ministers in Prague called together on President Benes, on the instructions of their Governments, to urge upon him the advisability of accepting the peace plan as it stands because 'time presses.' A Cabinet Council has been summoned.

Poland and Hungary are now pressing for their share if minority areas in Czecho-Slovakia are to be ceded, and Hitler's aid was invoked in interviews at Berchtesgaden yesterday.

THE SECOND VISIT TO HITLER

Mr. Chamberlain is going to see Hitler to-morrow at Godesberg, near Bonn. The announcement was made at 11 p.m. from Downing Street as follows:–

The Prime Minister and the German Fuehrer and Chancellor have decided to resume the conversation which they began at Berchtesgaden at Godesberg on Thursday, September 22, at 3 p.m.

154

The Prime Minister will again be accompanied by Sir Horace Wilson, his personal adviser, and by Mr. Strang, of the Foreign Office.

THE CZECH REPLY

The official communiqué announcing the dispatch of the Czech reply says:–

The Czecho-Slovak Government communicated this evening to the British and French Ministers in Prague a Note in which is set forth its attitude to the proposals brought forward by the British and French Governments.

The attitude adopted makes possible further diplomatic negotiations in the spirit of conciliation which the Czecho-Slovak Government has always shown.

AN ARBITRATION SUGGESTION

It is understood that the Czech Government stated that according to Constitution it was unable to acquiesce in ceding Czech territory to a foreign Power.

The Czech Government therefore suggested that the Anglo-French plan, so far as it refers to the conceding of Sudeten territory, should be referred to the Hague Tribunal.

A Prague communiqué issued earlier in the evening said that the Government, it was expected, would come to a decision on the Anglo-French proposals 'as soon as certain pending diplomatic negotiations yield a result.' It added:

These diplomatic negotiations consist of the exchange of opinions with all friendly Governments, particularly with London and Paris.

THE PARTITIONING OF CZECHO-SLOVAKIA
Significant New Moves

THE CRISIS NOW TAKING ON A NEW PHASE

From our Diplomatic Correspondent

London, Tuesday Night.

The situation of Czecho-Slovakia, desperate enough in any case, threatens to be made more desperate by the attitude of Poland. The Czechs could resist a German invasion for some weeks, perhaps for many weeks. But can they resist a combined

155

German and Polish (and perhaps Hungarian) invasion, seeing their frontier with Poland is very long and ill-fortified?

By abandoning her Czech alliance France has broken up the Eastern and Central European order. Her alliances with Poland, Yugo-Slavia, and Russia have become as worthless as she has made her alliance with Czecho-Slovakia. If the Czechs cannot rely on the French alliance Poland cannot either. Poland, abandoned by the Western Powers, feels obliged to compound with Germany.

A PARTITION AGREEMENT

There is to be a meeting between General Göring and the Polish Foreign Minister, Colonel Beck. Hitler received the Hungarian Premier and the Foreign Minister and the Polish Ambassador to Germany at Berchtesgaden to-day. It is believed here that the situation created by the recent discussion between Hitler and Mr. Neville Chamberlain has now been superseded, and that Hitler will henceforth speak not only on behalf of Germany but also on behalf of Poland and Hungary. It is believed that a German-Polish-Hungarian partition of Czecho-Slovakia is now intended.

In the recent Anglo-French discussions there was no serious opposition to Hitler's demand that all regions with a Sudeten German majority be transferred to the Reich. Indeed, what has really happened is that Hitler's demands have simply been communicated to the Czecho-Slovak Government by the French and British Governments. A proposal for an international guarantee of what little may have been left of Czecho-Slovakia has been added merely to make these demands seem less crude and to create an impression that the Western Powers are trying to do something for Czecho-Slovakia (and France something to respect her alliance), whereas the truth is that they are merely abandoning the Republic to Hitler. The prospect of a Four-Power pact is being held out quite vaguely as a further concealment of the total capitulation of the Western Powers.

POLAND'S INTENTIONS

It now remains to be seen whether Poland will co-operate in a German invasion of Czecho-Slovakia, hoping in this way to postpone her own partition (which is inevitable if Czecho-Slovakia is partitioned). But if Poland stands aside (even if only for a while) and Germany undertakes the invasion alone, and the Czechs offer armed resistance, what will France do? It is believed here that she may yet honour her alliance with Czecho-Slovakia (she has not repudiated it formally). Russia is bound by her alliance with Czecho-Slovakia only if the Franco-Czech alliance comes into operation.

As for Great Britain, she is bound, now as before, by her obligations to France, and will no doubt respect them. It is clear that the Czecho-Slovak Government must have time to press for modifications, seeing that they are of such a momentous character.

What if Hitler takes the action he has several times threatened to take and begins military operations? Does the Franco-Czech alliance still stand in that event? If so, then the international crisis, so far from having ended, will merely have begun.

p.12

DAYS WITH THE CZECH FORCES
Formidable Defences and a Fighting Nation

By a Military Correspondent

Bismarck called that mountain salient which is now Czecho-Slovakia 'a fortress built by God in the very heart of Europe,' and with the men who defend that fortress I have recently spent some most interesting days. They have an army under peace conditions of some fourteen divisions, with six cavalry brigades. The Czech, the Slovak, and the German stand side by side in the ranks; an army entirely loyal to the Republic, and officered by a well-trained, hardworking, and conscientious body of the upper middle class. Many of the seniors served in Czech legions fighting for the Allies in Russia during the war. Of these, General Ludendorff spoke most highly when the Bolsheviks were giving way before the German divisions. Others served in the Austro-Hungarian armies, and when this empire was broken up rejoined to serve their new republic.

For many years a French mission, now under General Fuscher supervised the training of the force until the Czech generals found their feet; then many Czech officers went for several years' instruction in the French Staff and military colleges, and now the Army has its own school with its own instructors. Now as to the morale of men which compose the force; they are intensely patriotic, hardworking, clean, sober, and read every paper, military or otherwise, they can find. They face the present position calmly, are well disciplined, respect their officers, and obey them gladly. Even the German in the ranks will undoubtedly serve as loyally as his Czech comrade. There are no Sudeten German officers.

THE FRONTIER DEFENCES

The divisional artillery has not yet been mechanised; it is well horsed (the heavy artillery is mechanised), and when I saw them on the road and in action at a practice range a few days ago I considered them good but not up to the average of French or British gunners. The batteries are grouped, and in the divisional artillery there are four guns to a battery. The cavalry are well mounted, for it is a great country for horses, and are recruited from ideal material – young farmers and labourers. The air arm, which is part of the Army, is large and efficient, consisting of fifty or more squadrons, divided into heavy bombers, light bombers, fighters, and mixed units for army co-operation. The country is particularly suitable for the horse in military operations behind the natural defences on the frontiers.

The frontiers of Czecho-Slovakia form a natural fortress. Bohemia is entirely surrounded by a mountain range with the exception of the 'gate' through which the Elbe flows, a pass which it would be extremely costly to capture. On the crests of these ranges the Czech has a series of strongly fortified positions. But this first line of defence might fall, for inside the strong positions lies the country of the Sudeten Germans, who though most of them have Czech names or are Czech by descent are now thoroughly Germanised and would be actively unfriendly to the army of defence.

On the east side of Bohemia come the Bohemian–Moravian heights, a range completely dividing these two provinces; the Moravian gateway at the northern end of the line has been made one of the strongest fortresses in Europe. Southern Moravia is again naturally defended by mountains and rivers, in addition to carefully prepared forts and strong posts along the entire line. I visited this area a few days ago, and there is every evidence of military knowledge and skill displayed in the defences. The northern frontier of Moravia is similarly protected.

Such is the line over which the enemy has to cross. It will be a costly operation if the Czech Army puts up the resistance expected of it, but superior numbers must in the long run gain the day. In two months, perhaps three, the Germans would hold all the principal tactical positions if no other nation intervened. But the Czechs would certainly fight on stubbornly.

Czecho-Slovakia is a self-supporting country. There are ample food supplies for both the Army and the nation. Moreover, the immense arms factories would keep the nation well supplied with arms and ammunition. The Skoda works, it is true, are near the frontier. These works supply most of the heavy material and heavy guns. The Z works at Brno manufacture medium and small arms. I visited them a few days ago. It is a wonderful organisation, working day and night and capable of immense output, a keen and efficient management controlling over 70,000 men. Many Continental Powers allied to Czecho-Slovakia make their purchases here. No trade or workers' troubles in factories like these; the men work hard and make good money, are contented, happy, and well fed.

Neither in Prague, nor anywhere in the country is there any apparent preparation against hostile air attack. The inhabitants of the cities would get what cover they could find in their cellars or scatter in the open country and villages around. The fear of gas does not exist, and retaliation is looked upon as the surest means of preventing the continuance of air attacks on the cities.

Every Czech general or civil official I have talked with is quite convinced that the nation will fight, and fight well, if the country is attacked. They have all worked together since the creation of their State; they have made it what it is, a prosperous, happy land; they are intensely proud, as well they may be, of what they have done, and they will not relinquish their greatly valued possession without a bitter struggle. This is the spirit of every Czech, and they will take up arms to a man.

They look to England more than to any other nation. She is spoken of everywhere, in the barracks, hotels, and streets. They say over and over again, 'We have no alternative but to fight, but we shall die if England does not help us.'

Thursday 22 September   *p.4*

CONDEMNATION OF 'PEACE PLAN'
A Cambridge Resolution

DEMAND FOR RECALL OF PARLIAMENT

An emergency meeting at Cambridge on Tuesday night of a group of societies affiliated to the Cambridge Peace Council passed the following resolution:

Believing that the London plan initiated by Mr. Chamberlain after his conversations with Hitler, and as reported in the press, so far from being a peace plan, is a proposal which increases the danger of war in the future by giving yet a further sanction to aggression and thus strengthening the hold of militarism not only in Europe but throughout the world, believing further, that the plan, prepared without consultation with the Czech Government, is an insult to every principle of honour, decency, and peaceful co-operation in international affairs in that it betrays Czecho-Slovakia, as previously Abyssinia, Spain, China, and Austria were betrayed, to military invasion; we, the undermentioned societies wish to call for

(a) The immediate summoning of Parliament;
(b) The repudiation by the British people of the dismemberment of Czecho-Slovakia under the threat of force;

159

(c) The promotion of an international guarantee of the territorial integrity of Czecho-Slovakia against violation by armed force.

The societies represented included:— League of Nations Union, Cambridge; Council of Action for Peace and Reconstruction, Cambridge; Cambridge Trades Council and Labour Party; Communist Party, Cambridge; Scientists' Anti-War Group, Associated Society of Locomotive Engineers and Firemen.

p.11

'WE ARE SACRIFICING OURSELVES TO SAVE PEACE'

The following is the text of a broadcast made from all loudspeakers in the streets of Prague last night:—

This afternoon the Czecho-Slovak Government's reply was handed over after the Government had been exposed to pressure for which there was no precedent in history and which amounted to a 'Diktat' such as is imposed upon a vanquished people.

But we are not a vanquished people. We submitted in order to avoid greater losses, misery and bloodshed. We are sacrificing ourselves to save peace as Christ sacrificed himself to save humanity.

We shall not attempt to throw blame where it belongs, but leave this to the judgment of history.

We stand alone, but we shall be Czechs together.

A new life is now before us.

THE CZECHS GIVE WAY
'Sacrifice for Peace Under Unprecedented Pressure'

MR. CHAMBERLAIN'S TASK TO-DAY
Poland and Hungary in Hitler's New 'United Front'

After two days of painful deliberations and under strong and increasing pressure from Britain and France, the Czecho-Slovak Government, at five o'clock yesterday afternoon, accepted the Anglo-French plan.

The reply was handed to the British and French Ministers, who twice during the day had visited President Benes to urge acceptance without further delay. It made no reservations or stipulations, but (Reuter learns from official sources) concluded with an appeal:

If Czecho-Slovakia should nevertheless be attacked, the Czecho-Slovak Government trusts that Britain and France will come to her aid.

There were demonstrations against Britain and France in the streets of Prague last night, and slogans were shouted in support of the Army.

Last night a moving message to the people was broadcast to the crowds in the streets. This spoke of the Czechs, as an unvanquished people and of the sacrifice for the cause of peace made under pressure unprecedented in history.

MR. CHAMBERLAIN AND THE NEW FACTOR

This afternoon at three o'clock Mr. Chamberlain will meet Herr Hitler again, this time at Godesberg, on the Rhine, near Bonn.

But since the Anglo-French plan was drawn up after the first Chamberlain–Hitler meeting at Berchtesgaden a new complication has arisen – the demand of the Poles and Hungarians, now officially put before the British Government, that they also shall have ceded to them their minority areas in Czecho-Slovakia.

That demand, it is being said in Budapest, following on Hitler's interviews on Tuesday with Hungarian and Polish representatives, has the backing of the Fuehrer 'with all the means at his disposal.' ...

The German press now says that Mr. Chamberlain to-day will find himself confronted with a Hitler leading a united front of Germans, Hungarians, and Poles, with the backing of Mussolini. One Berlin paper dismisses the Anglo-French plan as already obsolete.

MUSSOLINI, HUNGARY, AND POLAND

Without mentioning Hungary and Poland specifically, Mussolini in a speech yesterday implicitly demanded a settlement in a way satisfactory to those two countries.

Although Berlin says that there will be no 'precipitate action' on the part of Germany against Prague, the German press has not yet called a halt to its campaign of abuse against Czecho-Slovakia, and the demand is beginning to appear that with the coming 'settlement' the present rulers in Prague must be replaced by men more favourable to Germany.

Yesterday Poland denounced its minority treaty with Czecho-Slovakia.

BRITISH POLITICAL LEADERS' CRITICISMS

Mr. Anthony Eden, the late Foreign Secretary, declared yesterday that the conviction is growing that continued retreat

CZECHO-SLOVAK TERRITORY FOR TRANSFER TO GERMANY

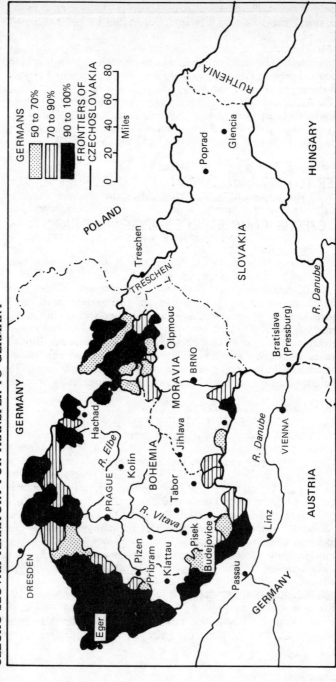

Embodied in the Anglo-French peace plan for Czecho-Slovakia is the transfer of all regions with a population of more than 50 per cent Sudeten German

can only lead to ever widening confusion. 'The people know that a stand must be made. They pray that it be not made too late.'

Mr. Churchill, on his return from a visit to Paris, spoke of the 'complete surrender by the Western democracies,' and said the menace was not to Czecho-Slovakia but to the cause of freedom and democracy in every country.

Sir Archibald Sinclair, Leader of the Liberal Opposition, spoke of 'Britain's humiliating rout.' ...

p.14

HITLER TO LEAD UNITED FRONT AT GODESBERG TO-DAY
Anglo-French Plan 'Obsolete'

CZECHS 'COMPLETELY ENCIRCLED' BY NAZIS AND THEIR ALLIES

Berlin, September 21.

Mr. Chamberlain will be confronted to-morrow at Godesberg with a Hitler leading a united front of Germans, Poles, and Hungarians, with Signor Mussolini as an additional support, according to the German press to-night. This new situation follows yesterday's diplomatic activity at the Berghof and Signor Mussolini's speeches.

Czecho-Slovakia and her Government are treated in to-night's papers as a factor which now carries little weight. ...

CRITICISM OF THE LEAGUE
Litvinoff at Geneva

PROMISE TO HELP CZECHS
Assurances Recalled

Geneva, September 21.

A bitter attack on the League for its failure to protect its members was made to the Assembly by Mr. Litvinoff, the Soviet Foreign Minister, to-day.

The League, he said, was created to replace the old system of military alliances by collective assistance to the victim of aggression, but it had done nothing in this sphere. Abyssinia and Austria had lost their independence. China was a victim of aggression, and Spain was in the midst of a sanguinary war owing to the intervention of armed aggression.

At the present time a fifth State, Czecho-Slovakia, is suffering from interference in its internal affairs at the hands of a neighbouring State. ... 'The sympathies, if not of all Governments, at any rate of all the peoples represented in the Assembly go out to the Czech people in this terrible hour of trial.' (Cheers, mostly from the public galleries).

'There is nothing surprising in the fact that the general discussion in the Assembly has centred on what the League ought to have done but did not do. The League is still active enough to resist aggression. It is only necessary for the obligations of the League to be confirmed and the machinery of the League to be brought into action in conformity with the Covenant.'

RUSSIA'S ASSURANCES

Mr. Litvinoff revealed that when asked by the French Government a few days before the meeting of the League what was the Soviet attitude in the event of an attack on Czecho-Slovakia, he replied that the Soviet intended to fulfil its obligations and to afford assistance to Czecho-Slovakia by the ways open to them. The Soviet War Department was ready immediately to take part in a conference with representatives of the French and Czecho-Slovak War Departments in order to discuss the measures proper to the moment.

'It was only two days ago,' he added, 'that the Czecho-Slovak Government addressed a formal inquiry to the Soviet Government whether my Government was prepared, in accordance with the Soviet–Czech pacts, to render Czecho-Slovakia immediate and effective assistance, to which my Government gave a clear answer in the affirmative. Unfortunately other steps were taken which have led, and could not but lead, to such a capitulation as is sooner or later to have quite incalculable and disastrous consequences. ... To avoid a problematic war to-day and receive in return a certain and large-scale war to-morrow was not to act in the spirit of the Covenant of the League.' ...

'BONUSES TO SABRE-RATTLING'

... Mr. Litvinoff's speech was well received and he concluded amid loud applause.–Reuter.

A GREAT DAY IN GODESBERG

From our Correspondent

Berlin, September 21.

Godesberg, the quaint little town picturesquely situated on the banks of the Rhine – 'Germany's stream but not Germany's frontier' – has suddenly become a beehive of activity as it has leapt into world history. Its few hotels are crowded with journalists and press photographers, and almost every language under the sun can be heard. The streets are decorated with Swastikas, and many Union Jacks are seen.

The Hotel Dreesen, where the meeting will take place, is a fine building with an imposing terrace overlooking the Rhine. Here it was that Hitler rested after his release following the abortive uprising in Munich in November 1923. Since then there has arisen a friendship between the owner of the hotel and the man who to-day is the head of the German Reich. Hitler has his own permanent suite at the hotel, and often stays there.

Three rooms will be used for the conference between Mr. Chamberlain and the Chancellor – his private suite, the big reception hall commanding a glorious view over the river of the Seven Hills mountains, and a special conference room with a long table around which 18 chairs are placed. The British guests will stay on the other side of the river at the Hotel Petersburg. The rooms of the British delegation of 14 are on the first floor. Three rooms have been reserved for Mr. Chamberlain, from which he can see Herr Hitler's quarters at the Hotel Dreesen across the river if he steps up to the window.

HITLER'S CZECH VICTORY
Consequences to the Western Powers

From our Diplomatic Correspondent

London, Wednesday Night.

It is generally accepted that the main points of the Anglo-French peace plan are the transfer to Germany of the regions with a population more than 50 per cent Sudeten German and the international guarantee.

Nothing in the proposals has any real meaning except the demand – or rather order – to transfer territory to the Third Realm. Hitler's victory is absolute. The capitulation of the Western Powers is absolute also. Czecho-Slovakia will soon cease to be a Power at all. The Western Powers have suffered a prodigious loss in strength (relatively to the Third Realm), influence, and prestige.

Their defeat and the storm that is gathering over the so-called 'peace' that has been 'won' are admitted by all serious observers.

If, as has been stated, the guarantors of the new Czecho-Slovakia include Germany and Italy, then it is obviously in their power to make the guarantee meaningless. It is as though the viper and the scorpion were to guarantee the wellbeing of the shorn rabbit. The guarantee means the end of the alliances between Prague and Paris, and between Prague and Moscow. It also means the end of the Little Entente.

If the French and British Governments imagine that they will have the slightest influence on the execution of the order they have given to the Czecho-Slovak Government they are living in a world of complete illusion or self-deception. The details and modalities will be determined by Hitler, and by Hitler alone.

Yesterday Czecho-Slovakia was still in a mood to fight rather than to accept such shameful terms. She was prepared to resist a German invasion, terrible as the odds against her might be. But her Hungarian frontier is ill-fortified, while her Polish frontier is unfortified. Against a combined German–Polish–Hungarian invasion, no fight was possible. The end of the Czecho-Slovak Republic is at hand. It may be that a remnant will enjoy a nominal independence (although even that is doubtful) under German domination. But Hitler has made himself complete master of what was, until now, the only free country east of the Rhine.

There ought to be no illusion with regard to the consequences. They are certain to be disastrous, quite apart from ethical considerations and merely in terms of real politik. It is widely supposed that Hitler, having secured an eastern and south-eastern 'outlet' will ignor the west. He will do nothing of the kind. On the contrary, his western plans will be taking concrete form even now. The importance of the German–Italian–Japanese alliance – that is to say, of the Anti-Comintern Pact – is evident only now.

Hitler is not primarily interested in Eastern or South-eastern Europe. He has to secure his rear against attack, and he requires access to the raw materials of the Danubian Basin, especially Rumanian oil, so that he may be immune to blockade. He will have achieved both these objects now that he will have passed the 'strategic barrier' formed by the forest-clad mountains that separate Bohemia from the Third Realm. ...

ANGER ON THE LEFT IN FRANCE
Socialist Deputies Concentrate Criticism on M. Bonnet

DIVISIONS IN THE POPULAR FRONT AND THE GOVERNMENT'S FUTURE

From our own Correspondent

Paris, September 21.

What is described as 'Bonnet's ultimatum to Benes' is in the centre of all political discussions in Paris to-day. It is stated that late last night such an ultimatum was sent to Prague warning the Czech Government that if they did not accept the London plan they could face German aggression alone without relying on any French help. It is reported here that this French ultimatum was supported by a message from London demanding from the Czechs immediate surrender.

At any rate M. Bonnet's step (which it would appear, was taken without the approval of the Cabinet) caused intense indignation among the Socialist deputies who at their meeting at the Chamber this afternoon, singled him out for particularly severe criticism. He was treated as the principal culprit of the present capitulation of France. Among other things, he was accused of having at a particularly critical moment given a wrong conception to the Cabinet of the part Russia would have played had France made up her mind to defend Czecho-Slovakia. In the Chamber lobbies this evening the speech of Mr. Litvinoff at Geneva to-day was widely quoted as a clear denial of the views of Russia's position in the Czech crisis that M. Bonnet had expressed in Paris after his last meeting with Mr. Litvinoff at Geneva ten days ago. ...

FOREIGN OPINION ON THE CZECH CRISIS
Russian Attack on France and Britain

HELP FOR THE CZECHS ONLY IF THE FRENCH COME IN

From our Correspondent

Moscow, September 21.

On the day on which Mr. Litvinoff reaffirmed at Geneva the Soviet Government's position, to-day's Soviet press becomes more outspoken in its condemnation of the Franco-British proposals. A contrast of policies is implied in the 'Pravda's' assertion in its heading 'Playing with fire.' The Soviet Union, it says, stands alone in defending peace and international justice. Poland is significantly warned that White Russians and Ukrainians predominate in some regions of Poland and that these have the same right to raise the question of self-determination as have the Poles in Czecho-Slovakia.

Under the heading 'The fate of Czecho-Slovakia is the fate of France' the 'Izvestia's' Geneva correspondent declares that Czecho-Slovakia knows from the experience of Spain and China that it is possible to resist the war efforts of the totalitarian States.

There was nothing essentially new in Mr. Litvinoff's Geneva statement. Moscow's silence was broken only to reiterate the statement that the Soviet Government is ready to carry out its treaty commitment's to Czecho-Slovakia. He did not cast any new light on the question of how the Soviet Union proposes to take part effectively in the defence of Czecho-Slovakia and the statement clearly has no bearing on the possibility of the Soviet Union independently aiding the Czechs. Inquiries show that the Soviet Union would go to the help of the Czechs only if France did, and that this is what Mr. Litvinoff promises.

As the British remained apparently determined that they were not willing to go to war on Czechoslovakia's behalf, it is important to remember that Britain did not have any Treaty obligations which pledged her to defend Czechoslovakia. The French, however, most certainly did, but on 21 September 1938 they informed Benes that he had no hope of arbitration as he had expected under the terms of the German–Czechoslovak Treaty of 1925 and they further urged him to accept the Anglo-French proposals 'before producing a situation for which France and Britain could take no responsiblity.'

THE PEACE CAMPAIGN
To-day's Deputation

AN APPEAL FROM CZECHO-SLOVAKIA

The British section of the International Peace Campaign issued last night an appeal to the public calling for a united demonstration, in the biggest possible numbers, to support a deputation which will go from the I.P.C. to 10, Downing Street, at 8 30 p.m. to-day to deliver a protest against the betrayal of Czecho-Slovakia. This deputation will be in response to a telegraphed appeal from the Czecho-Slovak section of the I.P.C. which Lord Cecil, president of the movement, received yesterday. ...

LABOUR PARTY CAMPAIGN
Protest Meetings

THIS 'SHAMEFUL SURRENDER'

From our Parliamentary Correspondent

Fleet Street, Wednesday.

The united British Labour movement, representing the Trades Union Congress, the Labour party, and the Labour Parliamentary party, has done all in its power to-day to inform Mr. Chamberlain, on the eve of his second visit to Herr Hitler, of its detestation of the Government's policy towards Czecho-Slovakia and of its full support for a policy which would defend the integrity of that country. In the words of a resolution passed by the three Labour executives to-night, the Govenment's policy is viewed as 'not merely the sacrifice of a gallant democratic people; it is the sacrifice of the vital British interests involved in the sanctity of international law.'

The moves which have been made by Labour to-day were first the visit of Mr. Attlee and Mr. Greenwood, Leader and Deputy Leader respectively of the Opposition, to the Prime Minister, and secondly the visit of a deputation representing the three executives to Lord Halifax at the Foreign Office. ...

Friday 23 September   *p.9*

TALKS TO GO ON TO-DAY
Premier and Hitler Alone for Over Two Hours

ARMY CHIEF AS CZECH PREMIER
Mr. Chamberlain's Advice: The Danger of Incidents

Mr. Chamberlain was in conference with Herr Hitler for over three hours last night at Godesberg, and will see him again this morning at eleven o'clock.

For two hours and twenty minutes of that time, it was officially announced, Herr Schmidt, the interpreter, was the only other person present.

After the personal interview between the German Chancellor and the British Premier they joined a conference of the two full delegations, which lasted for 45 minutes.

No indication has been given of the ground covered at yesterday's meeting.

PREMIER'S APPEAL AFTER THE TALK

An appeal by Mr. Chamberlain for orderliness in Czecho-Slovakia was contained in a communiqué issued by the British delegation last night after the conversations were over for the day. the communique says:–

> The Prime Minister had a conversation with the German Führer, which, beginning at four o'clock, was continued until shortly after 7 p.m. It is intended to resume the conversations to-morrow morning.
>
> In the meantime the first essential, in the opinion of the Prime Minister, is that there should be a determination on the part of all parties, and on the part of all concerned, to ensure that the local conditions in Czecho-Slovakia are such as not in any way to interfere with the progress of the conversations.
>
> The Prime Minister appeals most earnestly, therefore, to everybody to assist in maintaining a state of orderliness and to refrain from action of any kind that would be likely to lead to incidents.

Last night the German wireless stations continued their abuse of the Czechs.

THE POLISH AND HUNGARIAN CLAIMS

Hungary and Poland yesterday both presented formal demands to Czecho-Slovakia that whatever was granted to the Sudeten minority should be accorded to their minority areas.

Lord Winterton, in a speech yesterday, made the first reference to the new demands of Poland and Hungary that has been made by any Cabinet Minister. He said:

> Unhappily, since the Premier's visit last week two European countries adjacent to Czecho-Slovakia and a large portion of the German press have put forward proposals which go far beyond and indeed have nothing to do with the Sudeten German question.
>
> These countries and newspapers should be under no delusion that there is any foundation for the belief that his Majesty's Government would in any way favour these proposals.

THE NEW CZECH CABINET

Yesterday morning the Hodza Cabinet resigned, and last night the formation of a new Cabinet of national reconstruction, with General Syrovy as Premier, was announced. General Syrovy is a veteran of the Czech Legion, of Great War fame, and is now Inspector General of the Army. He is one of the most popular personalities in Czecho-Slovakia.

The new Cabinet is on a wide national basis and includes Dr. Krofta, the former Foreign Minister, who keeps the same office, two other members of the Hodza Cabinet, and a number of officials, including the Mayor of Prague. There is no Communist member. ...

MR. CHAMBERLAIN'S STATEMENT

Before he left Heston at 10 47 yesterday morning Mr. Chamberlain gave the following message:–

A peaceful solution of the Czecho-Slovak problem is an essential preliminary to a better understanding between the British and German peoples. That, in its turn, is an indispensable foundation of European peace.

European peace is what I am aiming at, and I hope that this journey may open the way to get it.

DR. BENES

Nazi Demand for His Resignation

The 'Volkischer Beobachter,' the principal Nazi newspaper, joins in the demands for the resignation of Dr. Benes. It says:–

'The new spirit in those districts which are to be conceded to Germany forthwith would not be materialising. Prague would not abandon its measures of oppression or release the Sudeten German prisoners or hand over the power to the Sudeten Germans as long as Dr. Benes, who is responsible for the Prague murder system remains in office. The demands of the world should be 'Benes, you must go.''

p.10

REDRAW THE MAP

To the Editor of the Manchester Guardian

Sir,–The danger of war is not over, and supporters of the Left who retain their sanity need to urge two points immediately upon their more warlike colleagues.

First, 1914 must not be repeated. We were urged then to fight for Belgium, for the defence of democracy, and for the sanctity of treaties. We know what the results were; and in 1938 nobody in his senses should fight for Czecho-Slovakia, for the defence of democracy, and for the sancity of the Versailles Treaty. It is the same mouse-trap and the piece of cheese is not even changed. A war between Hitler's Germany and Chamberlain's British Empire, whatever be the intentions of those who support it, would in a few months become nothing but a conflict between two different forms of imperialism. All that we most detest, as anti-Fascists, would be installed in power here.

Secondly, though to keep the Sudetens under Czech control is not worth the blood of a single soldier of any country, the crisis will return in a new form. Under present leadership we shall continue to bluster and retreat until 'British interests' are affected. Then, having deserted Spain and compromised over Czecho-Slovakia, we shall plunge the world into war to keep German Togoland or some such place.

There is only one chance of stopping this miserable process. That is to make a bold attempt to redraw the map of Europe, tearing up the Versailles Treaty, and inviting every Power, including Russia and the United States, to sit in on another peace conference. ... Now may be our last chance.–Yours &c.

J.F. HORRAGIN, RAYMOND POSTGATE.
London, September 20.

p.12

'CHAMBERLAIN MUST GO'
Whitehall Slogan

DEMONSTRATIONS LAST NIGHT

From our London Staff.

Fleet Street, Thursday.

The International Peace Campaign's protest against the Anglo-French plan attracted three or four thousand people to Whitehall this evening, and for a few minutes it seemed as though there might be a serious disturbance.

It had been announced that a deputation organised by the I.P.C. would present a protest to the Foreign Office at 8 30, but the composition of the deputation caused some delay, and it did not reach Downing Street till soon after 10 30. Meanwhile a large crowd had gathered in Whitehall outside Downing Street, which was cordoned off by a dozen policemen, and passed the time by shouting such slogans as 'Recall Parliament,' 'Stand by the Czechs,' and 'Stop Hitler,' 'Save Britain,' 'Chamberlain must go.'

172

FIRST DAY OF TALKS
4 p.m. to 7 15

MR. CHAMBERLAIN'S POPULARITY

From our Correspondent

Berlin, September 22.

The historic Godesberg conference began this afternoon at four o'clock and ended at 7 15. Herr Hitler and Mr. Chamberlain spent the first two and a half hours alone in one of Herr Hitler's private rooms and then went downstairs and continued their talk in the presence of Herr von Ribbentrop, the German Foreign Minister.

When Mr. Chamberlain arrived at the Hotel Dreesen Herr Hitler was awaiting him in the lobby, and after welcoming him heartily went with him up to the room where their talks opened. At the end of the day's meeting Herr Hitler accompanied his guest out to the lobby, where he said farewell to him with another cordial handshake. The conversations will be continued to-morrow morning.

Herr Hitler's special train of eleven shining coaches had arrived at Godesberg at ten o'clock this morning. High Nazi officials were gathered on the platform to welcome him. The Führer, in brown uniform, drove in an open black car to his hotel. He stood most of the way and acknowledged the cheers of the crowd. Even the school children had a day off in order that they could line the streets.

'HEIL, CHAMBERLAIN!'

Two and a half hours later Mr. Chamberlain's aeroplane arrived at Cologne aerodrome after what he declared to have been a 'most interesting flight.' He was welcomed by Herr von Ribbentrop, and after inspecting the guard of honour of Black Guards sped by car to Godesberg. The cheers of the crowd which lined the road were repeatedly acknowledged by Mr. Chamberlain. In fact, the British Prime Minister is a most popular man in Godesberg. Wherever he appears in the streets shouts of 'Heil!' greet him from the waiting crowds.

Mr. Chamberlain and his advisers arrived at their hotel at 2 p.m. They immediately went up to their rooms, and Mr. Chamberlain repeatedly expressed his admiration of the beautiful view of the Rhine River. After a quiet lunch they prepared for their visit to the Hotel Dreesen.

The conference was not yet begun when the German people were informed by enthusiastic reports from Eger that 'Hitler's flag' had been hoisted through the Sudeten regions following upon Prague's acceptance of the proposals. The news of the resentment of the Czech Government was also prominently displayed, and was generally regarded here as a sign of the crumbling of Czecho-Slovakia.

DR. BENES'S APPEAL FOR CALM AND UNITY
Czech President Broadcasts Again

Prague, September 22.

President Benes, in a broadcast address to the nation to-night, said:

'In the whole of Europe changes are taking place, not only in our country. These changes have different forms in different countries. We must, therefore, face the changes with calm and unity. The Czech Government has had to act in accordance with the present circumstances.

'I have never feared, and I do not fear, for the future of our nation. I have made my plans and cannot be surprised by events. I am ready for any understanding that will be favourable for my country, for the pacification of Europe, and for collaboration with Great Britain, France, and Germany.

'Therefore I call upon you to preserve your calm and await developments without fear.

'We are prepared, if necessary, to fight to the last man for our rights, just as we are prepared to negotiate. If we have given way it is to our honour. I see things clearly and I have my plans. Our line of policy is firm. Your patriotic demonstrations I fully understand. They show your interest in the State. Do not lose your feeling of optimism and your common sense.

'Our adversaries expect trouble here and would take advantage of a situation of unrest. Therefore, I repeat that it is essential to keep calm. Have no fear about the future of our Fatherland.

'A new Government has been formed and the names will be made known to you later this evening. It will be a Government of national solidarity. Let everyone return to his post. Do not listen to rumours and provocations. Have no fear, for the nation and the State. The nation has deep roots, and I will close with the words of your national poet, "Czecho-Slovakia will not perish."

'I have a plan for all circumstances. I will not allow myself to be led astray. We desire an understanding on which we are to-day working, an understanding between the greatest nations of the world, and if this should be brought about and should this understanding be honourable our people would find great advantage therein, and there would be a general reconciliation of England and France with Germany and also a reconciliation of Germany and her neighbours, and also collaboration with other States, especially in Eastern Europe.

'Let us save our strength. We shall need it. I repeat once more we shall need it. Let us preserve our mental equilibrium. To-day we need it more than ever before.'

The declaration was preceded by a solemn fanfare of trumpets. Dr. Benes began to speak at 7 15 and spoke for five minutes.—Reuter.

GERMANS SWARM OVER THE FRONTIER

Selb, September 22.

This German frontier town, humming with excitement and rumour yesterday, has become deserted overnight. Like those of other German towns on the Czech frontier almost the entire population has swarmed into Sudetenland. Men, women, and children in every sort of conveyance, laden with bundles of flags, have already bedecked the Sudeten towns with the Nazi emblem and banners. This has given the countryside the air of a gigantic fête.

Czech barriers across the roads which until yesterday used to stop travellers have been converted into traffic regulators.

In Sudetenland to-day the Union Jack is a fine passport. With a Union Jack fixed on each side of our taxi (telephones Reuter's special correspondent) we drove through the streets in Sudetenland to the acclamations of crowds who shouted for England and Hitler.

The railway station at Eger, the post offices, and other buildings have been taken over by the Sudetens, and Czech ticket-collectors and other officials have handed over their duties to the Henleinist Ordnance Corps. Housewives are paying for their food in Eger with Reichsmarks, which they have been collecting for some time, and a number of banks have returned large sums of Czech currency to Prague. One bank this morning dispatched 30,000 kronen to Prague.

The church bells in Selb have been pealing since the evacuation of Sudetenland by the Czech military began at noon to-day. Everywhere there is joy except on the faces of Czech soldiers, resting in ditches by the roadside, and Czech police and gendarmes in their stations. These men are bewildered and sad.

On the Custom-house at Asch the Henleinist Ordnance Corps have mounted guard with fixed bayonets. Everybody is asking where is Herr Henlein and will he have a triumphant entry into Sudetenland. ...

PREMIER'S STATEMENT AT 2 A.M.
'Not a Complete Breakdown'

HITLER'S 'FINAL' PROPOSAL TO BE PUT TO PRAGUE
German Troops Move: Czechs Mobilise

At two o'clock this morning, as Mr. Chamberlain entered his hotel after three hours' conversation at Godesberg with Herr Hitler he told the press:

You cannot call this a complete breakdown. I am making proposals to the Czech Government. It is up to them now.

A communique issued by the German Foreign Office early this morning says:

The conversations between the Führer and Mr. Chamberlain, which were held in a friendly spirit, ended to-day with the handing over of a German memorandum containing the final German attitude to the situation in Sudetenland.

The British Prime Minister has undertaken to forward this memorandum to the Czech Government.

Mr. Chamberlain, accompanied by the British Ambassador, Sir Nevile Henderson, and Sir Horace Wilson, visited the Führer and Chancellor in the presence of the German Foreign Minister to say good-bye to him.

The Führer expressed to the British Prime Minister and the British Government on this occasion his sincere thanks and that of the German people for the efforts to bring about a peaceable solution of the Sudeten question.

The British Prime Minister will leave Germany early this morning by air to return to England.

GERMAN WIRELESS 'SETTLEMENT' REPORT

An announcement early this morning on the Berlin wireless, which must, of course, be treated with extreme reserve, said:—

An agreement has been reached on the basis of an immediate cession of the Sudeten territories. If Czecho-Slovakia disagrees with this, Mr. Chamberlain has promised that Britain and France will disinterest themselves.

A Paris report suggests that agreement may be reached on the basis of the immediate occupation of a section of the Sudeten territory as a 'symbolic' occupation.

MIDNIGHT MEETING

The crisis had become acute last night with the apparent breakdown of the conversations between Mr. Chamberlain and Herr Hitler and movements of German troops on a large scale from Munich towards Salzburg.

All through the day news had been awaited of the resumption of the talks between Mr. Chamberlain and Herr Hitler, but about 8 p.m. it became known that the British Premier was to see the German Chancellor later in the evening to say good-bye and that the British delegation was to return to London by air this morning.

But when the 'good-bye' visit, which began at 10 30 p.m., went on until 1 25 a.m., it seemed that a last effort might have been made to save the situation.

FRENCH PLEDGE

It was learned in Prague yesterday that Britain and France gave Czecho-Slovakia when they pressed her to accept the Anglo-French plan, guarantees of the present frontiers until the negotiations should be complete.

M. Daladier, the French Premier, stated last night that in the event of negotiations being adjourned or broken off France and Britain would certainly have to confer as to the appropriate measures to be taken.

M. Daladier added that if Czecho-Slovakia was the victim of unprovoked aggression France would immediately take the necessary measures for her assistance.

Though nothing has been officially disclosed, it is believed that Mr. Chamberlain had asked that German troop movements should cease during the negotiations and that this proved the crucial difficulty.

TROOP MOVEMENTS

All the while the negotiators at Godesberg were seeking a basis for a resumption of the talks troops and equipment were pouring through Munich by road and rail in a ceaseless stream towards Lower Austria and the Bohemian border. Aeroplanes also flew over, squadron after squadron, in the direction of the frontier.

Last night a proclamation by President Benes was broadcast ordering general mobilisation of the Czech Army.

RUSSIA WARNS POLAND

Soviet Russia yesterday warned Poland that she would abrogate the Soviet-Polish Treaty of Non-Aggression if Poland violated Czecho-Slovak territory and had announced assurances to Prague. ...

177

GERMAN TROOP MOVEMENTS
Roads from Munich to Austria Thick with Traffic

TEN RAILWAY SERVICES STOPPED

Thousands of German troops were moving from Munich in the direction of Salzburg all yesterday. All traffic on ten railway lines running from Germany to Czecho-Slovakia was stopped by the Germans, who alleged that the Czechs were dynamiting the lines. Apparently the lines were wanted for military traffic.

A WORRIED PUBLIC

Munich, September 23.

All day long columns of troops have been pouring through this city in the direction of the Reich motor road which leads from Munich to Salzburg. Trains loaded with troops and equipment have been leaving the station throughout the day. Traffic in Munich has been disrupted by movements of the troops.

One main tram-line has ceased running. Huge crowds have been standing in the streets watching the streams of troops. There is in the city a general atmosphere of anxiety and tension.

The stream of military traffic includes lorries, field guns, transport vehicles, and hundreds of requisitioned private cars and lorries. Soldiers and officers occupy the private cars, and lorries carry the supplies and petrol.

Late this afternoon several squadrons of bombing 'planes flew over Munich in the direction of the north-east. Several motorised columns have been seen on the Bavarian highway with the numbers of the regiments removed from their uniforms.–Reuter.

FULL CZECH MOBILISATION
'Within Six Hours'

'DECISIVE MOMENT ARRIVED'

Prague, September 23.

It was announced over the wireless at 10 20 p.m. that the Czech Government had ordered full mobilisation.

All men of military age up to 40 are to join the colours within six hours.

The mobilisation order – a proclamation signed by Dr. Benes – contained a demand for the immediate requisitioning of horses, motor-cars, and aeroplanes. All civil aviation is to cease immediately.

The announcement was broadcast from all stations in Czech, German, Hungarian, Slovak, Ruthenian, Polish, and Finnish.

The proclamation ends:

> The decisive moment has arrived. Success depends on everyone placing his whole strength at the service of the Motherland. Our fight is a fight for justice and freedom.

The streets are full of cheering crowds. Excitement and enthusiasm are intense. Every motor-car is stopped and either commandeered or requested to take reservists to their stations. Strong guards of police and military have already been placed in front of all the Legations, especially the German. Warning was issued to all shops and other establishments to be prepared for air raids and all windows were darkened.

All news of a military character is subject to a rigorous censorship.—Reuter and Exchange Telegram.

RUSSIAN ASSISTANCE FOR CZECHO-SLOVAKIA
Litvinoff's Reassurance on the Pact

Geneva, September 23.

Mr. Litvinoff, the Soviet Commissar for Foreign Affairs, stated here to-day that if fresh demands were made on Czecho-Slovakia and she decided to defend herself with arms the Soviet Union would only help her provided France did the same. 'Addressing the Political Committee of the League, he said:

'After it had already accepted the German–British–French ultimatum, the Czecho-Slovak Government asked the Soviet Government what its attitude would be – in other words, would it still consider itself bound by the Soviet–Czecho-Slovak pact if Germany presented new demands, the Anglo-German negotiations were unsuccessful, and Czecho-Slovakia decided to defend her frontiers with arms.

'This second inquiry was quite comprehensible since, after Czecho-Slovakia had accepted an 'ultimatum' which included the eventual denunciation of the Soviet–Czecho-Slovak pact, the Soviet Government also had the moral right to renounce that pact.

'Nevertheless the Soviet Government, which for its part does not seek a pretext for evading the fulfilment of its obligations, replied to Prague that in the event of France granting assistance under the conditions mentioned in the inquiry the Soviet–Czecho-Slovak pact will again enter into force.'

Explaining the origins of the pact, Mr. Litvinoff said: 'After the statement I made at the Assembly as to the attitude of the Soviet Government to the Czecho-Slovak problem, I have heard it said that as the Soviet Government makes its help to Czecho-Slovakia conditional upon similar help by France it would appear equally culpable of breaking its pact of mutual assistance with Czecho-Slovakia.

'People who say this obviously are unaware – or pretend to be unaware – that the Franco-Soviet and Soviet–Czecho-Slovak pacts of mutual assistance were the result of actions undertaken for the creation of a regional pact of mutual aid with the participation of Germany and Poland and based on the principle of collective assistance.

TWO BILATERAL PACTS

'In consequence of the refusal of the two countries I have just mentioned France and Czecho-Slovakia preferred instead of a single Soviet–Franco–Czecho-Slovak pact the conclusion of two bilateral pacts. Moreover, it was the Czecho-Slovak Government that at the time insisted that Soviet–Czecho-Slovak mutual assistance should be conditional upon assistance by France, and this was reflected in the treaty in question.

'Thus the Soviet Government has no obligation to Czecho-Slovakia in the event of French indifference to an attack on her. In that event the Soviet Government may come to the aid of Czecho-Slovakia only in virtue of a voluntary decision on its part or in virtue of a decision by the League of Nations but no one can insist on this help as a duty, and in turn the Czecho-Slovak Government did not raise the question of our assistance independently of assistance by France, and this out of not only formal but also practical considerations.'–Reuter.

SUDETENS WAIT
'Help from Reich' Soon

From our Correspondent

Berlin, September 23.

Czecho-Slovakia, in the view of German political leadership, is now a hotbed of Communism. Her Government, the press announces, is 'Red' and her new Prime Minister 'an old friend of the Bolsheviks,' so that Prague is 'acting completely under the orders of Moscow.' It is the same accusation which was raised against Spain, except that in this case it affects the German people more directly owing to the proximity of events both from the point of view of time and distance.

'Communists set fire to buildings,' 'Houses looted,' 'Anarchy reigns,' 'The inhabitants of the Sudeten German towns and villages wait longingly for help from the Reich,' are some of the alarming messages which have reached Berlin in the course of the day. 'Prague's new Government, following orders from Moscow, has let its bloodhounds loose on the defenceless Sudeten Germans,' the 'Berliner Tageblatt' writes, referring to the return of the Czech Army to the frontiers. ...

The line of argument is logical – Czecho-Slovakia in the hands of Moscow; Communists and Red troops inflicting suffering on the Germans; the Germans must have protection, and Bolshevism must be prevented from taking root in the heart of Europe. Now a new map will be drawn 'in a part of Europe,' as the 'Lokalanzeiger' writes, 'which for 20 years was first the military assembly ground of the Entente against Germany from the east and then became the military assembly ground of Bolshevism and its western friends against the Third Reich.'

FRENCH ARMY ON RHINE
Lines Manned

Strasbourg, September 23.

French soldiers on the Rhine frontier here were this evening seen to have their full field equipment. They are ready on their fighting positions to a depth of three kilometres in front of the Maginot Line.

The civil population, calm but serious, are standing about in Strasbourg streets in small groups. They have been told that in the case of an outbreak of hostilities they will at once be evacuated. ...

PLEDGES TO THE CZECHS
France and Britain

Paris, September 23.

In reply to questions asked by a delegation of the Radical Socialist group which he received this evening M. Daladier, the French Prime Minister, said that in the case of negotiations being adjourned or broken off France and Britain would certainly have to confer as to the appropriate measures to be taken.

In case of Czecho-Slovakia's being the victim of unprovoked aggression France would immediately take the necessary measures for her assistance.

M. Daladier added that if events rendered this necessary Parliament would be called in order to assume its responsibility at the same time as the Government.–Reuter.

It was learned authoritatively in Prague to-night that Paris and London have given Prague a definite guarantee that they will not allow the frontiers of the State to be violated in the course of negotiations or during the technical work needed to delineate the new frontier.

This is generally interpreted in Prague as meaning that Britain and France when pressing Czecho-Slovakia to accept the partition plan have promised aid if a German invasion were to take place.–Exchange Telegram.

p.16

ANXIOUS HOURS AT GODESBERG
Premier's Letter and the Long Wait for Hitler's Reply

LAST NIGHT'S FINAL INTERVIEWS

Godesberg, September 23.

As far as can be ascertained to-night that is what has happened in the past 24 hours.

The course of yesterday's conversations with Herr Hitler, coupled with conversations which Mr. Chamberlain had last night with London, gave rise to certin new considerations. It was decided to write a letter to Herr Hitler, and this letter was carefully drafted. Nothing is known of its contents.

The letter was dispatched at about 10 30 this morning, almost at the same moment that the motor-cars were drawing up outside the Petersberg Hotel to take Mr. Chamberlain across the river to see Herr Hitler. Half an hour later the cars were sent away. Then at about 11 30 Mr. Humphreys-Davies, private secretary to Mr. Chamberlain, came into the hall and announced that the morning's meeting was cancelled and that a letter had been sent to Herr Hitler.

FIVE HOURS' WAIT FOR HITLER'S REPLY

Officials on both sides, two hundred journalists from all nations, and large crowds of Germans held back by perspiring Black Guards, gathered outside the Hotel Petersberg and waited anxiously for five hours until Dr. Schmidt, the official interpreter, arrived with Herr Hitler's reply at 3 35 p.m.

Dr. Schmidt left the hotel just after five o'clock. Shortly afterwards the British Ambassador, Sir Nevile Henderson, accompanied by Sir Horace Wilson, the Premier's personal adviser, left the Hotel Petersberg to visit Herr von Ribbentrop, the German Foreign Minister, at the Hotel Dreesen, Herr Hitler's headquarters. The Chief of Protocol, Herr von Dörnberg, accompanied them.

Just after he had gone a girl secretary from the Foreign Office arrived at Mr. Chamberlain's hotel in another car with luggage and typewriter bearing the Imperial Airways label. Until then Mr. Chamberlain had stayed in his suite all day. There is tremendous pressure on all telephone lines. The British delegation had long talks with London and Paris late last night and throughout this morning. This evening it is impossible to get through to London or even to Berlin without hours of delay.

HITLER CONSULTED

Sir Nevile Henderson and Sir Horace Wilson saw Herr von Ribbentrop for two hours, beginning shortly after 6 p.m. During this time Herr von Ribbentrop left the meeting to see Herr Hitler. Later he returned and there was a further short talk. Then Sir Nevile Henderson and Sir Horace Wilson hurried back to Mr. Chamberlain's hotel on the other side of the Rhine. They saw the Prime Minister, and afterwards Sir Horace Wilson made the following announcement to the waiting journalists:–

Sir Nevile Henderson and I have been across to the Hotel Dreesen and I have had two interviews with Herr von Ribbentrop.

The present arrangement is for Mr. Chamberlain to go across late in the evening to see Herr Hitler.

Mr. Chamberlain's present arrangements are to leave for London by aeroplane in the morning.

LAST NIGHT'S CALL ON HITLER

When Mr. Chamberlain left his hotel to see Herr Hitler shortly after 10 p.m. he was accompanied by Sir Nevile Henderson and Sir Horace Wilson. He looked very serious.

Mr. Chamberlain was greeted with shouts of 'Heil!' from a large crowd at the ferry. Four cars were in the procession. The first was an open car full of S.S. Guards and the other three were closed cars.

Earlier in the evening after Sir Horace Wilson had made his statement he was asked whether it was to be taken as signifying a breakdown in the conversations. Sir Horace Wilson replied: 'You will know when you look at what I have told you'.–Reuter.

ANXIETY IN BERLIN

From our Correspondent

Berlin, September 23.

There is a feeling of anxiety and tension in Berlin to-night in view of the apparent deadlock at Godesberg, of which no explanation has so far been offered. The German view that first of all the Sudeten region must be cut loose from Czecho-Slovakia, and that the Sudeten Germans must be placed as soon as possible, if not immediately, under practical protection, undoubtedly played a considerable role in yesterday's first meeting and to-day's exchange of views.

'The question of guarantees is not half so important as the practical secession of the Sudetenland and the extermination of the war danger in Prague,' one commentator to-day says in describing Germany's views.

RUSSIA AND THE CZECHS
Litvinoff's Views

From our own Correspondent

Geneva, September 23.

Mr. Litvinoff has authorised me to say that the assertion in a French paper that about a fortnight ago the French Government asked for military conversations between France and Russia and that the Russian Government refused, is, to quote his exact words, 'an absolute lie.' The truth, he said, is exactly the countrary, as he said in his speech at the League Assembly on Wednesday.

The passage of the speech to which Mr. Litvinoff refers is as follows:–

When a few days before I left for Geneva the French Government for the first time inquired of my Government as to its attitudes in the event of an attack on Czecho-Slovakia. I gave the French representative, in the name of my Government, the following perfectly clear, unambiguous reply:–

'We intend to fulfil our obligations under the pact and together with France to afford assistance to Czecho-Slovakia by the ways open to us. Our War Department is ready immediately to participate in a conference with representatives of the French and Czecho-Slovak War Departments in order to discuss the measures appropriate to the moment.

'Independently of this, we should consider it desirable that the question be raised at the League of Nations, if only as yet under article 11, with the object, first, of mobilising public opinion, and, secondly, ascertaining the position of certain other States whose passive aid might be extremely valuable. It was necessary, however, to exhaust all means of averting an armed conflict, and we considered one such method to be an immediate consultation between the Great Powers of Europe and other interested States in order, if possible, to decide on the terms of a collective démarche.'

p.17

BRITAIN'S 'BLACKEST CHAPTER'
Labour Criticism

Speaking at Horden, County Durham, last night, Mr. Emanuel Shinwell, Labour M.P. for the Seaham Division, said that nobody who had watched the Chamberlain Government in Parliament need be surprised at the turn of events abroad. It was not so much the betrayal of the Czechs that disturbed them, however much that crime deserved condemnation; it was the gradual weakening of democracy and the readiness to yield to force which were the real danger. If the Prime Minister was seeking a general peace settlement he was going the wrong way to secure it. It would not be obtained by allowing Germany to terrorise the Czechs, for that would only encourage Hitler to look round for other victims.

'Does Mr. Chamberlain really believe that Hitler desires a lasting peace?' he asked, 'Does he believe that Hitler will be content with his latest victory? Surely the Prime Minister could not be so childish.'

The Czechs were now completely disillusioned, and other small nations were certian to take note of the situation and refuse to rely on the word of France and Britain in the future. If war should come we should be left to fight our battles unaided. It was the blackest chapter in British diplomatic history.

A WARNING TO AGGRESSORS
Moscow's Motives

From our Correspondent

Moscow, September 23.

The Soviet Government's warning to Poland of its intention to denounce the Non-Aggressive Pact if Poland invades Czecho-Slovakia is evidence that the Soviet Government proposes to maintain in the eyes of the world a policy of dealing firmly with aggressors.

Soviet quarters contrast Russia's attitude towards Japan at Changkufeng with the weakness of France and Great Britain in dealing with Germany, and make clear that Poland is a 'cowardly aggressor' for whom Soviet quarters have little respect. The Soviet press pictures Poland as a bully hiding behind Germany's skirts, or a little pickpocket behind grown-up bandits.

The Soviet Union has more reason than the Polish threat to Czecho-Slovakia to take a serious view of Polish aggression because of her special interest in the Baltic, where Lithuania at least is menaced by Poland in the view of the Soviet.

To-day's Note to Warsaw serves as a notice to the Baltic States that the Soviet Union does not believe in appeasing aggressors at the expense of small countries. An indication that the Soviet Government regards the matter as of the greatest urgency is seen in the fact that the Note was presented to the Polish Chargé d'Affaires at four o'clock in the morning.

BENES'S CALL TO ARMY
'Remain Firm'

Prague, September 23.

In a proclamation to the Army published to-day Dr. Benes says:–

Enemy propaganda both here and abroad is taking advantage of the situation to undermine the confidence of the people in the action of the responsible authorites and to create unrest and opposition among the people.

In this difficult moment the nation has naturally turned to its Army for the strength and organisation for which every-one has made sacrifices. Every true citizen sees in the Army not only his protection, but the salvation of the nation and State.

The Army will deserve this confidence of the population and will stand immovable by the decision of the Government and its Commander-in-Chief the President of the Republic. ...

HITLER'S FANTASTIC TERMS
Mutilation and Paralysis of Czecho-Slovakia

ARMS AND PLANTS FOR GERMANY

From our Diplomatic Correspondent

London, Sunday Night.

The German 'proposals' to Czecho-Slovakia are not 'proposals' at all, but an ultimatum – one of the most drastic ever known. If accepted, it would involve not only the mutilation of Czecho-Slovakia but her total economic, industrial, political, and strategical paralysis.

At Berchtesgaden Hitler demanded the regions where the Sudeten Germans are in a majority of over 50 per cent. Czecho-Slovakia, advised by the French and British Governments to give way, did so almost at once. The result was that Hitler increased his claims, as he had done several times before. What he now demands in his ultimatum (which reached Prague yesterday) is as follows:–

> The immediate cession of all the territories (with scarcely any considerable exception) where there are Sudeten Germans. There is no longer any question of only such districts where they make up more than 50 per cent. Districts where they are in conspicuous minorities or even where there are no Sudeten Germans at all are included.

The proposed frontier line would include large areas exclusively inhabited by Czechs.

All this territory is to be handed over on October 1 (in its present condition), so that, presumably, Czech war material and so on would pass intact into German hands. Germany would acquire all the defences of Bohemia and Moravia and the Czechs would, presumably, be unable to withdraw or even to dismantle their artillery.

Beyond this Germany demands a 'plebiscite' in a number of regions all but one of which have either no Sudeten German inhabitants at all or at the most a very small minority.

THE CONTROL OF THE PLEBISCITES

In the ultimatum it is suggested that the plebiscites be superintended by an international commission. But nothing is said as to how the commission is to be constituted. If it were formed at all, Germans would certainly preponderate (once her ultimatum is accepted she can decide how the plebiscite is to be carried out). The commission – or the commissions – would no doubt be accompanied by German troops or police (as a protection against 'Czech violence,' to prevent 'incidents'). There is every reason to expect that the plebiscite would, in fact, be 'run' by Germany. How otherwise could she hope to secure German majorities where there are no Sudeten Germans?

It is noteworthy, too, how the areas where the plebiscites are to be held have been chosen. Brno is the main junction between Eastern and Western Czecho-Slovakia. If Germany secures this area and the area north of it Czecho-Slovakia will be left with only a narrow corridor to connect her eastern and her western provinces – and in this corridor there is not a single railway.

By securing the region round Jihlava Germany would sever Bohemia from Moravia.

FANTASTIC IN ITS EXTRAVAGANCE

The German ultimatum seems fantastic in the extravagance of its demands, since Hitler is running the risk of a world war to procure in a few weeks what he would otherwise secure in, say, a year. The ultimatum if accepted would make him master of Czecho-Slovakia almost at once, whereas the previous demands which Czecho-Slovakia did accept would, had they been carried out, have made Hitler master of Czecho-Slovakia only after some time, though not, perhaps, a very long time.

Why is Hitler in such haste? If the ultimatum is accepted Germany's rear will be secured. She will soon make herself immune from blockade, she will be in possession of new industries and sources of raw materials, of some of the finest armament and aircraft factories in the world, of great stores of first-class war material (including some of the finest artillery and the finest machine-guns in existence). And of the twenty-five divisions which she has on the Czech border now twenty, perhaps, would be released.

And all this, it is thought, would happen within a few weeks. The next step in this argument is that Germany, with Italy for an ally (or perhaps even with Italy as a neutral Power), would be able to turn west. She would be able to present another ultimatum, demanding perhaps, colonies, or the surrender of the Maginot Line, or a 'plebiscite' in the Flemish regions of Belgium, and so on. She would be able to back this ultimatum with a vastly superior Air Force, a vastly augmented armament, and almost complete invulnerability. In other words, she would have achieved her maximum of offensive and defensive power in relation to France and Britain.

WHITEHALL SCENES
Huge Crowds

SEVERAL ARRESTS MADE

Large crowds gathered in Whitehall during the day to watch the movements of Ministers and officials. A column of youths and girls wearing Fascist armlets swung into Whitehall and in passing the Cenotaph raised their arms in Fascist salute. There were cries of protest from the crowd. 'Put those hands down' and 'No Hitlers here' they shouted. There were long queues all the afternoon filing past the Cenotaph to inspect the wreaths.

As the evening wore on Whitehall was invaded by the biggest crowd since the beginning of the crisis : its entire length was thronged. Small bands of demonstrators shouted 'Stand by the Czechs' and 'Concessions mean war.' The crowds were orderly, but just before the French Ministers arrived two men were arrested. Often the shouting of slogans was drowned by the singing of the 'Marseillaise.'

Hundreds of Fascists walked from a Hammersmith meeting to Whitehall accompanied by police. On the opposite pavement walked people who shouted 'Stand by the Czechs.' When the Fascists reached Wood Street, Westminster, they passed four stationary buses filled with policemen. They reached Whitehall at 10 20 p.m., and as they entered the street they shouted 'Britons fight for Britons only,' and 'Down with the Jews.' Immediately a man stepped forward and knocked one of the demonstrators to the ground. The man was chased for some distance by Fascist sympathisers but eluded them. There was some scuffling, and about six arrests were made. ...

PREMIER'S RETURN

The Prime Minister flew back from Germany on Saturday. There were loud cheers when the Prime Minister reached Downing Street, and these drowned the booing of a small section of demonstrators who were waiting near the Cenotaph. These demonstrators shouted in unison, 'Stand by the Czechs,' and a bundle of pamphlets bearing the slogans, 'Recall Parliament' and 'Stand by the Czechs' were thrown after the Prime Minister's car. ...

ANGLO-FRENCH PLAN
What It Proposed

Details were available from an authoritative quarter last night of the original Anglo-French plan for Czecho-Slovakia, which was accepted by the Czecho-Slovak Government. This plan proposed—

(a) Transfer without plebiscite of areas of over 50 per cent Sudeten German inhabitants with a proviso to arrange by negotiations adjustment of the frontier which circumstances render it necessary by some international body which would include Czech representatives.

(b) An exchange of population on a basis exercisng a right of option freely within some specified time-limit.

(c) If the Czech Government is prepared to agree in these measures, which involve material changes in the conditions of the State it is entitled to ask for assurances of its future security.

A general international guarantee is accordingly proposed in the plan safe-guarding the independence of Czecho-Slovakia against all possible aggression and this would be substituted for existing treaties of a reciprocal and military character.

The British Government has expressed its readiness to join in this international guarantee of the new boundaries of Czecho-Slovakia against 'non-provoked aggression.'

It is learned also that the Anglo-French plan contains a frank acknowledgement by the British and French Governments of the magnitude of the sacrifice which under the plan would be required of Czecho-Slovakia.

HITLER'S NEW DEMANDS
Prague Decides That They Are Unacceptable

FRANCE AND BRITAIN CONFER
Midnight Cabinet : French Army Chief In London To-day

Anglo-French consultations last night on Hitler's 'final' demands to Prague were followed by a midnight Cabinet.

M. Daladier and M. Bonnet had arrived from Paris shortly before 7 p.m. straight from a French Cabinet Council which had approved unanimously a declaration to be put before the British Government. No date has been fixed for their return to Paris.

When Mr. Chamberlain and Lord Halifax met the French Premier and Foreign Minister they were in possession of a message from the Czechs concerning Hitler's latest demands. Unofficially it was understood that the Czech Government had found the terms unacceptable; the text of its reply was being drafted at midnight.

The British and French Ministers began their discussions at 9 20 and were still in conference at 11 25, when this was interrupted for a meeting of the British Cabinet, which had sat for four and a half hours in the morning and afternoon.

After seventy minutes the Cabinet rose at 12 35 a.m. A few minutes later the French Ministers left Downing Street and it was announced that the discussions would be resumed at 10 this morning. M. Daladier, replying to an inquiry about the course of the talk, said 'I can only say it has not been bad.'

GENERAL GAMELIN COMING.

The French Embassy stated early this morning that General Gamelin, the French Commander-in-Chief, will travel to London to-day to join M. Daladier.

HITLER'S NEW DEMANDS

We give on another page the text of Hitler's latest demands, which our diplomatic correspondent describes as being fantastic in their extravagance. In the area to be ceded by Saturday are not only the districts over 50 per cent Sudeten German, but districts where Germans are in conspicuous minorities. There is no mention of a guarantee in the German proposals. ...

Tuesday 27 September   *p.9*

PREMIER'S PLEDGE TO HITLER
Proposal Early This Morning

AFTER FÜHRER'S INSISTENCE ON HIS ULTIMATUM
An Earlier London Appeal

AND WARNING OF 3-POWER SUPPORT FOR CZECHS

After reading Herr Hitler's speech last night Mr. Chamberlain issued the following statement from 10, Downing Street early this morning:–

I have read the speech of the German Chancellor and I appreciate his reference to the efforts I have made to save the peace.

I cannot abandon these efforts since it seems to me incredible that the peoples of Europe who do not want war with one another should be plunged into a bloody struggle over a question on which agreement has already been largely obtained.

It is evident that the Chancellor has no faith that the promises made will be carried out. These promises were made not to the German Government direct but to the British and the French Governments in the first instance.

Speaking for the British Government, we regard ourselves as morally responsible for seeing that the promises are carried out fairly and fully, and we are prepared to undertake that they shall be so carried out with all reasonable promptitude provided that the German Government will agree to the settlement of terms and conditions of transfer by discussion and not by force.

I trust that the Chancellor will not reject this proposal, which is made in the same spirit of friendliness as that in which I was received in Germany and which, if it is accepted, will satisfy the German desire for the union of Sudeten Germans with the Reich without the shedding of blood in any part of Europe.

Hitler, in his speech last night in Berlin, maintained that the Godesberg memorandum is Germany's last word and that Dr. Benes would have to surrender the Sudeten areas by October 1. The choice of peace or war was with Dr. Benes.

A BRITISH WARNING

A statement in authoritative quarters last night said:

During the last week Mr. Chamberlain has tried with the German Chancellor to find the way of settling peacefully the Czecho-Slovak question. It is still possible to do so by negotiation.

The German claim to the transfer of the Sudeten areas (it is added) has already been conceded by the French, British, and Czecho-Slovak Governments. But if, in spite of all efforts made by the British Prime Minister, a German attack is made upon Czecho-Slovakia the immediate result must be that France will be bound to come to her assistance and Great Britain and Russia will certainly stand by France.

It is still not too late to stop this great tragedy and for the peoples of all nations to insist on settlement by free negotiation.

Radio Prague announced yesterday that the Anglo-French recommendations accepted by the Hodza Government are for the present Government, too, the only basis for an understanding.

PREMIER'S ENVOY TO HITLER

Yesterday Sir Horace Wilson, the Premier's personal adviser, flew to Berlin with a 'personal communication' to Herr Hitler from Mr. Chamberlain. The communication was sent with the full approval of M. Daladier, the French Prime Minister, and M. Bonnet, the Foreign Minister, both of whom had been in a 90-minute consultation with Mr. Chamberlain just before Sir Horace set off on his mission.

Sir Horace was with Hitler for 55 minutes, and is returning to London this morning by air with Hitler's reply.

THE ANGLO-FRENCH CONSULTATIONS

Yesterday morning the conference between the French and the British Ministers was completed at 10, Downing Street. General Gamelin, Chief of the French General Staff, who had been called over for consultation, was present during the later stages of the talks and an official communiqué afterwards stated that 'full accord was established on all points.' A meeting of the British Cabinet followed.

General Gamelin later saw Lord Gort, Chief of the Imperial General Staff, and also consulted with French military experts at the French Embassy. Later he returned to Paris by air, whither he had been preceded by the French Ministers.

The King, who had cancelled his arrangements for his Scottish visit to-day at the request of the Premier, held a Privy Council meeting late last night. Earlier in the evening the King had seen the Premier.

At 10 p.m. the 'Inner Cabinet' met and had before them the important portions of Hitler's speech. The meeting ended at midnight.

ROOSEVELT'S APPEAL

President Roosevelt yesterday telegraphed to Germany, Czecho-Slovakia, Great Britain, France, Poland, and Hungary urging that negotiations should continue, recalling the Kellogg Pact, and emphasising the incalculable dangers of war to the social structure of every country.

Mr. Chamberlain and M. Daladier immediately replied welcoming the President's move. In Germany the President's appeal was ignored. No mention of it was allowed on the wireless or in the newspapers. Mussolini did not refer to it in his speech. In Prague, on the other hand, it was immediately broadcast. The appeal was not sent to Italy or to Russia. ...

LIMIT REACHED
No Going Beyond the Anglo-French Plan

GERMANY TOLD

From our Diplomatic Correspondent

London, Monday Night.

Hitler's ultimatum to Czecho-Slovakia is regarded as unacceptable both here and in Paris. Both the French and British Governments stand by the Anglo-French proposals that arose out of the conversation between Mr. Chamberlain and Hitler at Berchtesgaden. These proposals might be carried out more quickly than was originally intended, in which case Germany would occupy those regions of Czecho-Slovakia where the Sudeten Germans are in the majority sooner than was planned; indeed, almost at once, but this is the limit beyond which the French and British Governments will make no further concessions.

Hitler's essential demand, which amounts to immediate control of Czecho-Slovakia and the seizure of her main strategic points, of her main railway system, of many of her industrial centres and armament factories is rejected no matter what form it takes. The Czecho-Slovak Government has been left in no doubt in this respect, while Germany has been informed that if she conducts unprovoked war against Czecho-Slovakia, France and Great Britain will immediately go to war with her.

All hope of peace has not yet been abandoned. If Hitler were willing to engage in further negotiations war might still be averted. If he were to give way now and revert to the Anglo-French proposals he would still have won a prodigious diplomatic victory.

HITLER'S SPEECH

Whatever hope of peace there may still be, it is not to be found in Hitler's speech. He spoke under the stress of terrible emotion. At times his words came slowly and with long intervals between them. But when he spoke of democracy, of Czecho-Slovakia, and Dr. Benes, he worked himself into a passion of fury. At times he roared like a wild animal and his audience – evidently a huge crowd – roared with him. He insisted that his last proposals were final and that he would take the Sudetenland on October 1.

It is very difficulty not to regard his speech as a war speech.

DOMINIONS AND THE CRISIS

Reuter's Ottawa correspondent cables this morning that the Canadian Cabinet is to meet this morning to consider the latest developments in the crisis.

Last night the High Commissioners for Australia, Canada, South Africa and Eire went to No. 10, Downing Street with Mr. Malcolm MacDonald and heard from the Prime Minister the latest developments.

After their calls at No. 10 the Dominions High Commissioners went to the Colonial Office, where it is understood they listened to Hitler's speech.

STAND, WHATEVER THE RISKS
Mr. Attlee's Letter

The following letter from Mr. Attlee, Leader of the Opposition was delivered to No. 10, Downing Street yesterday:–

'Dear Prime Minister,–The terms of Herr Hitler's memorandum which you agreed to submit to the Czecho-Slovak Government have, I believe, profoundly shocked British public opinion.

'The Czecho-Slovak Government could not have done other than refuse these terms, acceptance of which would mean the sheer destruction of the Czecho-Slovak State.

'You will recall that on September 8 the three Executive bodies of the Labour movement declared that–

The British Government must leave no doubt in the mind of the German Government that it will unite with the French and Soviet Governments to resist any attack upon Czecho-Slovakia. The Labour movement urge the British Government to give this lead, confident that such a policy would have the solid support of the British people. Whatever the risks involved, Great Britain must make its stand against aggression. There is now no room for doubts or hesitations.

'These words express the considered and emphatic judgment of the Labour movement, and indicate the only means by which in our view peace may still be preserved. I earnestly trust that his Majesty's Government will now decide to adopt and vigorously to pursue a policy in conformity with this declaration.–Yours sincerely, C.R. ATTLEE.'

The letter was taken to No. 10, Downing Street by Mr. John Dugdale, Mr. Attlee's private secretary.

The National Council of Labour which held an emergency meeting in London yesterday, adjourned until to-day in view of Hitler's speech last night.

There was again a constant stream of callers at No. 10, among them were Mr. Attlee, Leader of the Opposition, and Mr. Arthur Greenwood, deputy leader. Mr. Winston Churchill was another visitor. Afterwards he went to the Foreign Office.

PRESIDENT ROOSEVELT APPEALS TO EUROPE
His Careful Effort to Time It

HINT TO AMERICANS THAT THEY ALSO MAY BE INVOLVED

From our own Correspondent

New York, September 26.

Mr. Roosevelt's appeal to Hitler and to Dr. Benes, as well as to Britain, France, Poland and Hungary, not to allow negotiations to break down and to avoid war was made public early to-day. Replies welcoming the President's move have been received from Britain, France and Czecho-Slovakia, but not from Germany.

The President spent last evening preparing the text of his appeal. Journalists, many of whom were routed from bed, were summoned to the State Department shortly after midnight this morning to receive the text. It is understood that the President had contemplated some such statement for a long time, but he felt it was important not to send it too early or too late.

It is believed that his declaration of two weeks ago that the United States had no commitments to France and Great Britain was intended to emphasise this country's neutrality and to make to-day's appeal the more effective.

The message is also partially intended to impress Americans with the fact that, as the President says, 'in the event of a general war no nation can escape some measure of the consequences of such a world catastrophe.'

While Mr. Roosevelt's message is ostensibly addressed both to Hitler and to Dr. Benes, it is universally assumed here that it is actually directed chiefly to Hitler. Virtually everyone in the United States, including, it is safe to say, the President, believes that the European crisis is almost entirely the result of the German Leader's actions.

An emergency session of the Cabinet is to be held at Washington to discuss the European situation.

DUCE SPEAKS AGAIN
Still Time

HOPES WAR WILL BE LOCALISED
Subjects Ignored

Rome, September 26.

'There are still some days left in which to reach a pacific solution. If this is not found it will need an almost superhuman effort to avoid a conflict,' declared Signor Mussolini in a speech at Verona to-day. He made no mention of President Roosevelt's appeal. Mussolini said:

'The development of events which at this moment are holding people in suspense permits us to-day to summarise the situation. It is necessary to recognise and appreciate the efforts which the British Prime Minister has made. Equal recognition is due to the long suffering which Germany has shown up to now.

'The German memorandum does not deviate from the lines which were approved at the meeting in London. It is evident that if the Czechs are left to rely on their own forces they will perhaps be the first to recognise that it is not worth while engaging in a fight of which the final outcome cannot be in any doubt.

ATTACK ON DR. BENES

'From the moment when the problem was set by the irrestible forces of history it has had a triple aspect – German, Hungarian, and Polish. It must be resolved integrally, and there is one man at the present moment in Europe who is the most indicated as being responsible for what happened. This man is the President of the Czecho-Slovak Republic. He was one of the most obstinate instigators, if not the greatest, of the disintegration of the Habsburg monarchy. He then spoke of a Bohemian nation; his review was called "the Czecho-Slovak nation." He (Dr. Benes) went about declaring everywhere, including at Geneva' – here the Duce's speech was interrupted by howls from the crowd, and he did not finish the sentence. 'Geneva is in the state which doctors call comatose. All the opponents of Italy have to finish thus,' said Mussolini.

HOPE THAT GENERAL WAR MAY BE AVOIDED

'Now the development of events may follow along these lines. There are still some days in which to find a pacific solution. If this is not found only an almost superhuman force can stop a conflict. If this breaks out it will in the first phase be localised. I still think that Europe will not wish to put herself to fire and sword, will not

THE FRONTIERS OF CZECHO-SLOVAKIA

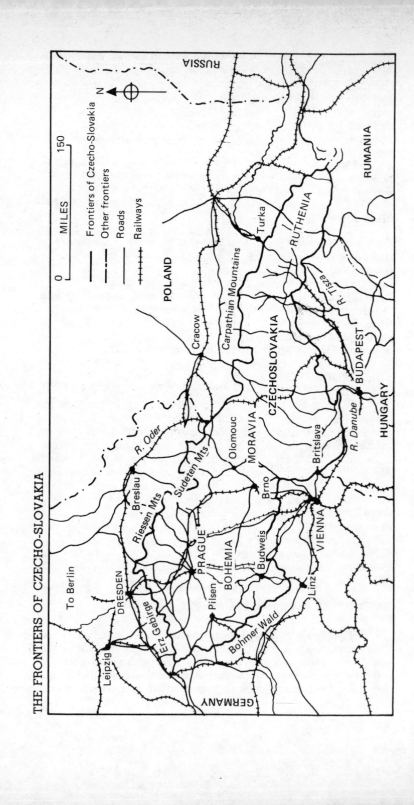

wish to burn herself in order to cook the rotten egg of Prague. Europe has many tasks in front of her.

'Certainly the least pressing of all is that of increasing the number of ossuaries which arise too frequently on the frontier of States. We must, however, foresee a third phase, that in which the extent of the conflict will be such as to involve us directly. It must be added that the progress of these phases can be extraordinarily rapid. ...

LAST CHANCE FOR PEACE
Joint Warning

BRITAIN, FRANCE, AND RUSSIA
Mr. Churchill's Call

Mr. Winston Churchill yesterday issued the following statement:–

'There is still one good chance of preserving peace. A solemn warning should be presented to the German Government in joint or simultaneous Notes by Great Britain, France and Russia that the invasion of Czecho-Slovakia at the present juncture would be taken as an act of war against these Powers. The terms of this Note should be communicated to all neutral countries, some of whom may be balancing their actions, and most particularly to the Government of the United States.

'If such steps had been taken a month ago it is improbable matters would have reached their present pass. Even at the last moment clear and resolute action may avert the catastrophe into which we are drifting. If the Government and people of the United States have a word to speak for the salvation of the world, now is the time and now is the last time when words will be of any use. Afterwards, through years of struggle and torment, deeds alone will serve, and deeds will be forthcoming.

'It will indeed be a tragedy if this last effort is not made in the only way in which it may be effective to save mankind from martyrdom.'

FRENCH OPINION OF THE SPEECH
'For Home Consumption'

Opinion in Paris and in Geneva last night was that Hitler had not burned his boats and that the position had favourable sides.

French officials who take the second view, say that after removing the rhetoric, and although the word 'war' is used for the first time, the speech did not exclude all hope of a peaceful settlement and left matters as they were. There is a distinct impression that the speech was very much impromptu and not one that the Chancellor had summoned 30,000 people to hear. As one Frenchman put it, 'It was an embarrassed and embarrassing speech which leaves matters as they were. The speech was essentially for home consumption.'

On the unfavourable side, French officials dislike the virulent personal attacks on President Benes. But the outstanding fact which makes French opinion pessimistic is that Herr Hitler stood by the exact terms of his latest memorandum and his time-limit.

Reuter's Berlin correspondent says that the tenor of the speech was more conciliatory than was anticipated and even appears to leave a door open for quick negotiation. However, the impression is that he will march on Saturday unless his demands are satisfied.

In Rome, Budapest, and Warsaw the speech was well received.

p.13

EXTENT OF RUSSIA'S OBLIGATIONS
Moscow Statements

From our Correspondent

Moscow, September 26.

To-day the 'Izvestia' prints the full text of the Soviet Union's mutual aid pact with Czecho-Slovakia in reply to numerous requests it has received from its readers for information about this country's commitments. 'Izvestia' draws attention to the fact that the aid is conditional on France's participation.

The Soviet public learned only to-day of the Soviet's warning to Poland against an attack on Czecho-Slovakia. 'Izvestia' follows a brief report of the Soviet's diplomatic action and the Polish reply with a leading article indicating the Soviet's distrust of the Polish assertion that her troops have been concentrated only for defence. 'Izvestia' remarks that time will tell whether Poland has adopted Japan's interpretation of the word 'defence.'

The map shows the area of Czecho-Slovakia of which Hitler demands the cession by Saturday and also the areas in which he would permit a plebiscite.

BRITISH FLEET TO BE MOBILISED
Efforts for Peace to the Last
–Premier's Broadcast

REPORTED GERMAN THREAT OF FULL MOBILISATION
'Prague Must Accept by 2 p.m. To-day'

The Admiralty last night announced that it has been decided to mobilise the Fleet as a purely precautionary measure. The announcement followed a late meeting of the Cabinet.

According to Reuter's correspondent, it was understood in Berlin last night that if a favourable message is not received from Prague by 2 p.m. to-day Germany will order general mobilisation.

Mr. Chamberlain, in a broadcast to the nation last night, declared his determination not to abandon his efforts for peace as long as any chance remains. He repeated the offer made in his statement early yesterday morning of a British guarantee of a prompt fulfilment by the Czechs of their promises. To-day Mr. Chamberlain makes his statement to the Commons.

Vital passages in his broadcast were–

However much we may sympathise with a small nation confronted by a big and powerful neighbour, we cannot in all circumstances undertake to involve the whole British Empire in war simply on her account. If we have to fight, it must be on larger issues than that.

I am myself a man of peace to the depth of my soul. Armed conflict between nations is a nightmare to me, but if I was convinced that any nation had made up its mind to dominate the world by fear of its force, I should feel that it must be resisted. Under such a domination the life of people who believe in liberty would not be worth living.

So long as war has not taken place, there is always hope it may be prevented, and you know I am going to work for peace to the last moment.

After Mr. Chamberlain had spoken last night the B.B.C. sent out on its medium-wave transmitters in German and Italian President Roosevelt's appeal and the replies of the British and French Premiers and Dr. Benes, Mr. Chamberlain's broadcast statement to the British nation, and his statement early yesterday morning after Hitler had spoken.

THE KING TO HIS PEOPLE

The Queen, in the course of her speech at the launching of the Queen Elizabeth at Clydebank yesterday, said:

> I have a message for you from the King. He bids the people of this country to be of good cheer, in spite of the dark clouds hanging over them, and, indeed, over the whole world. He knows well that, as ever before in critical times, they will keep cool heads and brave hearts. He knows, too, that they will place entire confidence in their leaders, who, under God's providence, are striving their utmost to find a just and peaceful solution of the grave problems which confront them.

Yesterday the American Ambassador, Mr. Joseph Kennedy, was received in audience by the King at Buckingham Palace.

'A CASE OF EMERGENCY EXISTS'

The Order in Council published in last night's 'London Gazette' authorising the calling up, announced on Monday, of defence units of the Auxilliary Air Force, contains the following words:—

> Now therefore his Majesty, by and with the advice of his Privy Council, doth hereby delcare that a case of emergency exists.

The War Office announced last night the formation of a women's Territorial organisation for non-combatant duties.

PEACE WITH VICTORY
German Hopes

THE ANGLO-FRENCH SUGGESTION

From our Diplomatic Correspondent

London, Tuesday Night.

The most careful examination of Hitler's speech only confirms the first impression – namely, that it offers no new hopes of peace. But does it close the door on peace altogether? The view taken here is that perhaps it does not.

The French and British Governments hold that the 'Anglo-French proposals' might still be a solution. They are, as they informed Hitler yesterday, willing to accelerate that solution if it is accepted. Could not the towns on the fringe between the Czech–German frontier and the Czech 'Maginot Line' be occupied by the Germans on October 1 and could not the rest of the territory to be ceded (that is to say, the territory where the Sudeten Germans are more than 50 per cent of the population) pass into German hands under the superintendence of an international commission, as provided for in the proposals, though with greater speed than was originally intended, while allowing the Czechs time to dismantle their forts and withdraw their war material and entrench themselves behind the new frontier?

GERMAN HOPES

In his speech last night Hitler did not differentiate very clearly between his ultimatum and the Anglo-French proposals (his German hearers could certainly not have gathered the nature of the ultimatum from his words alone). He might, conceivably, still accept the proposals while gaining the point he emphasises most in his speech – that is to say, the invasion of Czecho-Slovakia on October 1 – without appearing to have given way very much in the eyes of his German public.

It is on some such compromise or convenient interpretation that German observers base their hopes of peace with victory. There is a further suggestion that the Czech Army might withdraw from the Sudeten German regions while the German Army remains where it is on the frontier (or advances a mile or two across it on October 1). But either compromise conceals certain dangers. Once the Czech Army has evacuated its 'Maginot Line' what is to prevent the Germans from using the decisive strategic advantage they will have gained (and without a fight), the advantage of possessing the Czech 'Maginot Line' or the advantage of having secured the abandonment of that line by the Czechs? What is to prevent the Germans, once either of these things has happened, from advancing in greatly superior force into the heart of Czecho-Slovakia and making themselves masters of the whole country by a military campaign?

The answer is that there is nothing whatever to prevent them from doing so, for the intervention of the Western Powers would no longer be able to avert the 'fait accompli' of the German conquest of all Czecho-Slovakia.

PLEBISCITE ASSURANCES

The Germans deny that if there is a plebiscite they will use terrorism and the falsification of returns to secure a majority. And, indeed, it is just possible that these methods, though habitual in Germany since Hitler became Chancellor and Führer, would not be used or would be used in relative moderation. Some of the areas in which the Germans demand a plebiscite are purely Czech. But according to the German interpretation of Hitler's ultimatum and of the map that accompanies it the plebiscite will be held not only in the regions designated on the map for that purpose but in the whole of the territory claimed by Germany (whether through cession or through a plebiscite). In this way a majority would be achieved. The three and a half million Sudeten Germans who would vote for union with Germany (helped by a modest amount of terrorism and falsification of returns) would outweigh an almost equal number of Czechs and so enable Germany to annex a vast territory with a mainly Czech population (and including important industrial towns and railway junctions like Brno) in additon to the regions where the Sudeten Germans form the majority.

There is considerable optimism amongst German observers still. They believe that Hitler's ultimatum will yet be accepted in substance if it can be so interpreted that it will seem outwardly to resemble the Anglo-French proposals. They are convinced that Mr. Chamberlain is willing to grant what Hitler demands if only a form can be found which will conceal their essential character.

PARLIAMENT TO-DAY
Premier's Speech

FULL STORY OF THE CRISIS
Two Days' Debate

From our Political Correspondent

London, Tuesday Night.

The world, having heard Herr Hitler and Signor Mussolini several times expressing what they declare to be the will of their people on the issue of peace and war, will to-morrow see a free Parliament speaking for the oldest of the three remaining great democracies, discussing in the full light of day this country's choice. It should be a sight to fortify the human spirit wherever in the world it still stands by freedom as the indispensable condition of its true development.

It is tempting to pursue analogies between Grey speaking on August 3, 1914 and Mr. Chamberlain speaking to-morrow and there are certainly not a few correspondences. But Grey, though he knew 'the lights were going out in Europe' for a long time, could never have dreamt they would return only to light a stage for dictators more absolute than Kaiser or Caesar in Germany and Italy. Mr. Chamberlain has had to chart his course in a new and more dangerous world, and perhaps he has strained some constitutional doctrines rather severely, and no doubt he will be told so.

But that criticism will not be pressed. It is only too clear that final, if belated, declaration that Britain stands with France and Russia against a violent German solution of the Sudeten problem will unite the House from Right to Left (save for a few exceptions), and in those circumstances the House will be more anxious to exhibit its unity than to argue, say, whether the method of imposing the Anglo-French plan on the Hodza Government was right or wrong. This, of course, assumes that the position to-night will be the position to-morrow.

If, by a miracle, there were to be any new negotiations, some parts of the House, particularly on the Left, would be driven into a more reserved attitude. They would await the result of the new negotiations. But as things are Mr. Chamberlain, whatever question-marks some people would put against his personal adventures in diplomacy, wins the support of the great majority in Parliament. ...

SOVIET 'FULLY PREPARED'
The Two Marshals

From our Correspondent

Moscow, September 27.

No indication is given here that any special military measures have been taken in view of the gravity of the crisis, but foreign quarters in Moscow believe that the Soviet Government is fully prepared for any eventualities.

The Army newspaper the 'Red Star,' in its report on the opening of the Far Eastern Army's Communist party conference, mentions that Marshal Voroshiloff was elected to the praesidium (inner committee), from which it is assumed that the Defence Commissar is attending a meeting 4,000 miles from Moscow at the height of the European tension. Marshal Blücher's name fails to appear in the list, although Blücher is still the Far Eastern commander as far as is known. Reports circulated abroad recently that he had been transferred to the Ukrainian front were not confirmed in Moscow official quarters.

The press does not report Hitler's speech last night, and the wireless reception of it was completely jammed. The German memorandum was published under the heading 'Hitler Demands Actual Liquidation of Czecho-Slovakia.'

YUGO-SLAV SUPPORT FOR CZECHS
Sokols' Pledge

Belgrade, September 27.

Yugo-Slav Sokols (members of the great international athletic and gymnastic association) at a mass meeting here to-night passed a resolution declaring that they were ready at all times to join forces with the Czechs to defend their just cause. A copy of the resolution was sent to Dr. Stoyadinovitch, the Yugo-Slav Premier.—Exchange Telegram.

p.13

CZECH VIEWS ON THE NAZI DEMANDS
An Ultimatum for the Vanquished

WHY IT IS REFUSED

The text has now been made public of the Czech Note that was handed to the British Government on Sunday about Hitler's memorandum. The demands contained in it are described as 'new and cruel.' The reply says:

'Our national and economic independence would automatically disappear with the acceptance of Herr Hitler's plans.

'The Czecho-Slovak people have shown unique discipline and self-restraint in the last few weeks, regardless of the unbelievable coarse and vulgar campaign of the controlled German press and radio against Czecho-Slovakia and its leaders, especially Dr. Benes.

'H.M. and the French Governments are very well aware that we agreed, under the most severe pressure, to the so-called Anglo-French plan for ceding parts of Czecho-Slovakia.

'Nevertheless we accepted it because we understood that it was the end of the demands to be made upon us, and because it followed from the Anglo-French pressure that these two Powers would accept responsibility for our reduced frontiers and would guarantee us their support in the event of our being feloniously attacked.

VULGAR GERMAN CAMPAIGN

'The vulgar German campaign continued. While Mr. Chamberlain was at Godesberg the following message was received by my Government from his Majesty's and the French representatives at Prague:—

' "We have agreed with the French Government that the Czecho-Slovak Government be informed that the French and British

207

Governments cannot continue to take the responsibility of advising them not to mobilise.''

'My new Government, headed by General Syrovy, declared that they accept full responsibility for their predecessors' decision to accept the stern terms of the so-called Anglo-French plan.

'After the return of Mr. Chamberlain from Godesberg a new proposition was handed by H.M. Minister in Prague to my Government with the additional information that H.M. Government is acting solely as intermediary and is neither advising nor pressing my Government in any way. ...

'ABSOLUTELY UNACCEPTABLE'

'My Government wish me to declare, in all solemnity, that Herr Hitler's demands in their present form are absolutely and unconditionally unacceptable to my Government.

'Against these new and cruel demands my Government feel bound to make their utmost resistance, and we shall do so. God helping us.

'The nation of St. Wenceslas, John Hus, Thomas Masaryk will not be a nation of slaves. We rely upon the two great Western democracies, whose wishes we have followed much against our own judgment, to stand by us in our hour of trial.'

BELGIUM
'Not to be Europe's Battlefield'

Brussels, September 27.

The Great Powers have guaranteed Belgium's frontier and all recent information indicates that these engagements will be kept,' declared Mr. Spaak, the Belgian Prime Minister, in a broadcast to the nation shortly after Mr. Chamberlain's broadcast.

'Our territory will not be the battlefield of Europe. Belgium is independent and strong. We want to keep war outside all our frontiers. Our Army is magnificent and is the rampart of our independence. The Government has taken certain security measures during the last few days and has completed them to-day on a reinforced peace footing.'

The Prime Minister expressed admiration for President Roosevelt's appeal and said force was no solution for the future.' The more just is the cause the less is force needed. During the present tension, Belgium affirms her policy of independence and looks to the King's declaration of two years ago.

'Be united; be confident,' the Premier finally exhorted. The calling up of the six classes on which the Belgian Cabinet decided to-day affects about 200,000 men.—Reuter.

When Belgium opted for a return to her neutral status of pre-1914 King Leopold, in making the announcement on 14 October 1936, stated 'This policy should aim resolutely at keeping us apart from the quarrels of our neighbours.' For France this meant that she could not enter Belgium until Hitler had already invaded. This was yet another and probably the most important in the line of events which shattered her defensive strategy based as it was on the concept of the Maginot Line defence fortifications.

THE EXODUS FROM PARIS
Protection of Books and Works of Art

From our own Correspondent

Paris, September 27.

It has been another day of tension in Paris. Many political observers have been, as it were, examining Hitler's speech through a microscope, hoping to find some symptom of retreat from the Godesberg memorandum. Some have discovered the absence of any reference to the map attached to the memorandum and some other possible ambiguities in his speech. But on the whole the speech has created a deplorable impression, and the hopes that Sir Horace Wilson or Mr. Chamberlain or anybody can stop Hitler are not running high.

The authoritative British warning and the Premier's statement that the British Government would guarantee that the Czech Government carried out its obligations are considered to be of great importance, although it is wished that Mr. Chamberlain had made some friendly reference to Dr. Benes, if only as a contrast to Hitler's stream of abuse.

The French Cabinet met this morning and its deliberations were rather based on the assumption that in the absence of better news the worst must be expected. It is probable that unless there is a distinct improvement in the next 24 hours several hundred thousand more reservists will be called up.

The exodus from Paris increases in intensity and the stations are crowded with people going, or at least taking their children, to the country. The Louvre and other museums were closed to the public to-day and the manuscripts and the more valuable books are being sent away by the National Library.

There is much agitation at the Chamber in favour of an immediate summoning of Parliament, and feeling on the Left is running high against M. Bonnet.

The resignations of MM. Paul Reynaud, Mandel, and others who stood for a policy of firmness are no longer spoken of.

AMERICA HEARS PREMIER
Vast Audience

From our own Correspondent

New York, September 27.

Mr. Chamberlain's broadcast address is printed in full in the evening papers here to-night. It appears to have made a deep impression in the United States. It was broadcast throughout the country, and the listening audience has been estimated at anything up to 50,000,000 persons. While the broadcast was going on taxi-cabs could be seen parked along the streets of New York with their wireless sets turned on and knots of listeners grouped about them.

No comment has come so far from Washington officials on either Mr. Chamberlain's statement or Hitler's reply to Mr. Roosevelt's appeal, which was received here shortly before noon. It is known that the President studied Hitler's statement with care before attending the emergency session of the Cabinet held to-day.

Thursday 29 September   *p.9*

GREAT RELIEF IN BERLIN
A Remarkable Change

PUBLIC EXPECTS AN AGREEMENT
Nazi Comment

From our Correspondent

Berlin, September 28.

The news of the Four-Power Conference at Munich to-morrow, the biggest piece of news Berlin has heard for a long time, dispelled with one slash the gloom and pessimism which had settled down. Expressions of relief are heard wherever the news is discussed, but it was not made known until half-past eight, thus coming too late for the evening papers. The few who have heard of it are saying 'Thank God that the danger of war has been averted.'

There could scarcely have been a greater anti-climax to yesterday's and this morning's despondency here than this piece of news. There is a difference like between day and night. Even political commentators for once abandoned their scepticism and have expressed themselves hopefully. They say that the final settlement has come nearer and a way will no doubt be found, for where four men talk the difficulties must thin down.

THE MEETING PLACE

Preparations in Munich are in full swing. It is believed, though not yet confirmed, that the imposing new Führer House on the likewise imposing Royal square will be selected. Mussolini was a guest there when he was in Germany last year.

To-night's 'Diplomatic Correspondence' once more quickly takes up some of the recent points in the argument and clarifies the German viewpoint before the conference begins.

If the Czechs complain that they must surrender valuable economic districts in Sudeten Germany, it writes the answer is that the Germans do not want any valuable Czech districts and expect a reciprocal attitude on the part of the Czechs. If, moreover, the Czechs worry about the loss of important strategical points and insinuate that Germany wanted to destroy Czecho-Slovakia,

they ignore intentionally Hitler's latest statements in which he declares that he rejected incorporation of Czech soil. ... In this respect every guarantee is given on the part of Germany for the security of the new frontiers.

The 'Diplomatic Correspondence' concludes by urging speed for two reasons, so it says. One is to prevent further suffering and destruction. The other is the lack of dependability of the Czechs, 'which permits no other choice but to take away immediately from them the power over foreign racial soil.'

ATTACKS ON DR. BENES

The press continues its attacks on Dr. Benes. Protest meetings all over the Reich have taken place. Banners of 'Make an end of Benes' and 'Benes tells lies Hitler is victorious' were carried in a demonstration in Frankfurt.

211

RESPITE IN THE LAST HOURS
Munich Conference To-day

PREMIER, HITLER, MUSSOLINI, AND DALADIER
German Mobilisation Postponed

'The crisis has once more been postponed and there is one more opportunity to try what reason and goodwill and discussion can do,' said Mr. Chamberlain in the House of Commons yesterday in announcing a new conference in Munich to-day.

The news, totally unexpected, reached Mr. Chamberlain only towards the end of a long speech in which the House felt itself on the brink of war. Then came a pencilled note handed to the Premier by Sir John Simons. It announced an invitation to Mr. Chamberlain to meet Herr Hitler in Munich to-day, together with Signor Mussolini and M. Daladier, the French Premier. This was in response to a suggestion made by the Premier, who had also written to Signor Mussolini.

There were remarkable scenes of enthusiasm in the House at this announcement, and after short speeches by Mr. Attlee and Sir A. Sinclair the House adjourned until Monday.

'THIS LAST EFFORT'

The Premier said that in response to an appeal by Signor Mussolini Herr Hitler had agreed to postpone mobilisation for 24 hours, and went on:

> This is not all. I have something further to say to the House yet. I have now been informed by Herr Hitler that he invites me to meet him at Munich to-morrow morning. He has also invited Signor Mussolini and M. Daladier. Signor Mussolini has accepted, and I have no doubt M. Daladier will also accept. I need not say what my answer will be. We are all patriots, and there can be no hon. member of this House who did not feel his heart leap that the crisis has been once more postponed to give us once more an opportunity to try what reason and goodwill and discussion will do to settle a problem which is already within sight of settlement. I go now to see what I can make of this last effort.

Mr. Chamberlain's announcement followed a long and frank recital of his conversations with Herr Hitler, conversations in which Hitler had made it clear that he was determined to have his way even at the cost of a world war.

Mr. Chamberlain will leave Heston by air at 8 30 this morning. Signor Mussolini accompanied by Count Ciano, left Rome by train last night. M. Daladier's acceptance of the invitation was announced by him in a broadcast speech last night. Herr Hitler left Berlin last night accompanied by Field Marshal Göering.

With the Premier will be Sir Horace Wilson, Sir William Malkin, of the Foreign Office, Mr. Ashton-Gwatkin, and Mr. William Strang.

It was learned last night that Mr. Masaryk, the Czecho-Slovak Minister in London, had asked Mr. Chamberlain that a representative of Czecho-Slovakia should be present at the Munich conference. Mr. Chamberlain replied that he was considering the matter, and would communicate with Dr. Benes.

PAVING THE WAY

The way for the Munich conference was prepared yesterday morning by the four Governments. In Berlin Hitler saw the French Ambassador for an hour and immediately afterwards the British Ambassador for over an hour. In Rome our Ambassador saw the Foreign Minister twice during the morning, the second time handing him a message from Mr. Chamberlain urging Mussolini to support the British efforts for peace. Mussolini got into contact with Hitler, and the Munich conference was announced.

FOOD HOARDING

As a result of information that there has been increased purchasing of foodstuffs in the last few days, the Board of Trade yesterday issued an appeal against hoarding and an assurance that supplies will be adequate and well controlled.

The Board of Trade yesterday made an order suspending until after October 16 the validity of outstanding export licences for war material for foreign countries. The order, it is explained, has been made to enable outstanding licences to be reviewed, but it is not the intention that all exports should be prohibited.

A STRANGE ATMOSPHERE
Contrast with the Temper of 1914

From our Political Correspondent

Westminster, Wednesday Night.

The unparalleled scenes in the House of Commons at the end of Mr. Chamberlain's speech are described elsewhere. They will live in memory's eye as the most remarkable that one Parliamentary journalist has ever seen at Westminster. The Commons standing on the benches and waving order-papers for Philip Snowden's Emergency Budget and his closing lines from

Swinburne's great rhapsody on England's faith in her stars – that, the most memorable scene in the House of Commons for years, was nothing to this.

The Tories were up and wildly cheering, not once but a number of times. Some Liberals joined them and one or two Labour men. The rest of the Opposition remained seated and constrained. Possibly they did not want to rush in and identify themselves prematurely with a four-Power move that might have darker objectives than a settlement of the Sudeten problem.

DIPLOMATISTS AND CHEERS

But their undemonstrativeness only heightened that of everybody else, for the clapping and the cheering were carried up to the roof. The side galleries were packed with cheering Tories. The Diplomatic Gallery was also on its feet applauding – the Diplomatic Gallery, if you please! – and Signor Grandi, with that handsome Italian Renaissance head of his, was admirably leading the clapping. Above them and taking their lead from the diplomatists were the general public, and they clapped with such resolution that the attendants came up in an attempt to stop them.

On the other side of the dock the peers were standing – Lord Baldwin, Lord Halifax, the Archbishop of Canterbury and the rest. But they just stood. They have been trained in a severe school of self-control.

CONTRASTS

But this tumultuous culmination to the speech was not the only unusual thing. This crisis has never for long escaped a touch of unreality. A world war for the difference between the Anglo-French plan and the Hitler memorandum has always carried gleams from the larger lunacy about it, and there was something about the atmosphere of the House to-day that did not quite match the momentous issues of peace or war. Why, it is not easy to say, because everybody was convinced up to Mr. Chamberlain's speech that only hours stood between us and war with Germany.

When Grey spoke in August 1914, they had to bring in chairs for surplus members and set them in the wide aisle leading up to the table. No chairs were necesssary to-day. Some Labour members found occasion for laughter during Mr. Chamberlain's speech. Nobody wanted to laugh in 1914.

WHY?

The House hung on every word of Grey. They did not hang on every word of Mr. Chamberlain. Twice Mr. Churchill conspicuously yawned. It was only the end of the speech that brought the House bolt upright.

This difference in temper between 1914 and now is baffling. Is it because the suspense has been almost unendurably prolonged and that even modern war is not more terrible than the everlasting anxiety? Whether this is the true explanation or not, the Romans knew something of the psychology of it. There is their saying, 'The fear of war is worse than war.'

'IT'S ALL RIGHT NOW'
Smiling Premier

Facing a cheering crowd in Downing Street last night, Mr. Chamberlain cried, 'It's all right this time.'

Mr. Chamberlain had just returned from making his momentous announcement in the House of Commons and his optimistic shout had an electrifying effect on the crowd. It was a changed Premier that the watchers saw, smiling and confident, in great contrast to the serious-faced figure which had left for Parliament only two and a half hours before.

Mr. Chamberlain seized his wife's hand and shook it warmly, and by a gesture claimed a share of the cheers for her.

p.12

TO-DAY'S MUNICH CONFERENCE
What Basis?

GERMAN CONCERN AT WAR DANGER

From our Diplomatic Correspondent

London, Wednesday.

The optimism of German observers is being justified, it would seem. Last night and this morning it was known here that concern over the prospect of a European war, with Great Britain as one of the belligerents, was rapidly growing in Germany, that it was spreading throughout the 'Labour Front,' and was getting very near those responsible for the conduct of German policy. Whether this concern has had any influence on the situation and whether it has compelled Hitler to suggest the new conference is not very clear, but it may well have had a certain effect. But there can be no doubt at all that, whatever the motives may be, Hitler's move has strategic value as a withdrawal carried out so as to occupy stronger positions than heretofore.

215

German mobilisation was to have begun at two o'clock to-day. That this was so has been known here since yesterday. It is a little difficult to understand what German mobilisation means, seeing that Germany had already mobilised.

What is to be the basis of the discussions in Munich? Presumably the 'Anglo-French proposals.' The German view is that Hitler's ultimatum to Czecho-Slovakia can be so interpreted that it is not so incompatible with the 'Anglo-French proposals' as it might seem to be. That is to say, these proposals will be the formal basis, while the ultimatum (and the map that goes with it) will be the real basis; or, to put it differently, the 'Anglo-French proposals' will be the shadow, Hitler's ultimatum the substance (in the manner explained in this correspondence yesterday).

The intervention of Mussolini raises a further question – namely, does he expect any advantages more tangible than increased importance or enhanced prestige? What does he want, in concrete terms, for his 'contribution to peace'? Is it Spain?

It may well be that Hitler will begin his occupation of the Sudetenland on Saturday (with the consent of the statesmen assembled at Munich) and take possession of merely the fringe (with towns like Asch and Eger) that lies outside the Czech fortified lines. In this way he will at least have fulfilled, or seem to have fulfilled, a promise he made to his audience on Monday.

BROADCAST BY DALADIER
France Accepts

M. Daladier, the French Premier last evening announced his acceptance of the invitation to the Munich conference in a broadcast. He said:

This afternoon I received the German invitation to see Signor Mussolini, Mr.Chamberlain and Herr Hitler to-morrow morning. I have accepted this invitation.

Before my departure I wish to address to the people of France my sincere thanks for the courage and dignity which they have shown in this difficult situation. My special gratitude and greetings go out to those citizens of France who were called to the colours in these last few weeks. I thank them for the calm, sang-froid, and resolution with which they have followed the call of their country.

The task ahead of me is still difficult. You will understand, therefore, that I cannot say much to you now, except this – since the beginning I have not for one minute ceased to work for this supreme aim, the preservation of peace and security for France and the world. To-morrow I will continue this task, and it will be a source of great satisfaction to me to know that I am in full agreement with the entire nation.

M. Daladier spoke only for three minutes.

WHY MOSCOW IS SO CALM
Crisis News 'Purged'

From our Correspondent

Moscow, September 28.

Moscow must be one of the calmest places in Europe to-day, thanks to the thorough way news from abroad is being kept from the public.

Only short messages from other capitals appear from time to time. One paper alone disclosed this morning that the British fleet is being mobilised, and even this item was dismissed in two lines without comment. Herr Hitler's speech on Monday was ignored altogether until to-day, when the Soviet press reported it in the single sentence: 'Hitler made a speech containing sharp attacks on the Czecho-Slovak Republic and on President Benes.'

Articles are published seeking to prove that Germany's economic position is unfavourable to a warlike venture and that her military strength has been exaggerated.

Foreign observers here comment on the complete absence of efforts through propaganda to stir up popular feeling in Moscow in preparation for Soviet Russia's possible entry into war. This is in striking contrast with the thousands of meetings and the flood of resolutions when foreign forces intervened in the Spanish war and when Japan invaded China.

SUGGESTED SOVIET APPEAL

Moscow, September 28.

The Soviet Union is willing to support President Roosevelt's proposal to hold an international conference and to play an active part in it, M. Potemkin, the Assistant Commissar for Foreign Affairs, stated here to-night.

He was replying to a suggestion from the United States that the Soviet should also appeal to Germany and Czecho-Slovakia to settle the Sudeten issue peacefully. The suggestion was made in the following communication to the Soviet Government submitted by Mr. Alexander Kirk, Counsellor of Embassy:—

'If the head of the Soviet Union or of the Government considers it necessary immediately to appeal to Germany and

Czecho-Slovakia as the United States did, calling attention to the extra-ordinary importance of not applying force for the settlement of the present conflict, the cumulative effect of such an expression of public opinion would influence the development of events and help in the preservation of the peace of Europe.—Reuter.

RUMOURS IN LONDON
Cheering Crowds

Rumours of a settlement at Munich spread all over London last night. There was applause at public gatherings, and at the theatre 3,000 people stood cheering wildly. At another there were special cheers for the Premier.

Crowds of women made Mrs. Neville Chamberlain the centre of an affectionate demonstration. She had been at St. Michael's Church, Chester Square, London, where the Archbishop of Canterbury had addressed a crowded broadcast midweek service. ...

AGREEMENT SIGNED AT MUNICH
Full Text of Terms

GERMAN OCCUPATION TO BEGIN TO-MORROW
New Czech State 'Guaranteed'

The Munich conference between Mr. Chamberlain, M. Daladier, Herr Hitler, and Signor Mussolini, which started soon after midday yesterday, ended at 1 30 this morning, and at 2 30 the terms of the agreement reached were issued.

Following is the official text of the communique as issued by the German News Agency:—

Agreement between Germany, Great Britain, France, and Italy concluded in Munich on September 29, 1938.

The conversations which the Chiefs of the Governments of Germany, Italy, France, and Great Britain began on Thursday noon have found their conclusion in the late evening.

The agreements which were reached, which are laid down in the following articles, have been immediately transmitted to the Czech Government.

Germany, the United Kingdom, France and Italy have agreed, taking into consideration the settlement already agreed upon in principle concerning the cession of the Sudeten German districts, on the following conditions and procedure and the measures to be taken, and declare themselves individually held responsible by this agreement for guaranteeing the steps necessary for its fulfilment.

1. The evacuation begins on October 1.

2. The United Kingdom, France, and Italy, agree that the evacuation of the region shall be completed by October 10 without destruction of any of the existing installations and that the Czecho-Slovak Government bears the responsibility for seeing that the evacuation is carried out without damaging the aforesaid installations.

3. The conditions governing the evacuation will be laid down in detail by an International Commission composed of representatives of Germany, the United Kingdom, France, Italy, and Czecho-Slovakia.

4. The occupation by stages of the predominantly German territories by German troops will begin on October 1. ... The remaining territories of predominantly German character will be ascertained by the aforesaid International Commission forthwith and be occupied by German troops on October 10.

5. The International Commission referred to in paragraph 3 will determine the territories in which a plebiscite is to be held. These territories will be occupied by international bodies until the plebiscite has been completed. The same Commission will fix the conditions in which the plebisicte is to be held, taking as a basis the conditions of the Saar plebiscite.

The Commission will also fix the date not later than the end of November on which the plebiscite will be held.

6. The final determination of the frontiers will be carried out by the International Commission. This Commission will also recommend to the four Powers, Germany, the United Kingdom, France, and Italy, in certain exceptional circumstances minor modifications in the strictly ethnographical determination of the zones which are to be transferred without plebiscite.

7. There will be a right of option into and out of the transferred territories, the option to be exercised within six months of the date of this agreement. A German–Czecho-Slovak Commission shall determine the details of the options, consider ways of facilitating the transfer of population, and certain questions of principle arising out of the said transfers.

8. The Czecho-Slovak Government will within the period of four weeks from the date of this agreement release from the military and police forces any Sudeten Germans who may wish to be released, and the Czech Government will within the same period release Sudeten German prisoners who are serving terms of imprisonment for political offences.

An annex to the agreement:

His Majesty's Government in the United Kingdom and the French Government have entered into the above agreement on the basis that they stand by the offer contained in paragraph 6 of the Anglo-French proposals of September 19 in relation to an international guarantee of the new boundaries of the Czecho-Slovak State against unprovoked aggression.

When the question of the Polish and Hungarian minorities in Czecho-Slovakia has been settled Germany and Italy for their part will give a guarantee to Czecho-Slovakia.

The heads of the Governments of the four Powers declare that the problems of the Polish and the Hungarian minorities in Czecho-Slovakia if not settled within three months by agreement between the respective Governments shall form the subject of a further meeting of the heads of Governments of the four Powers here present.

Supplementary declarations:

All questions which may arise out of the transfer of the territories shall be considered as coming within the terms of reference to the International Commission. Munich, September 29, 1938.

The agreement is, of course, between the four Powers only. Czecho-Slovakia was not represented at the conference, although two Czech diplomats were in Munich for information.

PLANS FOR EVACUATING LONDON AND BIG CENTRES
Ready to be Put Into Operation

TRANSPORT & 48 HOURS' RATIONS FREE: BILLETS IN PRIVATE HOUSES

Emergency evacuation plans for London and other big cities – to come into operation only when announced by the Government – were described last night in a Home Office statement.

There are two separate schemes, both voluntary – a general one for members of the public and a special one for school children in charge of teachers. The refugees would be taken thirty to fifty miles from London by train and thence to various villages and towns. At the beginning the Government would pay for the billets, which generally would be in private houses, but later those who could afford it would have to contribute. At the railhead each refugee would draw a 48 hours' food ration, and transport would be free. The Government would pay the cost of billeting school children under the second scheme.

The arrangements which were broadcast last night apply to London, but the Home Office points out that plans on similar lines are being made for some of the big cities and will be made known there.

FREE TRANSPORT

On the days fixed by the Government those wishing to leave by the special arrangements should make their way to announced railway stations. Everyone should take respirators. Only small hand luggage may be taken. Refugees should wear their warmest clothes and should take some food for the journey and a rug or blanket. No domestic animals, such as dogs or cats, could be taken.

At the 'pick-up' stations the refugees would be given a free railway ticket and then taken by train thirty to fifty miles from the centre of London. No one would be allowed to choose his destination, but a special franked postcard would be issued to every person, so that when billeted they could write to relatives or friends giving the address. Transport from railway stations to the billets would be free.

THE BILLETS

Billets would generally be in private houses. Householders would be required by the billeting officers to receive refugees up to the limit of one person for each habitable room in the house. If a house has six habitable rooms and there are four persons resident, that household would be required to take two refugees. At the beginning the Government would pay for the billets, though later it is expected that those who could afford to would contribute to the cost.

The 48-hour food ration drawn at the railhead would include canned milk, and would be free. After that refugees would be expected to buy their own food, and arrangements would be made for extra supplies in the local shops. Those in immediate need of money could apply to the nearest office of the Ministry of Labour, taking their billeting form.

The Government would pay to each householder upon whom a refugee is billeted 5s. a week for each adult and 3s. for each child under 14. In return the householder would have to provide shelter, water, and access to sanitation. The Government is confident that the householder would also provide cooking facilities and help the refugees in other ways.

SCHOOL CHILDREN

The second plan is one under which school children in the congested areas of London whose parents were unable or unwilling to leave could be sent away in the care of their teachers. The children would go to school in the ordinary way and be sent to their billets in groups.

Each child should have his or her warmest clothes, an overcoat or macintosh, a handbag, a blanket, food, an apple or orange, and a respirator. No drinks in glass bottles would be allowed. No one but teachers could go with them or be allowed in the trains or stations. All ordinary train services would be interrupted from about 10 a.m. to 4 p.m. on the days fixed.

The householder who takes the chidlren in would be expected to give them board and lodging and to look after them. It is hoped that they would be regarded as members of the family. The Government would pay the householder 10s. 6d. a week if one child were taken and 8s. 6d. for each child if more than one child were taken.

PARENTS' APPROVAL

If possible, groups from each school would be billeted close together. Notices would be posted outside schools telling parents where to write to their children.

The plan has received wide approval from parents, adds the Home Office. It would be entirely voluntary, and no parents need send children out under the scheme if they did not wish to do so. It is hoped, however, that as many as possible would be allowed to go.

The announcement adds that due warning and more precise instructions would be given when and if necessary.

Saturday 1 October p.7

THE THREE PLANS FOR CZECHO-SLOVAKIA
Anglo-French, Herr Hitler, and the Munich Agreement

Following is a comparison of the three sets of proposals for settling the Czecho-Slovak crisis – the Anglo-French plan, Herr Hitler's 'ultimatum,' and the Munich agreements:–

THE ANGLO-FRENCH PROPOSALS OF SEPTEMBER 19

1. All areas with over 50 per cent of Sudeten Germans to be transferred to the Reich. No time-limit mentioned.
2. No plebiscite.

222

3. Adjustment of frontiers by an international body, which was to include a Czech representative.
4. Exchange of population on the basis of a right of option within a time-limit.
5. An international guarantee to be given to Czecho-Slovakia by the United Kingdom and other countries against unprovoked aggression: this guarantee to take the place of existing treaties between Czecho-Slovakia, France, and Russia.
6. The French and British Government recognise how great is the sacrifice required of the Czecho-Slovak Government in the cause of peace.

HERR HITLER'S MEMORANDUM OF SEPTEMBER 23

1. These areas (and certain others, although they have not a majority of Sudeten Germans) to be occupied by German troops by October 1.
Czech troops and police, Customs officials, and frontier guards to withdraw.
The territory to be handed over intact, including fortifications, all plant and establishments, materials, railway rolling stock, aerodromes, wireless stations, utility services (gasworks, &c.,) food-stuffs, goods, cattle, raw materials, and so on.
A Czech plenipotentiary may be attached to the German Army headquarters to settle evacuation details.
1a. All Sudetens in the Czecho-Slovak Army or police to be discharged to their homes. All German political prisoners in Czecho-Slovakia to be liberated.
2. A plebiscite to be held, not only in these areas but in other specified areas, before November 25.
The plebiscte to be held under the control of an international commission.
Voters must have been born or resident in the plebiscite areas before October 28, 1918. The majority vote to determine the issue.
During the plebiscite both parties will withdraw their military forces.
3. Alterations to the new frontiers arising out of the plebiscite to be settled by a German–Czech or an international commission.
3a. An 'authoritative' German–Czech commission to be set up to settle all 'further details.'
4. No provision.
5. No provision.
6. No recognition.

1. The evacuation of these areas to begin on October 1 and be completed by October 10.
   No destruction of or damage to 'any of the existing installations.'
   Conditions of evacuation to be laid down by an international commission composed of representatives of Germany, the United Kingdom, France, Italy, and Czecho-Slovakia.
   Occupation by German troops to begin on October 1 and be completed by defined stages by October 10.
   International commission.
1a. Discharge from Army or police and release from prison to be effected within four weeks from September 29.
2. No plebiscite in the ceded areas, but the international commission will determine territories in which a plebiscite is to be held.
   The plebiscite will take place not later than November 30. In the meantime these territories will be occupied by international bodies. The plebiscite will be based on the conditions of the Saar plebiscite.
3. The new frontiers will be determined by the international commission. It will also recommend certain minor modifications in the zones to be transferred without plebiscite.
4. The right of option into or out of the transferred territories may be exercised within six months of September 29. A German–Czecho-Slovak commission shall settle details.
5. The United Kingdom and French Governments 'stand by the offer' of an 'international guarantee of the new boundaries of the Czecho-Slovak State against unprovoked aggression.'
   When the question of the Polish and Hungarian minorities has been settled, Germany and Italy will give a guarantee to Czecho-Slovakia. If this question is not settled within three months by agreement the four Powers will again confer.
6. No expressed recognition.

p.12

THE PEACE

The pacificators of Munich returned home yesterday to receive greater gratitude than has ever been given to any returning conqueror. They have done something that has hardly ever happened before in history – the snatching of the world at the eleventh hour from a universal calamity, from a return to barbarism, from untold cruelty and misery. The future may be dark and uncertain enough, but after all it is the future and mankind does not live in it. The instinct of the peoples to-day to praise (even to pitches of extravagance) the peacemakers is sound. It is also something for which to be thankful, for, however much civilisation has seemed to slip back in the last few years, it is shown that peace is still the greatest hope in the hearts of men. We need not therefore argue overmuch where the credit lies among those who brought peace. Italy is satisfied that the Duce has saved the world; Germany is not permitted any doubts about her Führer's part; Britain feels that Mr. Chamberlain's sincerity and pertinacity have made the largest contribution; France applauds M. Daladier, but with a fine sense of justice does not forget the victim of the peace, Czecho-Slovakia, at whose expense Europe has been saved. And whatever view we take about the policies and acts that led up to the crisis and the character of the settlement we cannot help sharing the common thankfulness. None of us, to be frank, can disguise from himself that even had a European war been fought on the deeper issues and Germany been overcome the boundaries of Czecho-Slovakia could not have remained intact. The nationalism of her minorities, by whatever artificial means it was inflamed, had made that impossible. And great as are the injustices that Czecho-Slovakia suffers under the Munich Agreement, and they are for her calamatous, they cannot be measured against the horrors that might have extinguished not only Czecho-Slovakia but the whole of Western civilisation.

But at the same time we must not delude ourselves that we have not paid a high price. Most of us would agree with the 'New York Times' that

> It is a price which enables a dictator who would willingly destroy the last vestige of democracy in Europe to claim with justice that he scored over the democracies of Europe the greatest diplomatic triumph of modern times – that he accomplished by a mere ultimatum what Bismarck failed to accomplish with armies.

That, we can be certain, is how it appears in Germany and Italy and to a growing number of people in this country and is shown by the statements of Sir Archibald Sinclair, Mr. Amery, and others last night. The realisation of it may be a little obscured by the new Anglo-German declaration that Mr. Chamberlain has brought back with him. It is a useful and important declaration, although actually it says little. Herr Hitler declares (as he has done many times before) that he does not want to go to war with us and is ready to pursue 'methods of consultation with us' and to join with us in 'efforts to remove possible sources of difference.' This kind of formula can only be tested by experience. Thus it is inconceivable that it could be operated as a matter merely between this country and Germany. The bilateral method of the Anglo-German Naval Agreement was gravely resented by France, to say nothing of Russia. Surely we are not to continue it and, by settling disputed matters (such as colonies) with Germany, present France with an accomplished fact. An Anglo-German understanding is only defensible if it accompanies close working with France and looks towards the broader international framework represented by the League. We cannot discuss colonies with Germany without regard to the parallel interests of France and to the international system under which mandates are exercised. That is not to say we ought not to take up the question with Germany. We ought to do so quickly. Better the initiative should come from us (in association with France) than that we should wait until Hitler makes his demand in his own way and at his own time. His response would be the test of his sincerity for the peaceful settlement of European differences. And if we are to draw the real lesson from the peace of yesterday we cannot make that test too soon.

For no one in this country who examines carefully the terms under which Hitler's troops begin their march into Czecho-Slovakia to-day can feel other than unhappy. Certainly the Czechs will hardly appreciate Mr. Chamberlain's phrase that it is 'peace with honour.' The terms are a little better than the Godesberg ultimatum but not much. The Czechs are to leave intact all the fortifications, all the private and public property in the surrendered regions. The Anglo-French plan pre-supposed an orderly transfer: this is impossible when German troops occupy almost at once and hundreds of thousands of Czechs, German Socialists and Jews have to flee for their lives. An international commission (of ambassadors in Berlin) is to regulate the details of evacuation; it has no force to see that the helpless minority is protected. The plebiscite areas are rather less than in the Godesberg plan, and there will be the safeguard of an international force until the voting is over. But it still remains possible for the plebiscite method to create fantastic enclaves, under German control, in the midst of Czech territory. Even if the voting in an area shows only a small German minority, the effect will be to make that minority a focal point of disturbance; for that purpose it may have been designed. There are serious omissions from the plan which make it more unjust than the much-abused Versailles Treaty. There is no provision for the assumption of responsibility for the State debt represented by the ceded territory or for compensation for the seized State property. If Germany's aim were the economic and financial destruction of Czecho-Slovakia the Munich Agreement goes far to satisfy her. Czecho-Slovakia loses some of her major industries; sources of supply and markets are cut off; her main railways passing from one half of the State to another run through an alien territory. Lord Runciman, realising the economic effects, suggested that there should be a commercial treaty on preferential terms between Germany and Czecho-Slovakia. Of this the settlement contains no word. But, it may be urged, while the Czechs may suffer economically, they have the political protection of an international guarantee. What is it worth? Will Britain and France (and Russia, though, of course, Russia was not even mentioned at Munich) come to the aid of an unarmed Czecho-Slovakia when they would not help her in her strength? Germany and Italy join the guarantee, but only after Poland and Hungary have been bought off. And what, again, would that be worth if Italy were to decline to act against German 'unprovoked aggression'? Politically Czecho-Slovakia is rendered helpless, with all that that means to the balance of forces in Eastern Europe, and Hitler will be able to advance again, when he chooses, with greatly increased power.

p.13

AN ANGLO-GERMAN PLEDGE
Consultation, Not War

SIX BRITISH BATTALIONS GOING TO CZECHO-SLOVAKIA
German Entry at Dawn To-day

Mr. Chamberlain, who returned to London yesterday from Munich, brought with him a no-war pledge signed by him and Herr Hitler yesterday morning. It is in the following terms:—

We, the German Führer and Chancellor and the British Prime Minister, have had a further meeting to-day, and are agreed in recognising that the question of Anglo-German relations is of the first importance for the two countries and for Europe.

We regard the agreement signed last night and the Anglo-German Naval Agreement as symbolic of the desire of our two peoples never to go to war with one another again.

We are resolved that the methods of consultation shall be the method adopted to deal with any other question that may concern our two countries, and we are determined to continue our efforts to remove possible sources of difference and thus to contribute to the assurances of peace in Europe.

The declaration was signed after a talk lasting an hour and a half – 'a friendly discussion on all subjects of European politics' – between Mr. Chamberlain and Herr Hitler. There was no one else present except the interpreter. Before reading the declaration to journalists at his hotel Mr. Chamberlain said, 'I always had it in mind that if we could find a peaceful solution of this problem of Czecho-Slovakia we should open the way to the general appeasement of Europe.'

Asked whether he thought there would now be general demobilisation, Mr. Chamberlain said, 'Well, we did not discuss dates, but we hope that will come about practically immediately.'

From Heston Mr. Chamberlain went to Buckingham Palace to report to the King, and then to Downing Street, where a Cabinet meeting lasting an hour was held.

MARCHING AT DAWN

The Czech Government yesterday accepted the terms agreed on at the Munich conference, and it was expected that the German occupation of Sudeten territory would begin at dawn to-day.

The Czecho-Slovak Government, which was not represented at the conference, was given only a few hours in which to accept the plan. That acceptance was announced in a brief statement issued in Prague that –

The Czecho-Slovak Government, after having considered the decisions of the conference in Munich, taken without and against them, find no other means but to accept, and have nothing to add.

General Syrovy, the Premier, said in a broadcast that they had to choose between the death of the nation and the loss of territory. An understanding with neighbouring States should now be easier.

In Prague the day was regarded as one of national mourning. A broadcast appeal was made to the workers not to demonstrate against the terms, and the crowds which did attempt to demonstrate were quickly dispersed. The Government is said to be in full control. The full terms have not yet been disclosed to the Czech people.

The International Commission held its first meeting in Berlin last night. There were present Baron von Weizsäcker, Secretary of State at the German Foreign Office (who was appointed chairman), the French Ambassador (M. Francois-Poncet), the British Ambassador (Sir Nevile Henderson), the Italian Ambassador (Signor Attolico), and Dr. Mastny and General Husareck, the Czech representatives. A plan for handing over the first zone was accepted.

BRITISH TROOPS GOING

The Munich terms provide for an international force to keep order in the plebiscite areas, and it was learned in London this morning that six British battalions are likely to go to Czecho-Slovakia in the next few days. They will probably consist of four Guards battalions and two battalions from line regiments.

LONDON'S WELCOME

London gave a tumultuous welcome to the Premier. From Heston, where his car was besieged by huge crowds, Mr. Chamberlain went direct to Buckingham Palace, and he appeared on the balcony with Mrs. Chamberlain and the King and Queen, remaining there for several minutes. There were dense crowds all the way from the Palace to Whitehall, and when the Premier returned to Downing Street the great crowd swept the police aside and continued cheering until Mr. Chamberlain had spoken from a window. 'My good friends,' he said, 'this is the second time in our history that there has come back from Germany to Downing Street peace with honour. I believe it is peace for our time.' ...

THE RECEPTION AT HESTON

From our London Staff

Fleet Street, Friday.

In all this protracted crisis – during which personalities have become clearer, and personal, sometimes intimate things have been said by public men – there has been no moment more personal or more unusual than that to-night when Mr. Chamberlain stood for the sixth time in fifteen days before a microphone at Heston, waving in the air his agreement with Herr Hitler for everyone to see. 'And here,' he almost shouted, 'is the paper which bears his name upon it as well as mine.'

One had just a glimpse of the heavy writing of those signatures. He read out the document and there was a lot of ragged feminine cheering. Then someone shouted 'Three cheers for Mr. Chamberlain.' And they gave three big cheers.

The police were just able to hold back the people as Mr. Chamberlain walked very slowly, black hat in hand, to his car. They sang 'For he's a jolly good fellow.' Three hundred yards farther on, at the aerodrome gates, they (even the polite Eton boys who were there) broke the police cordon and thumped their approval on the windows of the car. All down the road from the aerodrome the footpaths were crowded : flags were in the house windows and there was cheering all the way.

LETTER FROM THE KING

The evening was a dark unwelcoming one. Rain had begun a little before the Prime Minister's plane came in sight. The 'plane ran straight across the field and swung sideways across the space between wooden bars, where the Cabinet Ministers and the diplomats stood.

This was the first glimpse that people had of Mr. Chamberlain – smiling and nodding at the window as the 'plane swung across and stopped. Umbrellas came down, flags were waving, and the cheering began. Women were shouting wild words of eulogy.

As Mr. Chamberlain left the 'plane there was certainly a lightness, a new lightness, in his eye and smile, but he walked stiffly and under his eyes were large dark rings. The Lord Chamberlain, Lord Clarendon, gave him a letter from the King. Dr. Kordt, Chargé d'Affaires at the German Embassy, came forward, then Lord Halifax, Count Grandi, Mr. Malcolm MacDonald, Mr. Hore-Belisha, and then a host, the Dominion High Commissioners and members of Parliament.

PREMIER'S SPEECH

This was the fourth time that one had seen Mr. Chamberlain at Heston, and this time there was a relaxed look about him. He moved much more slowly; he was not tense; his smile was unforced. His words when he spoke into the microphone were casual this time, and not so measured. He said:

'There are only two things I want to say. First of all, I received an immense number of letters during all these anxious times. So has my wife. Letters of support and approval and gratitude: and I cannot tell you what an encouragement that has been to me. I want to thank the British people for what they have done, and next I want to say that the settlement of the Czecho-Slovakian problem which has now been achieved is, in my view, only a prelude to a larger settlement in which all Europe may find peace.

'This morning I had another talk with the German Chancellor, Herr Hitler, and here is a paper which bears his name on it as well as mine.

'Some of you, perhaps, have already heard what it contains, but I would just like to read it to you.' ...

230

PREMIER APPEARS ON PALACE BALCONY
London's Tumultuous Welcome

ADDRESS FROM WINDOW: 'PEACE WITH HONOUR'

From our London Staff

Fleet Street, Friday.

No stranger experience can have happened to Mr. Chamberlain during the past month of adventures than his reception back home in London. He drove from Heston to Buckingham Palace, where the crowd clamoured for him, and within five minutes of his arrival he was standing on the balcony of the Palace with the King and Queen and Mrs. Chamberlain.

The cries were all for 'Neville,' and he stood there blinking in the light of a powerful arc-lamp and waving his hand and smiling. For three minutes this demonstration lasted. It ended with the singing of 'For he's a jolly good fellow' and 'God Save the King.' But the crowd remained, and singing, chanting, and cheering continued until late in the evening.

Mr. Chamberlain arrived about 6 45, but for more than an hour before that people had been waiting to welcome him. They stood first in dry weather, but heavy rain came on. The people put up with it cheerfully, sharing umbrellas, covering their hats with newspapers, covering babes in arms also with newspapers.

TRAFFIC PROBLEM

It was a harassing time for the police who could not stop the flow of evening traffic. Matters were complicated by the unscrupulousness of those who hired taxis and drove slowly round and round the Victoria memorial, hoping that one of their circuits would provide a view of Mr. Chamberlain's car. The crowd amused itself by shouting, 'What! Again?' each time the culprits appeared.

There was a moment of relief when the rain stopped and the sun began to set in splendour behind Buckingham Palace, staining the clouds which moved slowly eastward. A rainbow was faintly perceptible over St. James Park, the arch embracing Carlton House Terrace, Whitehall, and Westminster.

But when Mr. Chamberlain arrived the bright colours had gone. A breeze kept the Royal Standard afloat over the Palace, and a faint, pearl-grey light emanated from the west. The crowd, however was concerned only to see Mr. Chamberlain. One City man in his zeal had brought a leather hatbox with him to stand on, and from this perch kept letting out an intermittent bellow.

Another welcome awaited the Premier in Downing Street, which he reached fifteen minutes later. With difficulty his car moved from Whitehall to No. 10. Mounted policemen rode fore and aft and a constable kept guard on the running board of the car.

Every window on the three floors of No. 10 and No. 11 was open and filled with faces. The windows of the Foreign Office across the way were equally full – all except one, which was made up with sandbags. Mr. Geoffrey Lloyd stood on the window-sill beside the door of No. 10 and everywhere were people cheering. One of the women there found no other words to express her feelings but these. 'The man who gave me back my son.'

'PEACE FOR OUR TIME'

Mr. and Mrs. Chamberlain stood for a few minutes on the doorstep acknowledging the greeting. Then Mr. Chamberlain went to a first-floor window and leaned forward happily smiling on the people. From his own house, where so many disquieting Cabinet meetings have been held, he spoke to the crowd outside – a different crowd in temper from many that have been there during the last month. 'My good friends,' he said – it took some time to still the clamour so that he might be heard – 'this is the second time in our history that there has come back from Germany ''peace with honour.'' I believe it is peace for our time. We thank you from the bottom of our hearts.' ('And we thank you,' came the response.) 'Now I recommend you to go home and sleep quietly.'

A DEPUTATION

There was no discordant note in the welcome which Mr. Chamberlain received himself, but before his arrival a deputation representing 27 London branches of the National Unemployed Workers' Movement delivered a protest at No. 10 at Mr. Chamberlain's action in 'coming to terms with Nazi Germany.' The arrival of these men, who stood on the doorway of No. 10 and who selected two of their number to go inside the building, was noted jealously by the crowd, who had been kept on the other side of the road. 'Why are they allowed to be there?' asked a woman. 'It's a free country,' replied a man standing near.

The National Unemployed Workers' Movement, under the leadership of Wal Hunnington had been founded in 1921. Along with most of the other leaders of NUWM he was an avowed Communist. The oath of the NUWM included the words 'to never cease from active strife against this system until capitalism is abolished and our country and all its resources truly belong to the people.'

OCCUPATION OF SUDETENLAND
Preparing a Welcome

It was said in Berlin last night that the march of the German troops across the Czech frontier would begin at dawn to-day. This will avoid the dangers of entering during the dark.

The press bureau of the Sudeten German party said (according to the German News Agency) that no men belonging to the Free Corps would be allowed to enter Sudeten German territory unless they were ordered to do so by the headquarters of the Free Corps.

HENLEIN TO HITLER

Herr Conrad Henlein, the Sudeten German leader, sent a telegram yesterday to Herr Hitler thanking him 'for the freedom you have won for us.' The telegram, which was sent from Bayreuth, reads:–

In the name of the people of Sudeten Germany who have been tormented and oppressed for 20 years I thank you, my Führer, with deeply moved heart for the freedom you have won for us. Children and children's children will bless the day on which, by the union with Greater Germany, thou, my Führer, changed the unspeakable misery of millions into a deep joy and proud confidence.

Words are too weak to express to you what we all feel at this moment for you. In deep gratitude the whole Sudeten German people stands for ever in most loyal fellowship behind its deliverer.

The German News Agency states that towns and villages are decorated with swastikas, pictures of Hitler, and emblems of the Reich. Everywhere the papers declare the thought is, 'We must prepare a joyful reception for the German troops.'–Reuter.

CHANCES OF CO-OPERATION IN EUROPE
Germans Look to the Future

EVEN A KINDLIER FEELING TOWARDS THE CZECHS

From our Correspondent

Berlin, September 30.

The German people are to-day basking in the happy feeling that peace has been assured. It is as if a great weight has been removed from them after weeks of depression developed into gloom and anxiety in the last few days. Even the attitude of the papers which so proudly talked of defiance in the past few days has somewhat melted. 'A deep sigh of relief passed through the whole world, a nightmare has been removed from the nations,' the 'Borsen Zeitung,' for instance, writes. And the 'Frankfurter Zeitung' exclaims:

> The world once more begins to breathe. The task has been completed. From the hands of the four statesmen Europe receives the assurance of peace – and for the first time this word means justice too.

Mr. Chamberlain is a most popular figure here to-day. People quite frankly say that everyone owes him a debt of gratitude. Great Britain altogether is most popular here this afternoon, for the Anglo-German communiqué drafted by Herr Hitler and Mr. Chamberlain after their conversation this morning in Munich is given great prominence. Political quarters are deeply gratified at the idea of better relations between these two countries for which they have been longing for a long time.

'Never again war between Germany and England,' a headline reads, and extra editions of the afternoon papers bearing the news were sold like hot cakes.

GERMANY'S NEW TASK

Germans have yet another reason to rejoice over the Munich agreement, for it adds to their country three and a half million people of their own kith and kin and also some very lovely country. No wonder that one paper calls Herr Hitler the 'augmenter of the Reich.'

On the other hand the Germans fully realise that this means that the matter, so far as they are concerned, is still in a state of development. The British and French may lean back and rejoice in peace preserved. Germany, on the other hand, has now the task before her of peacefully occupying the Sudeten region, a task which will fill the next ten days with no little activity.

The first troops are expected to move into the Sudeten region at midnight. ...

PARIS UNEASY ABOUT NEW PLEDGE
First Attempt by Germany to Weaken the Anglo-French Bonds?

M. DALADIER'S RETURN

From our own Correspondent

Paris, September 30.

'Paris Soir' publishes on its front page to-night a photograph showing Hitler and Göring looking on as M. Daladier signs the Munich agreement. One wonders how many people in Paris have looked at this photograph with any sense of historical perspective and have realised its ominous significance from the French point of view.

It marks for France the end of a great many things – of her system of alliances, of her influence and prestige in Central and Eastern Europe, and of her role as the potential nucleus in an anti-Fascist coalition. One wonders how many people thought of all that. Perhaps more than one imagined as one looked at the Paris groups who lined the streets and waved and cheered as M. Daladier, standing up in an open car, drove this afternoon from Le Bourget Aerodrome to the War Office.

Never before had the wireless announced the route along which a Premier would drive into Paris, and it was only natural that large crowds of people should have gone to see M. Daladier drive past. The streets were decorated with flags, including some Union Jacks, but the cheering was rather conventional, lacking any real emotional quality. Shop-girls were standing on the balcony of the Galerie Lafayette holding tri-colour flags, and a street-sweeper waved a broom with a handkerchief tied to it – which caused much amusement in the group.

UNEASINESS

Some cried 'Vive La Paix!' and others cried 'Vive La France!' A workman next to me remarked rather ironically, 'Vive la France malgré tout,' and a messenger boy with a bicycle said that since the Boulevard Haussmann had been closed to traffic half an hour earlier there was now a terrible traffic jam higher up the avenue where it runs into the Grands Boulevards, and the drivers were all 'cursing like blazes.' A grimmer touch of irony was added a few minutes before M. Daladier's car drove down the Rue Lafayette by the appearance of a brewer's lorry labelled 'La Sédan Bières, Extra-Fines.'

In spite of the cheering, in spite of the profound relief that war had been averted, there was an undercurrent of uneasiness in Paris. And one doubts whether the leading article in the 'Paris Soir' (next to the photograph of M. Daladier signing the Munich agreement) really reflected the feelings of the man in the street.

As a result of this terrible crisis (it said) France could have died or might have come out much reduced in authority. She has come out of it with her head erect, with her friendships strengthened, with the Anglo-French friendship definitely sealed, and with new friendships in prospect.

M. Daladier personally is not blamed for what has happened, except that it is felt by many that he might have managed his Cabinet better a fortnight ago than he did. It is felt that at Munich he must have put up a fairly good fight in order to save the little that could still be saved. To what extent he merely seconded Mr. Chamberlain or took any independent initiative during the talks is not known yet. The seeming cordiality with which he was received by the people of Munich – perhaps a spontaneous reflection of the German people's desire for peace – and the jovial pats on the back he received from Göring, who, according to one report, exclaimed, 'You are the sort of chap I like,' have no doubt caused much pleasure to many Frenchmen, though to some others it all sounds a little too good to be true. The Nazi leaders can well afford to be jovial now. Sober observers would argue that France is being dragged – very much as a 'fourth partner' – into a four-Power pact, and that Göring is trying to revive in M. Daladier the illusions he once entertained on the possibility of a direct Franco-German 'settlement.'

FEARS FOR THE FUTURE

But again, as happened to M. Laval at the time of the Anglo-German Naval Agreement, many Frenchmen, and perhaps M. Daladier himself, must be wondering after to-day's Anglo-French communiqué whether France has not again been 'kept out of it' – and rather deliberately at that. Certainly in official quarters this evening this communiqué was not commented on with as much enthusiasm as some might have expected. Mr. Chamberlain, it is felt here, probably hoped by this communiqué to improve the possibilities of an orderly transfer of the Sudeten country and also to weaken Hitler's open threat – made twice in the last months – to denounce the Anglo-German Naval Agreement; but the French, nevertheless,

236

feel rather hurt in their dignity and see in the communiqué a first attempt by Germany to weaken the present bonds between England and France.

And it is wondered what Mr. Chamberlain's policy will be in the months to come: Will he frankly adopt a four-Power pact policy and possibly try to divert Germany's new energies towards the east – in spite of Hitler's pledge that the Sudeten country was Germany's last territorial claim in Europe? Altogether it is expected that all sorts of subjects will before long come up for discussion – the Franco-Soviet Pact and Spain and many more. But if these discussions take place on a four-Power pact basis it is doubted whether France and Britain will collect many of the tricks.

M. FLANDIN'S FATE

In France the Army will probably remain mobilised until the Czech problem is more or less settled in practice. What political changes there will be it is still too early to say, but there probably will be some. A number of politicians will have been completely 'sunk' as a result of this crisis – in the first place, M. Flandin, who preached defeatism and denounced the Government as liars at the most critical moments of the past week.

Parliament is meeting for a short session on Tuesday. Foreign affairs will be discussed, and possibly also the financial situation, for the events of the past weeks have certainly not been without effect on that.

In the meantime the greater part of the French press is full of praise for Mr. Chamberlain, and the 'Paris Soir' is even proposing to raise a public subscription for a villa to be called 'the House of Peace' to be presented to the British Premier as a token of gratitude from the people of France.

It is said that Daladier expected to be stoned on his return to Paris from Munich, whereas he was treated as a hero and had flowers strewn in his path. For France, Munich meant that her pre-conference weakness was paralleled by the post-conference ones, i.e. a completely defensive military strategy, out-dated tactics and an unwillingness to fight. The abandonment of Czechoslovakia, rather than 'buying time' had, in fact, achieved the opposite effect.

UNITED STATES OPINION
Relief and Regret

HOSTILE VIEWS OF THE TERMS

From our own Correspondent

New York, September 30.

Profound relief that the danger of an immediate war in Europe has passed was the predominant feeling here to-day, and everywhere in New York one heard the remark 'Thank God for peace.' At the same time there is the deepest sympathy with Czecho-Slovakia, and the belief is often expressed that what has been obtained is only a postponement and that the issue will have to be faced again, perhaps next year.

A remarkable feature in the past few days has been the increased popularity of Mr. Chamberlain. There has been almost a revolution in sentiment regarding him within the past ten days. His picture is enthusiastically applauded in the cinemas. In spite of the suggestions that the maintenance of peace was really the work of President Roosevelt or of Signor Mussolini, most Americans evidently attribute it chiefly to Mr. Chamberlain.

The actual terms of the Munich Agreement, have, of course, had hostile reception. Herr Hitler is violently unpopular in the United States, which always had a friendly feeling towards Czecho-Slovakia. Publicly and privately one hears the belief expressed that Czecho-Slovakia is doomed to extinction and poignant regret that this must be so. ...

INDUSTRY'S THANKS TO PREMIER

The following telegram was sent to the Prime Minister yesterday by Mr. W.M. Wiggins, president of the Federation of Master Cotton Spinners' Associations:–

In the name of cotton-spinning employers in Lancashire, Yorkshire, Cheshire, and Derbyshire, employing 150,000 workpeople, I offer you profound gratitude and congratulations upon your indomitable and successful efforts to save a world-wide catastrophe. Fervently hope your health may not be impaired as a result of your herculean endeavours in the interests of humanity in general.

In an interview later in the day, Mr. Wiggins expressed his gratification at the happy ending of a crisis 'which for the past few weeks had threatened to throw the whole of the world into the vortex of war with its consequent universal privation and suffering,' and added that he had nothing but the greatest praise for the way in which Mr. Chamberlain had paved the way to a settlement honourable to all parties concerned.

He welcomed the settlement also from the trade point of view, because he believed that with the passing of the war clouds industry would resume its normal activity. During the weeks of the crisis orders had naturally been withheld, and he trusted that the settlement would quickly have the effect of restoring general confidence in the world and bring about the resumption of international trade which would mean increased prosperity to all.

'CAPITULATION ROUTINE'
Moscow's Views

From our Correspondent

Moscow, September 30.

The Soviet press reports the Munich decisions without comments, but the Soviet attitude is amply explained by the Moscow journalist who has accompanied Mr. Litvinoff to Geneva. He develops the Marxian interpretation 'of the routine Anglo-French capitulation' as meaning that the nations fear to put arms into the hands of the masses.

The profound pessimism of the Moscow leaders over the future is reflected in the warning that only fools think that Munich laid the basis of a lasting peace and that Hitler's appetite is appeased. Two observations by the journalist now in Geneva are of interest in considering the future probabilities. The first is that France has lost significance as a Great Power, and the second is that the League of Nations during the crisis did not exist in fact.

'Izvestia' declares that Lord Runciman's letter to Mr. Chamberlain proves that his sympathies were with the Henleinites and insinuates that he instigated the secession movement.

The strong Soviet press comments are perhaps more understandable in the light of Russia's exclusion from the Munich negotiations.

HITLER'S NEW POWERS
Czecho-Slovakia at His Mercy

By Our Diplomatic Correspondent

London, Friday.

The Munich agreement gives Hitler everything he wants (to begin with) except in so far as it does not perhaps quite enable him to get it as quickly as he would have done under the untrimmed ultimatum of Godesberg. He will begin the invasion of Czecho-Slovakia to-morrow exactly as he threatened to do in his speech on September 12. He is free to occupy all the regions where the Sudeten Germans are in a majority and to do so by rapid stages.

All the misery and outrage that followed the German occupation of Vienna are now certain to follow the German occupation of the Sudetenland. Prague has, even now, begun to fill with refugees – Sudeten German Socialists, Jews, not to speak of Czechs – which is natural enough, seeing that for months the German newspapers, wireless, and Hitler himself have referred to the Czechs in terms that have been one prolonged incitement to acts of violence and oppression.

By October 10 Hitler will have annexed a vast area with great natural and industrial wealth, and is not even to pay compensation for Czech property, whether private or Government. He will be master of Czecho-Slovakia's main defences, and there is nothing to stop him from making himself master of all Czecho-Slovakia in course of time.

THE PLEBISCITE

To give him control over the regions where the Sudeten Germans are in a minority the device of the plebiscite (which was rejected under the Anglo-French proposals) has been used. Did Mr. Chamberlain and M. Daladier ask Hitler what the plebiscite was for and how, without intimidation, he could hope for a Sudeten German majority in regions where they are known to be a minority? Elections and plebiscites held under Hitler offer many examples of the way in which they can be manipulated.

The areas selected for the plebiscite are not quite the same as in the Godesberg ultimatum. For example, the industrial town and railway junction of Brno is not included. But the Germans will be so close to this town that it will be at their mercy. Besides, it has a small German minority (about 12 per cent of the total population), which, under pressure from Hitler, will be its real administrators. Any village or township with a German majority (and there are many such scattered throughout Czecho-Slovakia and right into Carpathian Ruthenia) in regions where the Czechs are the vast majority can, through the device of the plebiscite, be made to become a German stronghold, dominating the surrounding country like the castle of a mediaeval robber baron. With the help of the plebiscite Hitler can get control of factories, railways, and strategic points. In a short time he can make himself master of Czecho-Slovakia, without war and without any serious opposition from the Western Powers. ...

Monday 3 October   *p.8*

London, Sunday Night

RESPONSIBILITY

Mr. Duff Cooper's resignation is not expected to be followed by that of any others from the Cabinet, although considerable pressure is being exercised on at least three of them from their constituents and friends. Their personal admiration for Mr. Chamberlain may have turned the scale against their doubts about his international policy.

Public opinion is more sober to-day, and the extravagant claims of Saturday are less heard. Thankfulness for peace and a desire not to look too far into it is now the 'note.' Two points are urged. Speakers in to-morrow's debate should seek to make the most of the military guarantee which, with France, we have given to Czecho-Slovakia. Its importance and our responsibility should be stressed. The other point in our responsibility is financial aid to the Czechs, who are losing vast amounts of property and plant to the Germans under our agreement. It is argued that a trifle out of the cost of the war that their surrender has saved us from might be the national peace offering.

'PEACE WITH HONOUR'

Mr. Chamberlain, influenced, no doubt, by the force of historic circumstances, set the results of his work at Munich alongside those of Beaconsfield, who told the Downing Street crowd on his return from the Berlin Congress in 1878 that he had brought back 'peace and honour.' Mr. Chamberlain made the same claim for himself on Friday night. Not every statesman would choose Disraelian diplomacy as the standard of excellence, but even by that standard Mr. Chamberlain's claim seems pitched too high.

The objects of Lord Beaconsfield's policy were to separate the interests of the Emperors of Germany, Austria, and Russia and to prevent Russia from getting too near the Mediterranean after her victory over Turkey. His weapon, like Mr. Chamberlain's, was the threat of force, and he reached his mark without war,

241

securing for the conquered nation more territory than the victory wished.

Mr. Chamberlain's avowed object was to prevent German aggression, and he had only two autocrats to contend with. He reached his mark without war, securing for militant Germany more territory than she had asked for three months ago.

WHERE THE SUDETENS LOSE

A minor but interesting point in the relations of Czecho-Slovakia with other States is pointed out to me by an American friend. The Sudeten manufacturers, who are now incorporated in the Reich, will lose their present trade advantages with the United States. Czecho-Slovakia still exists as a separate country, and it has a trade agreement with the United States. Its benefits were, of course, enjoyed by the manufacturers in the Sudeten provinces, but it now lapses there as Germany has no such agreement.

When Germany annexed Austria a test position arose. Austria had an agreement with the United States under the 'most favoured nation' clause. Germany hoped that the United States would not accept the Anschluss, as it had never accepted the Japanese occupation of Manchukuo or the Italian conquest of Abyssinia. President Roosevelt, however, accepted the Anschluss and struck Austria out of the list of countries with which the United States had trade agreements, explaining in a Note why he had done so. There are several reasons why the Sudeten manufacturers and their employees will do worse under Berlin than they did under Prague. This is another.

Mr. Duff Cooper's letter of resignation and Chamberlain's reply to it appear in the extracts of Monday 3 October.

KEPT IN THE DARK

One aspect of the vast disturbance of the last fortnight must strike anybody who reflects on its history. In the three most powerful States of Central and Eastern Europe the peoples were not allowed to know what was being said and done outside. In Russia there seems to have been very little news. In Germany and Italy the news was deliberately falsified when it was not suppressed. The German people were not allowed to know of President Roosevelt's message. The Italian people were led to believe that Chamberlain was in agreement with Hitler and only anxious to put pressure on Benes. Of one of his speeches they were given a false version. When you look at the population of Europe you find that almost one half of it was thus left in ignorance or deceived. Of the four Powers represented at Munich, France and Great Britain have between them a population of about ninety millions and Germany and Italy a population of one hundred and fifteen. The people of France and Great Britain knew everything and the people of Germany and Italy very little. It used to be said that the first casualty in war is truth, but there are countries in which truth is killed long before war begins. During the war between Russia and Japan we were told as a dramatic indication of the dense ignorance of the Russian peasant that there were villages in which nobody knew that a war was going on; that was cited as an illustration of the primitive state of Russian civilisation. To-day the most alarming fact is the ignorance of the best-educated peoples, an ignorance that is the result of deliberate policy on the part of their rulers. ...

Leader   **FOR OUR TIME?**

Now that the first flush of emotion is over it is the duty of all of us to see where the 'peace with honour' has brought us. The Prime Minister claims that it has brought us 'peace for our time.' It is an inspiring claim, and if it proves to be a just one he will have earned a high place in history. It falls to Parliament to-day to analyse it and to secure from Mr. Chamberlain the grounds on which he bases his belief. To many of us they are not obvious. What we cannot escape is that Europe to-day is an entirely different place from what it was a fortnight ago, before the visit to Berchtesgaden. Then there was a virtual alliance of the totalitarian States, assertive on the German side, weak on the Italian, embarrassed on the Japanese. Against them France and Britain offered a common front on the west; the co-operation of Russia was assured, neutralising Poland and threatening Japan; in Central Europe Czecho-Slovakia hung on Germany's flank, and Hungary behind was neutralised by the other members of the Little Entente; outside Europe was the imponderable influence of the benevolent neutrality of the United States. It was not an unequal balance of forces; Britain and France, especially the latter, might be relatively unprepared in a military sense, but their reserves of strength were enormous. All these anti-Fascist forces had, moreover, an ideal to fight for, to preserve liberty in the world. To-day the links that bound these countries have gone. Czecho-Slovakia has disappeared as a military force; Poland has become a German client; the Little Entente has been forced into acquiescence in German and Italian domination. Russia has lost her means of intervention in Central Europe and has every excuse for falling back into isolation and self-protection. The two Western nations stand alone. Britain has accepted Germany's offer of a consultative understanding; France is to be offered one. Similar understandings are supposed to be on the way with Italy. The transformation is fundamental.

In terms of power politics it seems to mean the crumbling of a 'democratic front' which, whatever its shortcomings, did hold tenuously to the League and did embody the idea of co-operation between peace-loving States to maintain international law. This is replaced by the new conception of a European order governed by four States holding two opposite views of life. It is Parliament's business to find out what is the basis of this new Four-Power Peace Mr. Chamberlain is trying to give us. The only condition on which it would be tolerable would be a change of heart on the part of the dictators – a sign, after their years of sabre-rattling and organisation for war, they are prepared to return to the path of international co-operation. One apologist for Mr. Chamberlain asserts that that condition exists. 'The brutal methods of national aggrandisement,' says the 'Times,' 'have been publicly renounced by their principal exponents, to whom peace-loving peoples should be ready to give full credit for their professions.' We should all be willing to give full credit, but where are the proofs? They do not appear in the Munich agreement. We can see now that two things saved us from war: the realisation, even in the militarised States that the common people do not want war, and the realisation by Germany and Italy that they would be faced by the combined resistance of Britain, France and Russia. (The mobilisation of the Fleet and the minatory tone of President Roosevelt's message added the last touch.) But that did not save Czecho-Slovakia. Hitler and Mussolini got (and loudly claim) a bloodless victory. Central and Eastern Europe come under the German might, and with the thrusting aside of Russia, France and England lose the support of the Power which acted as the main check on German aggression on the west. We start the new order therefore, having enormously enhanced the influence and strength of Germany and Italy and reduced those of the 'peace loving peoples.' Is that offset by the value of the proffered friendship of the dictators, on the cultivation of which Mr. Chamberlain's entire policy now rests?

For that there are a few searching tests. The initial difficulty is that Herr Hitler never keeps a promise if it suits his incalculable mood to break it. This is only the fourth time he has renounced the seizure of territory by force – he renounced it in May, 1933, in March, 1936 (after the seizure of the Rhineland) in March 1938 (after the seizure of Austria). But Mr. Chamberlain thinks he is honest this time. In that case, if the time of anxiety is past, we must begin to see results. First, are we to be able to relax our part in the armaments race and to stop digging burrows for ourselves? (No one else is likely to bomb us except Hitler's men.) Secondly, are we to see a quick attempt to get the volunteers out of Spain and to avert the threat to our own vital interests caused by Italian and German invasion (Mr. Chamberlain's former condition for his friendship with Mussolini)? Thirdly, are we to make a beginning to get the remaining grievances of Europe cleared up by international conference? Herr Hitler wants to discuss colonies by peaceful consultation. Is Mr. Chamberlain prepared to propose that colonies and raw materials and other grievances of the 'have nots' be dealt with in the only reasonable and just way, in association with all the interested States and the League? Mr. Chamberlain must have some constructive programme if he expects this country to overcome natural prejudices and make full friends with those whose ideals and practice it hates and fears. It must be said that Mr. Duff Cooper's resignation suggests strongly that this programme is lacking and that Mr. Chamberlain has nothing to offer us except the timid hope that he can save our skins by keeping in with the dictators at no matter whose expense. Parliament must find out. It would be desperate indeed if this much-vaunted 'peace for our time' were to be a cringing peace, a peace gained by throwing sops to the dictators – Czecho-Slovakia, Alsace, Schleswig, Tunis, a British colony or two. Mr. Chamberlain can disprove it in two ways. The first was stated by Mr. Cordell Hull in his warning comment on the Munich Agreement.

It is to be hoped that, in any event, the forces which stand for the principles governing peaceful and orderly international relations and their proper application should not relax, but redouble their efforts to maintain these principles of order under law, resting on a sound economic foundation.

In short, Mr. Chamberlain must stick to British principles and assert them. In the second place, the non-Fascist forces must stand together, which means that in the highest self-interest if for no other reasons Britain and France must keep and strengthen their association with Russia and with the United States. To discard Russia (which has seemed to be Mr. Chamberlain's aim) would be to tie ourselves bound to the Berlin–Rome axis. If indeed we gained 'peace for our time,' it would be the peace of the shorn lamb.

p.9

MOVING APPEALS FROM CZECHO-SLOVAKIA
The Price of Dismemberment

PREMIER'S REASSURANCE TO FRANCE
Cabinet Minister Resigns

While German Troops were marching into Czecho-Slovakia on one side and Polish troops on the other dignified and moving declarations and appeals were being made yesterday by the leaders of the Czecho-Slovak people, spiritual and political.

The President of the Upper and Lower Houses of the Prague Parliament have sent an appeal to the British and French Parliaments in which they say:

245

We appeal to them to understand the moral revolution which has caused the punishment of a State and a nation which wanted nothing more than to fulfil its obligations, a nation which had real faith in the high principles of human co-operation, a nation which committed no other wrong than the desire to live in its own fashion in the cultural community of nations and States.

We bequeath our sorrow to the French and English people. ...

PREMIER'S MESSAGE TO FRANCE

Mr. Chamberlain sent the following message to M. Daladier, the French Premier, on Saturday:—

On my return to London I wish to express to you my grateful appreciation of your loyal and helpful co-operation throughout these recent days of anxiety, and my admiration of the courage and dignity with which you have represented your great country.

In the declaration which the German Chancellor and I signed yesterday we have agreed that our respective peoples are united in their desire for peace and for friendly consultation in all differences that may arise. Closely united as are the hearts of our peoples, I know that these sentiments are true of your country no less than of my own.

I look forward to renewed and continuous co-operation with you in further efforts for the consolidation of European peace through an extension of the goodwill and confidence which so happily inspires the relations between our two countries.

The Anglo-German pledge which Mr. Chamberlain brought back with him from Munich has caused uneasiness in France. Reports from Berlin suggesting that a similar Anglo-French pledge may be signed soon are not confirmed from any French source.

CABINET MINISTER RESIGNS

Mr. Duff Cooper, First Lord of the Admiralty, has resigned from the Government because he 'profoundly distrusts the foreign policy which the present Government is pursuing and seems likely to continue to pursue.' Mr. Duff Cooper will, it is expected, make a statement in the House of Commons to-day.

Mr. Duff Cooper apologies in his letter to the Premier for 'striking a discordant note at the moment of your great triumph.' ...

Mr. Chamberlain returned to Downing Street last night after a brief rest at Chequers to prepare for to-day's meeting of the House of Commons. He left it on Wednesday with the words, 'I go now to this last effort.' He returns to give an account of the Munich conference and to explain the agreement reached and his new understanding with Herr Hitler. His claim that he has brought back 'peace for our time' will be critically examined by the House.

MR. DUFF COOPER'S LETTER
'Profound Distrust' of Foreign Policy

It was announced on Saturday that Mr. Duff Cooper, First Lord of the Admiralty, had resigned from the Government on account of his disagreement with its foreign policy. His resignation has been accepted by the Prime Minister.

Mr. Duff Cooper's letter of resignation was as follows:—

Admiralty. Whitehall.
October 1, 1938

My Dear Prime Minister,

It is extremely painful to me in the moment of your great triumph to be obliged to strike a discordant note. For reasons with which you are acquainted, and which I propose to explain to the House of Commons in due course, I profoundly distrust the foreign policy which the present Government is pursuing and seems likely to continue to pursue.

Feeling as I do, I have considered that honour and loyalty demand that I should offer you my resignation. I do so with profound regret, because I have been so proud to hold my present office, the one I envied beyond all others in the State, and I have been so grateful to you for having placed such confidence in me and for having shown me such invariable kindness and patience.

Yours very sincerely,
DUFF COOPER

The Right Hon. Neville
Chamberlain, M.P.

The Prime Minister replied:

10 Downing Street, Whitehall.
October 1, 1938

My Dear First Lord,

I have received your letter, in which you tender your resignation from the Government, with great personal regret.

247

But, knowing that you are sincerely convinced that the foreign policy of the present Government is mistaken, I agree with you in thinking that it would not be proper for you to remain a member of the Government.

Before submitting your resignation for the approval of his Majesty the King, I should like to thank you for your work in the great office which you are now giving up, and to express the conviction that differences over public policy will make no breach in our personal relations.

Yours sincerely,
N. CHAMBERLAIN.

Right Hon. A. Duff Cooper,
D.S.O. M.P.

Duff Cooper's was the only resignation from the Cabinet over the terms of the Munich Agreement.

PARLIAMENT AND THE PEACE
To-day's Debate on the Munich Agreement

From our Parliamentary Correspondent

London, Sunday Night.

The resignation of Mr. Duff Cooper from the office of First Lord of the Admiralty means that Mr. Chamberlain has now defined his new foreign policy – the Munich Agreement has made that possible – and that he intends to stake his political career upon it. The process of definition has been going on for some time, and the first public sign of it was the Anglo-Italian talks, which caused Mr. Eden's resignation.

It may be wondered why Mr. Duff Cooper did not resign at the same time. His letter of resignation to the Prime Minister makes it clear that his differences from Mr. Chamberlain are not new. 'For reasons with which you are acquainted,' he wrote, 'I profoundly distrust the foreign policy which the present Govenment is pursuing and seems likely to continue to pursue.' Perhaps Mr. Duff Cooper thought that the Italian agreement was stillborn, and hoped that the policy which it foreshadowed would not thrive.

Mr. Chamberlain, clearly, will not let himself be disturbed by Mr. Duff Cooper's resignation. He is absolutely convinced that he is on the right lines, and told the House of Commons during the debate on the Anglo-Italian agreement that he had never been more sure of the merits of any action he had taken than in his approach to Signor Mussolini. The Munich Agreement represents a development of that policy. Furthermore, if Mr. Chamberlain was prepared to lose Mr. Eden, who was a popular Minister, he will certainly not pine for Mr. Duff Cooper, who is not.

A DISRAELI PARALLEL

There is a parallel between Mr. Chamberlain's present attitude and that of Disraeli when he was framing his Balkan policy in 1878 before the Berlin congress. Disraeli was quite ready, indeed anxious that he should lose three dissident Cabinet Ministers, including Lord Derby, who was then Foreign Secretary.

The effect of Mr. Duff Cooper's resignation on Conservatives in the House of Commons is likely to be much more disturbing, for he is an exemplary party man with no dubious antecedents and with an independent position in the Cabinet. He does not start with a bias towards the Chamberlain policy, as all the members of the inner Cabinet do. Lord Halifax was brought in expressly to carry out a policy which Mr. Eden resisted. ...

OPPOSITION PARTIES

Mr. Duff Cooper is an independent witness and a Conservative witness. His personal statement to-morrow will be heard with special attention by Conservative members. His protest against the policy of the Government will have the support, whether expressed or not, of Mr. Eden. Mr. Amery is also dubious about Munich. Mr. Harold Nicolson, who has already attacked in the House the Anglo-Italian agreement, holds that Mr. Chamberlain has brought back not 'peace for our time,' as he himself thinks, but peace for six months. Mr. Winston Churchill has no love for the Chamberlain policy either.

The official Opposition parties are sure to express the sense of humiliation and shame which many people in this country feel at the treatment of Czecho-Slovakia, which has received a series of what were virtually ultimatums from the Western democracies. Sir Archibald Sinclair, the leader of the Liberals, has already voiced his resentment. Mr. Attlee and other Labour leaders are to settle their line of action to-morrow morning.

Mr. Lloyd George intends to speak during the course of the debate. He is under no illusions as to the faults of the Czecho-Slovakian Government, but equally he is under no illusion as to the gravity of the decisions on foreign policy taken by Mr. Chamberlain at Munich without consulting Parliament.

A GENERAL ELECTION?

It is expressed that there will be a demand for assistance to the Czech State in its new weakness. The least, it is felt, that Britain can do now, having forced dismemberment upon her, is to succour the remnant.

It is impossible to estimate how far these criticisms of Government policy will detach supporters from the loyal phalanx of Mr. Chamberlain's followers. A great deal depends on Mr. Chamberlain's defence of his new policy and his forecast of its results. It is probable that he feels so sure of himself as to appeal to the country if Parliament shows great hostility. Munich is the gateway to a four-Power pact, excluding Russia, which has apparently been one of his chief objects, and he is not the man to evade a fight.

One effect of Munich has been to stimulate the campaign in this country for national service and more armaments. ...

THE KING'S MESSAGE TO THE NATION*

The following message from the King to the nation was issued from Buckingham Palace last night:–

The time of anxiety is past and we have been able to-day to offer our thanks to the Almighty for His mercy in sparing us the horrors of war.

I would like to thank the men and women of this country for their calm resolve during these critical days, and for the readiness with which they responded to the different calls made upon them.

After the magnificent efforts of the Prime Minister in the cause of peace, it is my fervant hope that a new era of friendship and prosperity may be dawning among the peoples of the world.

GEORGE, R.I.

---

p.11

'DEMOCRATIC IDEA BETRAYED'
Mr. Harold Nicolson and Results of Munich Conference

AN UNNECESSARY SURRENDER

'We have betrayed a valient little country and a great democratic idea. There are many people who feel that in so doing we have achieved peace for a generation. They are wholly mistaken. We have not achieved peace for a generation: we have achieved it only for eight months.'

This statement by Mr. Harold Nicolson, M.P. was made at a luncheon held in Manchester on Saturday by the National Labour Area Organisation, at which Mr. Nicolson discussed the recent crisis.

* The King's Message in the original 'Guardian' report appeared in the middle of the above article.

Mr. Nicolson, who made it clear at the outset that the opinions he was expressing were his personal opinions and not those of the official National Labour party, said that at the moment we had not got the official text of what was agreed to at Munich. We had got the words, but we had not got the map, which was the vital thing, because without the map we were not able to see how the Munich settlement differed from the Godesberg settlement rejected by the Prime Minister.

MISSED OPPORTUNITY

But to his mind it was quite apparent that the Prime Minister misunderstood the feeling in Germany, the feeling in Italy, and, above all, the feeling in this country. He was offered one of the greatest opportunities that ever fell to the lot of any British statesman. He missed that opportunity. He had behind him in this country a force of national resolution such as had seldom been united. He had with him the opinion of the whole civilised world. And, if he had only understood the situation, he was faced by opponents who knew that our resolution was greater than their resolution, our unity greater than their unity, and our power greater than their power. Had he taken a firm line at Munich he would have established, perhaps for ever, the superiority of democratic faith over Fascist conceptions. He did not question the Prime Minister's sincerity or his courage, but he had been ill-advised.

'I think, in regarding this crisis,' continued Mr. Nicolson, 'we ought to differentiate carefully between what I may call our physical, personal momentary feelings and our intellectual, moral, and permanent feelings. Obviously, when we heard that the war had been postponed there was an immense feeling of physical relief, an absolutely overwhelming feeling of relief, a feeling which I regret to say, manifested itself in the House of Commons by a demonstration of mass hysteria such as that great institution has never witnessed.'

FORCE OR LAW: A TEST

Proceeding to a detailed discussion of what the crisis was about, the speaker said that Herr Hitler well knew that this Czecho-Slovak question had become a test case which would demonstrate to the world opinion and establish to other smaller Powers which of the two theories, whether the theory of force or the theory of law, was determinant in Europe. He knew if he won upon this issue all the smaller Powers from the North of the Black Sea and from the Baltic to the Mediterranean would say to themselves, 'The two Western democracies are not strong enough to resist this tremendous force. We must, before it is too late, make our terms with the future master of Europe.' This again was a theory which the French and British Governments desired to oppose.

'I feel the public in this country, and in fact throughout the world, was under the illusion that the British Prime Minister was the champion of their own theory. By going to Berchtesgaden, Godesberg, and Munich he himself accepted this championship and took upon himself the weight of responsibility either for its triumph or for its defeat. We all felt that such courage on his part was highly commendable, and necessitated the sympathy and support of all men of good will. At the same time many of us were convinced that the violence of the dictator states could only be countered by a show of force on the part of the democratic peoples.

'We urged two course upon the Prime Minister. We begged him urgently to make it quite clear at Berlin that in the event of any aggression upon Czecho-Slovakia, or in the event of any terms imposed upon Czecho-Slovakia by a threat of force, he would find arrayed against him the combined forces of France, England and Russia. We also urged upon him the necessity of demonstrating our own resolution of some overt act, and we begged him to believe that those of us who had experience of German and Italian mentality were absoutely convinced that once he mobilised the British Fleet we should cause perturbation in Rome and thereby break the Berlin–Rome axis. The Prime Minister, at the eleventh hour, accepted this advice. The effect was immediate. Signor Mussolini realised at once that he would be faced by the might of the British Navy and at once he intervened at Berlin to prevent any forceful conclusion.

'It was at that moment, had the Prime Minister realised it, that we held all the cards in our hands. We well knew that opinion in Italy and Germany was alarmed and indeed terrified by the prospect of being faced by a war on two fronts and by a conflict in which the whole democratic opinion of the world would be united against them. Had the Prime Minister exploited his advantage he would have obtained peace with honour. He did not, however, understand the psychology of Germany and Italy and surrendered to them at the very moment when surrender was least necessary.

VOICE OF THE PUBLIC

'I cannot but feel that in so doing the Prime Minister did not interpret the real wishes of the British people. If, instead of relying upon the advice of the Inner Cabinet and his own industrial expert [Sir Horace Wilson], he had summoned the House of Commons to discuss the matter he would have learnt the British public had a far more vivid sense of realities, a far more clear conception of the needs of peace than was implied in his own doctrine of realism and appeasement. He managed to short-circuit the House of Commons upon an emotional appeal, and I am still unaware that his final surrender had the approval of his own Cabinet.'

Mr. Nicolson, who added that the Peace Pact which the Prime Minister had signed with the Führer was 'not worth the paper it is written on,' since Herr Hitler had himself stated that agreements were signed for war only and not for peace, said that within the course of a few days public opinion in this country would realise that it had been faced with a surrender of which it was not prepared to approve and which was wholly unnecessary.

At this time Harold Nicolson, a formidable former diplomat and man of letters, was National Labour M.P. for Leicester and only he along with Churchill, Eden and Duff Cooper on the Government side of the House of Commons did not cheer Chamberlain either as he set off to Munich or, even more significantly, on his return.

p.12

A PEACEFUL OCCUPATION
German Troops Followed by Returning Refugees

VIEWS ON AGREEMENT WITH BRITAIN

From our Correspondent

Berlin, October 2.

The German troops have begun their march into the Sudeten region with that military precision for which the German Army is famous. Thus Chancellor Hitler kept his word that he would commence with the liberation of the Sudeten Germans on October 1, and it is noted here with satisfaction. But still greater satisfaction – in fact relief – is felt that the occupation is a peaceful one and that the German soldiers can advance without firing.

The occupation of zone 1, in the South-west, began at 2 p.m. on Saturday, and of zone 2, in the North, at 1 p.m. to-day. So far no untoward incidents have been reported. The evacuation by the Czechs, and the occupation by the Germans is, to all appearances, progressing peacefully. Symbolical perhaps of this is that the first larger bodies of soldiers marching into zone 1 were headed by military bands, one of which halted at the frontier and played the German National Anthem before going any farther. Meanwhile reports are beginning to pour in from all sides of flowers being presented to the marching soldiers, of gaily decorated houses, shops and streets.

THE MUNICH MAP OF CZECHO-SLOVAKIA (Monday 3 October)

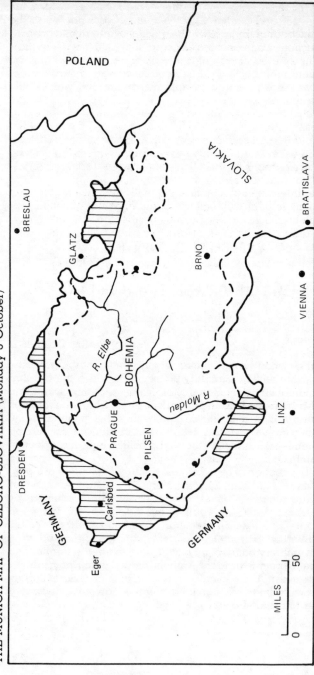

The map shows the four Sudeten territories of Czecho-Slovakia to be occupied by Germany in stages, according to the terms of the Munich Agreement. Territory No. 1 was occupied on Saturday and yesterday, and the occupation of Territory No. 2 will be completed to-day; Territory No. 3 will be occupied during the next three days, and Territory No. 4 during Thursday and Friday. The remainder of the predominantly German territory is to be occupied by October 10. The broken line is the frontier demanded by Herr Hitler in his Godesberg ultimatum.

COMMISSION'S GOOD WORK

At the back of the military movements of retreat and advance there watches the international commission that was set up in Munich. In the calm of a quiet room in the Foreign Office in Berlin its members meet to work out the plans and to smooth out the difficulties.

The commission is doing everything to keep the sand out of the wheels. It has, for instance, stipulated that a zone, two kilometres broad, shall remain between the Czech and the German forces. To-day it issued a proclamation to the Sudeten German population asking that they do everything to enable the passage of Sudeten Germany from Czecho-Slovakia to the Reich to take place without friction and without incidents.

The international commission will form itself into sub-commissions to deal with economic and financial questions and with the plebiscite. In order to prevent disorder the Sudeten German refugees are told that they may only pass into their home country after its occupation by German troops. Thus it happens that the troops are frequently followed by large bodies of returning refugees.

HENLEIN'S OFFICE

Meanwhile the Third Reich, with its talent for organisation, has already worked out its scheme for running the Sudetenland. For the time being Herr Hitler has entrusted the military commanders directing the occupation with its administration, but already the civilian successor has been nominated. It is Conrad Henlein, who has been appointed by Chancellor Hitler High Commissioner for the Sudeten region. He is directly under the orders of Herr Hitler, and will attend to the 'political, economic, and cultural building up' of the Sudetenland.

To-day Henlein issued a proclamation to the population of the Sudeten regions in which he says that the foremost task is the coming plebiscite in districts with mixed populations. Once more, he says, the Sudeten Germans will prove to the world that they stand behind Adolf Hitler. Surprise is voiced by the population here at the peacefulness of the Czechs after the many reports to the opposite about them in recent weeks.

ANGLO GERMAN UNDERTAKING

In retrospect political quarters here find many points in the Munich talks, aside from the solution of the Sudeten question, which fill them with great content. Thus the Munich conference is beginning to assume an ever-increasing importance in German opinion. Apart from the saving of peace and the solution of the Sudeten issue, the Anglo-German agreement not to go to war rises like a pinnacle high above all other results of the talks. 'One of the finest fruits of Munich,' one commentator calls this agreement.

It has been the Chancellor's wish for a long time to come to an understanding with the British people, and it is generally felt that a great step in this direction has now been taken. There are still a number of points of disagreement between the two nations it is admitted, the most acute still being the colonial problem. Herr Hitler himself pointed out that the Reich had not renounced its claim when he said in his speech last Monday that after the Sudeten question had been settled 'he would have no more territorial claims in Europe.' People here now hope that this problem, which in their opinion has been intensified by the fact that Germany now numbers 80,000,000 people, can now be tackled and settled by friendly negotiation.

The personal contact between M. Daladier and Herr Hitler will lead, it is hoped, to an improvement of Franco-German relations, possibly resulting in a similar agreement not to go to war against one another, as the one made between Mr. Chamberlain and Herr Hitler.

Finally, there is much talk here to-day of a closer co-operation of the four Powers which, as it is said, might lead to a limitation of armaments and the settlement of many other points close to the heart of the four nations.

Prague's acceptance of Poland's demand to occupy the region inhabited by its minority was welcomed here as removing a strain and a danger point. Prague is told that if it cuts loose from Moscow and enters no military alliances – which are considered here in any case as incompatible with an international guarantee – and that if it instead maintains good-neighbourly relations all may go well with Czecho-Slovakia.

AN ANXIOUS STOCKTAKING IN FRANCE
Misgivings About Britain's New Policy

THE MUNICH PLEDGE AND THE ANGLO-FRENCH ALLIANCE

From our own Correspondent

Paris, October 2.

Last night large crowds, including ex-servicemen's delegations with their banners, assembled in the Champs-Elysees and the Place de l'Etoile to see M. Daladier rekindle the flame on the tomb of the Unknown Warrior. And as the hundred thousand people present sang the 'Marseillaise' one felt that there was in the hearts of all these people – or most of them – a struggle between two different emotions – gratitude because France had been spared a terrible war and an intense anxiety for her future.

After the joy and the relief of the last two days the time has come in France for taking stock. 'Apart from England we have got nobody left' is a phrase more and more frequently heard in Paris to-day. Together with Czecho-Slovakia France has lost the Polish alliance and probably also the Russian alliance, and treaties bearing her signature have lost much weight. The 'Temps' already admits that 'the Polish and Russian alliances have lost much of their practical meaning.'

What is more, it is widely felt that even the British alliance is no longer what it used to be after Mr. Chamberlain's talk with Herr Hitler on Friday morning. It was a severe blow to France and not least to M. Daladier himself, who apparently had not expected anything like that at Munich. It is said that a similar Franco-German declaration 'may shortly' be made, but there is no evidence of any steps being taken in that direction – not that anyone in France can have many illusions about the value of such a German promise to France. But the Anglo-German declaration is considered here to be of much more than academic interest. It is believed to be the first clear indication of that new British policy which has already brought about the resignation of Mr. Duff Cooper.

A NON-AGGRESSION PACT

Although the Anglo-German declaration is not a legally binding document, it has been remarked in Paris that it is in effect something like a non-aggression pact, and the question is asked how such a bilateral non-aggression pact can be reconciled with Britain's guarantee to France and Belgium. Whatever the answer to this, it is strongly felt that the Anglo-German declaration clearly marks a weakening of the Anglo-French alliance as the keystone of Britain's Continental policy.

In this connection M. de Kerillis quotes a remarkable statement which 'one of the most eminent British Conservatives' (one guess is Mr. Winston Churchill) made to him a fortnight ago:

The Czecho-Slovak affair (he said) may have much graver consequences than is imagined. For three centuries British policy has been based on the balance of power in Europe. We have always fought against the hegemony of any one Power. But this policy was possible only because we always had a strong point of support which we used as our basis. In reading your papers, in looking at your reactions, we are for the first time beginning to wonder whether such a point of support exists any longer. It is therefore possible that the time will come when we may be obliged to break away from our traditional policy, and instead of resisting against the dominating Power in Europe we shall endeavour to come to terms with it.

257

M. de Kerillis adds: 'It is only fair to say that he did not add "At your expense." But nevertheless his words have worried me greatly; and I also remembered "Mein Kampf" with the isolation and destruction of France as Hitler's ultimate aim.'

SECOND THOUGHTS ON MUNICH

Altogether since pondering over the Anglo-German declaration the French papers are no longer as enthusiastic about Munich as they were. No doubt 'Paris Soir' is still collecting money for 'a villa in France with a river where he can fish' which is to be presented to Mr. Chamberlain, and the President of the Paris Town Council has asked Mr. Chamberlain to visit Paris and to receive the gratitude of the Paris people. But many of the papers are now in a state of confusion.

The isolation of France is keenly felt, and the question persistently asked after the Anglo-German statement is: 'What is England's policy going to be?' If it is to be the four-Power pact, then France can clearly play in it no part except that of England's satelite, with no will and no initiative of her own; and in any case this four-Power pact can produce nothing good for France and Britain, it is felt here.

FOUR-POWER PACT POLICY

Already the first result of the four-Power pact agreement at Munich has been to strangle Czecho-Slovakia. The second result was Poland's ultimatum to Czecho-Slovakia – a move which showed that four-Power pact decisions will either not be observed at all or else be violated only at the expense of France, England, and their friends. In any case the four-Power pact, which had always been regarded by France as a dangerous heresy, is Signor Mussolini's most cherished invention – which alone is enough to make it suspect.

In the view of French observers the alternative to a four-Power pact policy in Mr. Chamberlain's mind is an Anglo-German policy. This at least would have the 'advantage' of robbing Italy of her ambition to play the balance-of-power game hitherto played by England. In either case, however, France, it is felt, would be in an extremely precarious position. Under the four-Power pact she would be the reluctant and helpless 'fourth partner'; under the Anglo-German policy she would be even more at the mercy of England's and Germany's good graces, with nothing to fall back on except the more than doubtful friendship of Italy (the cultivation of which, by the way, is now being again advocated by the press of the Right, but this time without the old conviction).

No doubt the policy of Anglo-German friendship would not be directed against France but against Russia. But ultimately such a deliberate aggrandisement of Germany's power would hardly save France – or England for that matter. And the question is also asked whether Mr. Chamberlain, while no doubt considering the Rhine frontier essential to British security, will not expect France to foot the greater share of Germany's colonial bill.

FRENCH DEFENCES

Altogether there are few Frenchmen who doubt that if such a policy is pursued it will result in the isolation of France, to be accompanied, or followed, by the isolation of England. A patriotically-minded Frenchman like M. de Kerillis, who fears the worst, holds that France can now be saved only by a complete reorganisation, by the establishment of what he calls an 'Authoritarian Republic' by the building up of 'three new Maginot lines,' by the purchase wherever possible of 3,000 of the fastest bombing aeroplanes, by the thorough organisation of A.R.P., &c. – otherwise, he says, France, left almost entirely to herself, will be doomed.

The internal consequences of Munich in France are still incalculable. The idea of building up a tremendous defence machine now that all allies have been lost has gained ground; and with it all sorts of theories about an authoritarian regime, a military dictatorship, a totalitarian financial system, and what not. Among the working class, on the other hand, there is profound disgust with the 'Republican regime' as it has functioned in the last months and a great loss of loyalty to 'democracy.'

WAS HITLER BLUFFING?

Looking back on the Czech crisis some interesting new reflections and suggestions have been made – one, for instance, is that Herr Hitler was bluffing to the bitter end. Germany clearly could not afford to fight against a vast coalition (a point blatantly admitted in Field Marshal Göring's paper to-day).

Secondly it is whispered that the Munich meeting was in reality discreetly suggested to a certain important person in Rome by a neutral diplomat – who was clearly acting on Germany's behalf. If so, Munich would be much less of a triumph for Mr. Chamberlain than is commonly supposed.

Finally the reflection is made that if Herr Hitler was really prepared to go to war with France and England he would not have acted as he did this time: he gave them several weeks to prepare for war. But his favourite war theory, on the contrary, is that the war should start 'like a bolt from the blue.'

The aftermath of Munich could be described as a period of progressive disillusion in Great Britain and France. It had finally become apparent that Hitler could not in any real sense be appeased and that, whatever his professed views on the preservation of the British Empire might be, he was intent on a revanchist policy in Continental Europe.

Appeasement had been shown to be a dismal failure. The Democracies, if they were now to fight, would do so from a markedly weaker position.

WORKING OUT THE MUNICH PACT
Big Task Before Commission

GERMANY AND ITALY

From a Diplomatic Correspondent

London, Sunday.

The international commission composed of the Ambassadors in Berlin of Great Britain, France, Italy, the Minister of Czecho-Slovakia in Berlin, and the Under Secretary of State in the German Foreign Office will have to decide (as was stated in the 'Manchester Guardian' on Saturday) in which Czech and Czech–German districts plebiscites are to be held. During the negotiations in Munich the big four were not able to come to an agreement on this question.

German quarters are extremely optimistic with regard to the decisions of the international commission. It is believed that the commission will make no attempts to alter in any considerable measure the extreme Godesberg demands. It is felt in Germany that now, after the German demands have in principle been accepted and internationally corroborated by the marching in of the Germans in the Sudeten districts, no Power will want to bring on another crisis about 'trifles' and 'questions of interpretation.' It cannot be entirely ruled out that this opinion of the German leaders was supported by the proceedings in Munich.

The task of the international commission comprehends considerably more than has been laid down in the wording of the Munich agreement. It appears that the commission has been authorised to decide all those questions on which full agreement could not be brought about in Munich. Among these, for example, are such important questions as the methods of the plebiscite and the treatment of the war material in the Czecho-Slovak fortresses.

ITALIAN SYMPATHY FOR FRANCE

It has been said that the conversations in Munich have shown that Italy has no military agreement with Germany. This impression is certainly not correct. The proceedings in Munich have proved on the contrary – that the German–Italian military alliance is a fact.

How this alliance would have worked if war had broken out is another question. It is probable that Mussolini and Count Ciano, as Foreign Minister, would have had to face certain internal difficulties if they had made an attempt to put into force immediately the military alliance with Germany. In particular some of the non-Fascist population in Northern Italy is opposed to the pro-German policy.

It has been confirmed that when the announcement of the discussions in Munich became known on the Milan Stock Exchange members began to sing the 'Marseillaise.' More important than these influences was the opposition of the King during the last few days. It is said that the King went so far as to refuse his signature to the mobilisation order requested by Mussolini. This attitude explains Mussolini's attempts to avoid war.

p.13

SOUTH AFRICAN TRIBUTE TO THE PREMIER

General Hertzog, the Prime Minister of South Africa, has sent a congratulatory cable to Mr. Chamberlain in which he says that the Union of South Africa has received the outcome of the Munich conference with immense relief.

The message continues:—

'I sincerely trust that the conference will be the first of many others at which the problems which lie at the root of a dangerous position will be faced courageously and honestly and with a steadfast determination to solve them on a basis of justice and goodwill to all concerned.'

GENERAL SMUTS

General Smuts paid tribute to Mr. Chamberlain in a speech at the opening of a royal Scottish gathering at Johannesburg on Saturday. He said 'Once more the occasion has produced the man. Mr. Chamberlain appeared at the last moment to save the world from war, God bless him. Without thought of the difficulties and danger to his future he risked all and, I trust, has won all.'

General Smuts said that the world was grateful to the four leaders of Europe for doing something which ended the most dangerous crisis in recent history.

'We are now in a position to build up peace in future on a wide scale: it can only be peace with understanding, confidence, and the negation of violence and resort to superior force. On this basis of understanding and systematic conference as laid down in the Covenant of the League can we rebuild the peace which we failed to make in 1919. The moment has arrived for great advances, and the world should not let it pass unused.'

Mr. Mackenzie King, the Canadian Prime Minister, has received the following acknowledgement from Mr. Chamberlain to the message of congratulation sent him on Friday:–

'I have been greatly touched by the terms of your telegram. My efforts to ensure a peaceful settlement of the problem, which threatened all the horrors of war, have been greatly strengthened by the knowledge that I had the support of all men of goodwill, both here and in all parts of the British Commonwealth. I share your hope that the agreement now reached may prove a stepping-stone towards general appeasement in international relations.'–Reuter.

It should be noted that just prior to the Munich meetings the High Commissioners for Australia, New Zealand, South Africa, and Ireland had met Chamberlain on 26 September and according to one authority had all 'felt that the German proposals should not be allowed to wreck peace. Therefore it could be argued that as Chamberlain's appeasement policy reached its apotheosis at Munich it enjoyed the support of the vast majority of his Commonwealth colleagues.

PRAGUE PARLIAMENT APPEALS TO BRITISH AND FRENCH
Problems the Agreement Ignored

Prague, October 2.

The Presidents of the Czecho-Slovak Chamber of Deputies and the Senate have addressed the following telegram to the Speaker of the British House of Commons and to the President of the French Chamber of Deputies:–

'The Parliamentary representatives of the political parties forming the Government majority in the Czecho-Slovak Government appeal to the conscience of the French and British Parliaments at a time so painful for the Czecho-Slovak nation. We do so after the conference in Munich, where a decision was made about us and without us in a manner unparalleled in history.

'Our hearts urge us to unburden our feelings to the representatives of the French and British peoples, convinced as we are that you are the exponents and representatives of the ideals which we too still hold dear.

'From the time of the restoration of our State after the world war we put our faith in the noble ideals of democracy, right, justice, honour, humanity, and especially, peace among the nations and States. For those ideals we sacrificed much, spiritually and morally. We strove for peace in the world. We stood for peace at home, supporting our Government with all our strength to reach a just solution in our nationalities question. Never did we break the obligations which we assumed for this purpose.

1,000 YEAR OLD FRONTIERS

'Under tremendous pressure the Czecho-Slovak Government accepted the proposals of the French and British Governments on September 19 this year. We did this in spite of the fact that these proposals disrupt boundaries untouched for a thousand years, given by God and Nature, and consecrated by the blood of the Czech nation.

'It must be clear to the whole world that the decision of the Czecho-Slovak Government was one of the greatest sacrifices made for the peace of Europe. We supposed, however, that the application of the principles of the secession of our territory would be carried out, so that it would be tolerable, over a certain period of time.

'In particular, we supposed that the vital interests, economic, transport, livelihood, would be properly respected. We were all the more unpleasantly affected when the conference paid no attention to the promises given to us as to the defence of our vital interests, especially our most important communications and supplies and the most essential raw materials.

'Instead of this the territory has to be transferred within a few days. There has been no final settlement of the question of compensation for State property or the interests of thousands and thousands of people. The question of minorities is left in complete obscurity.

'This is the painful fact which leaves an ineffaceable scar in our hearts, and so we turn our minds to-day to all the noble spirits of Europe and of the world, demanding that they should recognise our position.

'We appeal to them to understand the moral revolution which has caused the punishment of a State and a nation which wanted nothing more than to fulfil its obligations, a nation which had real faith in the high principles of human co-operation, a nation which committed no other wrong than the desire to live in its own fashion in the cultural community of nations and States.

'We bequeath our sorrow to the French and English people.'

DECORATIONS RETURNED

General Medek, a Siberian war veteran, who was decorated with the D.S.O. and the Legion of Honour, has returned the insignia of these decorations to the British and French Governments, saying that his conscience will not permit him to wear them.

One or two other persons holding French decorations have returned them to the French Government.–Reuter.

TRIBUTES TO MR. CHAMBERLAIN
A Blackpool Gift

Mr. William Parkinson, chairman of Blackpool Football Club and president of Blackpool Cricket Club, has offered to build and present to the corporation twelve houses to be occupied by ex-servicemen or their families free of rent as a means of commemorating the successful efforts of the Prime Minister to preserve European and world peace.

The offer is contained in a letter to the Mayor of Blackpool, Alderman J.R. Quaile. Mr. Parkinson's solicitors expressed the view in making the offer, that as many towns as possible should do something by way of a tribute to Mr. Chamberlain. 'This is a noble and characteristic action by Mr. Parkinson and is a magnificent and generous gesture', the Major told a reporter.

Mr. William Parkinson is a brother of the late Sir Lindsay Parkinson, former Mayor of Blackpool and first M.P. for Blackpool Parliamentary Borough.

MORE HOSPITAL BEDS

The chairman of Westminster Hospital, Mr. Bernard Docker, has given £1,000 to name one of the beds in the new hospital in perpetual remembrance of the victory of peace. The hospital has received the Prime Minister's permission to name the bed 'The Neville Chamberlain Bed.'

An anonymous benefactor has endowed a 'peace' bed at the Manchester and Salford Home for aged Jews, in honour of Mr. Neville Chamberlain. Prayers for the Premier will be recited at the dedication service.

FREEDOM OF VERSAILLES

The freedom of Versailles is to be conferred on Mr. Chamberlain, according to a decision reached at a meeting of the Versailles Municipal Council on Saturday. The council also decided to name one of the avenues in the town 'Avenue Chamberlain.'

The subscription opened by the 'Paris Soir' for presenting a house to Mr. Chamberlain exceeded 100,000 francs (£500) in the first twenty-four hours. Aix-les-Bains suggests that the site of the house should be on the shore of Lake Bouget.

A public subscription for a monument in a Lisbon park to Mr. Chamberlain is to be opened by the 'Dairio de Noticias' to-morrow.

THE NOBEL PRIZE

The proposal that Mr. Chamberlain should receive the Nobel Peace Prize, says the Stockholm 'Tidningen,' is warmly supported in all quarters in Sweden, Norway, and England. The newspaper publishes views which its London correspondent obtained from the Archbishop of Canterbury, the Lord Mayor of London, Mr. Lansbury, and others. Persons qualified to propose candidates according to the Nobel testament have expressed support of the proposal.– Reuter's telegrams.

Tuesday 4 October   *p.11*

NO HALT IN BRITAIN'S REARMAMENT
Premier Warns the Country

GOVERNMENT'S WEAKNESS IN THE CRISIS
No Clear Warning to Hitler

–Mr. Duff Cooper.

Mr. Chamberlain, who returned from Munich on Friday with the claim that he had won peace with honour – 'and, I believe, peace for our time' – warned the country when he met the House of Commons yesterday that there can be no halt in our rearmament programme. He said:

> Lasting peace is not to be obtained by sitting still and waiting for it to come. It requires active, positive efforts to achieve it.
> No doubt I shall have plenty of critics who will say that I am guilty of facile optimism and that I should disbelieve every word that is uttered by rulers of other great States. I am too much of a realist to believe that we are going to achieve our paradise in a day. We have only laid the foundations of peace. The superstructure is not even begun.
> For a long period now we have been engaged in this country on a great programme of rearmament, which is daily increasing in pace and volume. Let no one think that because we have signed this agreement between these four Powers at Munich we can afford to relax our efforts in regard to the programme at this moment.
> We must renew our determination to fill up the deficiencies that yet remain in our armament and in our defensive precautions, so that we may be ready to defend ourselves and make our diplomacy effective.
> I say with an equal sense of realism that I see fresh opportunities of approaching this subject of disarmament opening up before us.

Mr. Duff Cooper, who has resigned his post of First Lord of the Admiralty because of his 'profound distrust' of the Government's foreign policy, preceded the Premier with his 'personal statement.' He complained that the Government had for weeks allowed the country to drift nearer and nearer to war with Germany by failing to make our position clear. The first real warning given to Hitler, he said, was the mobilising of the British Fleet. Points from his speech were:–

I have always thought that in any international crisis our first duty was to make it plain exactly where we stood and what we were doing.

I believe the great defect of our foreign policy in recent months and weeks has been that we have failed to do this. During the last four weeks we have drifted day by day nearer into war with Germany.

We never stated until the last moment, and then in the most uncertain terms, that we were prepared to fight. We know that information to the opposite effect was being poured into the ears of the Germans, that in no case would Great Britain fight.

I had hoped the Premier after his meeting with Hitler at Berchtesgaden might have made the position plain. He did not do so. Again at Godesberg I hoped that a statement might have been made in unequivocal language. Again I was disappointed.

Hitler had another speech to make in Berlin, and there was another opportunity of telling him exactly where we stood. Again the opportunity was missed. It was only after the speech that he was told through a distinguished English civil servant that under certain conditions we were prepared to fight.

A message with at least three qualifying clauses was not likely to produce on him, on the morning after his great ovation, the effect that was desired.

It was only when the Fleet was mobilised that Hitler realised that what his advisers had been assuring him was untrue and that the British people were prepared to fight in a great cause.

It was only then that there was the first sign that he was prepared to yield something.

The Premier believes he can come to a reasonable settlement with Herr Hitler on all outstanding questions. He may be right. I hope he is. But I cannot believe it.

Mr. Chamberlain made no reply to Mr. Duff Cooper. He announced that he was going to deliver the speech he would have made if Mr. Duff Cooper had not resigned. Mr. Duff Cooper's criticisms and others could be answered later. The answer made by Sir Samuel Hoare, who wound up for the Government, was that 'if we had gone farther than we did there would have been a world war in progress to-day.'

Defending the Anglo-German pledge, which Mr. Duff Cooper had criticised, Mr. Chamberlain said there was no cause for suspicion. He had made no new commitments; there was no secret understanding. But he believed there was sincerity and goodwill on both sides and that the significance of the declaration went far beyond its actual words.

HELP FOR THE CZECHS

Mr. Chamberlain paid a warm, if belated tribute to Czecho-Slovakia's 'restraint, dignity, and magnificent discipline in the face of such trial,' and announced some immediate financial assistance. The Czech Government, he said, had asked the British Government to help it to raise a loan of £30,000,000 by a British Government guarantee. The Chancellor had already asked the Bank of England to provide credits of £10,000,000. How that £10,000,000 would be related to the final figure of the loan was a matter for the future.

The National Council of Labour issues an appeal 'to all classes and parties' to support the International Solidarity Fund to relieve distress in Czecho-Slovakia. The council has opened the fund with a gift of £2,000. The Lord Mayor of London will decide within the next day or two whether to open a Mansion House Fund. Subscriptions began to arrive yesterday for the Council of Action's fund.

HITLER'S TRIUMPHAL ENTRY

While German troops were occupying the third zone of Sudetenland yesterday Herr Hitler was entering the country in triumph. He crossed the frontier near Asch, where he received a tumultuous welcome, and went on to Eger, where the demonstrations were repeated. He later visited other villages, and will continue his tour to-day.

It was revealed in Rome yesterday that during the crisis Italy had secretly mobilised three military classes and the reservists of three Alpine divisions. Their demobilisation will begin on Monday. This was the first disclosure of any military measures by Italy during the crisis.

A contingent of the British Legion, 1,000 strong, is being sent to Czecho-Slovakia for police duty in the plebiscite areas. The volunteers, representing all areas of the Legion, are to assemble at Olympia, London, on Thursday.

THE PREMIER'S AIMS
Four-Power Pact?

PARTIES AND THE PEACE
Labour's Indecision

From our Political Correspondent

Westminster, Monday Night.

One sought for the answer to two questions in to-day's debate. First, is Mr. Chamberlain finally bidding for a four-Power pact as 'the sheet-anchor' (in Lord Baldwin's time 'the sheet-anchor' was the League) of British foreign policy? Secondly, how does his party stand towards the Munich settlement? Does he carry it with him?

Take the first question. There was not a syllable in Mr. Chamberlain's speech that is inconsistent with the theory that he is set on a four-Power pact for Europe. Certainly, he spoke in warm praise of President Roosevelt's intervention at the height of the crisis last week, but expression of a sentiment of that kind is not in necessary conflict with the aim of attempting to secure peace in Europe through a concert of the four Western Powers.

RUSSIA IGNORED

Most damning of all, if you are looking for evidence of this new orientation of British policy, is Mr. Chamberlain's complete ignoring of Russia. He never once mentioned her. Mr. Maisky was in the Diplomats' Gallery during the speech and made some notes. Their tenor is not difficult to guess. On the other hand there was something like a pledge for Herr Hitler's sincerity and there was unreserved praise for Signor Mussolini and his part in the Munich negotiations. As for France, Mr. Chamberlain commended M. Daladier for the excellent way in which he had played a difficult role at Munich. No more than that. Nothing about France herself. If it had not been for his statement of yesterday seeking to reassure the French Government on the point one might have thought that Mr. Chamberlain was seeking something even narrower than a Four-Power Pact – a straight deal with the two dictators.

PREMIER AND HIS PARTY

As for Mr. Chamberlain's position in his own party, he has nothing to fear. The party rose to him when he came in. That was almost as good as a division. Who remains seated? Mr. Churchill, Mr. Sandys, Mr. Harold Nicolson, Commander Bower, and Mr. Cartland.

It is the old Churchillian group (plus Mr. Harold Nicolson) and they have been routed on so many Parliamentary fields. There may be a few more to add to them. Sir Roger Keyes, for instance. But it would take a revolt of 200, not 20, Tories to disturb this Government.

That is not to say that every Tory likes the Munich settlement. There are quite a number who think it an unpleasant business, but they will swallow a lot of unpleasantness before voting against the Government. There remains the great bulk of the party, and it shares the more general view that Mr. Chamberlain saved us from war last week, and on better terms than those of the Godesberg ultimatum – in short, through wringing some concession from Herr Hitler.

To them, as to so many of the general public, Mr. Chamberlain has become the deliverer, and they will vote for him to a man. Mr. Chamberlain will have a huge majority in the division.

THE LABOUR PARTY

The Labour party met to-day to decide what motion to put down. It could not reach a decision and will try again to-morrow. The truth is the Labour party is not at one. Like the Liberal party, it has one or two members who would let their approval of Mr. Chamberlain's peace outweigh everything else. It is also true, of course, that a big body of the party is so strongly moved by hatred of Fascism that it takes Mr. Duff Cooper's line that the 'mailed fist' can only be answered by the 'mailed fist' and not by the Premier's 'sweet reasonableness.'

Between these two wings is another group, more concerned with the management of the party, that is nervous about doing anything that might make it possible for the Conservatives to represent Labour at the next election as the war party.

The Government late to-night put down its vote of confidence, and this leaves the way clear for the Labour party to reply with a reasoned amendment instead of what could be construed as a vote of censure. In that way Labour will offer the Government no excuse for plunging into an immediate general election, which it is assumed the Government would win.

ONLY A RESPITE

The logic of most of the speeches to-day was that we have secured, not peace, but a respite and that there is nothing left but to rearm at much greater speed. Even Mr. Chamberlain, though he believes we may be entering a longish period of peace, also called for steady rearmament. This debate was a world removed from the ebullient optimism of Friday.

LETTERS TO THE EDITOR

'THE FUNERAL OF BRITISH HONOUR'

To the Editor of the Manchester Guardian

Sir,–The flowers piled before 10, Downing Street, are very fitting for the funeral of British honour and, it may be, of the British Empire. For sheer degradation the frenzies of last Friday beat even the night of Mafeking.

I appreciate the Prime Minister's love of peace. I know the horrors of war – a great deal better than he can. But when he returns from saving our skins from a blackmailer at the price of other people's flesh, and waves, laughing with glee, a piece of paper with Herr Hitler's name on it, if it were not ghastly, it would be grotesque. No doubt he has never read 'Mein Kampf' in German. But to forget, so utterly, the Reichstag fire, and the occupation of the Rhineland, and June 30, 1934, and the fall of Austria! We have lost the courage to see things as they are. And yet Herr Hitler has kindly put down for us in black and white that programme he is so faithfully carrying out. (For he keeps his threats, though not his promises.) Alliance with Italy and England: the annihilation of France: the conquest for the German plough of the Ukraine: a Reich of 250,000,000. And then?

I may be wrong. No one can tell. There are no sure prophecies in politics, as even Bismarck owned. But just because all roads lead none knows whither, all the more reason to keep the straight path of honour. This is the really unpardonable thing in the conduct of Mr. Chamberlain. Even if what he did were the right thing to do, this was not the way to do it. Any really great man who had felt forced to sacrifice a small nation that trusted in him would at least have returned full of anguish and of shame. But Mr. Chamberlain, though he has good intentions, has no finer sense of honour. He lent himself with complacency to the shrieking adulation of a London that had lost all dignity, without one thought for the agony of Prague. Leaders should have some touch of finer mettle. Mr. Chamberlain, chanting of 'peace with honour,' has debased the moral currency of England. And not for the first time: and not, I fear, for the last.

Meanwhile the past is past, however shameful. What now? If we have any remaining particle of self-respect we shall remedy at once that outrageous omission by which all Sudetens in Czech prisons are to be liberated, while no word is said of the Czechs dragged across the frontier into German captivity or arrested in Germany. Secondly we shall compensate Czecho-Slovakia for the property we have forced her to leave to the invader – the machinery in Czech-owned factories, the fortifications, and their artillery – which belonged to the Czech State as a whole, not to the Sudetens, as indefeasibly as the very streets of Prague. Thirdly, unless we propose to barricade ourselves behind pieces of paper kindly autographed by Herr Hitler, we shall look a little better to our defences, even if it means conscription in the near future.

As I watched last week in the villages of Alsace-Lorraine the young men sadly but loyally leaving their fields for the colours it was impossible to feel that we in England were doing our share. And a citizen army is to some extent a safeguard, which we may yet need against Fascism at home,–Yours, &c.,

F.L. LUCAS.
Kings College, Cambridge, October 1.

THE MUNICH AGREEMENT — AND AFTER
Mr. Chamberlain's Great Opportunity:
Can He Be Trusted to Use It?

To the Editor of the Mancheter Guardian

Sir,–For the present we are safe but what of the future?

In 1919, when the Treaty of Versailles was being hailed with nation-wide enthusiasm and acclaimed by a virtually unanimous House of Commons, I incurred many abusive letters and a few threats of violence to life and limb – one from a Cabinet Minister – because I publicly protested againt certain of its clauses. I welcomed a treaty of peace, even an unjust and unwise peace, brutally imposed on a helpless and unheard nation, as preferable to war, but I protested against certain provisions as likely to perpetuate the misery of Europe and cause further trouble in the future. They did so; they proved unworkable: and they have almost all been gradually annulled or dropped.

There is now a similar widespread enthusiasm, partly due to relief from immediate fear, partly, I think, to nobler causes, over another unjust peace treaty, imposed with needless brutality on a nation similarly helpless and similarly unheard. This peace also is vastly preferable to war, and the terms, however unsatisfactory, probably less unjust and unwise than would have resulted from war, which ever side had the victory. Consequently I welcome it. But I would add two cautions.

The Treaty of Versailles, however faulty, was only made intolerable owing to the fraudulent and violent methods by which it was carried out. We do not yet know how the Hitlerite troops will carry out their occupation; how far they will use their undoubted skill in creating 'incidents' to provide an excuse for 'tearing Czecho-Slovakia to pieces,' as suggested by the Nazi official press; or even how far the international commission in the plebiscite areas will succeed in counteracting Nazi terrorism.

Secondly, we do not know, we can only tremble to think what may be meant by Mr. Chamberlain's warm and affectionate assurances of co-operation and friendship given to the two dictators. We know what the dictators want and on what their power is based. Hitler has told it in 'Mein Kampf'; Mussolini tells it daily in the bronze map of the new Roman Empire set up in the Forum. Not only 'Die Vernichtung Frankreichs'; the making of the Mediterranean again into mare nostrum; and the repartition of the British Empire. Worse than all these, the utter corruption of the soul of Europe, government by delation and persecution, the abolition of law and morality in politics, and the consequent dissolution of the League of Nations.

What the dictators mean or have hitherto meant is clear. What Mr. Chamberlain's co-operation means is not clear. We have some dim idea what it has meant in the past; a continual complaisance which to large sections of his own party appeared neither far-sighted nor honourable but which at least kept his own country out of war. Such a course may or may not have been unavoidable in the past, but now the Prime Minister has a nobler choice. His last-minute personal efforts to save the peace of Europe have appealed to the imagination of the whole world and made suddenly visible and articulate that profound horror of war, of its wickedness and blindness as well as its misery, which has for long formed a bond of inward and unconscious union between all the peoples of the earth. He has in his hands the same instrument of world emotion that President Wilson had in 1918.

Is that emotion a passing thing or is it deep, permanent conviction which Governments can be compelled to obey? If it is a deep conviction, can Mr. Chamberlain be trusted to use it, to understand it, to see that peace means something better than merely running away from war, and that, however great the majority of people who want peace, they cannot have it unless they stand together as one?

A tremendous opportunity is there: will it be used? Yours, &c.,
GILBERT MURRAY.
Yatscombe, Boar's Hill, Oxford. October 1.

Murray was Regius Professor of Greek at Oxford University from 1908–1936; he was also Chairman of the League of Nations Union from 1923–1938.

EUROPE'S NARROW ESCAPE FROM WAR

To the Editor of the Manchester Guardian

Sir, The days of terrible anxiety through which we have passed have brought to light significant and sometimes strange facts and taught lessons which should not be ignored:

1. It has been possible for this and other nations to be brought to the very verge of war for reasons incredibly inadequate.

2. The dangers and drawbacks of a military alliance with France have been revealed fully. We have been shown that a pledge to defend France if she attacked can be interpreted as an undertaking to attack a country with whom we have no quarrel if France decides to attack her because another ally of France's has become embroiled with that country on an issue concerning which France's other ally is more in the wrong than in the right. This somewhat involved sentence may serve to demonstrate the extent to which the term 'defence' can be stretched.

3. We have been given a disturbing example of the strange and sheeplike willingness of our people to be led, or driven, to the slaughter for a cause even in their estimation inadequate. This time the majority of our nation accepted the virtual inevitability of war with no hysteria of militant fervour and with a recognition that those whom they might have to kill were, like themselves opposed to war. With heavy hearts and no hatred they went off sadly to prepare to kill or to prepare to give what assistance might lie in their power to the victims of destruction on a scale unequalled in history, but hardly any seemed disposed to rise up in flaming indignation and declare, 'This thing is monstrous: such evil folly shall not be!'

4. We have had revealed to us the appalling inadequacy of the great majority of our political leaders in wise statemanship and ability to weigh accurately grave moral and practical issues. One man and one man alone, and he a member of a practical party usually characterised by incapacity to do much of value in the cause of peace, displayed at the eleventh hour a courage, an originality, and a breadth of human friendliness which make him at the present moment probably the most deservedly popular figure in the civilised world.

But what hope would there have been for us if the leaders of those parties which are supposed to be the special champions of progress and humanity had been in power? Labour leaders, with a few honourable exceptions, in an ill-judged effort to 'call the bluff' of a strong man who was not bluffing, would have involved millions of innocent people in destruction that they might gratify their hatred for a Fascist dictator and a Fascist regime. Liberal leaders would have done the same, partly from misplaced zeal for what they quaintly term 'collective security' based on force, a policy which the events of present-day history and the searching criticisms of more than one able mind have demonstrated to be impracticable before the day arrives on which it becomes unnecessary.

5. The great though often disputed truth that armaments by their very existence are not a defence but the main cause of war has again been demonstrated. Because both Germany and Britain were confident of a good chance of victory by reason of the power of their great fighting machines and the strength of their alliances they came to the very verge of war, not on a grave issue but on a trifling one. I do suggest that the destructive power of rival armaments did not influence the statesmen at all in their decision for peace, but it was our armaments that made our Government ready to fight Hitler on account of his championship of the Sudeten Germans and it was our Prime Minsiter's friendliness and reasonable appeals, and not fear of our armaments, which were the main factor in persuading ultimately to choose the way of peace.

Others no doubt will call attention to the tremendous opportunity that lies before us if we will only make the best of the new spirit in international relationships, and will refrain from the accursed apathy and folly which refuse to right any injustice before compulsion is applied and which will not do the right thing by a large section of humanity for fear lest our motives be misunderstood or the interests of some small minority be sacrificed.

Finally, let us take to heart the lesson the Prime Minister has taught us, never, no matter how much we may dislike his past record or present policy, to regard a man personally unknown to us as of necessity a brute incapable of goodness or good feeling on any issue and as one upon whom any approach in the spirit of friendliness must of necessity be wasted.—Yours, &c.,

TAVISTOCK.
Cairnsmore, Newton Stewart, Wigtownshire, September 30.

According to the sentiments expressed in the final paragraph of his letter Lord Tavistock still did not appreciate the full enormity of Hitler's philosophy and naked ambition.

BRITAIN'S DEBT TO THE CZECHS

To the Editor of the Manchester Guardian

Sir,—You refer in your letter this morning to the sacrifices which Czecho-Slovakia has had to make for our peace. The sacrifices are individual (on the part of those refugees who must leave behind their goods, their stock, or their livelihood) and collective (on the part of the whole nation, whose economic position will be disastrously impaired).

Will the British people in their gratitude share in this sacrifice? Our Government might bear the financial cost to the

274

Czecho-Slovaks to the extent of a hundred million pounds (or two or three hundred millions, whatever be the most). The money might be raised by special taxation for this special object. This is the least that we can do to share the material part of the sacrifice involved. The alternative was war.

Let us not wait for others to act. A subscription list is not enough. It is a collective obligation.–Yours, &c.,

T.E. CLARKE,
Brookland Methodist Church, Lower Ashley Road, Bristol.
October 1.

THE PRAYERS FOR PEACE

To the Editor of the Manchester Guardian

Sir,–While we have been appointing days of prayer to God for peace in England, has any one of us reflected that thousands of the Czech nation have also been praying to God? We are now rejoicing in peace, however procured, and have appointed a day of thanksgiving. What of the Czechs and their day of mourning? Are the devout of England merely to send them the complacent message that 'whom the Lord loveth He chasteneth'?

Ought not our thinking to be a little clearer somewhere and our jubilation less strident?–Yours, &c.,

GERTRUDE BONE,
October 1.

A FABLE OF ÆSOP

To the Editor of the Manchester Guardian

Sir,–During the past days of obviously impending surrender to the threat of violence the accompanying fable of Aesop has been very present to my mind. It might perhaps be re-read usefully by the democracies:

THE TREES AND THE AXE

A woodman went into the forest and begged of the Trees the favour of a handle for his Axe. The principal Trees agreed at once to so modest a request and unhesitatingly gave him a young ash sapling, out of which he fashioned the handle he desired. No sooner had he done so than he set to work to fell the noblest Trees in the wood. When they saw the use to which he was putting their gift they cried, 'Alas! alas! we are undone, but we are ourselves to blame. The little we gave has cost us all: had we not sacrificed the rights of the ash we might ourselves have stood for ages.'

–Yours, &c.,

D. SMITH,
Ocean View, Rhos-on Sea,
September 30.

TO WHOM GRATITUDE IS CHIEFLY DUE

To the Editor of the Manchester Guardian

Sir,–More than to anyone else the demonstrations of gratitude for peace now taking place in all countries should be directed to the Czecho-Slovakians and to their Government for the noble way in which they have controlled and restrained the temper and behaviour of their people under the greatest provocations. Their quality is shown in every pronouncement they make.– Yours, &c.,

C.H. REILLY,
The Athenaeum, Pall Mall, London, S.W.1, October 2.

Wednesday 5 October   *p.9*

MORE PRESSURE ON CZECHS
Breaking Up Country

From our own Correspondent

Berlin, October 4.

Czecho-Slovakia is depicted here as already breaking up. Following the yielding of the Teschen area to Poland and the latest demands of the Slovak autonomists, the Czechs, it is reported here, are evacuating the areas claimed by Hungary and the Ruthenians are stated to be joining their voices with those of Germany for the abolition of the Czech pact with Russia. Whatever their accuracy may be, these reports are worth recording, for they probably correspond with German intentions towards the future Czecho-Slovak State. ...

GERMANY'S DIPLOMATIC VICTORIES

It is assumed here, however, that the Russian pact with Czecho-Slovakia is already dead and past resurrection. The

276

'diplomatic revolution' against Versailles, declares the official newspaper 'Angriff,' which began with the German pact of non-aggression with Poland, ended in victory at Munich by Mr. Chamberlain's visit and its sequel. The paper says Germany has broken this encirclement, Russia has been pushed back into Asia, and Europe established. A full list of the victories obtained in the 'diplomatic offensive' against Versailles and the treaty edifice built around it is given.

Institutions and treaties, either destroyed or rendered inoperative, include, according to the list, the League of Nations, the Little Entente, the Locarno treaties, the Rome agreement, the Franco-Belgian military agreement, the Polish-Czech military agreement, the Franco-Czech pact, and the Franco-Russian-Czech pact of mutual assistance.

p.12

NAZI DEMANDS FOR RESIGNATION OF DR. BENES
Some Urgent Questions from Prague

HELP AGAINST FURTHER DISRUPTION OF THE REPUBLIC

From a Correspondent

Prague, October 4.

Mr. Duff Cooper's resignation has received a great deal of publicity in the Prague press, but Czech opinion awaits the result of the debate in the House of Commons without much hope. Anxiety is expressed lest certain vital questions should be overlooked.

What is going to be done to protect the German minority in the districts that have been ceded? What safeguards will be made against further disintegration of the new Czecho-Slovakia when the plebiscites are over? Will the Western democracies take any steps to protect Czecho-Slovakia against the demand – repeated over the German wireless and taken very seriously in Prague – that President Benes should resign and that the Government should be reorganised in accordance with German ideas, even to the extent of including a representative of the Reich in the new Cabinet?

The Czechs do not forget that as a rule, the children of Social Democrat families grow up into Nazis, and the continuance of any German minority in the country is seen as a possible pretext for further demands by Germany in a year or two's time.

AVOIDING ECONOMIC DISASTER

But the vital question is how to avert an economic disaster.

277

The loss of vital industries is not all. New railways will have to be built where the old ones are being cut by the cession of territory. This is particularly true of the main line to Slovakia. New roads will be needed for the same reasons.

At the moment refugees from the plebiscite areas are being sent back into those areas so that the Czech vote may not be diminished. But after the plebiscite these refugees and many more may return like a flood and new industries will be needed to employ them. If loans from England and France are not on a sufficiently large scale then Czecho-Slovakia will inevitably become economically dependent on Germany.

In the same way, commercial treaties to the Czechs form one of the few means now remaining whereby the democracies can prevent a virtual economic alliance of Czecho-Slovakia and Germany. Whatever the answer to these questions may be, the effect of recent events on Czech opinion will remain. The loss of provinces and industries is perhaps less deeply felt by some Czechs than the moral shock they have received from the conduct of their friends.

It is expected that a full account will be published in Prague during the next few days of the precise manner and terms in which pressure was applied to the Czech Government by England and France. It is even said here that this publication will include a statement that the French and English Ambassadors told President Benes that if the Munich terms were resisted by Czecho-Slovakia and Russia, then England and France would support Germany. This, it is said, effectively prevented Russia from supporting Czecho-Slovakia in resistance to the Munich terms.

GROWING PROBLEM OF REFUGEES IN CZECHO-SLOVAKIA

From our Diplomatic Correspondent

London, Tuesday.

The situation in Czecho-Slovakia grows more appalling hour by hour. There is an exodus from the Sudetenland of those Sudeten Germans who opposed Henlein and the union with Germany. It was chiefly they who wrecked Hitler's scheme to take Czecho-Slovakia 'from within' by armed insurrection. They number tens of thousands, and as they not only thwarted Hitler's plans but were prepared to take part in the armed defence of the Czecho-Slovak Republic they are regarded as traitors by the German invader. They are fleeing from persecution in the Sudetenland, but are not allowed to seek refuge in purely Czech areas. As in Vienna, an epidemic of suicides is spreading.

EMPTY GUARANTEE

It is still uncertain how Germany means to dismember Czecho-Slovakia. A good deal will depend on the intentions of the Poles and the Hungarians, though the Germans mean to make themselves masters of the republic. A certain reconciliation between German and Czech has already begun. The Czech has no choice in the matter. It is the intention, no doubt, to detach Slovakia from the purely Czech regions, in reality even if not in a formal sense. The future of Carpathian Ruthenia remains obscure. The 'neutrality of Czecho-Slovakia' is already being made a term without any meaning, and the 'international guarantee' of that neutrality is known to be an empty phrase by everyone who has given any serious attention to the events of the last few days.

The Czecho-Slovak Government is trying to promote some sort of order amid the wreckage. The problem of the refugees grows more and more intractable. Unemployment is increasing rapidly, and threatens to become overwhelming. The financial burden created by the prodigious national effort of the last few weeks, by the mutilation of territory, by the fearful losses in factories, plant, rolling stock, mines, and so on, not to speak of deposits, savings, and all kinds of property, is incalculable in its immensity.

NO CONDITIONS MADE

In their haste to meet the wishes of Hitler the representatives of France and Great Britain seem to have been quite unable to make any sort of conditions or to originate any sort of proposals that would prevent the German seizure of the Sudetenland from becoming an act of spoliation as well as a transfer of territory.

In the Munich Agreement it was said that all the Czechs' 'installations' were to be left. This seems to be a translation of the German word 'Einrichtungen.' The word is entirely vague and may cover every kind of immovable property, fittings, and even the movable appurtenances of factories, mines, railways, and so on.

SOVIET UNION AND MUNICH
Complicity Denied

From our Correspondent

Moscow, October 4.

Soviet quarters believe that attempts are being made to link the Soviet Government with the Munich conference and to put the stamp of Soviet approval on its decisions. 'Pravda,' the organ of the Communist party, and 'Izvestia,' the official Government newspaper, have issued strong denials, and have restated the Soviet position.

In leading articles both newspapers grow indignant at the reports that the Soviet Government was informed of the Munich negotiations, and asserts that, in fact, the Soviet Union was the only ally of Czecho-Slovakia that remained true to its obligations.

The selection in the Soviet press of foreign comment on the settlement emphasise how unpopular is the Anglo-French policy outside the Fascist countries. The vigorousness of the denials of Soviet complicity shows the determination of the Russians to clear themselves, especially in the eyes of the small countries.

There is no doubt that the Soviet Union was consciously excluded from the Munich negotiations by both sides of the negotiating table.

HITLER SPEAKS TO SUDETENS
Must be United

NO DIFFERENCES TO BE ALLOWED

Carlsbad, October 4.

A programme of reconstruction for the Sudeten territories was announced in a speech by Herr Hitler during his visit to Carlsbad to-day. He was continuing his tour of the Sudeten areas which he began yesterday. Hitler said:

'The misfortunes of the Sudeten Germans began twenty years ago. I have been faithful to the racial ideals for twenty years, and I have been faithful for twenty years to my belief in my own people. We are now united in our racial union in our greater Reich, which nobody can break again.'

Hitler referred to the attitude of mind which the Sudeten Germans would have to adopt. They would have to put behind them, he said, everything that had separated them and deepen their sense of national community. 'The creed of the Sudeten Germans,' he said, 'finds response in the creed of 75,000,000 Germans.'

Herr Hitler referred again to 'the resolution which had inspired the entire German people to liberate the Sudeten Germans, if necessary by force. I did not know how I would reach this point, but I knew that I should come here in due course.

Herr Hitler then mentioned measures which would have to be taken in the Sudeten German territory as well as the reconstruction programme, which would be vigorously instituted forthwith. 'We can be proud of this great German Reich,' he said, 'whose leader I am, and this Germany is equally proud of you

Sudeten Germans. At this moment we cannot do anything more than think of our eternal German people and our great German Reich.'

GERMAN TROOPS HURRY IN

After his speech Herr Hitler stood for several minutes on the balcony of the theatre, with Herr Henlein by his side, returning the enthusiastic applause of the crowd. Hitler entered the famous spa town this afternoon only a little more than eight hours after the last Czech soldiers had left. While he was speaking the Czech Army was barely five miles away. His arrival in the town was enthusiastically cheered by the population, which had been lining the streets for some hours. He drove through the main streets to the square.

The Czechs began evacuating the city at eight o'clock last night and the last contingent of troops had left by five o'clock this morning. German troops and tanks were by then already moving into the town, which they had fully occupied by eight o'clock. So closely did the German troops follow on the heels of the Czechs that there were actually some 1,800 Czech Government officials in Carlsbad when the Germans entered. These officials withdrew rapidly and joined the retiring troops. The incoming troops under the command of General von Reichenau were loudly welcomed by dense crowds, which lined the streets to cheer them and to await the arrival of Herr Hitler. ...

p.18

LETTERS TO THE EDITOR

So many correspondents in all parts of the country are writing to us on various aspects of the situation created by the Munich Agreement that we regret it is impossible to print more than a small selection from the hundreds of letters we are receiving.

THE MUNICH AGREEMENT — AND AFTER
Hitler and Britain: A Forecast

To the Editor of the Manchester Guardian

Sir,—In one tragic week the world's course has changed. Yesterday democracy was in possession of a righteous cause, and had the power to enforce it. To-day the bastion of Czecho-Slovakia has gone, together with our righteous cause, and we spurn Russia.

When Britain's own turn comes, as come it will, despite all the protestations of Herr Hitler – for colonies, ours and others, are essential to his declared purpose of world domination, – the course which the triumphant dictator will pursue is not difficult to forecast. Strengthened by his conquests in the east, nothing will be easier than to mobilise an immense army on the Dutch and Belgian borders and demand a dominating share in the Dutch Indies, the Belgian Congo, and such British and French possessions as he has a mind to take.

If, with the help of France, Czecho-Slovakia, and Russia and with the backing of the United States and the moral support of the whole world we had to bend to his will in the matter of Czecho-Slovakia, what chance of resistance remains when Hitler's armies thrust themselves onto the Dutch and Belgian shores and threaten England with bombardment? We shall meet them almost singlehanded, and backed by scanty world support. For Russia threatens to retreat into isolation and prepare the defences of the Ukraine. The United States may naturally be expected to withdraw from interest in Europe's concerns and arm to the teeth against her own day. England and France will stand alone, bound by weakened links.

The prospect is terrible, and I see but one glimmer of hope. A rally, even at this eleventh hour, of all who oppose the suicidal foreign policy of the Government with a request to France and Russia to join us once more in the formulation of determined resistance to further aggression, and then a drive, as persistent as Herr Hitler's own, to provide the material means of defence, might yet succeed. Britain could be rallied to such a lead and world conscience would support it. The way is yet open for collective security. Can the lead be given? Or has the hour passed?—Yours, &c.,

HEWLETT JOHNSON,
The Deanery, Canterbury, October 3.

Obviously not for nothing was Hewlett Johnson popularly referred to as the 'Red Dean.'

NO GENERAL ELECTION
The Many Rumours Finally 'Laid' Last Night

PREMIER TO 'PURGE' HIS CABINET

From our Political Correspondent

Westminster, Wednesday Night.

The general election, if it was ever 'on' (which, as we suggested here yesterday, was improbable), is certainly 'off' to-night. In indirect ways the rumour has been finally and officially 'laid' and the extinguishing process had begun before Mr. Churchill satirised the project as 'an inverted khaki election.'

But there was never any justification to be offered for an election now. Mr. Chamberlain would have been almost criminally dividing the country at the moment when unity is essential and when unity is still obtainable for a decent foreign policy. Again, an election could not improve his Parliamentary position. The Government could not possibly hope to increase its present huge majority. Would it even maintain its present majority? There are differing views about the election values of the Munich Agreement, but even the greatest admirer of that achievement cannot believe that it would bring the Government a bigger representation in Parliament than it has to-day.

A LABOUR REPORT

The people who subscribed last Friday night to the dictum of the Premier that he had returned with 'peace with honour' are fewer to-night by very many than they were then, and so are the people who were inclined to think with Mr. Chamberlain that the Hitler–Chamberlain declaration might mean 'peace for our time.' Indeed the value of the Munich Agreement as an electoral trump card does not look anything like as high as it did.

No doubt some allowance is to be made for the desire to convince by emphasis, but an important official of the Labour party told me to-day that the reports from the constituencies (London excluded as being predominantly pro-Chamberlain) had almost persuaded him that the Labour party ought to have challenged the Government to an election. Make every allowance for exaggeration and it is surely evident that the Government would be making a great error if it thinks the whole country and everybody in it is thanking God for Munich and only longing for the chance to vote for Mr. Neville Chamberlain.

There is one thing, however, that Mr. Chamberlain, I am told, would certainly like to do, that is to 'clean up' his Cabinet as it is called. There are several Cabinet Ministers who have little sympathy with his new foreign policy, and he regards them quite honestly as dangerous men, because of their views. Mr. Duff Cooper was not alone in differing with the Prime Minister. There were at least three other Ministers who began along with Mr. Duff Cooper in differing with the Premier, but they have felt they were justified for one reason or another in not taking the extreme step with Mr. Duff Cooper.

Mr. Chamberlain is not the man easily to tolerate colleagues who are doubtful on the only question that matters at this time, and with to-morrow's division over and the big majority secured it would not be surprising if he found occasion to reconstruct (polite word) or 'purge' his Cabinet. It is scarcely necessary to say that none of these Ministers belongs to the 'inner' Cabinet, that combination described by Mr. Dalton as consisting of 'one man who admits he knows nothing of foreign affairs, a Foreign Secretary who is not allowed to discharge his duties, and two ex-Foreign Secretaries whose record at the Foreign Office is known and regretted.' The Ministers in question are lower in the hierarchy.

ALL OUR RESOURCES FOR REARMING
Mr. Churchill's Urgent Demand

'THE EMPIRE'S INDEPENDENCE THREATENED'

Mr. Winston Churchill made a striking speech in the House of Commons yesterday on the Munich Agreement and its consequences as he sees them. Mr. Churchill was speaking to the Government's vote of confidence which Sir J. Simon had moved.

Mr. Churchill summed up his view in a picturesque phrase: 'The utmost the Prime Minister has been able to secure,' he said, 'has been to secure that the German dictator instead of snatching his victuals from the table has been content to have them served to him course by course.' We were, he said, in the presence of a disaster of the first magnitude which had befallen Great Britain and France, and he demanded a secret session so that the House could be taken into the Government's confidence. 'The House,' he said, 'has a right to know where we stand and what measures are being taken to secure our position.'

We had, said Mr. Churchill, been left in the hour of trial without adequate national defence or effective international security. He went on:

Many people no doubt honestly believe they were only giving away the interests of Czecho-Slovakia, I fear we shall find that we have deeply compromised and perhaps fatally endangered the safety and even the independence of Great Britain and France.

The sense of our country falling into the power orbit and influence of Nazi Germany and our existence becoming dependent on their goodwill and pleasure is unendurable.

An effort at rearmament the like of which has not been seen ought to be made forthwith, and all the resources of this country and all its united strength should be bent on that task.

Do not suppose this is the end. This is only the beginning. It is only the first foretaste of a bitter cup which will be proffered to you year by year unless by a supreme recovery of martial vigour we rise again and take our stand for freedom as in the olden times.

RUSSIA NOT EXCLUDED

One of the passages in Sir John Simon's speech was devoted to the possibility of further Four Power talks and the suspicion that Russia may be excluded. He said:

Mr. Eden has asked whether the development of the Munich meeting would be a Four Power Pact. If the question is whether we are willing to enter into friendly consultation with France, Italy, and Germany upon the problem of Europe, then I say most emphatically that we do not rule out such consultations at all.

If, on the other hand, the question is whether we are contemplating an exclusive Four Power Pact that would attempt to disregard all other States, great and small, and without communication to them to impose our will upon Europe. I say, on behalf of the Government, that is not, and never has been, the policy of the Government.

It is our hope that Russia will be willing to join in the guarantee in Czecho-Slovakia. It is most important that she should do so. The Government has no intention whatever of excluding Russia, or trying to exclude Russia, from any further settlement in Europe.

If outstanding differences are to be resolved it must be on the basis of free communication with all European Powers.

Mr. Eden was right in emphasising the importance of securing the co-operation of the smaller Powers in Europe. They are always valuable allies for peace. Our object is to buttress and strengthen peace in every way we can.

It does not follow that because we have pacts with France, Germany, and Italy we will not have close contact with other nations.

Sir John Simon said the great significance of the Munich Agreement was the fact that 'for the first time Herr Hitler has made some concession. Whatever we may think of the agreement it certainly is very different in tone and substance from the Godesberg document.' 'The Prime Minister,' he concluded, 'has started a movement which may have immense developments, which we hope and believe may save the world for peace.'

The Labour amendment, calling for a world conference, was moved by Mr. Greenwood. The vote will be taken this afternoon. The Liberal Opposition decided last night to vote for the Labour amendment. ...

40,000,000 GAS MASKS

Mr. Geoffrey Lloyd stated in the House of Commons yesterday that 40,000,000 gas masks had been issued and that further large deliveries were being received each week. Precautions for the civil population must be carried out thoroughly and must be extended. Business firms who had begun schemes for the protection of their workpeople should press on steadily with them.

p.13

WHY DR. BENES RESIGNED
German Pressure

'ESSENTIAL FOR ME TO WITHDRAW'
Changed Conditions

Prague, October 5.

Dr. Benes, President of the Czecho-Slovak Republic for the past three years, submitted his resignation to the Council of Ministers to-day and it was unanimously accepted. General Syrovy, the Czech Prime Minister, will act as President until a successor to Dr. Benes has been elected by the National Assembly – that is, the Chamber of Deputies and the Senate jointly.

President Benes offered his resignation in the following letter:–

The eventful three years of my Presidency have culminated in the very sad events of these last days. They have weighed upon our spirits and our hearts, but they have not broken our faith or our ideals towards our people, our nation, and our State, ideals which have inspired and which will always inspire our people.

The historic events have changed the whole basis of our existence. I have played such a large part in those developments that I have to consider seriously what should be my duty under the changed conditions.

I came to office under circumstances which were entirely different, and I must take this fact into account. The circumstances have changed so completely that I feel that my remaining in office might constitute an obstacle to the new conditions which now confront the State, chiefly in regard to the international situation and with a view to the rapid development of a collaboration with our neighbours. We have now constituted a new Government which will be a Government of calm, of order, of economic efforts, and of social reconstruction; a Government which will aim chiefly at internal development, and I am convinced it will succeed in its efforts.

NOT EVADING RESPONSIBILITY

But I realise that in these new conditions it is essential for me to withdraw from office. That does not mean that I evade my responsibility in this difficult situation, or that I am leaving a vessel that is in a storm.

I wish only to facilitate the development of the policy of the Government both in external and internal affairs. That is why I place my resignation in your hands, Mr. Prime Minister, in order that you may take the necessary steps which the situation calls for. I thank you and your colleagues for your collaboration, and I wish you every success. I am fully convinced that a better period is now before us, a period of successful labour and of prosperity for the new State and for all our Czecho-Slovak people.

NEW CABINET'S AIM

In a broadcast later General Syrovy announced the policy of the new Government which was formed last night. He said:

Our policy will aim at friendly relations with everybody. In order to live in security it is necessary to cultivate good relations with our neighbours. We propose to reorganise our Administration and seek the support of all our people, Czechs, Slovaks, and the Sub-Carpathian Russians. This is the objective of the new Government.

Our policy will be based on a wide decentralisation of the Administration. We hope that there will be no unemployment. The country is able to provide work for everybody. Work and bread for everyone will be the objective of our policy. Agriculture, which is the foundation of the State, will be the special concern of the Government. We plan to realise our programme on a basis of social justice.

I appeal to you all to work in calm and confidence. We shall do everything in our power to give satisfaction to the justified claims of the Slovaks and Sub-Carpathian Russians.

Our State will be based on the equality of the three peoples. We commence a new era to-day. Czechs and Slovaks are brothers.

At this point the National Anthem was played and there was a four minutes' silence in the broadcast transmission.—Reuter.

HITLER SAYS 'THANK YOU'
Praise of Mussolini

NEXT OBJECTIVE TO END DISTRESS
Speech in Berlin

Berlin, October 5.

Herr Hitler and Dr. Goebbels spoke in the Sports Palace to-night at the opening of the Winter Relief Campaign. Herr Hitler was greeted with thunderous applause and shouts of 'Heil' and an incessant chorus of 'We thank you, Führer.' Dr. Goebbels said:

'We welcome our Leader with our old battle-cry. "Adolf Hitler, Sieg, heil!" ' (victory, hail). Turning to Hitler he added: 'My Leader, you have just come back from the Sudeten German district. You greeted the liberated German people there. Our hearts accompanied you. If we think one week and a half back when Hitler last spoke here he raised categorical demands when he argued against Benes. If we consider that Benes resigned to-day – (cheers) – we can say that seldom in history has such a change taken place.

'If a few critics still existed they have now become your warmest admirers. The slogan first used in the Anschluss has become true: "One people, one Reich, one Leader." '

Dr. Goebbels announced that the winter relief fund had placed 45,000,000 marks at the disposal of the Sudeten Germans.

HITLER ON DECISIVE YEARS

Herr Hitler said:

'When I took over the leadership of the Reich six years ago one of the so-called statesmen of Germany said: 'Until now this man was popular because he was in opposition. Now he must govern and we shall see what his popularity will be like in six weeks.'

'Since then six years have passed. I believe they have been the most decisive in German history. What lends this time its greatest characteristic is, I believe, its colossal unity. Only if one man could speak and act in the name of the whole people could he be successful. We have just experienced this. On May 28 I set myself a great task. One thing all must understand – I sacrificed my quiet and my bourgeois comfort for the great object for which I believe I must fight – the nation.

'It would have been easier for me to have lived a quiet life. The decisive thing was that the people backed me. This unity is an organised, peculiarly German unity. Without this unity all our problems could not have been solved. It is important for me to know that the people will not desert me – not even in bad times.'

MUSSOLINI A 'GREAT HELPER'

'I have had in the last months and weeks a great helper in foreign affairs. I have already had occasion to thank the man who stood behind Germany – Benito Mussolini. In my last Sports Palace speech I thanked my friend Benito Mussolini. He used all his energy and power.

'I must also thank the other two statesmen who in the last minute realised the gravity of the hour and who enabled me to give my hand to an understanding. But above all my gratitude goes out to the German people. They have taken all the measures necessary to enforce a just claim. It will be a page of glory in the history of the German people. At a time when hundreds of thousands were drafted to labour and hundreds of thousands called to the colours, no man went to the savings banks. No woman doubted. I am proud of my people.

'Soon the problem will be completely solved. By October 10 we shall have occupied all German territories which belong to us. Thus one of the gravest crises has been ended. For the first time we shall be able to look forward to Christmas, which shall be a true festival of peace.'

'Nobody in the world will help us unless we help ourselves. This programme of self-help is a manly programme. It is a different programme from those of my predecessors who ran around in the world begging in Geneva and elsewhere.

'In the last few months many thousands of workmen were torn away from their jobs. They were told, "You must pack your little suitcase. You must go to the west." They were the men who erected a wall of iron and concrete for the protection of all of us in Germany. They had to put up with discomfort. We owe our gratitude to them, to the men who were called to the colours to the women, to all nameless people. We owe our gratitude to those persons who, despite persecution, kept their faith in Germany alive for twenty years.' ...

WEAKNESSES IN OUR DEFENCES
Inquiry Already Started

PREMIER'S HINT OF GREAT EFFORT AHEAD
The People's Desire to Serve

The four days' debate in the House of Commons on the Munich Agreement and the new international situation ended yesterday in a division on the Government's vote of confidence and the Labour party's amendment calling for a world conference. The amendment was defeated by 369 votes to 150 and the vote of confidence carried by 366 to 144. No Government M.P. voted against the Government, but there were some abstentions.

Mr. Chamberlain himself wound up the debate for the Government. He announced his decision (already forecast in the 'Manchester Guardian') not to have an immediate general election. 'Possibly,' he said, 'we may want great efforts by the nation in the months that are to come. If that be so the smaller the differences there are the better.' The Premier also repeated the pledge that the Government will not introduce conscription or compulsory national service in peace-time, but later gave a hint that some scheme such as a national register may be considered.

LESSONS OF THE CRISIS

Another passage in the Premier's speech modified his 'peace for our time' declaration.

Points in the speech were:-

I hope members will not read into the words I used on my return from Munich – words used in moments of emotion after a long and exhausting day and after I had driven through miles of excited, enthusiastic, cheering, people – more than they were intended to convey.

I had indeed believed that we might secure peace for our time, but I never meant to suggest that we could do it by disarming until we can induce others to disarm too.

Our past experience has shown us only too clearly that weakness in armed strength means weakness in diplomacy. I realise that diplomacy cannot be effective unless there is a consciousness, not only at home but elsewhere, that behind that diplomacy is strength.

One good thing at any rate has come out of this emergency. It has thrown a vivid light on our preparations for defence and their strength and their weaknesses.

We would not be doing our duty if we had not already ordered that a prompt and thorough inquiry should be made to cover the whole of our preparations, military and civil, in order to see in the light of what happened during those hectic days what further steps may be necessary to make good our deficiencies in the shortest possible time.

I know that everywhere there is a strong desire among the people to record their readiness to serve their country whenever or however their service can be most useful.

I would like to take advantage of that strong feeling.

I do not myself clearly see my way to any particular scheme at this moment but I am ready to consider any suggestions that may be made to me in a very sympathetic spirit.

The House adjourned until November 1, although the Labour Opposition wished to keep it in session. Sir A. Sinclair and Mr. Churchill suggested as a compromise that the House should reassemble after a ten days' break, but the Premier held that the usual provision for the special calling of the House together 'if occasion should arise' was enough.

HITLER GETTING HIS DEMANDS

The International Commission, which is sitting in Berlin, has delimited the fifth zone which the Germans are to occupy by Monday. This gives Germany almost all the territory demanded by Hitler in the Godesberg ultimatum.

It is reported that areas entirely inhabited by Czechs are to be handed out and that in all 800,000 Czechs will now be transferred without a plebiscite.

Important railway lines are also to be cut. These demands were made by the Germans for strategical reasons. The Czechs have accepted under protest.

The German press has begun a new anti-Czech campaign, accusing the Czechs of looting and of not carrying out the arrangements, although reports from officers with the German Army are that German and Czech officers are co-operating in a friendly manner and that the transfer is being carried out smoothly. ...

HITLER GETTING HIS GODESBERG ULTIMATUM TERMS
Decision of Berlin Commission

800,000 CZECHS TO BE TRANSFERRED BY MONDAY

From our own Correspondent

Geneva, October 6.

According to a statement made this evening by the permanent Czecho-Slovak delegation here, the decision arrived at yesterday by the international commission sitting in Berlin concerning the zone in Czecho-Slovak territory that is to be occupied by German troops between to-day and Monday as in direct contradiction with the letter and spirit of the Munich Agreement and entirely in accordance with the map annexed to the Godesberg memorandum.

In consequence of this decision districts almost entirely Czech are to be annexed to Germany without a plebiscite and without giving the population any possibility of defending itself against this abuse of force. This the statement declares is against law and justice and against the ethnical principal of self-determination to which Germany appealed in demanding the territory inhabited by the Sudeten Germans.

Thus the international commission has decided to annex immediately to Germany the districts of Opava in Silesia Zabrek, Breclava, and certain districts of Northern Moravia. The commission has also decided on an immediate occupation by the German Army of the linguistic enclaves of Svitavy. In consequence of this decision which is based purely on strategic grounds, several of the principal communications between Bohemia and Moravia have been cut, with the result that the economic life of Czecho-Slovakia and its future development are in danger.

It is said that 800,000 Czechs will be taken over by the Germans.

The Czecho-Slovak Government, seeing no other alternative, has noted the decision and decided to execute it.

The question of numbers of Czechoslovakians being taken over by Germany as opposed to the number of Germans previously under Czechoslovakian rule in the Sudetenland is further referred to on page 299.

WHAT WAS REFUSED HITLER AT GODESBERG AND WHAT HE NOW GETS (Tuesday 11 October)

Area occupied by the Germans
Hitler's claims at Godesberg
Frontiers
Railways

POLAND

SLOVAKIA

GERMANY

MORAVIA

BOHEMIA

Breslau
R. Oder
Ratibor
Teschen
Zwittau
Olomouc
Trubau
Glatz
Znaim
VIENNA
Bratslava
R. Elbe
PRAGUE
Jihlava
Leit merritz
Budejovice
Mohenfurth
Dresden
Linz
R. Danube
Carlsbedl
Asch
Mancabe Pilsen
Tachau
Taus
Bohemian Forest
Passau
Eger
Regensburg
GERMANY

MILES
0 50

A LETTER FROM PRAGUE

To the Editor of the Manchester Guardian

Sir,–I have received the following letter from a friend in Prague:

You cannot realise how sad we are. Our lives are not less dear to us than yours to you, nor are those of our wives and children. Still we were prepared to sacrifice them, to stand the terrible shock of aggression, such shock as neither France nor Great Britain would ever have had to sustain.

Seeing the 'Great' Western Powers receding once more in the face of the blackmailer's threats, seeing the triumph of brute force over law and order, seeing the holiest covenants and treaties defaulted, all the recent promises and confirmations of alliances forgotten, makes you despair of the justice and honour of mankind. Can you imagine how abject I personally feel, who have always devoted my feeble efforts to the furthering and promotion of knowledge and understanding of Western ideas among my friends? I induced my staff to learn English; for three years they have been taking lessons at the office. I sent my engineers to England, I introduced British goods. I have been often laughed at because of my zeal and fervour for all that is British.

I feel terribly ashamed now, I am comforting everybody by saying that you must not judge countries and nations by the acts of individuals. The ideal of law and justice cannot be buried for ever. –Yours,&c.,

H.C. TURNER.
14, St. Austell Road, Manchester 16, October 7.

LETTERS TO THE EDITOR

THE CHAMBERLAIN—HITLER NEGOTIATIONS
Why was Russia Ignored and Parliament Not Consulted?

To the Editor of the Manchester Guardian

Sir,–Now that the hymns to the Prime Minister and his peace show some signs of dying down it is not irreverent, I hope, to examine in mere prose the events which have inspired these melodious exercises. The view which we take of the proper policy for the next decade must depend, to a considerable degree, on our interpretation of them. Hence some verdict on the crisis, however provisional, is a matter of life and death. We cannot merely leave it to the serene investigations of the historian of the future to disentangle its different aspects. If we do, his postmortem is likely to be held not only on it but also on us.

The authorised version of the story – if that term may be employed – is based on the narrative given in the Prime Minister's speeches of September 28 and October 3. In the former he stated that the Government had in July three alternatives before it, the first of which was that it could have threatened to go to war with Germany if she attacked Czecho-Slovakia. This alternative, he explained, was rejected on the ground that 'this country would not have followed us if we had tried to lead it into war to prevent a minority from obtaining autonomy.' In the latter he stated that, territorial concessions having already been agreed to by the Czecho-Slovak Government, the essential thing at Munich was that 'we should quickly reach a conclusion, so that this painful and difficult operation of transfer might be carried out at the earliest possible moment.'

The picture of Europe sliding swiftly to disaster and then rescued on the brink of the abyss by an inspired British statesman has obvious attractions. Unfortunately, however, it leaves a good deal out. Three points in particular require further consideration.

1. The Prime Minister's account of events was inadequate in two respects. It seems to have misstated the point at issue and it ignored the part played by force in the final settlement. The question from July onwards was not whether this country should engage in war in order 'to prevent a minority from obtaining autonomy.' It was whether Great Britain should do its utmost to secure that negotiations as to the future of Czecho-Slovakia should take place in an atmosphere of peace or whether they should be conducted to the noise of German troops on the march, raids on Czecho-Slovakia organised on the German territory, and a torrent of threats from the German Government-controlled press.

That difference was not a trifle. It raised the question whether, in the words of Mr. Duff Cooper, 'one Great Power should be allowed, in disregard of treaty obligations, of the laws of nations and the decrees of morality, to dominate by brutal force the Continent of Europe.' In such circumstances, the right steps to take were surely two. The first was to inform Czecho-Slovakia that the British Government expected concessions to be made, and that such concessions were the condition of its support. The second was at the same time to inform the German Chancellor that Great Britain, France, and Russia stood together on the points at issue, and, while prepared to take part in peaceful negotiations, would act as one in resisting violence and threats of violence.

The British Government took the first step; it did not take the second. The evidence of Mr. Duff Cooper, who attended Cabinet meetings as First Lord of the Admiralty, makes it clear that the British Prime Minister actually waited twice on Herr Hitler without a declaration of British intentions having been put before the latter in unequivocal language. To judge by the acount which Mr. Chamberlain gave of the Godesberg interview, he appears to have been taken aback by the intransigence of his host. If the facts were as stated by Mr. Duff Cooper, the only surprising thing is that Mr. Chamberlain should have been surprised. He succeeded at the last moment, when the British Fleet was mobilised, in somewhat mitigating the methods to be employed in dismembering the Czecho-Slovak State. It is hardly possible, however, to resist the conclusion that force remained the major premise throughout the negotiations.

2. The crucial point in the story is the absence of effective co-operation between Great Britain, France, and Russia. It is impossible for any outsider to say whether there is truth in French allegations of an 'inco-ordination voulue' between the British and French Embassies at Berlin; the French Government, for obvious reasons, is not likely to give publicity to them. But the failure to make use of Russian help is glaring. Whatever may be thought of the Russian version of Socialism, it can hardly be denied that Russia has been for several years a loyal member of the League and that her international conduct has been well above the average. The importance of her active co-operation in the recent crisis was so obvious that the failure to make the most of it must be regarded not as a mere omission but as a deliberate act of policy.

What was the reason for that attitude? That question, though asked in the recent debates in the House of Commons, remained unanswered. Two replies may be suggested. The first is that the British propertied classes have not yet recovered from their hysterics about 'Bolshevism,' and sacrificed the interests of their country and Europe to the reckless pursuit of a rather childish vendetta. The second is that co-operation with Russia would have thrown British policy out of gear. If the object of that policy was to put restraint on Herr Hitler, nothing clearly was more desirable than Russian co-operation. But what if its object was to strike a bargain with Herr Hitler at the expense of Czecho-Slovakia, with some face-saving thrown in? In that case, nothing would have been more embarrassing than joint action with a State which had the bad taste to mean business.

It that view is correct, the Prime Minister's conduct of affairs is intelligible enough. It is a further example of the technique employed – with unfortunate results – when he sought 'appeasement' by throwing his Foreign Secretary to the wolves. The public supposes him to have strained every nerve to check aggression by Herr Hitler. But, if so, why did he not play the strong hand which he held for all it was worth? Another possible explanation of his action cannot, unfortunately, be ruled out. It is that his main object was less to restrain Herr Hitler than to reach an agreement with him, and that the injustice on the Czechs was part of the price. If so, Mr. Chamberlain's means were well chosen and his success complete.

3. One feature of the whole business deserves more attention than it has hitherto received. That feature is the refusal of the Prime Minister to give the House of Commons the opportunity of discussing the Government's policy until the essentials of it had been settled between himself and Herr Hitler. The excuse given by him – that the negotiations were too important and his leisure too scanty to allow him to meet the House – will really not do. The Führer-Prinzip is not yet part of the British Constitution. If the Prime Minister of a Parliamentary State has not time for Parliament, he may be a deserving person but he is not fit to be Prime Minister. As it is, a revolution in foreign policy has been effected which may affect the life of the whole nation for a generation to come, without the nation's representatives being heard on the subject till things had gone so far that debate was almost useless.

It is on that revolution and its meaning that public attention ought now to be fixed. Its consequences are likely to be considerable. The League has received its coup de grace. The German dictatorship – concentration camps and all – has acquired an immense accession of strength. Every weak State has been taught that it has nothing to hope from the so-called great democracies.

Where and when Herr Hitler's next stroke will fall no one yet can say. It may be on the Ukraine; or again – since he appears to prefer blackmail to war – he may be satisfied for the time being to impose leonine contracts on the food, oil, and raw material producers of South-eastern Europe. Our position, in the meantime, is neither dignified nor safe. We have surrendered whatever claims to moral leadership we may once have possessed. In return we have got time. It is not clear yet we have got much else.

It is easy to make the Government the scapegoat for all this. Unfortunately, it is too easy. The Government has only behaved as it was to be expected it would behave. It is improbable that its members feel a positive enthusiasm for the manners of the dictators, which, after all, are pretty crude. It is only too probable, however, that they regard the alternative to them as infinitely worse. It is easy, again, to react into an attitude which assumes war to be inevitable and to acquiesce as a consequence in the mere piling up of armaments. That by itself is worse than futile: it represents the victory of Herr Hitler in our souls. Joint action with France, Russia, and all other States which accept as a basis of their policy united resistance to aggression and the peaceful settlement of all disputes; a clear statement of British aim, so that foreign Powers, friendly and unfriendly, can understand them, which at present they too often do not; a willingness to redress such genuine grievances as may exist, especially when that course involves some sacrifice by ourselves; a refusal to be frightened when gangsters brandish revolvers – these things, though doubtless difficult, are not impossible. They would, at least, be a beginning. Is there a chance of the present Government favouring them? Not the remotest. But the electors put the Government where it is. In spite of Herr Hitler's recent threats of his displeasure if we change it, the electors can turn it out, if they please, within two years from now.

If they do not turn it out, the presumption will be that they like it. In that case, a democrat must make the best of their taste. They ought, however, to know the real magnitude of the issues and to have a fair chance of getting what they want. Joint propaganda between members of different parties on limited and specific issues is a well-established practice of British politics. It compromises no one. The present situation is surely grave to justify a joint campaign of enlightenment by members of all parties who are not in agreement with the foreign policy of the Government.

In the meantime may the hope be expressed that we shall hear in future somewhat less of two topics? The first is the iniquity of the frontiers of Czecho-Slovakia fixed by the Treaty of Versailles. It is quite impossible that they were inequitable, though that was not a reason for consenting to their change under threats of armed force. If, however, as has been stated, some members of the present Cabinet were among the gallant three hundred who sent the famous 'no concessions' telegram to Lloyd George, the less now said about that subject the better. Reference to it merely serves to remind us that our rulers include men who were then insolent to the weak, as they are now servile to the strong.

The second topic on which we could do with less gush is the Prime Minister's peace. The unpretending courage of ordinary men and women is belittled by that stream of cant. We are all afraid of wounds and death, both for ourselves and for other people; but these emotions, though natural and human, are not among the major virtues. The Government's attempts to make capital out of them are nauseous. It is possible that prayers of gratitude prompted by relief at having saved our skins by the sacrifice of a brave and enlightened nation may be acceptable to God; but it is not so certain as it is now the fashion to suppose.–Yours, &c.,

R.H. TAWNEY,
Rose Cottage, Elcombe, Stroud, Gloucestershire, October 13.

Tawney, a leading thinker in the Labour Party in 1938, in his above letter, injects a necessary dose of deflation and uses his philosophical and logical skills to examine Chamberlain's handling of Munich in savage detail and thereby questions and exposes its policy deficiencies.

MUNICH 'SETTLEMENT' WORSE THAN VERSAILLES
The Facts About the Annexed Areas

CZECHS NOW LARGER MINORITY THAN GERMANS WERE
Why Some Districts Were Seized

From Our Diplomatic Correspondent

London, Tuesday.

The Czech minority in the region now annexed by Germany is over 34 per cent of the total population. The German minority in the Czecho-Slovak Republic before the Munich 'settlement' was under 25 per cent. The 'settlement' has therefore not improved but worsened the situation from an ethnological (or, as Hitler would call it, racial) point of view. In the regions now annexed by the Poles matters are even worse, for in those regions the Czechs are a majority of 55 per cent, while the Poles are only 35 per cent of the population.

When the frontiers of the Czecho-Slovak Republic were drawn after the Great War great care was taken not to break up regions that were organically united by industries, trade, railways, and by strategic needs. Under the Munich 'settlement' all such considerations, so vital to the welfare of the local inhabitants, no matter what their 'race' may be, have been wantonly disregarded, and even 'racial' considerations, although these are the professed basis of Hitler's foreign policy, have been disregarded, and no less wantonly.

WORSE THAN VERSAILLES

All that the Germans – and Hitler above all – have said about the Treaty of Versailles is true, only much more so, of the Munich 'settlement.' Indeed it is worse than Versailles, and much more a peace dictated and manipulated for the sake of exploitation and spoliation.

What is also much worse now than in 1918 is the treatment of the defeated enemy. Germany has taken proportionately much more Czech wealth and property than the Allied and Associated Powers took from Germany after four years of war. The behaviour of the Germans in the annexed regions is worse than that of the Allies on German soil after the Great War.

The Poles are, if anything, worse than the Germans. In their haste to grab all they could they have annexed a large and valuable mining area where the Czechs are in an overwhelming majority. They have taken the town of Bohumin because it is a powerful

299

A RACIAL FRONTIER IN THEORY AND PRACTICE

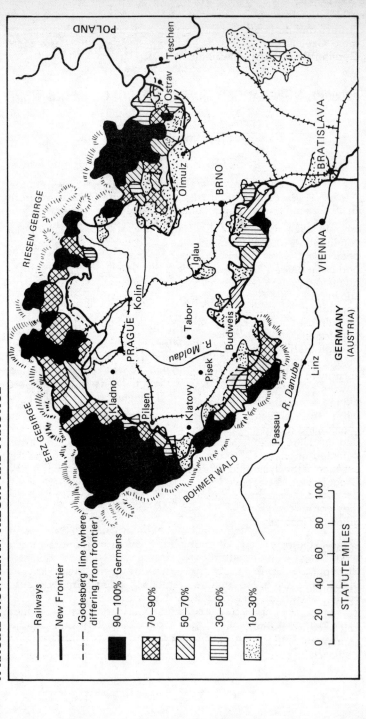

fortress and an important railway junction, although there are far
more Czechs than Poles in the town. Indeed, there are more
German than Polish inhabitants. ...

Saturday 22 October   *pp.13-14*

FRENCH POLICY IN EUROPE
[1919-1938]

IN SEARCH OF SECURITY
The End of a System

By L.B. Namier

In 1914 there were five Great Powers on the European
continent, in 1919 only one. Russia had collapsed, Germany had
been defeated, the Habsburg Monarchy had disappeared, and Italy
had been proved once more no Great Power. In this void France
attained a preponderance seemingly more complete than she had
known since the days of Napoleon I. But in 1815 she still had a
population larger than that of Austria, twice that of Great Britain,
and almost three times that of Prussia; now she has the smallest
population among the Great Powers. The victory of 1918 was won
through the intervention of the Anglo-Saxon Powers; it produced
Poland and the Succession States. France had the choice of seeking
security in political retirement under the wings of the Anglo-Saxon
Powers or of trying to remedy the disparity in numbers through
alliances with the new States. In victory the temptation to be once
more 'une puissance protectrice' proved irresistible – she
constructed a system based on satellite nations. France, Poland,
and the Little Entente were sufficient to hold in check the three
defeated enemies Germany, Hungary, and Bulgaria; it was the
essence of the system and its weakness that it contained only one
Great Power. A despoiled Russia and an ever hungry Italy were
left outside, antagonised; of uncertain value as military Powers,
they count through territory and numbers; dangerous potential
allies of Germany.

POLAND AND ITALY

Poland was the pivot of the French system, the Little Entente
its complement. Sentiment and interest seemed to bind Poland to
France. Culturally and politically Poland had gravitated towards
her, while all France had for over a century been pro-Polish, – her
Left because the Poles were victims of oppression and alleged
champions of liberty, her Right because they were devout Roman
Catholics. In 1919, through British action, Poland received less than

301

her due in Danzig and Upper Silesia; yet it was enough to earn her the bitter resentment of Germany. If a reconciliation between France and Germany had been possible the German–Polish conflict would have sufficed to prevent it. In 1919–20 with French connivance, Poland annexed extensive territories inhabited by White Russians and Ukrainians; it was henceforth a vital interest of Poland that Russia no less than Germany should remain an outcast among the nations. The result was the German–Russian Treaty concluded at Rapallo in 1922.

Italy always tries and usually succeeds, by acquisitions, to compensate for the absence of achievement. She received more than her due at the expense of Yugo-Slavs, Germans, and Greeks, and yet felt aggrieved. 'She has such poor teeth and such a large appetite,' said Bismarck about her. She started to play off Hungary and Bulgaria against the Little Entente and to construct a system rival to that of France. On one point, however, she agreed with France and the Little Entente: there was to be no 'Anschluss' of Austria to Germany, no German penetration of the Danube Basin, no German soldiers on the Brenner Pass. Otherwise Italy came to rank as a 'revisionist' Power.

APPEAL TO BRITAIN

France by her system had tried to redress her inferiority in numbers as against Germany; with Russia and Italy estranged this disparity threatened to become even worse. The French Army was still supreme; none the less France was afraid; for she did not want to fight again. There was no real 'militarism' in France, no aggressiveness, no lust for power; only the wish to be secure. Her 'system' was proving a liability; she therefore sought to make Britain share its burden. Our guarantee for all European frontiers was to be obtained at Geneva, through pacts and protocols. Since the war whoever wants to cajole Britain talks peace. But all that France obtained was the Locarno Treaty; no British guarantee for Poland. This was obtained from the Czechs who within their own frontiers, drawn by nature and history, tried to conciliate the German minority (from 1926 to 1938 there were German Ministers in every Czecho-Slovak Cabinet), and who, if left to themselves might perhaps have succeeded. The two standing conflicts on the Continent were between Germany and Poland and between Italy and Yugo-Slavia.

The rise of an aggressive German militarism showed up still clearer the insufficiency of the French system and the French unwillingness to fight. France now accepted Britain's leadership and joined in talks for a Four-Power Pact. At that stage Germany and Italy would have had to be satisfied at the expense of Poland and Yugo-Slavia; France did not mean to sacrifice her smaller allies, yet made them sour and suspicious. Why should they not in turn enter into direct negotiations with their hitherto hostile neighbours? The juncture was favourable to the Poles: Hitler was not a Prussian but an Austrian, and his first aim was not the recovery of the lost Prussian provinces but the "Anschluss." Moreover, both at home and abroad he was talking 'anti-Bolshevism.' The Russians became scared, entered the League and drew closer to France: one more reason for the Poles to work with Hitler. On his part this was a promise not to make them his first object of attack; on theirs, not to interfere with his operations elsewhere; neither seriously envisaged action against Russia.

YUGO-SLAVIA

The Nazi attempt in Vienna in July, 1934, alarmed Italy; by the 'Stresa Front' the Western Powers assured her of their support. But to the Yugo-Slavs the line Milan–Vienna–Budapest would have been as unwelcome as Munich–Vienna–Budapest to the Czechs. Most of all, Yugo-Slavia objected to a Habsburg restoration because of its attraction for the discontented Roman-Catholic Croats; and such a restoration came to be canvassed as the means for preserving Austria's separate existence. The Yugo-Slavs drew closer to Germany. France was losing two satellites but seemed to be gaining the co-operation of two Great Powers; exchanging pre-eminence for security.

When Mussolini invaded Abyssinia and England, in her disarmed condition, half-heartedly tried to fulfil the League Covenant France struggled to reconcile complaisance towards Italy with Geneva righteousness. The Western Powers neither satisfied nor checked Italy and lost themselves in half-measures. Sated and sophisticated, civilised, sensitive, and war-weary, the democracies have a conscience and no faith – the most dangerous condition for individuals and nations; and they encounter dictators, savage 'revivalists' without a conscience or sensibility. Political proclivities clash with international alignments: Germany is the ever-menacing enemy of France; Italy has become hostile to England: Russia has been turning into an ally. Yet large sections of opinion both in Britain and in France are pro-Italian, or even pro-German, and intensely anti-Russian. This confusion of purpose has produced the antics of the 'non-intervention' policy in Spain.

In 1936 Germany by remilitarising the Rhineland started a barrier against French intervention in Central and Eastern Europe – additional justification for the Polish and Yugo-Slav Governments to pursue their new policy, unpopular though it was with their poeple. Stalin started his 'purges,' which produced dismay among Russia's friends and raised doubts about her future military value – additional justification for those averse to a Russian alliance. Mussolini added Spanish entanglements to his Abyssinian commitment and launched a vicious anti-British campaign in the Near East. Meantime the armaments and policy of the Western Powers continue to display as much 'gaps' as substance. When Hitler invaded Austria there was no one to resist him. He is single-minded and ready to take risks, which makes him supreme over those who do not know their minds and cannot control their fears.

THE ANSCHLUSS AND AFTER

I wrote in the 'Manchester Guardian' on June 28, 1935:

Vienna is the focal point on the Danube. ... The moment the Nazis successfully set up their standard in Vienna ... the political balance of Europe would be destroyed. Czecho-Slovakia ... would either have to pass into the German orbit or cease to exist. ... Italy ... would have to think of her own safety. If then the Western Powers remained passive spectators German hegemony on the Continent would be re-established beyond anything known in 1914, more ruthless and more menacing, more brutal and more barbaric.

... Berchtesgaden is now the emotional centre of an incalculable German policy, and the storm which is brewing threatens Vienna. When it breaks it will not be a merely local disturbance.

Could the French system have survived the Nazi occupation of Vienna? The Czechs still adhered to it. But they asked the Western Powers; 'Do you want us? If not, tell us so, and we shall have to make our terms with Hitler.' They never received an honest answer. Had Poland and Yugo-Slavia stood by France, Germany could not have attacked Czecho-Slovakia; had the Western Powers stood by Czecho-Slovakia, Polish and Yugo-Slav public opinion would in the end have compelled the Governments to join them; had Czecho-Slovakia stood fast she could have forced France into action. For everyone war was fraught with incalculable risks: therefore no one wanted it; but the bluff of the democracies has been called; that of the dictators has not. Now it is all over. The French system has collapsed with unspeakable ignominy. What next?

East Central Europe will become a witches' cauldron. Poland, Yugo-Slavia, and Rumania are as composite as Czecho-Slovakia had been; all their 'Sudetens' are agog – there is scope for housebreakers. The security of the French system was collective; last month its quondam members have dug their own graves. And if Russia is ever added to the German system – by agreement with the Bolsheviks or by their overthrow – a Power will arise greater than the world has known.

France has 40,000,000 inhabitants, Germany has 80,000,000, Italy 40,000,000 to which Spain, when handed over to Franco, will add 20,000,000; a superiority of 100,000,000 for the 'axis'. Can Britain alone endure the integrity and independence of France, and therefore her own? It is idle to expect a victorious 'totalitarian' and his jackals to be satisfied with reasonable concessions.

The key to the situation is in the relations of the British Empire and France to the United States and Russia.

Namier's final paragraph is a most important one in that the attitude of the USA was partially shaped by the advice proferred by their Ambassader to Great Britain, one Joseph Kennedy. He spoke of his being a 'warm admirer' of the British role at Munich and that he understood Germany's Jewish policy completely, particularly as in his home town of Boston there existed clubs to which no Jew had been admitted for over 50 years. As late as the end of 1939 he recounted that he still had little idea as to why the war was being fought. His counterpart in France, William Bullitt, also had advised his government in 1938 that they ought to try and find some method of extricating France from her moral commitment to Czechoslovakia.

The diplomatic effects of the Munich Agreement were far-reaching in that they virtually compelled the USSR to find some means of ensuring its security without placing any reliance on Britain and France. In the context of Munich the Nazi–Soviet Pact of 23 August 1939 was always a distinct possibility and indeed mirrored the Stalinist conception of securing the revolution in its own country.

Monday 24 October   *p.11*

HITLER NOT RESTING ON HIS MUNICH VICTORY
Arms Gap Widening to Berlin's Advantage

From Our Diplomatic Correspondent

London, Sunday.

Although the Munich Agreement has created a new European situation, especially from a strategic point of view, the Governments of the Western Powers do not recognise that a new situation exists, or if they do recognise it their policies do not show it. While there is inertia here and in Paris, the utmost energy is being shown in Berlin. The initiative has all along been in Hitler's hands – and it remains in his hands after the crisis too.

It would be humanly understandable if Germany were to diminish the speed and volume of her rearmament, seeing that she has, through the Munich Agreement, achieved the equivalent of a great increase of her own armament in so far as she will be much less vulnerable againt blockade, will have security in the East and South-east, will have access to new supplies of raw material, and will partly own and partly control the Czech war industry, one of the finest in the world.

305

But she is not reducing the speed and volume of her rearmament. She is going forward with unabated energy and resourcefulness. She is not resting on her victory. British and French foreign policy, on the other hand, is being conducted as though Munich had been a victory for the Western Powers and not one of the great defeats in their history, as though the Europe of to-day were the Europe of a year ago. There appears to be no question of an active foreign policy. Indeed, everything is being done to avoid what might be regarded as 'active,' for any 'action' that might conceivably promote the interests of the Western Powers would at once be interpreted as hostile in Berlin and Rome and is therefore deprecated in advance as not being conducive to 'appeasement.'

There are three international problems that may have to be faced in the near future.

I.—THE LIMITATIONS OF ARMAMENTS

The disparity between German armaments on the one hand and French and British armaments on the other is growing, so that Hitler is getting more and more interest in any agreement that will help to stabilise this disparity – that is to say, will perpetuate the inferiority of the Western Powers, especially in the air. If Hitler does not succeed in negotiating an agreement with regard to aerial armaments he may denounce the Anglo-German Naval Agreement and challenge the Anglo-French command of the sea. He will be able to count on the support of Italy and Japan – both of them great naval Powers.

Germany is using the present time to augment her armaments as much as possible. The same time is being used by the Western Powers to augment their armaments as little as possible – that is, only so far as the most immediate necessities of the hour demand, and perhaps not even so far. This they are doing in the hope that an agreement for the limitation of armaments may be negotiated the more successfully, or rather, in the hope that an agreement will render unnecessary the rearmament which they now know to be necessary.

II.—COLONIES

There is as yet no intention here of making any definite proposals; the reports that France may make Germany an offer lack confirmation. It is known that Hitler demands the return of all Germany's former non-Asiatic overseas possessions. When he demands anything it is always a minimum, a starting-point for further demands. Germany wants her former colonies not so much that a 'wrong' may be 'righted' but so as to have a nucleus for an overseas colonial empire. The former colonies are to be that nucleus.

Thanks to persistent and skilful propaganda the demand for colonies is very popular in Germany; far more Germans take an interest in the colonial question now than before the war. ...

GERMANY AND THE CZECHS
Change of Outlook?

From our own Correspondent

Berlin, October 26.

... ANOTHER CHANGE OF POLICY?

Immediately after the Munich Agreement every sign pointing to the break-up of the Czech State was welcomed here, but afterwards Germany began to show interest and even friendliness in the consolidation of what was left.

The diplomatic contest over the future of the Czech State has been taken a stage farther by the departure of Herr von Ribbentrop, the German Foreign Minister, for Rome to confer with Signor Mussolini. The 'Angriff's' attack, coming at the present time, is striking and may presage another change of German policy. There are, however, no other signs of any change of the German attitude towards Hungary's claims, which are supported here so far as they do not go beyond the ethnical principle.

RUSSIAN PRESS ON PREMIER
Ground Shifted

From our Correspondent

Moscow, October 26.

The daily attacks in the Soviet press on the Munich Agreement and its consequences have taken more and more the character of denunciations of Mr. Chamberlain's part and his personal policies.

The original explanation offered to the Soviet public was that Mr. Chamberlain avoided war at all costs from a fear of arming the working classes. A writer in the Government organ 'Izvestia' this week pictured Mr. Chamberlain as 'the candidate for the gendarme of Europe,' with missionary zeal paving the way for making Europe Fascist and for laying low the forces of democracy.

An entirely new version is now provided by a writer in the Leningrad 'Krasnaya Gazeta.' He has discerned a deep-laid plot not only against the Soviet Union but also against Germany and Japan. Mr. Chamberlain's attitude on Austria and Czecho-Slovakia is attributed to his desire of clearing the way eastward for Herr Hitler and so of making easier an attack on the Soviet Union and diverting Herr Hitler's attention from the West. Viewing the Soviet Union, Germany, and Japan as Britain's greatest enemies, Mr. Chamberlain, it is declared, is seeking to embroil all three in the hope that the Soviet Union will be destroyed and Germany and Japan reduced to dependence on Britain. 'England,' it is added 'hates the Soviet Union and dreams of destroying it. She wants to turn loose the Fascist aggressors against the Soviet Union.'

Although the language used by the writer in 'Krasnaya Gazeta' above might be regarded as intemperate, future events would bear witness to the accuracy of his pronouncements.

Thursday 3 November p.12

FRANCE AND MR. CHAMBERLAIN
Some Apprehension

CRITICISM BY THE RIGHT WING

From our own Correspondent

Paris, November 2.

Not only the Left in France but even large sections of the Right, who in the days after Munich showered their blessings and compliments on Mr. Chamberlain, are becoming anxious. The Parliamentary group of the Republican Federation, which under the leadership of M. Louis Marin represents the largest Right-wing group in Parliament, to-day passed a resolution in which it said that 'it had carefully examined Mr. Chamberlain's speech in the House of Commons yesterday and had found several of its points particularly disquieting.'

Without specifying what these 'points' are the group in this resolution called upon the French Government to make a new declaration in addition to that already made by M. Daladier at Marseilles last week refusing to negotiate on the transfer to Germany of any parts of the French colonial empire, including the mandated territories. It even threatened to vote against the Government if it failed to do so.

TOO TRUSTFUL?

But this, I understand, is not the only, or even the chief, cause of concern in the minds of the Republican Federation. Its views on Mr. Chamberlain's speech are well reflected in the article in to-night's 'Journal des Débats' by M. Bernus, who is clearly taken back by Mr. Chamberlain's claims that Munich was a normally negotiated treaty and by the show of unlimited confidence in the goodwill of Herr Hitler that Mr. Chamberlain made in the course of his speech yesterday.

Other French commentators are perturbed by the complete freedom of action that Mr. Chamberlain is apparently giving Germany in Eastern and Central Europe by his faith, not justified by anything except Munich – and what kind of justification is that? – in the virtues of the Four-Power Pact. They are disturbed too by the way in which he almost ignored the existence of France throughout his speech. 'With all our faults,' one Frenchman rather bitterly remarked to-day, 'Mr. Chamberlain should not forget that we provide England with an army.'

Mr. Chamberlain's whole handling of the Spanish problem is causing the greatest anxiety here.

What has also surprised many French observers is the manner in which Mr. Chamberlain's speech was delivered – a manner which drew from Sir Archibald Sinclair the rebuke that he could not accept the 'Prime Minister's totalitarian standards' and 'preferred the British tradition of free speech.'

APOLOGISTS

The Premier's speech has, of course, some apologists. Among them is the rather disquieting M. Fernand de Brinon, of the Comité France Allemagne, who in the 'Information' to-night warmly approves of Mr. Chamberlain's Four-Power Pact policy, with which he says M. Bonnet and M. de Monzie, two of M. Daladier's Ministers, are in complete agreement.

Small wonder that M. Bonnet should, like Mr. Chamberlain in England, be regarded by Herr Hitler as one of the most desirable people to work with; so at least he said to M. Francois-Poncet at Berchtesgaden last week, according to the information published on the subject by M. Lamoureux, one of M. Bonnet's Radical colleagues.

By the time the sentiments expressed in the above article were framed it was too late to have any effect on the Munich Agreement. The die was already cast.

LETTERS TO THE EDITOR

BRITAIN'S LOST REPUTATION
'Perfidious Albion'

To the Editor of the Manchester Guardian

Sir,–The record of the Baldwin–Chamberlain 'National' Government must surely be unique in the annals of England. The pursuit of what some call 'British interests' and Mr. Chamberlain now calls 'appeasement' has led us into a morass of ignoble folly. For this narrow materialism, and it is nothing else, has lost us the greatest of all British interests – viz, British honour, credence, and faith, i.e. reputation.

During the sixteenth, seventeenth, and eighteenth centuries we, being Protestant, supported the Protestant cause in Europe with our diplomacy, money, and, when necessary, with men and armies and leaders. Why are we not supporting the democratic cause in Europe to-day?

1. In Abyssinia we betrayed a weak member of the League of Nations into the hands of its destroyers. We refused even to supply the means of defence to a people rightly struggling to maintain their independence.
2. We have allowed, and are allowing, the democratic cause in Spain to be imperilled and strangled by foreign Fascist invaders.
3. We have allowed our own creation, Czecho-Slovakia, to be sacked, violated, and murdered. More, we compelled it to submit.
4. We have refused both arms and money to China, rightly struggling to repel an invader.

Have we ever asked ourselves what will happen to us if in the next war the United States gives us our own medicine?

Every small nation that was our friend, that believed in England, if in nothing else, has hidden its head in fear; and every great nation laughs in derision; and the whole world echoes to-day with the accusation 'Perfidious Albion.' And now when he is shown up Mr. Chamberlain wants to muzzle us like a dictator. No wonder!–Yours, &c.,

EDWARD HUTTON,
London, November 3.

Appendix: Dramatis Personae in 1938

Amery, Leopold S.: MP (Unionist) 1911–1945. A Government Minister in Conservative administrations in the 1920s, he was without office in the 1930s and was a constant critic of appeasement policy.

Ashton-Gwatkin, Frank: A senior British civil servant who was both a member of the Runciman Mission to Czechoslovakia in 1938 and a member of Chamberlain's party at the Munich negotiations.

Attlee, Clement: Labour MP 1922–1955; Leader of Labour Party 1935–1955; Prime Minister 1945–1951. Mild-mannered appearance masked a 'steely' character.

Benes, Eduard: Son of a peasant and one of the founders of the Czechoslovakian state, Benes had worked tirelessly for its creation. He was President of his country at the time of the Munich Agreement.

Bevin, Ernest: Trade Union leader and leading figure in Churchill's wartime coalition cabinet and the postwar Labour Government. Founded and developed Transport and General Workers' Union. Destroyed Labour's lingering flirtation with pacificism, and its leader George Lansbury, by his devastating speech to the Labour Party Conference in 1935.

Blomberg, Field Marshal Werner von: Dismissed from office in January, 1938, when it was discovered that his recently-married second wife had a police record as a whore. His case was not helped by the fact that Hitler and Göring had acted as principal witnesses at his wedding.

Brauchitsch, General Walter von: Army Commander-in-Chief from 1938 in the wake of the Blomberg scandal. Although highly-regarded in Army circles he proved to be vaccilating and weak in Hitler's shadow.

Butler, Richard Austen: Conservative MP 1929–1965. Subsequently held great offices of state, but 1938–1941 was Under-Secretary of State for Foreign Affairs, having responsibility as spokesman on Foreign Affairs in the Commons. 'RAB' Butler was regarded by many as the 'nearly' man.

Cadogan, Sir Alexander: Civil Servant, Deputy Under-Secretary at the Foreign Office 1935–1937, Permanent Under-Secretary at the Foreign Office 1938–1946.

Chamberlain, Neville: Member of famous political family – son of Joseph and half-brother of Austen. He became an MP in 1918 at the comparatively late age of 49. Proved to be an able if uninspired Minister and one of the least likely Prime Ministers in the twentieth century. Although arguments continue to rage about the Foreign Policy pursued under his premiership, he did 'get it wrong'.

Churchill, Winston L.S.: Conservative and Liberal MP 1900–1955. Much of his present-day reputation depended on his, in some ways, fortuitous elevation to the Premiership in 1940 and his subsequent prosecution of the war. Out of office for all of the 1930s, he was one of the first and most determined opponents of appeasement policy. He was regarded as a 'maverick' at this time and was distrusted by other opponents of appeasement from both sides of the House. It was not therefore surprising when he accepted office in Chamberlain's government in 1939, although it was a bitter pill to swallow for his potential allies in the House.

Ciano, Count Galleazzo: Son-in-law of Mussolini and his Foreign Minister at the time of the Munich Agreement. He was reportedly as vain and stiff-necked as his mentor and father-in-law.

Cripps, Sir Stafford: Barrister and Labour MP 1931–1950. Held many important offices of state in both the war-time coalition Government and the post-war Labour Government, where he was identified with austerity in economic matters, a role for which his outward demeanour was admirably suited.

Daladier, Edouard: French Prime Minister in 1938. He expected to be both physically and verbally abused on his return to Paris for his part in the betrayal of Czechoslovakia at Munich; instead he was greeted as the returning hero.

Dalton, Hugh: Labour MP 1924–1931 and 1935–1959. A firm critic of the foreign policy pursued by the National Governments during the 1930s. He had firm contacts and friendships with the Czech, Russian and Polish Ambassadors to Great Britain, i.e. Masaryk, Maisky and Raczynski, which probably explains his insight into the troubled area of Central Europe at this time.

Duff Cooper, Alfred: Conservative MP 1924–1929 and 1935–1945, Secretary of State for War 1935–1937 and First Lord of the Admiralty 1937–38. He was a critic of appeasement policy and he resigned as a result of the Munich Agreement – the only Government Minister to do so.

Eden, Anthony: Conservative MP 1923–1957, Foreign Secretary 1935–38; 1940–45; 1951–55; Prime Minister 1955–57. The 'golden boy' of the Conservative Party resigned as Foreign Secretary in February 1938 as a result of a fundamental disagreement between himself and Prime Minister Chamberlain for whose appreciation of foreign policy he had scant regard.

Göring, Hermann: A First World War hero and final commander of the famous von Richthofen Fighter Squadron. Joined Hitler in 1921. He became President of the Reichstag, Reichsmarshall and had responsibility as the Reich economic dictator. A sometime drug addict and looter of the art treasures of Europe.

Hácha, Emil: President of Czechoslovakia at the time of the Munich Crisis.

Hailsham, Lord (Sir Douglas Hogg): Conservative MP 1922–1928. Knighted 1922; Baron Hailsham 1928; Viscount 1929. Lord Chancellor 1935–38; Lord President 1938.

Halifax, Edward, Lord: Conservative MP 1910–1925. Created Lord Irwin 1925; succeeded 1934; created Earl 1944. War Secretary 1935; Lord Privy Seal 1935–37; Lord President of the Council 1937–1938; Foreign Secretary (at the time of the Munich Agreement) 1938–1940. On the resignation of Chamberlain in 1940, Halifax would have been a very strong contender to succeed to the premiership, but his seat in the House of Lords excluded him from the contest.

Henderson, Sir Nevile: Joined the Foreign Service in 1905 and was British Ambassador in Berlin 1937–1939. He was apparently a staunch supporter of the policy of appeasement. A fair measure of the man can be gleaned from an examination of his somewhat whining apologia, *Failure of a Mission* (1940).

Henlein, Konrad: Leader of the Sudeten German Party from 1933. His Party was subsidised in secret from 1935 and he was in reality merely a puppet ready to undertake Hitler's bidding.

Hertzog, General J.B.M.: Prime Minister of South Africa at the time of the Munich Agreement. Informed the British Government that South Africa could not support any British actions which might lead to war. An outspoken appeaser.

Hitler, Adolf: From very unprepossessing beginnings in terms of both family and political background, rose very quickly to become Führer of the Third Reich. Using as a basis for his actions his treatise *Mein Kampf* he plunged the world into a global war of unprecedented proportions. But could, and should, he have been thwarted in 1938?

Hoare, Sir Samuel: Conservative MP 1910–1944. Held many offices of state including that of Foreign Secretary in 1935, a post from which he felt compelled to resign as a result of public dismay over his proposed pact with Laval concerning the compromise with Mussolini over Abyssinia. At the time of the Munich Agreement he was Home Secretary.

Hodza, Dr. Milan: Prime Minister of Czechoslovakia in 1938. As a result of the Czech government's somewhat coerced agreement to the British–French proposals which emanated from the Berchtesgaden negotiations, Hodza resigned on 22 September

1938 as his Government fell. He was succeeded by General Syrovy.

Kennedy, Joseph P.: American Ambassador to Great Britain at the time of the Munich Agreement. Kennedy was a member of the famous Boston political family, famous also as the father of President John. F. Kennedy and in 1938 for his strong anti-semitic views.

Lansbury, George: Labour MP 1910–12 and 1922–1940. Leader of the Labour Party from 1931 to 35 when he was succeeded by Attlee. He was a life-long pacifist whose stance and standing within the Labour Party was virtually destroyed by Bevin's savage attack on him and his views at the 1935 Labour Party Conference.

Lloyd-George, David: Liberal MP, was first elected to Parliament in 1890 and remained in the Commons until 1945. He was Prime Minister from 1916–1922, thereafter he never again held office. He was a man of undoubted brilliance, though somewhat erratic, who seemed happiest when 'flying by the seat of his pants.' He found it difficult to understand why he was excluded from office, as did his many supporters. He opposed appeasement following the Munich Agreement.

MacDonald, James Ramsey: Labour MP. Born in dire poverty in Lossiemouth. Entered parliament in 1906. Prime Minister 1924; 1929–1931; of minority Labour Governments. Prime Minister of National (coalition) Government 1931–1935. Regarded as a traitor in the Labour Party when he formed the National Government; his reputation has been subsequently re-examined in a much more positive light.

Maisky, Ivan: USSR Ambassador to London at the time of the Munich Agreement.

Masaryk, Jan: Czechoslovakian Ambassador to London at the time of the Munich Agreement.

Mussolini, Benito: 'Il Duce'. Ruled Italy, almost unhindered, throughout most of the interwar and Second World War period. A complex man whom his biographers have had difficulty in explaining. Seems to fit, in the modern parlance, into the category of 'a chancer.'

Neurath, Baron Constantin von: Sometime Foreign Minister of Germany. His views were regarded as too 'moderate' and Hitler dismissed him in February 1938.

Papen, Franz von: One time Chancellor of Germany (1932). Regarded somewhat as a ludicrous choice for Chancellor, having no political background or acumen. He thought he could handle Hitler, but he couldn't!

Phipps, Sir Eric C.E.: Entered Diplomatic Service 1899. He was Ambassador to Berlin 1933–1937; and to Paris 1937–1939, i.e. at the time of the Munich Agreement. Ardent supporter of appeasement in both France and Great Britain.

Ribbentrop, Joachim von: German Ambassador to Great Britain 1936. Appointed Foreign Minister succeeding von Neurath in February 1938. Described by William L. Shiver as 'shallow and compliant', a prescient description.

Roosevelt, President Franklin D.: President of the USA 1932–1945. A heroic figure who won the Presidency on an unprecedented four consecutive occasions after making only a partial recovery from a crippling attack of poliomyelitis.

Runciman, Walter, (Lord Runciman of Doxford): Liberal MP 1899–1900; 1902–1918; 1924–1931; Liberal National MP 1931–1937. Having held several Ministerial posts during his time in Parliament, he was despatched to Czechoslovakia in July 1938 cast in the role of the 'honest broker' to try and secure a solution to the 'Czech' problem. He failed, not least because his mission was an impossible one.

Schulenberg, Friedrich Graf von der: German Ambassador to Russia at the time of the Munich Agreement.

Schuschnigg, Kurt von: Austrian Chancellor at the time of the 'Anschluss' with Germany in 1938.

Simon, Sir John: Liberal MP and Liberal–National 1906–1918 and 1922–1940. Held all the great offices of state (i.e. Home Secretary; Chancellor of the Exchequer; Foreign Secretary) with the exception of the Premiership. He was a supporter of appeasement up to and including the Munich Agreement but opposed a continuance of the policy in 1939.

Sinclair, Sir Archibald: Liberal MP 1922–1945. Leader of the Parliamentary Liberal Party 1935–1945. Disliked Nazism but also opposed rearmament proposals in 1935.

Smuts, General Jan C.: Minister of Justice in the South African Parliament and Leader of the South African Party at the time of the Munich Agreement. He also opposed South African involvement should Britain/France contemplate war in 1938.

Stalin, Josef: Leader of the USSR at the time of the Munich Agreement. Stalin was able to engender in people extremes of feeling. Cast surprisingly in the West in the character of 'Uncle Joe', in reality there was little if any avuncularity about him.

Stanley, Oliver: Conservative MP 1924–1950. He was the younger son of Lord Derby and President at the Board of Trade at the time of the Munich Agreement. Acquiesced in the policy of appeasement.

Vansittart, Sir Robert: Entered Diplomatic Service 1902. Permanent Under-Secretary of State at the Foreign Office 1930–1938. He was strongly opposed to the pro-German thrust of British foreign policy. Felt himself, not unreasonably, to be a 'lone voice crying in the wilderness.'

Wilson, Sir Horace: Civil Servant. Chief Industrial Advisor to the Government 1930–1939. Chamberlain's chief advisor and confidante throughout the latter's premiership. Much of the manner of appeasement in 1938 was as a result of Wilson's influence. It has been said of him that he epitomised the most questionable element of the Prime Minister/Civil Servant relationship, namely 'power without responsibility.'

Wood, Kingsley: Conservative MP 1918–1943. Secretary of State for Air 1938–1940. A close friend of Chamberlain. His views favoured co-operation with Germany rather than France.